FACING THE ABYSS

FACING THE
ABYSS

AMERICAN LITERATURE
AND CULTURE
IN THE 1940S

GEORGE HUTCHINSON

COLUMBIA UNIVERSITY PRESS

NEW YORK

Columbia University Press
Publishers Since 1893
New York   Chichester, West Sussex
cup.columbia.edu
Copyright © 2018 Columbia University Press

A complete CIP record is available from the Library of Congress.

ISBN 978-0-231-16338-5 (cloth: alk. paper)
ISBN 978-0-231-54596-9 (e-book)

Columbia University Press books are printed on permanent
and durable acid-free paper.
Printed in the United States of America

Cover design: Catherine Casalino
Cover image: H. Armstrong Roberts/ClassicStock/Getty Images

To Jim, Mindy, and Charlie

in memory of Mom and Dad, and Dave

Even in the darkest of times we have the right to expect some illumination, and that such illumination may well come less from theories and concepts than from the uncertain, flickering, and often weak light that some men and women, in their lives and their works, will kindle under almost all circumstances and shed over the time span that was given them on earth.

—Hanna Arendt, *Men in Dark Times*

Not just a specific knowledge, appetite, suffering, and delight of one particular people, not only that, but knowledge of the Whole, greater from having been at the abyss and freeing knowledge of Relation within the Whole.

—Édouard Glissant, *Poetics of Relation*

Is it a dream?
Nay but the lack of it the dream,
And failing it life's lore and wealth a dream,
And all the world a dream.

—Walt Whitman, "Song of the Universal"

CONTENTS

....

ILLUSTRATIONS

....

ACKNOWLEDGMENTS

·····································

I must admit that at times while working on this project I felt like I was writing ten books in one, venturing into new realms and sifting through way too many books. It helped to have friends. I would like to thank all those who have listened and responded over the last eight years as this project began to take shape and finally became what it is. First, my colleagues at Indiana University, Bloomington, and the lively, rigorous, and capacious intellectual atmosphere they sustained, most especially Susan Gubar, Don Gray, Christoph Irmscher, Shane Vogel, and Scott Herring. I learned a lot from the work of Judith Brown, and Shane gave excellent advice on one chapter and on ideas for a title. Thanks to Susan for letting me know my original title would not do and for her example as a scholar with rigor, imagination, and integrity. I enjoyed talking about the 1940s over Susan and Don's dinner table. The College of Arts and Sciences at Indiana substantially aided me while on a Guggenheim Fellowship in 2011–2012, and the Booth Tarkington Chair Endowment (now the Susan Gubar Chair Endowment) provided generous research funds throughout my time at IU.

The English Department at Cornell took me on midway through the project, providing a comfortable and welcoming environment. Daniel Schwarz, who befriended me on my first arrival at Cornell and made me feel that I belonged, gave helpful comments on chapter 5. I especially want to thank the department chairs during the years I have been at Cornell, Roger Gilbert and Andy Galloway, who have been kind to me and all. Others who took the trouble to read a chapter or more of this book in earlier versions and encourage and in some cases correct me include Paul Sawyer, Jenny Mann, Robert Morgan, Ishion Hutchinson, James Perrin Warren, and Christopher Berardino. Samuel Zipp of Brown University provided very helpful advice on the epilogue. I benefited from a residential fellowship in the Atkinson Center for a Sustainable Future at Cornell and conversations with scholars far removed from my usual academic neighborhoods: Neema Kudva, Annelise Riles, Kim Haines-Eitzen, Carolyn Goelzer, and Mildred E. Warner. Aaron Sachs drew my attention to the work of Lewis Mumford in the realm of ecology. David Taylor, of Stony Brook University, also read a chapter and came up to visit and speak at Cornell on the environmental humanities, inspiring me to think in new ways about the relationship of literature to ecology. I appreciate the Atkinson Center and its director, David Lodge, for supporting humanities types in the exploration of environmental justice and sustainability. They have made Cornell a special place for addressing the greatest challenges of our time.

Others who have provided crucial moral support for my work in recent years include Werner Sollors, Ross Posnock, George Bornstein, and Carla Kaplan. The late Daniel Aaron was an inspiration and example. Thanks to Yang Jincai, Liu Haiping, Zhu Gang, and Xie Youguang of Nanjing University, I was able to present portions of my work in a very different environment from the American academy and to visit some amazing places while doing it.

Leah Dickerman invited me to participate in planning phases for the exhibition on Jacob Lawrence and the Great Migration at the Museum of Modern Art and the Phillips Collection, and I learned from the many illustrious artists and scholars they brought together on the advisory committee. Years ago I was introduced to the art of Norman Lewis when invited to give a lecture at the first general retrospective of his work at the Wadsworth Athenaeum, organized by Lowery Sims. This experience proved an unplanned inspiration for ideas that ended up helping shape this book.

A Guggenheim Fellowship in 2011–2012 allowed me to make substantial strides early on. Versions of portions of this book have been presented in the Distinguished International Lecturer Series, University of Nanjing, and other lectures at Ho Hai University, Soochow University, the Reception Studies Society biennial conference, the Norman Lewis exhibition at the Wadsworth Atheneum in Hartford, the Faulkner and Yoknapatawpha Conference at the University of Mississippi, the Cornell University Department of English, and the West China Faculty Development Seminar in American Studies, hosted by Guangxi Normal University in Guilin and funded by the Ford Foundation.

I owe special thanks to Philip Leventhal, senior editor at Columbia University Press, for his excellent guidance, and to the readers for the press, who provided encouragement and very helpful, informed advice. Thanks also to Don Fehr of Trident Media for seeing promise in the project early on and pushing it.

I often discussed parts of this book and its general argument with Margo Natalie Crawford, who was helpful in more ways than I dare try to define. I remain grateful as well to our companions Oscar and Jazz. The love and faith of my sons, Spencer and Geoff, sustain me always. The book is dedicated to my sister and brothers, in memory of those we lost as I was writing it.

Permission was kindly granted to quote from the following poems:

John Berryman, excerpts from "Communist," "The Dangerous Year," "Rock-Study with Wanderer," and "Thanksgiving: Detroit" from *Collected Poems: 1937–1971* by John Berryman. Copyright © 1989 by Kate Donahue Berryman. Reprinted by permission of Farrar, Straus and Giroux.

Gwendolyn Brooks, excerpts from "the white troops had their orders but the Negroes looked like men," "Negro Hero," and "the progress." Reprinted by consent of Brooks Permissions.

Witter Bynner, excerpts from "Defeat," reprinted with permission from the Witter Bynner Foundation for Poetry.

Richard Eberhart, excerpts from "The Fury of Aerial Bombardment" and "Dam Neck, Virginia," from *Collected Poems, 1930–1986*. Copyright © 1987 by Richard Eberhart. Reprinted with the permission of Oxford University Press, USA, and Dikkon Eberhart.

Robert Hayden, "Middle Passage." Copyright © 1962, 1966 by Robert Hayden, from *Collected Poems of Robert Hayden*, edited by Frederick Glaysher. Used by permission of Liveright Publishing.

Robert Lowell, excerpt from "Concord," from *Lord Weary's Castle*. Copyright 1946 by Robert Lowell. Copyright Renewed 1974 by Robert Lowell. Reprinted by permission of Houghton Mifflin Harcourt Publishing Company. All rights reserved.

Edna St. Vincent Millay, excerpts from "The Murder of Lidice" from *Life Magazine* (October 19, 1942). Copyright 1942, 1969 by Edna St. Vincent Millay and Norma Millay Ellis. Reprinted with the permission of The Permissions Company, Inc., on behalf of Holly Peppe, Literary Executor, The Edna St. Vincent Millay Society, www.millay.org.

Marianne Moore, from *The Collected Poems of Marianne Moore*. Reprinted with the permission of Scribner, a division of Simon & Schuster, Inc. All rights reserved. "Keeping Their World Large" Copyright © 1951 by Marianne Moore, renewed 1979 by Lawrence E. Brimm and Louise Crane. "In Distrust of Merits" Copyright © 1944 by Marianne Moore, renewed 1972 by Marianne Moore.

Howard Nemerov, excerpts from "IFF," reprinted courtesy of Alexander Nemerov.

Excerpts from poems by Karl Shapiro by permission of Kathy Shapiro c/o Harold Ober Associates Incorporated.

Louis Simpson, "Carentan O Carentan," "Memories of a Lost War," "The Heroes," and "The Battle" from *The Owner of the House: New Collected Poems, 1940–2001*. Copyright © 2001 by Louis Simpson. Reprinted with the permission of The Permissions Company, Inc., on behalf of BOA Editions, Ltd., www.boaeditions.org.

Wallace Stevens, excerpt from "Of Modern Poetry," from *The Collected Poems of Wallace Stevens*, copyright 1954 by Wallace Stevens and copyright renewed 1982 by Holly Stevens. Used by permission of Alfred

FACING THE ABYSS

INTRODUCTION

······························

Warren French was undoubtedly right when he wrote that the decade of the 1940s was "one of the longest, unloveliest and most ominously significant decades in human history," beginning with Hitler's invasion of Poland in late 1939 and ending with the invasion of South Korea, encompassing the dawning global awareness of the Nazi concentration camps and the invention and use of the atomic bomb.[1] How did such epochal moments and events register in the contemporary literary culture, and how did writers and artists still armed with the tools and techniques of the early twentieth century attempt to bring shape and meaning to the world in their wake? That is the question from which this book began.

In the very center of the 1940s, anything seemed possible, from human extinction to the first real promise of universal peace: planetary consciousness, ecological awareness, world government. Subtending it all was dread—unprecedented, planetary dread. Maybe humanity would be scared into a functional unity to remake the world, or maybe everyone would die.

Decades are arbitrary designations, yet I was drawn to using the decade in this case as a frame. Studies of modern American literature and culture tend to end or begin at 1945, and they tend therefore to focus on what preceded or followed the 1940s—the modernism of the 1910s–1930s, the "Cultural Front" of the Great Depression, the Harlem Renaissance of 1920–1935, on the one hand, and, on the other, postmodernism, the Cold War, the Black Arts Movement, the New York School, the Beat Movement, the San Francisco Renaissance, and so forth of the 1950s and after. Because their center of gravity lies earlier or later in the century, the forties are screened out even as the year 1945 is regarded as pivotal. While hundreds of books have covered the political, social, cinematic, and military history of the United States during the 1940s, that decade has been the black hole of American literary history.

To take just one recent example, the nearly encyclopedic six-volume *A History of the Book in America* treats in volume 4 "The Expansion of Publishing and Reading in the United States, 1880–1940" and in volume 5 "Print Culture in Postwar America." The period 1940–1945 is barely mentioned, and the "postwar" volume scarcely touches on the late 1940s. Major overviews of American literary history fall into a similar pattern, one that tends to exaggerate a sense of total transformation identified with 1945. Some excellent exceptions to the rule have recently arrived, yet each of these focuses on a particular sector of the field—the discourse of a "crisis" over the nature of humanity, popular middle-class realist novels, ethnic literature, paperback books, or African American literature.[2] All of these themes play through this book but with different conclusions or emphases, arising from considering the situation more holistically— paying attention to how the different literary forms and concerns function in interrelation and within particular conditions of the literary field.

I set off on this study in 2010 with no particular thesis to prove. It was an exploration of a period about which I had always been curious, shortly preceding my birth and shaping my childhood, the era when my parents came of age. My aim was to discover the distinctive themes, motifs, and aesthetic tendencies of a murky period in American literature but a momentous one in "History" and how these both refracted and bore witness to the times. I ended up thinking of the project as ecological, bringing attention to relationships between different actors and sectors of the field, how they interconnected, rather than taking the specialist's approach to one particular feature. Intriguing patterns emerged, and by way of these the basic organization of this book.

Surprising connections also developed. Whereas, for example, philosophical pragmatism by most accounts was losing all purchase from the late 1930s through the 1940s, in some spheres of imaginative literature, art, and even human-rights activism it was going strong. Perhaps the authors and artists were "behind" the curve of theory—or simply relatively autonomous from it. Most of them were writing out of personal origins and experiences and trajectories that derived from childhood and early adulthood in the 1920s and 1930s. These connections met up with developments in racial, ethnic, and sexual orientation clustering about the desire for "universality."

Many have concluded that the universalizing discourse of the 1940s, so important to the first universal declaration of human rights, the first international war-crimes trials, and the creation of the United Nations, effectively excluded most nonwhite, nonmale (and by extension nonheterosexual) subjects from the realm of the "human." One critic has approvingly noted, in speaking of Mark Greif's recent book on the discourse of the "Crisis of Man" from 1933 to 1973,

> We have largely forgotten about all this rumination on the ethics, character, and ontology of the human, and Greif understands, of course, that much of the reason why is that in capitalizing (on) the figure of "Man" in various forms of existential crisis, writers of the period reified the exclusion of most men and women on planet Earth from whole departments of academic inquiry—particularly in the humanities and in literary criticism—as it was practiced in and out of the university.[3]

This may have been true in the universities, yet I had discovered in American literature of the 1940s an unprecedented level of attention, mainly outside the academy, to just such subjects, testing the limits of "universals" with particulars while maintaining universality as an aspiration. Attacks on antiblack racism, anti-Semitism, and homophobia were ubiquitous in the 1940s, along with fear for survival of life as we know it.

Often these emphases connected with pragmatism's dialectical conception of the relationship between individuality and community as well as between culture and democracy. Seen as shaping both the ethical consciousness of individuals and the communities in which they were formed, aesthetics was reconnected to common experience, with an emphasis on creative process and extending ethical boundaries beyond the fixed and traditional. In the context of a global war, it might extend toward an imagined planetary humanism.

One striking connection between now distinct fields of inquiry is the way black, queer, and Jewish authors in particular resisted minoritizing discourses in favor of universalizing ones, to borrow terms from Eve Kosofsky Sedgwick's *Epistemology of the Closet*. They did this because they came to believe, in an era shadowed by fascism, that all forms of minoritization and oppression interconnect and that the battle for liberation must always be fought on broader grounds than identity politics alone provides, even though oppression operates by way of particularizing identity—marking the Jew, the Negro, the homosexual for subordination or worse. The universal exists not in the abstract human being, the classical liberal subject, but as a potential emerging at the shifting crossroads of social identities—never a fixed point—and a guard against limiting chauvinisms, separatist idealizations, or calcifying and monumentalizing traditions that curb the reach and power of creative imagination and that support *inhumanity*, to use a common term. The heroes of identity politics were Hitler, Hirohito, Mussolini, and the Ku Klux Klan. They have their much-diminished avatars today.

The universalism and self-professed humanism of Richard Wright, Ralph Ellison, Jo Sinclair, Isaac Rosenfeld, Robert Duncan, Truman Capote, and many others in the immediate postwar period fly in the face of current academic prejudices. In his keynote address to the Modern Language Association at its 2016 Convention, the MLA president, Roland Greene, assumed the collective assent of the humanities professors he addressed when he asserted "that the war dealt a more decisive blow to universalist assumptions about literature than did any theory," above all because the European scholars who had fled to the United States felt that the unreflective universalism of Eurocentric scholars had been shattered. "What I mean to suggest is that the history of the larger discipline of literary studies in the twentieth century can be divided into the universalist and postuniversalist periods, roughly before and after World War II."[4]

The war, in this view, inspired such scholars as Eric Auerbach and René Wellek to resist "an unspoken universalism—a resistance that must be enacted afresh with every turn of method and articulated again in nearly every piece of scholarship." Behind this address is the assertion of incommensurability—the notion that historical experience has created gaps impossible to traverse between different groups of human beings. "Universalism haunts the study of literature, as the founding article whose repudiation, once unthinkable, came to be necessary for the field to maintain its connection to history and to lived experience."[5]

On the contrary, World War II profoundly reinforced aspirations toward universalism among suppressed peoples, in multiple registers that resonate in the present. Those aspirations were splintered by the Cold War and its residues, not by World War II. It was not universalism but Eurocentric and "white" bourgeois parochialism that had failed (and were revived during the fifties). In fairness, I should add that Greene later asks, "Are we connected to each other? And might literature be understood not as the sign of a connection determined elsewhere—say, in nationality, language, or education—but as the fabric of that connection itself? How can literary works (and, we would add, film, video, rhetoric, and so on) not merely assume but establish collectivity?"[6] That is precisely what important American writers of the 1940s were after, as are some artists today who are regarded as avant-garde in diverse media. The universal for these writers was not a fixed point, anterior or foundational, nor even a Platonic ideal, but an aspiration, even at times an ecstatic experience, always to be called forth in acts of making.

When Richard Wright narrates episodes of his youth in *Black Boy* (1945), he doesn't mean to say that the fear, shame, and hatred that haunted his childhood can only be true for *him*, nor are they only relevant to other African Americans. He writes as an embodied human being to other human beings—who also are afraid, shamed, and hateful for their own reasons—with a faith in the possibility that they will listen and come to a "human" (his term) understanding of his experience and also of themselves, whoever and wherever they are—and that they will be changed by that understanding as he was (so he said) in the very writing of his autobiography of 1945.

American authors from early on have entered the institution of literature from different social positions, for different purposes. In the history of the United States, that diversity of position and approach has inspired literary invention—from the early captivity and fugitive-slave narratives to the essays of Emerson (often shaped to appeal to far-flung lyceum audiences) and the chants of Whitman, the fascicles of Dickinson, the revolutionary use of point of view in *The Adventures of Huckleberry Finn* or the blues and jazz poetry of Langston Hughes and Sterling Brown, the stories of Sui Sin Far, the sentences of Gertrude Stein. The force of such inventions endures in endless recurrences and transformations.

In most European and Asian countries, the ethnic and especially class origins of authors were not as diverse as in the United States. This is not a "nationalist" claim but a simple and important distinction relevant to the subject at hand. When university professors sought to impose a selective set of evaluative criteria on American literature just as it was entering the academy in midcentury, they narrowed the field to a canon of texts by white and mostly middle-class men. They posited standards of literary excellence that narrowed the field of attention. Not coincidentally, they found the literature of their own time, the 1940s, lacking. The story took hold that the literature of this decade doesn't measure up to the enormity of its time. It is a main aspiration of this book to change that story.

The 1940s was a period of accomplishment—producing major works by established modernist writers as well as by new ones, including Richard Wright, Eudora Welty, Robert Hayden, Gwendolyn Brooks, Truman Capote, Carson McCullers, Arthur Miller, and Tennessee Williams. *Native Son* was a Book-of-the-Month Club selection, Margaret Walker won the Yale Series of Younger Poets Award, and Gwendolyn Brooks published the book that would win her the Pulitzer Prize. The plays of Williams and Miller, still considered "classics," gained instant fame.

The decade saw American literary and artistic culture become less insular and more deeply internationalized than ever before. It gave birth to film noir, abstract expressionism, and what later would be called postmodernism. It was the period in which the study of American literature became academically respectable, when American studies moved from a small hole-in-the-wall operation led by democratic socialists and New Deal liberals to an institutionalized and international field. Thus the 1940s is not only the vortex of the past century but a period in which literature—especially contemporary American literature—mattered to more people than ever before or since. Hovering around the abyss of meaning that the war opened up, literature of the forties is the most probing witness we have of the nation's history and character in that pivotal period. But not just that period: it opened up depths covered over in less extraordinary times.

The United States emerged as a dominant cultural force, New York replacing Paris and London as the culture capital of the Western world, in part because of the influx of European refugees and in part because of the devastation suffered by Europe and Asia in World War II. But another factor was the rising prestige of American literature in the preceding decade. American writing gained from its embrace by European trendsetters like Sartre, and American writers were huge on the international stage. Three Americans had won the Nobel Prize in Literature in the 1930s: Sinclair Lewis (1930), Eugene O'Neill (1936), and Pearl S. Buck (1938). (Lewis was the first American writer ever to win the award.) In 1940, 1941, 1942, and 1943, no prizes were awarded in literature; in 1948 and 1949 T. S. Eliot and William Faulkner won the prize back to back. Never before or after was American literature so dominant internationally. And much of the publishing industry of Europe had migrated to Manhattan, joining American firms in making it the center of international print culture.

The country was largely isolationist in the 1930s, despite fascism's ominous spread, but between Mussolini's attack on Ethiopia and the

Japanese attack on Pearl Harbor a dramatic reversal occurred. By 1941, as Allan Nevins pointed out in the 1948 *Literary History of the United States*, "National safety was seen to lie in international union. It was one of the most dramatic and drastic *volte-face* in all American history."[7] The conversion affected every area of American thought and work. In the course of the decade, a culture formerly reluctant to engage in international entanglements emerged as a superpower, and its financial and cultural capital, New York, became what many regarded, particularly as the UN took form, as the capital of the world.

Yet in the literary culture one finds very little triumphalism. Instead, the dominant emotion is a new sense of dread, a haunting sensation of radical evil both without and within. Against popular recent notions of the "good war" and the "greatest generation," authors engaged in the war as well as conscientious objectors and those largely uninvolved moved beyond the disillusionment of early modernists with World War I to a probing of existential guilt and the nature of "man," attacks on racism and homophobia, questions about the survival of the human race, and ecological concerns.

Throughout the 1940s, the social consciousness and collectivist ethos of the thirties and the imperatives of the Popular Front lived on even as the Left splintered. Trotsky was assassinated; Stalinism, exposed. Zionism drew Jewish radicals to the cause of Israel. A reaction against communism took hold, but not against social democracy. By the latter years of the Depression, Americans had chosen two new paths that carried through the 1940s. Under Roosevelt's leadership but with the help of leaders in both major parties, as the *Literary History of the United States* pointed out in 1949, the nation "had decided to seek domestic security in social measures, and world security in collective policies. National individualism and isolationism were seemingly forever dead."[8] The country had committed itself to a reshaping of the social order and a major recalibration of the relationship between the national government and society. There would be drastic curtailment of concentrated wealth at one extreme and a commitment to end poverty on the other, to free the poor from want, hunger, and fear and to make them consumers. Plutocrats like the

Rockefellers, Carnegies, and Morgans would no longer plot the course of society; elected federal, state, and local governments would.

Communism in the United States lost its intellectual cachet to other forms of social-democratic thinking that had more interest in aesthetics. One reason the influence of Marxism over writers waned after the 1930s is that, though a powerful mode of historical explanation, it failed in its aspirations to predict. Communist Party methods in both labor organizing and cultural directives also turned artists off. But more importantly, Marxism could not address the need to bring form to unprecedented experience. Many writers grew bored with it. Rather than seeing literature as a means of changing the world in line with a materialist theory of history, in the 1940s authors saw it as a mode of witnessing and seeking meaning in absurdity. But unlike the avant-garde of the 1920s, they also emphasized the importance of communicating with a public.

The "art film" became commercially viable at the same time the paperback revolution began—first with pulp fiction but quickly spreading to "literary" fiction. And for the first time books by African American authors became bestsellers. Refugee publishers from the European continent arrived, along with a host of other editors and writers who changed the literary culture of the United States.

This is the decade in which the universities began replacing journalism and pulp factories as the training grounds of creative writers—and as patrons. Before and during the war, most poets and novelists supported themselves with journalism, scriptwriting for Hollywood, stories for slick magazines, adaptations of their novels for film, or pulp fiction. At the end of it, the returning soldiers inspired an expansion of creative-writing instruction in universities and the establishment of faculty lines and fellowships for novelists and poets—a main support for American literature since.

Literary scholarship in the United States tried to reconnect with contemporary life and letters. The pursuit of imaginative literature came under the purview of English departments just as creative writers grew more restive about their vocational reliance on journalism, advertising, and film. A renewed attention to aesthetic form rapidly gained stature as a crucial concern for antifascists. The so-called New Criticism gained hold not as an apolitical scholasticism, as it later became and is most often remembered, but as part of a reclamation of the centrality of the humanities to higher learning and a mode of training critical, democratic citizens. Motivating this shift was a belief that concern for values and meaning had been subordinated in Western culture to scientific method, with catastrophic results. This interest in values and meaning was believed to distinguish the arts and humanities from journalism and the social sciences.

While the United States emerged as a global power, its most important writers questioned its moral bases. Fascism was not seen as only existing in Europe. Authors as diverse as Hemingway, Faulkner, Bulosan, Tolson, Mailer, and Rukeyser recognized and worried about forms of fascism at home, often identified with antiblack racism and, specifically, lynching. Two runaway bestsellers in nonfiction during the war concerned native fascism: *Under Cover*, by John Roy Carlson—pen name for Arthur Derounian, an underground spy who had infiltrated the ranks of the far right—and *Sabotage: The Secret War Against America*, by Michael Sayers and Albert E. Kahn, about the profascist activities of several congressmen, which the Dies committee attempted to suppress. Martha Gellhorn often expressed her belief that fascism would never have gained ground, nor a second world war have ultimately broken out, had the ruling elites of England and the United States not been secretly in favor of it (as a buffer to socialism) throughout the 1930s, which is one of the themes of her 1940 novel set in Czechoslovakia, *A Stricken Field*. In fact, the theme is one that links the writing of the 1940s to that of the 1930s, when Sinclair Lewis published his lacerating attack *It Can't Happen Here* (1935). In this period, the Bollingen Prize of the Library of Congress, intended to be the nation's highest poetry award, went to an unrepentant fascist, Ezra Pound, for a book of poems, blatantly worshipful of Mussolini, he wrote while detained in an open cage awaiting trial for treason. The controversy convulsed the republic of letters.

In some of the best of the war novels—by Norman Mailer (*The Naked and the Dead*), John Hersey (*A Bell for Adano*), and John Horne Burns

(*The Gallery*)—American officers are characterized as fascists. A broad-based critique of antiblack racism and anti-Semitism, both of which were perceived through the lens of antifascism, was central to the literature of the decade from early on, continuous with leftist strains of the 1930s.

Critiques of the suppression of homosexuality inspired an extraordinary amount and quality of literary invention, in part because of the sexual energies and opportunities created by the war. Yet, as with African American and Jewish writers, "queer" writers resisted identity politics and aspired to universality. All forms of oppression, they stressed, interlocked. Alienation was the universal modern condition, and national minorities exemplified it.

No feminist identitarian movement like that of the 1970s emerged, either, but the critique of misogyny (which was epidemic in the forties) and of the hypersexualization and disempowerment of women constituted one of the most characteristic features of literature by women, in which satire and wit, perennial tools of the powerless, found a place at the table of the New York literary establishment—a subordinated one, provoking serious, sometimes self-lacerating indignation.

The 1940s is the period in which conservationist thinking turned ecological, partly in response to the war. Aldo Leopold's *Sand County Almanac* and its essay on a "land ethic," long revered in the modern ecological movement, were composed during the war and are rife with metaphors deriving from it. The war fundamentally shaped not only Leopold's metaphorical arsenal but the very form of his thinking. Also striking in Leopold's work is its emphasis on aesthetics in the struggle to preserve the balance of the natural world that people inhabit. As in Hemingway and Wright, the need for an aesthetic transformation supersedes purely political-economic approaches to the current situation. Attachment to the land is anchored in its beauty.

I have found much of the work treated here both unexpected and inspiring, yet I do not claim that the views of these artists suffice for our time nor that they represent the common sense of their own. We can never climb back into the many common senses of that era. Yet neither are their responses merely specific to their moment. They tapped into and took inspiration from earlier experiments and have had both acknowledged and (mostly) unacknowledged repercussions ever since.

It is difficult to resist the rhetorical drama of the revolutionary change, singular "event," or historical "break" around the date 1945, what the historian Ian Buruma has called "Year Zero." It was one of the most extraordinary moments in modern history. But a fundamental and paradoxical finding of this book is that even through an "event" or historical turning point as dramatic as World War II, cultural forms tend toward recurrence, despite previously unimaginable changes. The fifties put a lid on many of the energies of the late 1930s and 1940s (which have antecedents in the 1850s and the 1910s–1920s), but that lid, too, would soon be blown off. We need new ways of thinking about cultural transformation, ways less dependent on narratives of radical rupture and historical periodization, which tend to screen out the role of habit, processes of incremental cultural change, and the recursive nature of experience and expression.

This book covers a broad swath but is necessarily selective; I bring attention to books and poems that reward reading today, some well known and others not. It is organized by what I have found to be the most important themes and motifs, especially those that would have an enduring importance in American culture to the present day. I also talk about changes in literary form, the melding of realism with surrealism, and the interplay between modernist abstraction and vernacular forms. Both thematically and institutionally, literature worked in close relationship with other realms of artistic and intellectual endeavor that were part of what might be called the "literary ecology" of this extraordinary period. In thinking ecologically, so to speak, about the literary field, I hope to suggest how these various themes and motifs intersect.

Ecology involves studying relationships among organisms and between organisms and their nonorganic environment. To separate organisms and study them individually has merit but also contributes to specialization, hypercategorization, and, ultimately, myopia. Here I take the American literary-cultural field during a slice of time—the time considered epoch making—and investigate what seem to me its most significant features in interrelationship and across specialties. I do not always group authors by the social identities that are now routine (gender, race, sexuality, class), although each of these is fundamental to my argument. Most authors of the time would appreciate this, which means something in itself, regardless of what we might make of it today—realizing that whatever we make of it today is not what they would have made of it. The major concerns of the time are both like and unlike ours.

The literatures in each of what many scholars now think of as separate literary traditions turn out to be less separable from one another than we have come to assume, even as the authors created works that have been used to define those traditions. The authors functioned in specific artistic and social environments and intersected in the field of the "literary," which cannot be easily mapped, for the very reason that artists are drawn to boundaries. They usually come from or address the borders of social categories, reaching for new resources of language. That may be one reason we find some literary work unfixed in meaning and having an aura of timelessness, regardless of how particular and formative was the social ground in which it arose. Significant artists, in postfeudal societies at least, emerge from the interstices, from shadows cast by what is understood, a threshold position that affects their relationship to common time. The point here is not that traditions are unimportant but that they are always retrospective and consolidating. Invention happens at the edge of cultures and their temporal orderings. Like biotic communities, cultures are always imbricated with others, changing in relationship to others, in process, yet they adapt and persist if possible.

As pivotal as the decade of the forties was, as profound its political and economic contortions, it was a turn not a break, culturally speaking. Cultures reconstitute themselves; language, habit, and memory persist across catastrophic shifts. They interconnect and remake themselves in relation. We can see this, from the long view, in the national cultures and structures of power that survived World War II, in altered form, particularly those of the United States. This takes me beyond my subject but not beyond the method of this book, which finds both succession and repetition amid change even through what Isaac Rosenfeld called an Age of Enormity. Finally, in drawing attention to American literature of the 1940s I hope to demonstrate its distinctive qualities and what it accomplished that no other medium could during a high tide of both patriotism and planetary consciousness.

1

WHEN LITERATURE MATTERED

···

One of the first writers to emerge from World War II was Gore Vidal, whose debut novel, *Williwaw* (1946), drew on his experience as a naval officer in the Aleutian Islands. It was a surprise bestseller, and after his second novel, *In a Yellow Wood*, came out the next year he found himself "very much on view with the other young lions of the second postwar generation. Journalists were eager to know if we would be 'lost,' too." The magazine *Life* featured several of these "young lions," including a sultry full-page photo of Truman Capote. "Thus began his career as a celebrity," in Vidal's words. He was twenty-one; Vidal, twenty. "In those days works of literature were often popular," he reminisced in his 1995 memoir, "something no longer possible." Vidal moved to Paris in the late 1940s and stayed in the hotel where Sartre and de Beauvoir held court after they'd been driven from the Café Flore by hordes of tourists who came to look at them. "Now," Vidal continued, "I find it hard to believe that I once lived in a time when writers were world figures because of what they wrote, and that their ideas were known even to the vast perennial majority that never reads. . . . [W]riting was still central to the culture if not *the* culture."[1] In the 1940s, literature mattered.

Popular radio shows featured literary critics talking about recent poetry and fiction. The *New Yorker*'s book-review editor hosted one of the most popular radio shows in America, and his anthology, *Reading I've Liked*, ranked seventh on the bestseller list for nonfiction in 1941.[2] At the Democratic Primary Convention in 1948, F. O. Matthiessen, a professor of American literature, delivered a nominating speech for Henry Wallace, the late FDR's vice president. Writers were celebrities. Literature was popular. The 1940s was the most intensely literary decade in American history, perhaps in world history.

Books symbolized freedom. Posters of 1942 quoted the president: "Books cannot be killed by fire. People die, but books never die. No man and no force can put thought in a concentration camp forever. No man and no force can take from the world the books that embody man's eternal fight against tyranny. In this war, we know, books are weapons."[3] During the Blitz, Muriel Rukeyser recalled, "newspapers in America carried full-page advertisements for *The Oxford Book of English Verse*, announced as 'all that is imperishable of England.'"[4] For the first and only time in history, protecting books in war zones became an official aim of armed forces.[5]

The Writers' War Board, founded two weeks after Pearl Harbor as an independent propaganda agency, spotlighted modernist books as the targets of Nazism. American publishers gladly joined the crusade. To buy a book, particularly a "modern" book, was to defend liberty. "This book, like all books," read the back of the dust jacket to Muriel Rukeyser's volume of antifascist poetry *Beast in View* (1944), "is a symbol of the liberty and the freedom for which we fight. You, as a reader of books, can do your share in the desperate battle to protect those liberties—Buy War Bonds."[6] The front of the dust jacket featured an abstract rendering of the inside of a rifle barrel (fig. 1.1).

This was the golden age of the public library. From the 1910s through the 1940s, libraries sprang up in rural towns across the states, neighborhood branches sprouted in the great cities, and librarianship multiplied. During the Depression and "the War," the libraries offered free shelter, entertainment, and education, harboring readers rich and poor. Writers' memoirs of the 1930s and 1940s often feature tributes to the public library, whether neighborhood branch or metropolitan temple.

FIGURE I.I Dustjacket for the first edition of Muriel Rukeyser's *Beast in View* (Doubleday, 1944). *Source*: Reproduced by permission of Random House LLC.

Richard Wright got his education through the public libraries, beginning with the whites-only Memphis library, where he borrowed books on a white friend's card, posing as an errand boy. Jo Sinclair, from a desperately poor Jewish family in Cleveland, used the neighborhood branch of her public library as her first writing school.[7] Then, as a WPA employee digesting foreign-language newspapers, she worked at the main branch downtown and stayed long hours after work to explore its treasures. The "New York intellectuals" grew up in the public libraries even if their formal education came from City College, NYU, or Columbia. Alfred Kazin is just one of many who spent his days in the New York Public Library's palatial reading room:

> There it was, as soon as you walked up the great marble steps off Fifth Avenue. "ON THE DIFFUSION OF EDUCATION AMONG THE PEOPLE REST THE PRESERVATION AND PERPETUATION OF OUR FREE INSTITUTIONS." It said that to you as you

entered the great hall, in gold letters on the pylons facing the Fifth Avenue entrance. The entrance also read: "THE LIBRARY IS OPEN EVERY DAY OF THE YEAR 9 A.M.–10 P.M., MONDAY–SATURDAY. 1–10 SUNDAY.

Year after year I seemed to have nothing more delightful to do than to sit much of the day and many an evening at one of those great golden tables acquainting myself with every side of my subject. Whenever I was free to read, the great Library seemed free to receive me.[8]

Karl Shapiro's "Public Library," in *V-Letter and Other Poems* (1944) extols: "What is it, easier than a church to enter, / Politer than a department store, this center / That like Grand Central leads to everywhere?" Shapiro was planning to become a librarian before the draft intervened. For both Kazin and Shapiro, the library is the central institution of democracy: "Is it more civic than City Hall? . . . / Its one demand is freedom, its one motto / Deep in the door, Read, Know, and Tolerate."[9] The diversity of patrons and incongruous temporal juxtapositions in the library struck the refugee Claude Lévi-Strauss in the early 1940s: "I went to work every morning in the American room of the New York Public Library. There, under its neo-classical arcades and between walls paneled with old oak, I sat near an Indian in a feather headdress and a beaded buckskin jacket—who was taking notes with a Parker pen."[10]

The 1930s and 1940s also saw a profound expansion of book distribution across the United States as increasing numbers of Americans took up reading in their spare time. The market for books expanded dramatically, despite constraints. Books from the first half of the 1940s are not pretty. With rationing, they had to be printed on cheap paper, in small type within tight margins. Trade books had to be cut back, deterring risk and forcing shorter print runs. Yet the hunger for books grew. William Jovanovich later recalled that "publishers were able to sell practically everything to war workers, who had plenty of money and not much to spend it on."[11] James T. Farrell partly attributed the expansion to the scarcity of consumer goods; gas rationing, which cut down on pleasure trips; and restrictions on new film production. Gertrude Stein, recounting her first encounter with American GIs during the liberation of France, contrasted them with the soldiers of World War I, who "did not read much not those we knew." They told her they thought it was because they didn't have much to do in the 1930s, and the radio quizzes and crossword puzzles "kind of made them feel that it was no use just being ignorant."[12] The anecdote matches publishers' suspicions. Book publishing developed into a mass industry with new distribution techniques, eventually making the business attractive even to financial markets.[13] The expansion of demand inspired experiments. When the war ended, literary publishing boomed.

Priming the pump for demand for "modern" literature was a publishing enterprise that dated back to 1917, the Modern Library. Horace Liveright, the chief of Boni and Liveright, had started it as a self-consciously modernist venture—a reprint operation focusing on international modernism and attempting to make the best of recent literature available in an affordable and matching format to a growing intellectual class through the 1920s. With careful editorial selection, it quickly established a reputation for quality as well as affordability. Liveright's risky publishing and other ventures simultaneously made him famous and put him in hock by the early 1920s, however, and in 1925 he sold the imprint to two of his junior associates, Bennett Cerf and Donald Klopfer.

Cerf and Klopfer cannily moved to modern marketing and distribution techniques while building further the editorial distinction of the series, and within five years sales quadrupled. In the course of the 1930s the Modern Library solidified a revered status among intellectuals even as it used mass-production and -distribution techniques to sell its wares, foreshadowing the paperback revolution of the late 1940s.[14] They promoted the notion that they provided a reading list of the best contemporary writing, so that one couldn't go wrong buying one of their books and that reading them on a regular basis would constitute an education. They imitated Alfred A. Knopf's Borzoi colophon concept with a torchbearer motif designed initially by Rockwell Kent. But Modern Library, as mainly a reprint publisher, had a different mission.

Cerf and Klopfer tested the limits of respectability with mail-order schemes, a Book-a-Month plan, and other ideas usually disdained among the "high-class" publishers like Knopf—and their audiences. They risked being taken for "pushy Jews," something no one would say of the lordly Knopf (who was also Jewish). To maintain their reputation with critics and readers they kept titles that sold as few as two thousand copies a year, yet to maintain their reputation with the booksellers they cut any titles expected to sell less than that. Sales went through the roof in the course of the Great Depression as Cerf and Klopfer hit the roads to win over bookstores, college campuses, and department stores, implanting in retailers' minds the assurance that their books would not waste shelf space. You can sell a one-dollar book over three times easier than a three-dollar-book, they told the retailers, and it turned out they were right.

Worried about their image, however, they avoided newsstands and drugstores (which sold pulp fiction and comic books), and they never looked beyond the cities. By the end of the 1930s Modern Library supplied a large share of the books for college literature courses while also appealing to nonacademics and maintaining their all-important reputation for "class." But in addition to making their own fortunes and reputations, Cerf and Klopfer had helped expand the market for modern literature across the urban United States.

In the early 1930s, Cerf and Klopfer founded Random House as a limited edition "fine press," separate from the Modern Library, reinforcing their literary prestige. But in the mid-1930s they began to open up the list and turn it into a trade house, which became a behemoth in the course of the 1940s. Cerf, the gregarious one of the two (later a regular on the popular TV show *What's My Line?*), rubbed elbows with movie stars and directors and wrote a column, "Trade Winds," for the *Saturday Review of Literature*. Meanwhile, Klopfer enlisted in the army in 1942, serving until Germany's surrender and earning a chestful of medals, including the French Croix de Guerre.

Their correspondence during the war reveals plenty of back-and-forth with the movie studios. One evening, Cerf found himself sitting beside a beautiful German woman at a friend's dinner party and introduced himself. She was Greta Garbo.[15] When studios bought the rights to a novel, both publisher and author got a cut, and so movies became another cherished source of income in the literary world. Sinclair Lewis got a whopping $150,000 for the movie rights to *Cass Timberlane* in 1945.[16] Marketing machines brought attention to the books on which movies were based, not infrequently featuring a blow-up of the dust jacket on marquees and posters. Bookstores, in turn, exploited the glamour of the movies in their displays, linking books to the stars who played the characters.[17] Not only did Hollywood rewrite novels into scripts that could pass muster with the Hays Office Production Code and draw huge audiences, but publishers began "novelizing" popular films, often using ghostwriters. The Metro-Goldwyn Mayer prize for the "Novel of the Year" paid $100,000 to the winning author, assuring financial independence for life.[18]

The democratization of taste had its counterpart in the class backgrounds of authors. James T. Farrell, after noting that "far more people of the lower-middle class and even workers are reading seriously," added that "with ever greater frequency the more vigorous American writers are of plebeian origin, and . . . writers of the upper classes try to imitate them."[19]

Time called 1943 "the most remarkable [year] in the 150-year-old history of U.S. publishing." It added that "the whole vast literate population of the United States" was "for the first time buying and reading books"— surely an exaggeration but indicative of a major shift in consumption. Orders from bookshops and department stores, their shelves free of overstock, poured into publishers' offices.[20] With consumption of other goods curtailed by rationing, people were staying home and reading. And into the midst of this boom came what was arguably the most imaginative and transformative initiative in the history of American literary publishing. The Armed Services Editions put over 123,000,000 free books into the hands of a captive audience of soldiers and sailors who had little to do between battles (or in the hospital) but read, and read they did. What they read, overwhelmingly, was contemporary American literature.

Men read books in tanks, in hospitals, on bombers heading for the skies over Berlin, in ditches under fire, in tents and dormitories. Under the auspices of the Council on Books in Wartime, organized by American publishers, the Armed Services Editions published 1,322 titles between the years 1943 and 1947. The only books available to many soldiers, they created thousands of new readers in the course of the war, not a few of whom went on to write themselves. The series also primed the market for the paperback explosion of the postwar period, which blew the gates open for modern literature. These books profoundly altered both publishers' and audiences' perceptions of paperback books, sweeping a path for the armada of twenty-five-cent books that landed in welcoming stores after the war, cheap as soap and cheaper than soap as freight.

The idea began in the army in 1942 with Ray L. Trautman, an officer who headed the army's Library Section. With the help of an army graphic-arts specialist, he figured out that expendable paperbacks could be turned out for less than ten cents a copy on magazine and pulp-fiction rotary presses then idle because of wartime rationing. The books were made to fit the pocket of fatigues and conceived as purely recreational reading, mostly current titles at all levels of taste. Since rotary presses were built to print magazine pages, the plan was to print double-copy pages and then slice them horizontally to make pocket-size books. Short books were printed on *Readers Digest*–size presses and longer books on regular magazine-size presses. After slicing, the smaller ones were five and a half inches long by three and seven-eighths inches tall and the larger ones six and a half by four and a half. The text was printed in double columns and the pages bound on the short edge by one or two staples. A radio drama by Stephen Vincent Benet (an iconic literary figure during the war) publicized the effort and was later published by Farrar & Rinehart: *They Burned the Books*.[21]

The colorfully paper-bound, featherweight volumes came out in sets of between thirty and forty titles, each set including a variety of "genres." One set went out each month for every 150 men or fifty hospital beds. At its peak, the program distributed 155,000 sets of forty books per month.[22] Contemporary nongenre fiction by the likes of Steinbeck, Cozzens,

Marquand, Faulkner, Hemingway, Parker, Cain, Chandler, and others predominated. Next were "Westerns," followed by "Humor" books (e.g., Thurber), "Mysteries," and historical novels. Nearly a hundred short-story collections, many by now-canonical modernist authors and "made" specifically for the ASE, went out in the monthly shipments. An anthology of short stories entitled *Bedtime Tales* gives some sense of the fiction canon. It included Faulkner's "A Rose for Emily," Fitzgerald's "Winter Dreams," Hemingway's "The Short Happy Life of Francis Macomber," and fiction by a gamut of *New Yorker* authors along with James T. Farrell, Erskine Caldwell, and William Saroyan—authors who then loomed large.

To conservative congressmen the whole initiative smacked of "socialism" and even "communist propaganda." Lillian Smith's *Strange Fruit* and Henrietta Buckmaster's historical novel *Deep River* took aim at racism. The left-leaning historian Charles Beard's popular book on the American Constitution, *The Republic*, drew fire. The army and navy wanted nothing that would arouse racial, religious, political, or ethnic tensions, which is probably a main reason books by the likes of Richard Wright were not included (nor any others by black authors), as well as those with insulting racial, religious, sectional, and ethnic stereotypes. Zane Grey's *Riders of the Purple Sage* was nixed because of its negative portrayal of Mormons. As the presidential campaign of 1944 neared, Republican congressmen wanted no reading for soldiers that might cause them to favor FDR and passed the Soldier Voting Law, which prompted the council to assign Rosemary Carr Benét, the widow of the famous author of *John Brown's Body* and *Western Star*, the job of reading each potential selection for possible problems; she was later joined by Louis Untermeyer and eventually nine others.[23]

"Council Books," as the GIs called them, had a big impact on morale, especially in the periods before invasions and battles when soldiers needed distractions. One corporal wrote, "The books are read until they're so dirty you can't see the print. To heave one in the garbage can would be tantamount to striking your grandmother."[24] In the lead-up to the Normandy landings, when the troops were camped in the marshaling areas of southern England, each soldier received a book; few were discarded during the embarkation, when men cast off anything they didn't need. A. J. Liebling, a *New Yorker* journalist, boarded a landing barge on July 1, 1944, and two days later noted, as another one pulled alongside: "The soldiers were spread all over the LCIL [landing craft, infantry, large] next door, most of them reading paper-cover armed services editions of books." A private from Brooklyn charged with dynamiting enemy pillboxes during the landing told him:

> These little books are a great thing. . . . They take you away. I remember when my battalion was cut off on top of a hill at El Guettar, I read a whole book in one day. It was called "Knight without Armor." This one I am reading now is called "Candide." It is kind of unusual, but I like it. I think the fellow who wrote it, Voltaire, used the same gag too often, though. The characters are always getting killed and then turning out not to have been killed after all, and they tell their friends what happened in the meantime. I like the character in it called Pangloss.[25]

Liebling noted that early in the war, when the Red Cross gave pocket editions of books to the troops landing at Greenock, many were discarded, but a couple of years later the very same troops "had become book readers, traders and hoarders. . . . Largely, they had to turn to books . . . because there were no towns with jukeboxes to go to, no jive to tune in on, no liquor to be had, etc."[26] One infantryman had picked up a copy of Lytton Strachey's *Queen Victoria* just before a battle and put it in his pocket. "The next time I became cognizant of it," he wrote his wife,

> it was some two days later. We had advanced through enemy artillery fire and had finally been pinned down in a field by their mortar and machine gun fire. . . . After some close ones, I just dove head first into what appeared to be a solid growth of brambles and bushes. They broke under my weight, and I found myself in a rather deep narrow ditch below the surface of the ground. Soon I became cramped and started to move a little; a lump in my pocket turned out to be *Queen Victoria*. It

was pretty "hot" above. . . . There was nothing I could do except wait. I started to read and found it a rather good substitute for just "sweating." There was a two-way traffic above me, our shells going, theirs coming and bursting, and I kept reading of Victoria's "dear, beautiful Albert" and his soft flowing mustache that she admired so much. . . . Many times I wondered if I would ever finish it. The shelling lifted, we moved on, and days later I finished the book in a hospital somewhere in England.[27]

"The Council Books," another enlisted man remembered, "were our mainstay. They arrived punctually wherever we were throughout the Normandy campaign and later during the buzz-bombing months in Antwerp. They were the backbone and the chief attraction of the company day room wherever it was and however otherwise inadequate."[28] During the Battle of Saipan, another soldier later remembered, he carried a copy of Sandburg's *Storm Over the Land* in his helmet and read it during lulls in the battle.[29] Thousands of soldiers wrote the authors of books they enjoyed, many having "read a book straight through for the first time in their lives."[30]

For the first time in history, the American armed forces maintained libraries for soldiers on the bases. Stationed in Alaska, the devout Trotskyist Irving Howe found himself devouring books on subjects he would never have normally looked for: "Never before or since have I read in so wonderfully purposeless a way. The camp library had a few serious books in each of a range of subjects, which encouraged learning and discouraged specialization. . . . [H]ere I could read for the unalloyed pleasure of knowledge." He would attribute to this reading "a slow intellectual change," as his mind opened to subjects other than politics, discovering "a multitude of new interests leading to that taste for complication which is necessarily a threat to the political mind. It was not my ideas that changed so much, it was my cast of thought. . . . [It] was here in Alaska that I lost the singleness of mind that had inspired the politics of my youth."[31] By 1947 he was writing literary criticism for magazines such as *Commentary* and *Partisan Review.*

Many of the soldiers began aspiring to write themselves or were already published authors. Katherine Anne Porter, whose *Selected Stories* was made for the Council Books series, got six hundred letters within six months of its appearance in the spring of 1945, some from aspiring writers seeking guidance on technique. A. R. Ammons, from backwoods North Carolina, came across a paperback anthology of poetry while on patrol in the Pacific and began writing poetry himself. He never stopped, going on to win a National Book Award and teach creative writing at Cornell. Wallace Stegner found himself lecturing right after the war to "a flood of G.I. students" who had read the abridged ASE edition of *Big Rock Candy Mountain*. They inspired him to found the creative-writing program at Stanford, the second one in the United States.[32] James Dickey, an engineering student before the war, read the Armed Services Editions as an enlisted man in the Philippines and later became a writer.[33] The series helped make and revive reputations. The Fitzgerald revival that began in the late 1940s likely owes much to the Armed Services Editions of *The Great Gatsby* and *The Diamond as Big as the Ritz and Other Stories* (a book made for the series; see fig. 1.2).[34]

The Council on Books in Wartime also launched a series of motion-picture newsreels based on books, titled *Books in the War*. And NBC ran a popular radio program called *Words at War*. Bennett Cerf, one of the business's most effective publicists, had a *Books Are Bullets* program on WQXR, the *New York Times* station. The council started a paperback reprint series similar to the Armed Services Editions, called Overseas Editions, for distribution to people in newly liberated areas of Europe. This had a propaganda function but was also motivated by a desire to stimulate a European market for American books in the postwar era at a moment when the European publishing industry was in ruins.

In the spring of 1944, Bennett Cerf wrote Donald Klopfer that Modern Library sales were growing fast, and he predicted a rosy future:

The hundreds of thousands of Modern Library books that have been distributed through Army and Navy channels have introduced the

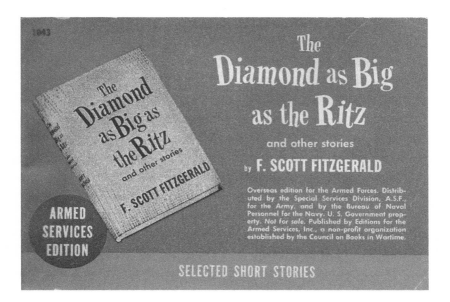

FIGURE 1.2 Cover of Armed Services Edition of F. Scott Fitzgerald, *The Diamond as Big as the Ritz and Other Stories*. *Source*: Charles Scribner's Sons. All rights reserved.

series to God knows how many millions of new readers. If only one half of one percent of these boys retains an interest in books in general and the Modern Library in particular, our potential market will have multiplied about five times over pre-war standards. This isn't just dreaming, it is hard, cold facts.[35]

One small but growing segment of the market was for literature by, about, and/or for African Americans. The Johnson Publishing Company in Chicago rode the wave of the Great Migration, a rolling revolution in black literacy, and founded *Negro Digest* in 1942 on the model of *Readers Digest*. Richard Wright's *Native Son*, Ann Petry's *The Street*, and Willard Motley's *Knock on Any Door* were all bestsellers. Margaret Walker's first book of poetry, *For My People*, was one of the best-selling titles in the Yale Younger Poets series. And this is not to mention Frank Yerby's first four novels, none of which would be considered "Negro fiction."

In the course of the 1940s, the paperback revolution reached "hundreds of thousands of people who had seldom read any kind of book before," according to the *Harpers* editor Cass Canfield.[36] Paperbacks had briefly found success in the nineteenth-century United States, but American publishers had given up on them until the founding of Penguin Books in England in the late 1930s. Emulating Penguin, Pocket Books started in 1938 with Pearl S. Buck's *The Good Earth* and was followed by Avon (1941), Dell (1942), Popular Library (1942), Bantam (1945), and New American Library (1947–1948). In the course of the 1940s, more and more "literary" titles came out in paper, particularly through New American Library, and the cover art modulated from lurid, pulp-like illustrative styles to more modernist designs borrowing from expressionism and surrealism.[37] As Paula Rabinowitz has recently argued in a book devoted to paperbacks of the midcentury, "pulp linked high modernism to the vernacular."[38]

These books sold where books had never been seen before—in drugstores, newsstands, smoke shops. Most were formula fiction—mysteries, detectives, romances, and the like, a step up from the earlier pulps, but not a big step. Yet "literary" titles got increasing attention and soon formed the core of New American Library (NAL), which took over the role of the Modern Library for the postwar era. NAL fundamentally changed the perception of paperback publishing and vastly expanded the market for modern American literature.

Before the forties, before Penguin, Germany had a respected paperback industry. Tauchnitz press in Leipzig even had a paperback collection of British and American authors that dated back to the mid–nineteenth century and in the interwar period brought out editions of work by Hemingway, Joyce, Sinclair Lewis, and others, copies of which American and British tourists smuggled home rather than buy the more expensive hardbacks published in New York and London. The Nazis shut them down. Another German paperback publisher from Hamburg, Kurt Enoch, who was Jewish, moved to Paris in 1937 to escape the Nazis but had to abandon the enterprise, fleeing first to London and then, penniless but well connected, to New York. Perceiving a niche for nonfiction and high-quality fiction in paperback, and with money borrowed from family and friends, he opened his own house.

Then he met Allen Lane, the British publisher of Penguin Books. With the advent of the war, Lane needed his American wing (headed by Ian Ballantine) to run semi-independently with books printed in the United States, but because he could not transfer funds out of England, Enoch bought into Penguin's American division with money loaned by his fellow refugee Kurt Wolff (a founder of Pantheon Books) and split the executive duties with Ballantine. After the war, Ballantine wanted to move the firm "down market" to compete with Pocket Books. This conflicted with Lane's vision as well as Enoch's, so he left to found Bantam Books; Enoch took over the American Penguin.[39] Not long afterward, Victor Weybright showed up at the New York Penguin office with an assurance from Lane that he could have some sort of executive position. He had met Lane during the war while connected with the U.S. embassy in London. Enoch sold half of his 40 percent equity in the American Penguin to Weybright, and they became partners, with Weybright as editor-in-chief and Enoch in charge of production and marketing. After two years they bought the Penguin equity in the company and in the course of 1947–1948 renamed the operation "The New American Library of World Literature."[40] While Avon, Dell, and the Popular Library were all connected with the pulp-magazine publishers, NAL would cultivate connections with the likes of Knopf and Cerf, whom Weybright emulated in his own way.

Weybright had a vision of a paperback reprint house along the lines of Modern Library but going where Modern Library had never gone, into the drugstores and newsstands where only magazines had been sold before, in small cities, towns, and hamlets across the United States. Under the slogan "Good Reading for the Millions," the firm also deliberately marketed the modernists. By 1948, Weybright came to the conclusion that their most successful books were those of what he called "genuine literary quality or dynamic contemporary appeal," not those written by the popular magazine writers like Edna Ferber.[41] The firm deliberately set out to expand readership for modernist writers. Their edition of

William Faulkner's *Sanctuary* in 1947 opened with a prefatory statement highlighting the lurid aspects of Faulkner's fiction—"full of rape, incest, violence, death and corruption," comparable to Bierce and Poe "in the category of the horror story." They compared the plot to that of a gangster novel and then emphasized that what made Faulkner's work different was its symbolism and psychological complexity.[42] Playing up the action, violence, and horror of Faulkner's fiction was undoubtedly necessary to meet the sales requirement for a 25-cent book. NAL needed to sell at least 75,000 copies of a short book and well over 100,000 of a longer one to avoid raising the price. And they succeeded. *Sanctuary* sold 148,000 copies in the last six months of 1947 alone; by April 1948, it was in its seventh printing.

Weybright also wanted to expand the market for writing by and about African Americans. On the last page of *Sanctuary*, the firm advertised Richard Wright's *Uncle Tom's Children* and Lillian Smith's *Strange Fruit* as other Signet titles in which readers might be interested. Among novels by black authors, in 1949 alone Signet/NAL also published Ann Petry's *The Street*, William Gardner Smith's *The Last of the Conquerors*, Chester Himes's *If He Hollers Let Him Go*, and Willard Savoy's *Alien Land*. Weybright also urged distributors to expand their marketing strategies to African Americans and to hire agents with knowledge of black neighborhoods. In 1950 he launched his new Signet Giants imprint—for unabridged long books of special literary significance selling at 35 cents— with Richard Wright's *Native Son*:

> The New American Library . . . is especially proud to launch SIGNET GIANTS with *Native Son*. The book was hailed by the critics as "an outstanding novel," a "contemporary classic," "a novel of tremendous power and beauty," "the most powerful American novel to appear since *The Grapes of Wrath*." It joins a distinguished list of Signet books by leading Negro writers, or which deal with racial themes.[43]

Other advertising compared the novel with *Crime and Punishment* and *An American Tragedy*.

In 1950, when angling for the rights to Willard Motley's *Knock on Any Door*, Weybright could claim that NAL had "garnered acceptance for substantial literature in the mass market to a degree not approached by anyone else in our field. . . . We have developed acceptance and enormous sales for authors, like Motley, in the top flight of contemporary literature."[44] Motley split a $25,000 NAL advance with Appleton-Century-Crofts for the reprint rights.[45] Thus NAL succeeded in winning the respect of prestige trade publishers, bookstores, and reviewers, helping give paperback publishing a new image. By the early 1950s, both authors and hardback trade publishers badly wanted NAL to reprint their books and were partly dependent on money from reprint rights. Before long, even New Directions was publishing paperbound books for good business reasons, and in 1953 the war veteran Lawrence Ferlinghetti founded the first all-paperback bookstore in the United States, City Lights—soon to spawn a paperback imprint wholly identified with the avant-garde, with books small and light enough to fit in a shirt or jeans pocket.

The growing popularity of literature in the United States coincided with its rising international prestige. The evisceration of literary publishing on the continent and the duress of Great Britain were not all: refugees from fascism across Europe helped make New York the cultural crucible of the midcentury. Refugees from the Soviet Union were soon to follow. But American writing also gained from its embrace by European trendsetters like Sartre, who wrote in an essay published in the *Atlantic Monthly* in 1946: "The greatest literary development in France between 1929 and 1939 was the discovery of Faulkner, Dos Passos, Hemingway, Caldwell, and Steinbeck. . . . At once, for thousands of young intellectuals the American novel took its place together with jazz and the movies, among the best of the importations from the United States."[46] During the Nazi occupation, reading Hemingway became a sign of resistance in itself. According to Sartre, French writers subsequently experimented with the new American narrative techniques, revolutionizing the existing forms of French literature, which they found inadequate to the contemporary situation.[47] French existentialist novels in turn became major influences on postwar American writing. In China, too, scholars attempting to construct a national literary tradition took great interest in American literature during the 1940s, beginning a translation project in 1941 that lasted until the 1950s, when the triumph of the People's Republic put an end to the project, redirecting intellectual energies toward political writing and turning scholars away from the culture of the imperialist United States.[48]

Alfred Kazin later reminisced about his trip to Europe in 1945 due to interest in his book *On Native Grounds*:

> I wanted fiercely to learn Europe. It turned out that Europe was crazy to learn the latest American writers. So I went to Paris, on my first airplane ride, just before Bastille Day in 1945 to address the first postwar congress of French professors of English and American literature. . . . The French intellectuals I met didn't know whether they loved America more than they hated it or hated it more than they loved it but either way they were obsessed with us.[49]

One reason for this was the internationalism of American literature during the period. Many American writers were or had been expatriates or foreign correspondents; many were fluent in multiple languages and used them in their writing. American publishers actively sought out new and established authors from other countries. Writers and publishers from Europe lived in the United States to escape persecution. In 2008, the permanent secretary of the Nobel Prize Committee charged that American literary culture had become too insular and that it isolated itself from writing elsewhere. Whatever the merits of that charge, it could not have been imagined in the 1940s.

The German publishing industry had been immolated after Hitler's seizure of power, with book banning and book burning heralding a general hegira of (especially Jewish) publishers. Some moved to Holland, France, and England in the 1930s, but when Germany attacked those countries they fled to the United States. The same was true of French publishers who were Jewish. They began by publishing translations from their earlier lists, but they also introduced new authors translated for the first time, which, as John W. Tebbell has written, set off "an unprecedented outpouring of books in the exiles' own languages."[50] Founded in 1940, Les Editions de la Maison Française was founded in 1940 to publish French authors in their own language. Frederick Ungar arrived in New York in 1940 from Vienna and published the work of Goethe, Schiller, Heine, Rilke, and others in the original German. Roy Publishers, founded in Warsaw in 1925, moved to New York in 1942; they had been one of Poland's most important houses and the publishers in Polish of Pearl S. Buck, Sinclair Lewis, Ernest Hemingway, and the like. To the American public they brought the work of Polish and Slavic authors. L. B. Fischer of Germany came to New York by way of Stockholm; J. P. Didier of France also moved to New York in 1942.

Of greatest impact was Pantheon Books, launched in 1942 by the German refugees Helen and Kurt Wolff in partnership with the American Kyrill Schubert. In Europe, the Wolffs had published Max Brod, Kafka, Werfel, Gorky, Chekhov, and Sinclair Lewis, along with an eighty-six-volume series of avant-garde expressionist poetry. In New York they helped define European intellectual life, appealing to both refugees and Americans. Jacques Schiffrin joined them in 1943. He had founded La Bibliothèque de la Pléiade in Paris (which merged with the prestigious Éditions Gallimard) but was fired under Nazi pressure by Gallimard in 1940. Under his influence, Pantheon began publishing new books by André Gide and an edition (in French) of Camus's *L'étranger*. Pantheon also started the influential Bollingen Series for books on psychology, art, and the humanities. The German-reading market was much larger than the French and was Pantheon's larger initial target. They scoured the New York Public Library for European titles to translate into English, aiming to bring the best of European culture to American audiences.[51]

In 1945 Schocken Books was founded in New York by Salman Schocken, a German Jew and friend of Martin Buber. He and his brother had owned one of Europe's most successful retail empires in the 1920s, which he had to abandon in 1936. He had also founded Schocken Verlag, which was put under Nazi censorship in 1937. He arrived in New York, by way of Tel Aviv, in 1941. His main goal was to publish Jewish titles and spread Jewish studies. Among his early books were ones by Kafka and Scholem. Hannah Arendt joined as editor in 1946 (having arrived in the United States in 1941) and continued in that capacity through 1949, just when her influence on American intellectual life was reaching its peak.[52]

One can barely come to a proximate understanding of the American literary culture in the 1940s without knowing a great deal of non-American literature, especially Russian, French, German, and British—and particularly Kafka, Dostoevsky, Koestler, Orwell, Auden, Malraux, Gide, Proust, Sartre, Camus, Mann—the list goes on. Mann's reputation was so secure in the 1940s that Knopf felt advertising was superfluous for his books. Mann, who had come to the United States in 1938, attested that "the American public is to a large degree replacing my lost German readers."[53] To Alfred Kazin, Kafka was the essential author of the decade, a judgment with which Anatole Broyard agreed in his Greenwich Village memoir *Kafka Was the Rage.*

New Directions Press both picked up on and encouraged the internationalist trend by deliberately setting out to Europeanize American audiences. As soon as he could get to Europe after the war James Laughlin went on an extensive trip there to work out distribution networks for his books, to locate inexpensive printers, and to scout out new authors worthy of translation. Upon his return he noted that "a great many Europeans read English and are hungry for good American books."[54] He also found plenty of good writers in France and Italy for translation, and the anthology *New Directions 10* (1948) included many of them.

The professionalization of imaginative writing in the United States began in the 1940s, when preparation for a writing life moved from journalism to the universities. One reason for this move was a rising regard for such writing in, of all places, English departments. In the course of the 1940s, a new phenomenon called "writers conferences" sprang up in universities across the country.[55] Literary prizes and fellowships proliferated. There had been some creative writers in English departments before, and most of the "Southern Agrarians" were professors in the 1930s at places like Vanderbilt, LSU, and Kenyon College. But in terms of creative-writing programs, only the Iowa Writers Workshop (then housed in the University of Iowa's English department) had existed before the war. Between 1945 and 1950 programs sprang up at Johns Hopkins, Stanford, Cornell, Denver, Florida, and Indiana; they now blanket the country. The return of veterans inspired most of these programs, but another factor was a transformation in the conception of American literary scholarship coincident with the rise of the so-called New Criticism but not to be equated with it.

In an influential 1941 book entitled *Literary Scholarship: Its Aims and Methods*, the case was made by five influential scholars, including the head of creative writing at Iowa, for reconsidering the "proper ends and means" of literary study. Dissatisfied with the dominance of a "scientific" approach to language and an old-fashioned form of literary history, the authors proposed a fundamental reorientation of universities' relationship to contemporary letters. Literary scholars had removed themselves from the life and letters of their time, from contemporary ideas, and from writers and critics. Literary scholarship, wrote Norman Foerster in the opening essay, needed a rapprochement with creative writing and criticism and to be "more concerned with the values which the humanities have to offer a world threatened with a barbarism expertly scientific in war and peace."[56] He called for restoring the importance to literary scholarship of "aesthetic sensitiveness, the ability to write firmly, a concern for general ideas, and an insight into the permanent human values embodied in literature," along with a "rigorous discipline in the specialized types of literary activity"—in which he included the theory and practice of literary criticism and "the art of imaginative writing."[57] Literature as a subject, he emphasized, lies "in the realm of values," and by retiring to a scholastic enclave of philology, influence study, or other forms of literary history, scholars had abandoned that most important of realms, leaving it unoccupied except by philosophers. Literary scholarship must itself become literary again, and this called for restoring imaginative writing to its domain. Abdicating their responsibility to values and purposes, scholars had cut themselves off from the life of their time. As if to prove the importance of literature, European fascists had meanwhile exiled numberless men of letters, recognizing their central role in educating a critical citizenry.[58]

Literature concerns the forces that guide action, feed the imagination, and provide resolution, Foerster argued, shaping "the immeasurable forces of human preferences and beliefs." The "dignity of the individual" might ultimately depend on teaching the humanities, keeping values accessible to the individual and helping each person develop the critical faculties required for modern citizenship. Value judgments in the arts and literature were connected with competencies in choosing wisely among competing values in private and public life.[59] This did not support a valorization of didactic literature but rather interpretive and analytical rigor and the appreciation of complexity.

The entry of creative writing into the universities was connected with defending democracy and with a rising emphasis on literature as something most worthy of study for its shaping of meaning and value. Subordinating literature to the history of ideas or of language, to social history, to biography, or to psychoanalysis missed its very reason for being, a crucial one: "Signs are multiplying that a grave responsibility may be placed, gradually or suddenly, upon American professors of literature and the other humanities," wrote Foerster. "Are they prepared to receive it?"[60] The 1940s was in many respects, as Randall Jarrell later pointed out, "The Age of Criticism."

Impressed by French *explication de texte*, or "close reading," and by the methods of the Russian formalists, the authors of *Literary Scholarship* were cognizant of what was just coming to be known as the New Criticism but placed a greater emphasis on the relationship of literary meaning and values to contemporary society and to personal experience. Thus the promotion of New Critical methods of reading in some quarters derived from resistance to a prior apolitical, "scientific," dryly academic approach to the very arts that, the critics often said, made life meaningful. Indeed, the New Criticism of the academics hardly dominated the field of criticism in general. In this moment when this new criticism was just acquiring a name and its methods were being codified and distributed through English departments with such textbooks as *Understanding*

Poetry (1939), formalist analyses emerged alongside a growing interest in psychoanalysis and interdisciplinary American studies. By the end of the 1940s, the New Criticism had become something close to a doxology in the English departments, but it also was eliciting passionate critiques by the likes of Edmund Wilson, Lionel Trilling, F. O. Matthiessen, and Alfred Kazin. The Modern Language Association was not then the guardian and guarantor of literary criticism as such. Nonetheless, it is useful to understand why the "new criticism" seemed so exciting a development in its nascent moment.

Writing in the *Kenyon Review*, Arthur Mizener noted that English departments were full of literary historians who had no critical ability whatever and no means of explaining what made some literary works "better" than others.[61] Indeed, they had little ability even to analyze the structure of literary works. They were therefore of no use to budding writers and critics. The editors of the *Kenyon Review* and the *Southern Review*, sympathetic to this critique, jointly devoted their fall 1940 issues to the topic "Literature and the Professors."[62] Out of this ferment grew one of the most important developments in the teaching of literature in the United States of the twentieth century. Yet it is important to point out that the *Kenyon Review*, edited by John Crowe Ransom and gaining its greatest influence precisely during the 1940s, was not only hospitable to the "new critics." They published work by the Marxist critical theorist Theodor Adorno, held symposia on Freud and psychoanalysis, and published early American-studies scholarship. The journal was by no means hostile to various approaches to literature, including historicist ones. Ransom was politically conservative, but his student Randall Jarrell certainly was not, nor was John Berryman, another regular contributor to the journal who, like Jarrell, had been deeply impressed by Marxism. Lionel Trilling, another of the journal's main contributors, anticipated reader-response criticism in a contribution to the 1940 symposium on psychoanalysis:

There is . . . no single meaning to a work of art and this is not true merely because it is better that it should be true—because, that is, it makes art a richer thing—but because historical and personal experience show it to be true; changes in historical context and in personal mood change the meaning of a work. . . . The meaning of a work cannot lie in intention alone; it must also lie in its effect. In short, the audience partly determines the meaning of the work.[63]

In the work of such emerging poet-critics as Randall Jarrell and John Berryman, the mentorship of the New Critics (particularly Ransom and Tate) is plainly evident, yet one finds a turn away from the stress on "impersonality" and a more left-wing political orientation. Moreover, paralleling the rise of New Criticism in the academy, nonacademic critics grew in influence elsewhere, like Alfred Kazin, whose *On Native Grounds* (1942) made him instantly famous. That book concluded with a strong blast against the "new formalists." Shortly after the book came out and he was adjusting to his success (a kind of success no literary critic today can imagine), he wrote in his journal: "The new barbarians. One of John Crowe Ransom's emissaries comes to see me. We talk of our disagreements. He says that Beethoven's *Eroica* is nasty. He uses the word 'stomach' when he means courage, militancy, personality: Viz: 'Van Wyck Brooks has no stomach.' But when I use the word 'shit,' he is shocked. I say it again—shit!"[64] Such passion, such clarity, stoked the fire of literary criticism.

Attention to aesthetic form rapidly grew among antifascists, even in reviews that in the 1930s had been mainly Marxist, like *Partisan Review*—a major venue for poetry and literary criticism in the 1940s under the leadership of Philip Rahv and Delmore Schwartz. To publish criticism was one of the chief missions of New Directions Press, the other being poetry. The so-called New Criticism's formalist agenda gained hold as an argument for the importance of the humanities to higher learning. It was yoked, however, in important respects to Southern Agrarian politics, which would not have endeared it to so many if not for a belief that a concern for values and meaning had been subordinated in Western culture to scientific method, with catastrophic results. This interest in values and meaning was believed to distinguish the arts and humanities from journalism and the social sciences. And the New Criticism lent itself well to a programmatic form of teaching introductory courses in literature to the swelling enrollees in postwar colleges.

Consider the development of new college-based literary reviews. *Kenyon Review*, founded in 1939 by John Crowe Ransom, came from an inspiration of the wife of the president of Kenyon College. The president recruited Ransom specifically to establish such a review. It quickly became one of the major literary reviews of its time, especially for poetry and criticism. Probably only *Partisan Review* had an equivalent impact. When the *Southern Review* folded in 1942 because of the war, *Kenyon Review* took over its unexpired subscriptions and named its editors as advisory editors.

Sewanee Review, founded in 1892 at the University of the South, reached its greatest influence in the 1940s. It first began publishing poetry in the mid-1920s and fiction in the mid-1930s, becoming a standard-bearer of the Southern Agrarians and then a major venue of the New Criticism (along with *Kenyon Review* and *Southern Review*), particularly under the leadership of Andrew Lytle and Allen Tate in the early to mid-1940s. In 1944 Tate officially became editor and redesigned the journal into the form it has had to the present day. *Antioch Review* was founded in 1941 over concerns about the rise of fascism. Left-wing but not communist in orientation, publishing work by the likes of John Dewey and Carey McWilliams, mainly on political and social issues, it added fiction in 1942 and poetry in 1945. Ralph Ellison's famous essay "Richard Wright's Blues" appeared in the journal in 1945, when he was at the beginning of his career.

If one justification for the rise of formalist criticism was that it could aid creative writers, the case for teaching creative writing in the universities was also in part based on an argument that modern writers themselves devalued literature, emphasizing instead a "cult of experience"—as if they had nothing to learn from the writers of the past, let alone literary critics. Wilbur L. Schramm, the director of Iowa's creative-writing workshop, argued that any aspiring writer needed to learn the art of criticism, that the best contemporary literature was not simply a record of "experience" or the product of romantic inspiration but a result of study and craft. The university English department was a better place for a budding writer to develop than the city room of a newspaper or the dispersed pulp-magazine stable. Journalism and pulp writing subordinated the creative imagination to reporting and formula fiction. Teaching, editing, and professional criticism were better supplementary vocations for the writer than journalism or writing potboilers or advertising copy. In university English departments aspiring writers could get to know one another and share their work, sometimes but not always under the supervision of more established authors.

Creative writing and scholarly criticism approached each other more closely than at any time before or since, particularly in the field of poetry. The disdain many creative writers have felt toward literary criticism in recent decades was certainly not shared by the likes of John Berryman, Randall Jarrell, Delmore Schwartz, Yvor Winters, and others of the World War II generation. Scholars of poetry—many of them poets— regularly published in and cited articles in the same reviews that poets most revered. The decade of the 1940s became the age of the poet-critics.

Criticism and creative writing thus established themselves together in the universities, inspired by the challenge of "totalitarianism" (fascist or Stalinist) and a belief in the importance of literature. And by the veterans. Wallace Stegner had earned a "creative" Master of Arts degree at Iowa (one of the first), where he roomed with Wilbur Schramm, and found his way to Stanford in 1945. There he found inspiration in the returning GIs, who had plenty to write about, and those who wanted to write had integrity. As he faced his bloated classes, he learned that some of them had read his work in Armed Services Editions. He founded the writing program at Stanford in 1946 with the help of fellowships funded by a wealthy woman donor, and the "Stegner Fellowship" remains one of the most prestigious awards for graduate-student writers to this day.

The rise of creative writing in the universities has been called by Mark McGurl "the most important event in postwar American literary history." Attending to "the increasingly intimate relation between literary production and the practices of higher education," he adds, is the key to understanding the originality of postwar American literature."[65] The codification of the New Criticism in tandem with the growth of creative-writing programs and the expansion of higher education with the G.I. Bill led to a dramatic expansion and diversification of the writing profession as well as a strengthening of what McGurl terms the "social functionality" of modernist literature in the United States. On a related if more mundane note, John Aldridge pointed out in 1951, young writers after World War II, unlike their predecessors, could find jobs related to their literary ambitions and could get training in the universities before graduating and having to support themselves.

> The universities alone are doing much to prevent the outbreak of another exile movement, at the same time that they are, as Stephen Spender said, "subsidizing American contemporary literature." . . . Instead of starving in Montparnasse, the young man [*sic*] of ability can take up residence on the campus, work under the tutelage of such writer-scholars as Wallace Stegner at Stanford, Robert Penn Warren at Minnesota, Mark Schorer at California, R. P. Blackmur at Princeton, and Lionel Trilling at Columbia, and even prepare himself for jobs like theirs so that if his writing should not pay off he will always be assured of a steady income.[66]

By the 1950s, what Irving Howe called "a major shift in cultural demography" had begun, as literary people were enticed away from "urban centers and bohemian enclaves to university towns across the continent."[67] The scope and significance of American literature and criticism in the general society, in the United States and abroad, had expanded exponentially since 1939. Modern and contemporary literature began taking a larger and larger role in the postwar academy. But as the effects of this dispersion and academicization set in over the decades to follow and as other media drew leisure-time attention, the importance of literature in the general culture declined. It became increasingly (but not exclusively) a professional specialization supported by universities. This is the context in which many Americans read it today.

2

POPULAR CULTURE AND THE AVANT-GARDE

···

As the 1940s saw the institutionalization of modernist aesthetics in popular styles, popular American culture assumed the role of things to come. "America is not small potatoes!" yawped Le Corbusier: "In the last twenty years, facing the old continent, it has set up the Jacob's ladder of the new times. It is a blow in the stomach that strikes you like a hurricane." This was in a chapter titled "I Am an American!" Internationalism and American cultural nationalism were not opposed tendencies in the 1940s, when American literature became an object of advanced study and training and the term "American Renaissance" was coined to name the era of emergence of a national literature. This is not a "nationalist" claim but a statement of widely, and internationally, recognized fact. "Once you have opened the door on America," Le Corbusier's Parisian compatriots confided, "you cannot close it again."[1]

The publication of F. O. Matthiessen's *American Renaissance: Art and Expression in the Age of Emerson and Whitman* (1941) put American literature on a level never accorded it before in the proliferating archipelagos of academe. It remains foundational (if controversial) to American literary study to this day.[2] Matthiessen identified the greatest American literary achievements of 1850–1855 with the struggle for a democratic culture and aesthetics consonant with such a culture. Suddenly even scholars had to take Whitman and Melville seriously, on a par with the greatest European authors going back to Shakespeare, and the case was made on a basis that Emerson and Whitman would have approved: that a new kind of society demanded and depended upon a new kind of aesthetic sensibility, a "democratic" one. Matthiessen essentially agreed with Whitman's conviction that American democracy's advent required a fundamental shift in the notion of the beautiful, portending changes in the distribution of social power.

Reviewing *American Renaissance* in the *Kenyon Review*, Daniel Aaron hailed it as the first truly critical estimate of American literature, emphasizing literary analysis over intellectual history (although making use of the latter). Deeply versed in the economic, political, and social backgrounds of the nineteenth century, Matthiessen had sought out the aesthetic principles guiding his five major figures (Emerson, Thoreau, Melville, Hawthorne, and Whitman) to show how they arrived at a "functional aesthetics." "And it is here," Aaron noted,

> that literary criticism imperceptibly passes into social criticism. For the ideas of these men were running counter to an age which divorced form and function and habitually divided language into the coarse and the refined, which saw beauty and utility as antithetical and equated culture with wealth and leisure. In discovering strength and beauty in the language of truckmen, in the shape of an ax or steamboat, in the slim graceful lines of a clipper ship, these men were denying that art was simply the "ideal" transcending the "useful."[3]

Aaron's analysis connects social-political values with literary ones without subordinating either the "aesthetic" or the "social" to the other, and at the same time he sees the relationship between functional objects of everyday life and "high" art. He closes with the postscript that "a sympathetic awareness of the American experience is indispensable for the elucidation of our literary culture," a culture weakened by the isolation of the educated class from the American masses and their country.[4]

There was, then, a growing strain in American intellectual culture positing connections between what was sometimes called vernacular culture and "high art." Melville and Whitman, after all, were the avant-garde of their day, breaking the forms of European fiction and poetry and reassembling the pieces with those of the American vernacular. Matthiessen's work had demonstrated how a modern, democratic literature had arisen out of a popular substratum of social consciousness and creative expression, in the midst of the rise of American capitalism and in tension with it. But Matthiessen himself would barely outlast the decade. A gay Christian socialist who was despondent over world affairs and the death of a lover, under suspicion for "un-American" activities and vulnerable to exposure as a "pervert" while the Cold War turned frigid, Matthiessen jumped to his death in 1950 from the window of a twelfth-floor hotel room in Boston.

There is something peculiarly of the 1940s about both Matthiessen's achievement and Aaron's analysis, marking a movement away from the Marxism of the 1930s but not from its insight into political and economic structures and highlighting a rising interest in aesthetic form in relation to "democratic" values and popular culture, such as one will later find in, for example, the essays of Ralph Ellison. Whitman's "Democratic Vistas," composed in the immediate aftermath of the Civil War as a stinging critique of the classist, antiegalitarian culture of his time, had struck the keynote, calling for artists and writers to address above all "the average, the bodily, the concrete, the democratic, the popular, on which all the superstructures of the future are to permanently rest"—like skyscrapers, perhaps.

Gertrude Stein called America the oldest country in the world because it was the first to enter the twentieth century—in the 1880s:

And now what is the twentieth century that America discovered. The twentieth century is a century that found out that the cheapest articles should be made of the very best material. . . . The Americans knew that if you wanted to make a lot of things that is things that will sell cheap you had to make them of the best material otherwise you could not turn them out fast enough, that is series manufacture because cheap material could not stand the strain. So America began to live in the twentieth century in the eighties with the Ford car and all that other series manufacturing.[5]

The culture industry—so called for the first time by Max Horkheimer and Theodor Adorno in 1944—was not far behind.

What was the relationship between "art" and "mass culture"? As European forms of modernist art took hold in North America, they became part of the general culture and the market economy, aspects of popular styles, including advertising, that foreigners found distinctly "American" and modern. Was American popular culture, existing between and merging these poles, really a culture (and genuinely "popular"), or was it just an effect of capitalist exploitation and consumerism? One strong strain in European thought, and Marxist criticism, has been to see popular culture as an "authentic" people's culture, rather like folk culture. Mass culture, on the other hand, is inauthentic because it does not grow from the people but is distributed to them by mass marketing that entices consumption, passivity, and allegiance to capitalist social relations. As I was once asked by a gathering of German professors, magistrates, and government ministers after giving a talk about American cultural pluralism, what is American culture other than fast food and Hollywood film?

One is forced to recognize the complex and not always antagonistic relationship between avant-garde and vernacular culture in the United States of the 1940s. This is where American popular culture took form. Linguists speak of a phenomenon called "dialect interference," in which a word with particular connotations in one dialect of a language gets confused with its connotations in another. Such may be the case with Marxist views of American popular culture, which developed in relationship to market forces virtually from the start, in blackface minstrelsy, medicine shows, and other forms. One of William Carlos Williams's insistent points was that American popular culture simply could not equate with European or British conceptions. It was the job of artists to help create a popular culture between the mass produced, the vernacular, the advertisers, and the cosmopolitan avant-garde.

Horkheimer and Adorno, German refugees in New York and then Los Angeles, wrote a powerful attack on the "culture industry" during the very time that avant-garde methods were gaining traction in that industry. To Horkheimer and Adorno, mass culture threatened the "negative" function of art, which is to evoke a critical perspective on the everyday workings of ideology from a relatively autonomous, alienated position; it grew from marketing considerations and the needs of capital, rather than being a spontaneous expression of people's interests and desires. As entertainment, it served the status quo, shaping desire to the needs of consumer capitalism and preventing people from conceiving of a society different from that in which they lived. In contrast, genuine art preserved a utopian quality and critical function independent of market considerations.[6]

Yet the market seemed continually to overwhelm art's autonomous critical function. It was difficult, if not impossible, for the avant-garde to stay ahead of it. Some avant-gardists did not even try. While the Frankfurt School theorists lamented the loss of art's aura in "the age of its mechanical reproducibility" (as Walter Benjamin had termed it before his death at the Spanish border), Gertrude Stein celebrated series manufacture and basked in the aura of celebrity. Aaron Copland, after a gestation period in avant-garde Paris in the 1920s, absorbed American folk music in his friend Alan Lomax's New York apartment and composed *Fanfare for the Common Man* (1942), *Rodeo* (1942), and *Appalachian Spring* (1944, commissioned by Martha Graham), making symphonic music popular. He believed it made no sense for serious composers to ignore the new media of radio, the phonograph, and cinema. Clement Greenberg had famously attacked "kitsch" in 1939 with an argument coincident with Adorno and Horkheimer's and in the course of the 1940s helped turn Jackson Pollock and a few other abstract expressionists into household names. Theodor Adorno loathed jazz as a debased product of the culture industry. Meanwhile, a new style of self-consciously avant-garde jazz called be-bop emerged in the 1940s and became a subject of serious political and cultural rumination for young soon-to-be Beats and for their elder, Langston Hughes, whose most ambitious poetic composition, *Montage of a Dream Deferred* (1951), would use be-bop and cinematic montage as its formal inspirations. In 1949, in his "Jesse B. Semple" column for the *Chicago Defender*, the eponymous working-class philosopher and social critic gave his theory of how be-bop got its name. The characteristic scat exclamations aren't just "nonsense" syllables: "Every time a cop hits a Negro with his billy club, that old club says 'BOP! BOP! . . . BE-BOP! . . . MOP! . . . BOP! . . . That's where Be-Bop came from, beaten right out of some Negro's head into them horns and saxophones and piano keys that plays it. Do you call that nonsense?"[7] Perhaps be-bop was exactly the kind of music Adorno was waiting for, even if he had trouble hearing it.

Contemporary fiction shaped new styles of cinematic entertainment, most notably what contemporary French intellectuals first began calling film noir. However, there were also profound differences between popular film and literature, as a comparison between the film *The Big Sleep* (scripted by Faulkner) and the novel by Raymond Chandler reveals. Subjects such as homosexuality, extramarital sex, and subversive political ruminations were "screened out" because of Hollywood's production code, imposed out of fear of what energies mass entertainment might provoke. In war novels one therefore finds repeated references to the movies as dangerously misleading and false. The relationship between avant-garde modernism and mass culture was, to say the least, both contradictory and ubiquitous.

Abstract styles of art and design were institutionalized in everyday environments on a purely instrumental basis: "beauty" and "utility," or the "refined" and the "useful," as Daniel Aaron had pointed out, need not be antithetical. In 1941–1942, on Roosevelt Island in New York's East River, Goldwater Hospital—a "welfare hospital"—was nearing completion and needed interior decoration. Before this, the norm in public buildings was to commission social-realist murals in the style of American regionalism, exemplified by Thomas Hart Benton, or that of the Mexican muralists José Clemente Orozco and Diego Rivera. Here, the choice was for abstraction, formerly considered a bizarre elitist trend tied to European decadence—too "unnatural" for the Right, too apolitical for the Left.

The rationale was not market based but therapeutic. Form follows function. Scenes of the outside world might be depressing for someone confined to a hospital over time, according to the artist Ilya Bolotowsky, and medical references might cause the patient to dwell on her condition:

> Consequently, the most suited design for a hospital mural should contain no definite subject matter but should be generally decorative and soothing in its line and color. The day room of the hospital is circular in shape. It is a very unusually beautiful room. However, its roundness might give some patients a feeling of being walled-in and fenced off from the rest of the world. Therefore, in the mural I have sought to create a feeling of free, open space. . . . The shapes of the doors and windows all around the day room have been woven into the design. . . . Since straight lines are the most restful things to contemplate, this mural is of straight lines and geometric shapes. The day room, its architecture, and its mural form one plastic unit. . . . The patient may enjoy the subdued colors with some emotion but with no unrest. I believe the Chronic Disease Hospital should have a mural in its dayroom as modern and progressive as the structure of the building and as the medical science of its staff.[8]

The shapes and lines of the mural would be purely geometrical, but they would interact with the constantly changing light streaming into the room from the semicircle of windows opposite. Bolotowsky's mural for Day Room D-31 functioned in this way (fig. 2.1). Over the course of a day, as the earth turned on its axis, lines of the window frames and casings would cast varying parallelograms and other geometrical designs over the floor and walls, in constantly shifting relationship with the mural's geometrical patterns, while also altering the mural's visible colors. The sensual experience of the patient in this "day room" is thus

FIGURE 2.1 Ilya Bolotowsky, *Abstraction*, 1942. Mural in Day Room D-31 of Goldwater Hospital, New York City. *Source*: Art © Estate of Ilya Bolotowsky/Licensed by VAGA, New York, NY. Photograph © Andrew L. Moore 2017.

contingent on the progressive interaction between natural light, architecture, painting, and individual point of view—a constantly changing visual synthesis of diverse material effects.

And what about literature? Paula Rabinowitz has written recently of the role of the paperback-book revolution in spreading modernist sensibilities and encouraging "demotic reading."[9] This is one important aspect of a broad transformation, but that transformation also depended in part on what modernists themselves were writing. Moreover, if the modernism the paperbacks distributed was "secondhand" (they were in fact all reprints), as Rabinowitz asserts, something else was going on at first hand in response to contemporary conditions, as first-generation modernists felt moved to communicate with a broader public. Frederic Jameson, too, has written of what he terms "late modernism" as essentially secondhand in the sense that it was no longer aesthetically radical, for it followed in the wake of the early-twentieth-century avant-garde.[10] In short, I think this is an understandable mischaracterization that derives, in part, from the Eurocentric habits of many *American* literature professors.

Jameson differentiates "late modernism" from the "classical modernists" or first-generation modernists on the basis that the latter were not making an ideological argument for the autonomy of art. Furthermore, they were operating without models for the type of artist they were becoming, and "form is never given in advance" but is rather "generated experimentally in the encounter, leading on into formations that could never have been predicted." Joyce had no model to follow, for example, but Nabokov had Joyce to follow. Or: "What separates late modernism's certainties from Mallarmé's groping discoveries is precisely the historical Mallarmé himself and his lapidary hints, which they already know in advance and repeat."[11] The argument resonates with the critique of the "culture industry" by Horkheimer and Adorno. Thus late modernism reuses the forms and strategies of the "original" modernists but necessarily with a different ideological meaning and force, that of aesthetic autonomy, which offers no resistance to the status quo.

This argument cannot accommodate such work as William Carlos Williams's *Paterson*, to take just one example, which develops new poetic strategies experimentally and has slight investment in aesthetic autonomy. And if it is true that someone like Charles Olson, emerging in the late 1940s, has Pound and Williams behind him, and Mallarmé or Baudelaire behind them, it is also true that Mallarmé and Baudelaire had Whitman and Poe behind them—both of whom sought "mass" audiences but produced experimental writing. Among early German expressionist poets, artists, and film directors, as among French symbolists, Whitman and Poe were heroes.

Jameson fully identifies the "modernist ideology" (which the classical modernists did *not* have, in his account) with late modernism and specifically the New Criticism, which he also sees as hegemonic after World War II. This ideology emphasized artistic autonomy, he argues, and was specifically an American product. Clement Greenberg's theory is paradigmatic, here. It argued for divorcing "art" from "culture," which was connected with mass culture, the culture industry (in Adorno's sense), and kitsch. Despite longing for artistic autonomy, however, late modernism is plagued by the need for an "anecdotal core," some "unassimilable empirical content" that short-circuits the attempts at autonomy. "Late modernist contingency is then precisely this dialectical process and constitutes the experience of the failure of autonomy to go all the way and fulfill its aesthetic programme."[12] This narrow characterization of American late-modernist criticism and creative practice cannot accommodate even the arguments of such major critics of the 1940s as Edmund Wilson and Alfred Kazin.

Jameson also concludes that the diminished aims of the late modernists as they moved toward aesthetic autonomy and away from the more radical aspirations of the early modernists toward the utopian and the absolute opened up a space of the middlebrow.

> It does not seem unduly restrictive, in an age of mass education, to suggest that the public of such a middlebrow late modernist literature and culture can be identified as the class fraction of college students (and their academic trainers), whose bookshelves, after graduation into "real life," preserve the souvenirs of this historically distinctive consumption which the surviving high modernist aesthetes and intellectuals have baptized as the canon, or Literature as such. But that canon is simply modernism, as the late modernists have selected and rewritten it in their own image.[13]

There are several problems with this formulation, beginning with the fact that Jameson is talking about something going on chiefly within English departments and the Modern Language Association, which had a far less dominant role in American literary culture (let alone American culture writ large) in the 1940s than today. His hypothesis also seems incapable of accommodating the fact that the surviving modernists themselves shifted tactics in response to the crises of the 1930s and World War II; this was not about valorizing aesthetic autonomy, in the sense of severing artistic creation from the larger social sphere, nor was it about meeting a manufactured consumer demand in the form of the "middlebrow." It had to do with engaging the social sphere in new ways and adapting previously avant-garde methods to new contingencies.

The modernists of the 1940s emphasized the importance of communicating with a public. Famously "difficult" modernists, including Stein,

Faulkner, Marianne Moore, and others experimented with more broadly accessible styles. Despite his loathing of Hollywood hackwork, experience writing Hollywood screenplays affected William Faulkner's "serious" fiction.

Kenneth Rexroth wrote at the time: "I think it was the events of the years 1935–36–37, more than any literary factors, which forced the issue of communication, the person to person responsibility of artistic creation, back into prominence."[14] Marianne Moore (a public librarian) considered the war a turning point in her career, making her "much more aware of the world's dilemma. People's effect on other people results, it seems to me, in an enforced sense of responsibility—a compulsory obligation to participate in others' problems."[15] Randall Jarrell needed the concrete subject matter and urgency of the war to break out of an artistic impasse.[16] His style and tone changed immediately after he joined the army in 1942 and landed at Chanute Field in Illinois: "I felt so strongly," he wrote Allen Tate,

> about everything I saw (the atmosphere was entirely one of lying, meaningless brutality and officiousness, stupidity not beyond belief but conception—the one word for everything in the army is *petty*) that stiff, sore, and sleepy, I'd sit up at night in the day room . . . writing poems, surrounded by people playing pool or writing home or reading comic-strip magazines.[17]

The obscurity of his early poems gave way to passionate engagement.

Wallace Stevens, one of the most recondite and abstract of modernist poets, spoke before Pearl Harbor of poetry as "resisting or evading the pressure of reality"; by August 1943 he had changed his mind: poetry required an "agreement with reality."[18] "Of Modern Poetry" (1942) registers the shift:

> It has to be living, to learn the speech of the place.
> It has to face the men of the time and to meet
> The women of the time. It has to think about war

And it has to find what will suffice. It has
To construct a new stage.[19]

Translated into French, Stevens's poetry, with his approval, was soon being dropped into occupied France by RAF pilots to encourage the Resistance.[20] Who could have imagined such a "stage" a few years before?

The interest in other people's problems differed from that of the mid-
1930s. Rather than seeing literature as a means of changing the world, in
the 1940s authors saw it as a mode of witnessing and attempting to make
sense of the incomprehensible (which is not the same as *explaining* it).
Martha Gellhorn, thinking back on her novel *A Stricken Field* (1940) in
1985, wrote: "Novels don't decide the course of history or change it, but
they can show what history is like for people who have no choice except
to live through it or die from it. I remembered for them."[21] Alfred Kazin,
meditating on the literary situation in 1945, put it another way: "The mind
can describe many processes in nature, but sooner or later the mind, despite what science boasts, cannot be satisfactorily correlated with all that
exists outside it. This is the abyss that great literature fills, though never
so fully that we cannot still hear the wailing of Job and Lear."[22]

The advances of fascism and Stalinism chastened the early-modernist
contempt for common sense and the public sphere. What came to be
called the "cult of impersonality" in poetry gave way to an emphasis
on communication even in the work of Eliot. The pragmatist aesthetic
theory of John Dewey—a far cry from pure formalism—displaced the
Marxist aesthetic theory of the thirties for many artists as they grew
bored with social realism and became more interested in creative process,
of "art as experience" (to borrow the title of Dewey's book), an activity of
discovery for both artist and reader/viewer, rather than illustrating or
delivering predetermined political messages. At the same time, previously avant-garde styles, like avant-gardists themselves, became familiar
to American readers. When the Museum of Modern Art moved to its
permanent home in 1939, the president of the United States delivered the
opening address, and the Picasso exhibition launched both the museum's
and Picasso's subsequent international reputations.

In the months and years to come, the experience of World War II baffled realist narrative and description, but other modes were at hand. Surrealism, futurism, imagism, and abstraction entered mainstream consciousness as modes of registering the extreme experiences of regular Americans from all walks of life—and surrealists themselves migrated to America in force. This does not mean that European abstract styles were imposed from "above" by a cultural elite; they were absorbed and redeployed in the new environment—as in the welfare hospital on Roosevelt Island. European avant-garde styles became "American," and American literature gained its greatest international prestige just as Americans became readers on a scale never known before.

Jameson's reflections on the relationship between early modernism as canonized by the late modernists, the New Criticism, and the culture industry offers a provocation for redescribing the shifting relationship between the avant-garde and popular culture in the 1940s, an era in which the theorization of this relationship was itself a matter of intense interest and debate. For Jameson "popular culture" is not a viable term for the era when peasant or folk cultures were transformed into other class forms by advancing capitalism and Soviet communism—a view that, again, matches Horkheimer and Adorno's thinking. Yet some exiled Marxist intellectuals of the time, on the contrary, found popular culture in the United States more disparate, anarchical, and fascinating than any popular culture had ever been.

Claude Lévi-Strauss came off the boat in 1941 fleeing Vichy France— long, lean, and unknown, seeking his intellectual bearings as he started work at the New School for Social Research, in New York City. He was enthralled by a city that could change in time, class, and culture from block to block. European folklorists who "had once combed the most remote countryside of central and eastern Europe looking for the last surviving storytellers, made some astonishing discoveries, right in the middle of New York, among their immigrant compatriots." In the evening they might go to the Savoy Ballroom in Harlem, hopping with jazz and the jitterbug. American popular culture was a "different" phenomenon from the start, impossible to pin down. "New York . . . was then a city where anything seemed possible. Like the urban fabric, the social and cultural fabric was riddled with holes. All you had to do was pick one and slip through if, like Alice, you wanted to get to the other side of the looking glass and find worlds so enchanting that they seemed unreal."[23] This description is a far cry from the Frankfurt School theorists' view of a mass culture that, in its underlying uniformity, matched serial manufacture and was managed from above.

One way of slipping through the looking glass was by following the adventures of the new superheroes. The decade of the 1940s was the Golden Age of comic books. In their endless battles against the bad guys the comic-book superheroes seemed to bear out Lévi-Strauss's view of how American popular culture provided recipes for making do under intolerable conditions.[24] The inventors of the superhero comic books were virtually all Jewish sons of working-class immigrants born between 1912 and 1920. Irreligious, they thought of themselves as ethnically Jewish American, like the Irish Americans and Italian Americans who beat them up walking home from school. They were misfits in their own communities. Influenced by pulp detective and crime fiction, the bodybuilding fad of Bernarr MacFadden, and radio shows like *The Shadow* and *Zorro*, they lacked father figures either literally or emotionally. Tangled relationships to masculinity, power, sexuality, and authority made them feel the anxieties of modern life acutely and from an outsider perspective.[25]

Robert Finger took modernist styles and themes from expressionist film and modernist art to remake *The Bat-Man* (1938) into *Batman*. He and Robert Kahn ("Bob Kane"), schoolmates at DeWitt Clinton High School, borrowed from modernist literature in developing the title character and his antagonists—all complex, traumatized, modern psychopaths. In the earliest issues (1939), the criminals tended to be gangsters, corrupt city officials, businessmen, and bankers. The illustrative "cells" were designed in the conventional rigid grid pattern and the characters crudely drawn as "realistic" figures. But with the third issue, Jerry Robinson was brought on for the artwork. Finger, who had studied creative writing at Columbia and aspired to be a "serious" writer, took him to the Metropolitan Museum of Art and to art houses showing German expressionist films. Robinson soon took over *Batman*'s design work, Fritz Lang on his mind. So when the first issue of a comic book dedicated solely to Batman was planned, he wanted more than a pulp-style gangster. He wanted internal contradiction, a supervillain with a sense of humor, someone like the "The Man Who Laughed" in Paul Leni's film of that name. The Joker was born. Similarly, Finger would create the villains Two-Face (influenced by Poe's "William Wilson"), the Penguin, Catwoman, the Riddler, and Clay-Face. Back-stories would come into play in subsequent issues, in which these supersociopaths would prove to be one-time innocents diverted by childhood traumas and social inequities toward mayhem and revenge.

The design of the pages changed—cells departed from the simple grid pattern, at first with overlapping or dovetailing corners, then taking on geometrical shapes other than the rectangle—triangles and circles, for example, to create visual dynamism. Robinson used color in rhythmic counterpoint between cells and began using the page spread as an allover composition, plastic and dynamic, no longer "square" and rigid. In the opening spread of *Batman #37* (October–November 1946), a Jokermobile on the splash page faces, across the stapled binding, a matching but darker Batmobile in the lower-right-hand cell of the facing page (fig. 2.2). They seem aimed at each other. The title "The Joker Follows Suit" is a nice pun but also suggests how the villain shadows the stoic hero as his grinning twin. Yellow circles around the joker's head, cast by a spotlight, combine with Robin's yellow cape to create a "V" design across the two pages.

If the comics were partly inspired by avant-garde literature and art, modernist aesthetics were sometimes shaped by the comics. Flannery O'Connor's first publications were cartoons in the 1940s, and comics profoundly affected the fictional aesthetic she developed in the 1950s, with figures like the Misfit or the nihilistic conman and seducer disguised as a bible salesman and named Manly Pointer (fig. 2.3). The popularity of the form held no meaning for or against modernist aesthetics, as George Grosz had already demonstrated early in the century.

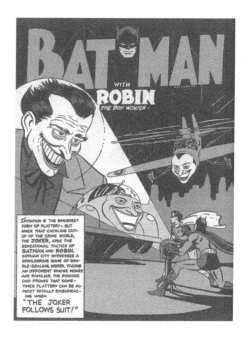

FIGURE 2.2 Splash page of "The Joker Follows Suit," *Batman* #37 (October–November 1946). *Source*: Art: Jerry Robinson. Letters: George Roussos.

FIGURE 2.3 Flannery O'Connor cartoon in *The Spectrum*, 1945 (Yearbook of Georgia State College for Women). *Source*: © 1945 Flannery O'Connor renewed by Regina Cline O'Connor. All rights reserved. Reprinted by permission of the Mary Flannery O'Connor Charitable Trust via Harold Matson Co., Inc.

Popular comics since the thirties had borrowed ideas from the same detective novels that inspired popular films, for which Hollywood producers hired writers needing a regular paycheck. While authors including William Faulkner, Lillian Hellman, and Ben Hecht got busy writing screenplays, agents were also moving back and forth between literature and film. In 1943, the William Morris Agency, until then one of the top show-business agencies, opened a literary department. Donald Friede, who had been centrally involved in modernist publishing in New York since the early 1920s, switched careers around 1940 to become a Hollywood agent. Ernest Hemingway allowed him to handle the sale of *For Whom the Bell Tolls*, the movie rights to which went for nearly $150,000.[26]

Hemingway, a friend and hunting partner of Gary Cooper, was a celebrity in his own right. So was Gertrude Stein. The reputations of both, even James Joyce's, had been growing throughout the 1930s. Stein's had risen since her American tour of 1934, and *The Autobiography of Alice B. Toklas* (1933), her most accessible book to that time, was a surprise hit. Throughout the thirties, publishers had coaxed American consumers to appreciate "highbrow" literature.[27]

Random House's pitch for James Joyce's *Ulysses* played to Americans' cultural insecurities, connecting modernism with tradition by convincing people that modernist titles were already becoming "classics" as they interpreted the chaos of the present. Advertisements showed boring men losing out to well-read ones in the dating competition and hyped modern fiction as a path to sophistication. Random House gave out booklets as guides to reading and placed a two-page advertisement in the *Saturday Review* entitled "How to Enjoy James Joyce's Great Novel *Ulysses*."[28] Viking, a major trade press by now, published Joyce's famously impenetrable *Finnegans Wake* in 1939, evidence to James T. Farrell of a rise in reading tastes: "The publication of *Finnegans Wake* by a trade publisher would have been unthinkable in 1925." Even *Ulysses*, before its publication by Random House, had circulated outside the channels of "commercial and best seller culture."[29] In the spring of 1944, Bennett Cerf of Random House informed his partner Donald Klopfer that Gertrude Stein's *Wars I Have Seen* had been getting wonderful reviews, including one on the front page of the *New York Times Book Review*, "and we'll sell out our full two printings of 14,000. That's more than her first five books together did!"[30] It hadn't been many years since a sale of 28,000 copies of any book would have qualified it as a bestseller. Reviewing *Wars I Have Seen* for *PM*, Richard Wright mused, "Wouldn't it be strange if in 1988 our colleges made the reading of *Wars I Have Seen* mandatory, so that our grandchildren would learn how men felt about war in our time? Wouldn't it be simply strange if Miss Stein's grammarless prose was destined for such a strange destiny? Would it not be strange if anything strange like that did happen?"[31] It seems her prose was as infectious as a popular song.

Stein was no longer a joke in the newspapers and popular magazines but a respected cultural icon. The first GIs to reach her at her home in the south of France were prepared: "We held each other's hands and we patted each other and we sat down together and I told them who we were, and they knew."[32] *Life* even sent her with American troops to report on what was left of Germany after the Allied victory. The result was an extensive feature in the August 6, 1945, issue, of which she was both author and subject (fig. 2.4).[33]

In the closing pages of *Wars I Have Seen*, Stein marvels at how "conversational" the soldiers are and attributes it to their reading: "The American men had at last come to be interested and to be interesting." She exchanged books with them: "I was interested that they were a bit tired of detectives, I like them as much as ever but that is because I am so much older and they do like Westerns and then they like adventures, and any longish American novel."[34] For Stein there was no battle between modernist style and pulp fiction. Three years later, the avant-garde limited-edition Banyan Press published her stab at a murder mystery, *Blood on the Dining Room Floor*.[35]

The rapprochement of modernist style with popular American culture—and of Stein with that culture—becomes the ultimate theme of *Wars I Have Seen*. She paces the book to lead to her first meeting with American soldiers: "What a day what a day of days, I always did say that I would end this book with the first American that came to Culoz, and to-day oh happy day yesterday and to-day, the first of September 1944."[36]

FIGURE 2.4 Gertrude Stein and others at Hitler's bunker, the "Eagle's Nest," Berchtesgaden, Germany, in *Life*, August 6, 1945. "Gertrude liked Hitler's radiators and wanted to take one home for a flowerpot but was talked out of it." *Source*: Photo credited to "Troop Carrier Command," *Life*. Courtesy of Getty Images.

The United States had difficulty achieving a cultural identity, according to Stein, because the people did not have their own language; in this the country was exceptional: "it had a certain difficulty in proving itself American which no other nation has ever had." Everybody in the United States already read and wrote English by the time "America became itself," so the language did not change the way Italian, French, German, and other vernacular languages developed over time before everyone could read and write. "So the only way the Americans could change their language was by choosing words which they liked better than other words, by putting words next to each other in a different way than the English way, by shoving the language around until at last now the job is done, we use the same words as the English do but the words say an entirely different thing." It was precisely the World War II generation that had overcome the problem:

Yes in that sense Americans have changed, I think of the Americans of the last war, they had their language but they were not yet in possession of it, and the children of the depression as that generation called itself it was beginning to possess its language but it was still struggling but now the job is done, the G.I. Joes have this language that is theirs, they do not have to worry about it, they dominate their language and in dominating their language which is now all theirs they have ceased to be adolescents and have become men.

When I was in America in '34 they asked me if I did not find Americans changed. I said no what could they change to just to become more American, No I said I could have gone to school with any of them.

But all the same yes that is what they have changed to they have become more American all American, and the G.I. Joes show it and know it, God bless them.[37]

So ends Stein's most popular book in her lifetime. What Stein claims for the G.I. Joes and American idiom is exactly what William Carlos Williams had earlier credited her with achieving and what he was attempting in his evolving epic *Paterson*, where he first came upon a new measure for American verse, what he called the "variable foot." What *Wars I Have Seen* also suggests is her feeling of being at one with her "Americanness" as she and the GIs encountered each other and they asked her to write about them: "Write about us they all said a little sadly, and write about them I will."[38] She kept her promise in her next and last book, *Brewsie and Willie*, published by Random House shortly after her death. Van Wyck Brooks had once hoped for "America's Coming of Age," which in a Whitmanian sense would mean the achievement of a "popular" culture. Stein had seen it happen, the culmination of a merging of "modernism" and the vernacular.

The problem, however, was interpreting the manifestations of popular culture in relationship to capitalism and class rule. When did popular culture work against antidemocratic class interests that concentrated power in the hands of a few, and when was it an expression, indeed tool, of those interests? Stein seemed oblivious to such questions. Marxist-leaning Claude Lévi-Strauss, on the other hand, found in American popular culture itself a partial, if temporary antidote: the European refugees at the New School and environs observed

a mass culture that, already far advanced in America, would reach Europe a few decades later. This may be the reason so many aspects of life in New York enthralled us: it set before our eyes a list of recipes thanks to which, in a society becoming each day ever more oppressive and inhuman, the people who find it decidedly intolerable can learn the thousand and one tricks offered, for a few brief moments, by the illusion that one has the power to escape.[39]

Such hints would be expanded in the work of the Canadian Marshall McLuhan, who began in the 1940s to work out the argument he would develop in *The Mechanical Bride: The Folklore of Industrial Man* (1951). McLuhan was inspired by Poe's story "A Descent Into the Maelström," in which a man tells of surviving an oceanic maelstrom not by fighting it but by studying the properties of its vortex, hanging on to a cylindrical barrel while his mates, grabbing differently shaped objects, were spun down to the depths and drowned. The story is also a portent of the strategy of Andy Warhol, who in 1949 began his career in commercial art and advertising. "The hyperaesthesia of the ad-men's rhetoric," wrote the Canadian McLuhan in "American Advertising" (1947),

has knocked the public into a kind of groggy, slap-happy condition in which perhaps are cushioned a good many of the brutal shocks felt more keenly by the realistic European. Viewed merely as an interim strategy for maintaining hope, tolerance, and good humour in an irrational world, this orgy of irrationalism may not be without its cathartic function.

Advertising had provided

a world of symbols, witticism, and behavior patterns which . . . comprise a common experience and a common language for a country whose sectional differences and technological specialisms might easily develop into anarchy. . . . Moreover, by various means, the whole technique and hallucination of Hollywood has been assimilated to the ads *via* pictorial glamour, so that the two are inseparable. They constitute one world.

McLuhan did not think this was all bad. The sadism purveyed by crime novels and films appealed to basic human instincts and, rather than causing people to act on them, provided a harmless sort of pleasure in a "lethal and chaotic world." Men with "a penchant for strong-arm political methods are not given to this form of fantasy life." The intellectual (Adorno, perhaps?) has it wrong, imagining he can arm himself with keen perception and analytical brilliance against the impact of commercial culture, but he is no more than a Quixotic guerrilla warrior, "a sort of noble savage free-lancing amidst a zombie horde." It makes more sense to take stock carefully of the products of our appetites, so ably demonstrated by the ad-men with their "totalitarian techniques" of market research, than to cast stones at the people smart enough to exploit them. "That the highbrows have been content merely to cock a snoot at the fauna and flora of popular commercial culture is sufficient testimony to the superficiality with which they have envisaged the nature of politics." There is nothing in the ads, driven not by dreams of tyranny but merely cold hard cash, that the people have not been desiring for some time as "a compensation and a promise for beauty denied."[40]

Not all the writers and critics, of course, were happy with the popularization of modernist style, comic-book literacy, and the encroachments of mass marketing. In tune with Horkheimer and Adorno, literary journals expressed anxiety about the commodification of literature and art in general, with Hollywood serving as a specter of what may come. In the late 1940s, Random House and the Modern Library drew hostile fire from those who feared the "Hollywoodization of literature."[41] Attacks on the commercialization of publishing by New Directions Press founder James Laughlin and his stable of authors were implicitly directed toward

Random House. James T. Farrell took deliberate aim at the Modern Library and the other large houses in *New Directions 9*, in an article entitled "Will the Commercialization of Publishing Destroy Good Writing?"—reprinted in pamphlet form under the title *The Fate of Writing in America*.[42]

However sincere, such attacks were also a form of self-branding in a diversifying industry. Laughlin conceived his press as a highbrow, cutting-edge "art house." He disdained the American public and believed education had spread too rapidly to the general population, preventing good taste from filtering gradually from the elite to hoi polloi. According to Laughlin, "The tradition of quality *has* been interrupted because we leapt in a few generations from the small cultivated élite of the Eastern seaboard to a huge mass of citizens, many of diverse immigrant origin, who have been taught *how* to read, but not *what* to read."[43] Next he blamed commercialism, the "mass production of culture."

New Directions had been founded by Laughlin as an undergraduate at Harvard, at Ezra Pound's urging, in 1936 with money Laughlin had inherited from his family's steel fortune. Pound (already a follower of Mussolini) had told him he was a lousy poet and should do something useful, like found a publishing company for avant-gardists like himself and his friends. New Directions, starting as a small-press annual anthology, quickly became an art press focused on avant-garde writing, in part distinguishing itself by publishing poetry and criticism, including translations of European work. Pound immediately made New Directions his American publisher and brought William Carlos Williams and H.D. aboard. Soon Laughlin was signing on many of Pound's friends and discoveries and branching out as his authors became his scouts. In the course of the 1940s New Directions established its position as a trend-setting (and finally profitable) institution, closely identified with emerging schools and movements as well as with the now-canonical modernists.

Laughlin called himself "strongly antipathetic to . . . the visual and aural vulgarities of the USA—things that so constantly offend the eye (the ugly buildings and almost everything that the automobile has brought to us), and the ear (what comes out of the radio and the juke box)."[44] He posed as proudly anticommercial, never worried about making money—which was crucial to his reputation and much ballyhooed by his authors. Yet even New Directions was subtly picking up marketing tips from those Laughlin publicly attacked.

New Directions addressed a newly profitable niche for contemporary "avant-garde" writing, prepared for by Cerf and Klopfer's Modern Library. Records of the business now housed at Harvard's Houghton Library reveal that Laughlin accrued symbolic capital by posing as the antithesis of the commercial publisher, disavowing an interest in marketing while constantly trying to think up new marketing techniques. The New Directions reader, his advertisements and circulars announced, belonged to an elite club. His anthologies published only his authors. Meanwhile, he tried a "pamphlet poets" subscription series run distinctly like a book club in the late 1940s and held a contest to come up with a name for it, in addition to publishing introductory books on New Directions authors to help educate readers in how to read avant-garde writing.[45]

Laughlin developed a whole series in the 1940s on "The Makers of Modern Literature," knowing, as Knopf and Cerf had known in the early 1930s, that he would sell more books if more people knew how to read them. In fact, New Directions worked hand-in-glove with the leaders of the New Criticism to build a reputation on college campuses in the late 1940s for publishing the best of contemporary writing. Consciously or not, it was modeling itself on the earlier Modern Library (which began losing market share in the late 1940s, mainly to the paperback houses). Laughlin succeeded in getting his books ensconced in college bookstores and on syllabi as Quonset huts and temporary trailer parks sprang up on campus outskirts everywhere and matriculation doubled after the war. Carrying a New Directions book in hand was a mark of being literarily up to date, at war with what Clement Greenberg famously called "kitsch" in a defining essay of 1939. "On several fronts," read an advertisement in the January 1940 issue of *Decision*, "the New Directions Press is fighting for the unconventional writer—for the poet, for the serious literary critic, for the 'advance-guard' writer who feels compelled to experiment, for all writers who refuse to compromise with the existing 'system' of the large commercial publishers."[46]

This did not keep Laughlin from appealing to prurient interests in marketing his books. Paul Bowles's "art novel" *The Sheltering Sky* was unrecognizable as a novel to Doubleday, which had originally contracted it. One publisher after another rejected it until Tennessee Williams, one of Laughlin's scouts, brought it to him. A surrealistic novel, it furthers certain strains of the 1920s and early 1930s avant-garde exploring "exotic" locations and disorienting personal experiences. It later impressed the Beats. The manuscript marginally featured a female American protagonist who, after her husband's death, ends up roaming the Sahara desert with a handsome Tuareg nomad and settling into his harem.

Laughlin trusted Williams's judgment of the manuscript but did not know how to sell it. He decided to get "corny" and play up the sex angle: "by being a little bit corny and sexy, we might drag in some readers from other groups who are attracted to the idea of the beautiful white girl going into a harem, or whatever you call those places."[47] Bowles washed his hands of the marketing strategy and gave his permission, adding (quite accurately) that there was really nothing "sexy" about the book.[48] Laughlin replied that mentioning an American girl ending up in a harem "ought to lure all kinds of suckers into the book stores."[49] *The Sheltering Sky* became New Directions' first bestseller, indicating the existence of a large-enough market for *très avant-garde* titles to sustain a house dedicated to them. In the 1950s New Directions became a profitable enterprise in time to prevent Laughlin from exhausting an inheritance built on and enabling the advent of the automobiles and skyscrapers he disdained.[50] By 1950, the press was publishing not only the high modernists of the first postwar generation but a number of the significant authors of the next: Carson McCullers, Tennessee Williams, Thomas Merton, Conrad Aiken, Kenneth Rexroth, and Richard Eberhart, among others.

While quite open to authors born outside the United States, particularly Europe and Great Britain, as well as Anglo-American rebels like Henry Miller, Laughlin published no black authors and no authors who would be called "ethnic" in orientation. This has some bearing on the midcentury distinction scholars made between "modernism" and African American and "ethnic" literatures, which would hold well into the 1980s—unlike the 1920s and 1930s, I might add.

The distinction between Stein and Pound in choice of publisher (Random House versus New Directions), literary tendency, and in rapprochement with American culture pertains, in the course of the 1930s and 1940s, to the discussion of literary institutions, as modernism diversified and a niche was carved out for an elitist avant-gardism, supported by New Directions and smaller limited-edition presses like Banyan and hoping to distinguish themselves from the all-consuming "mainstream"—a term soon to become an epithet. Ironies ensued: suffice it to say here that while Stein was conversing with her newfound friends in uniform, her old collaborator in the founding of American literary modernism was being held by another group of GIs in an open cage in Pisa, where he was penning impenetrable cantos eulogizing Mussolini and descending into madness. The *Pisan Cantos*, regarded by many of his admirers as Pound's greatest single achievement, was published by New Directions in 1948.

Related to the successes of New Directions was a proliferation of new "little magazines" and limited-edition presses in the late 1940s that incubated such movements as the San Francisco Renaissance and the New York School. Their authors overlapped with those of New Directions, which sometimes subcontracted books to the small presses for special editions—and advertised that fact, further establishing its distinction from the larger trade presses. One example is the Banyan Press, founded in 1946 by Claude Fredericks and Milton Saul in New York. Banyan published the early work of many soon-to-be famous poets, such as John Berryman, Robert Duncan, William Everson, Stephen Spender, Thomas Merton, James Merrill, and others, as well as new work by Gertrude Stein and Wallace Stevens (*A Primitive Like an Orb*). From 1946 to 1950 they published seventy-four titles, then vanished until the late 1970s, when they published fourteen more.[51] New Directions, meanwhile, became predominantly a paperback business. For the time being, then, the expansion of the book trade into mass outlets was not threatening the work of the emergent postwar poetic avant-garde that would later be canonized in Donald Allen's *The New American Poetry, 1945–1960*. The metastasizing market and proliferation of creative-writing classes had helped make such work publishable.

In contrast to Laughlin, not to mention Horkheimer and Adorno, C. L. R. James of Trinidad, who had come to New York in 1938, saw in American popular culture something immensely important from an independent Marxist point of view. Disillusioned with Trotskyism, which he had come to feel was irrelevant to the American situation and world development in general, in the course of the 1940s he developed an argument about American popular culture in relationship to his readings of Whitman's and Melville's work that would eventually be published as the book *American Civilization*. According to the editors of the book, it constituted

> a decisive break with the European tradition, what James called "old bourgeois civilization" with its oppositions between art and culture, intellectuals and the people, politics and everyday life. In it he sought to fuse the different elements—history, literature, political struggle, popular art, and detailed observations of daily life—into a dense work of startling originality. . . . [T]he movement of the narrative, the shift from established literary sources to the lives of ordinary men and women, reflected his understanding of the general dynamic of history. In short, he aimed to distill the universal progress of civilization into a specific contrast between the nineteenth and twentieth centuries. The culture of the intellectuals was giving way to the emergence of the people as the animating force of history.[52]

In a world growing increasingly interconnected by markets, capital accumulation, and new communications technologies, the relationship between the freedom of the individual and the social fabric was being redrawn, and the United States was at the forward edge of this global development. While human personality came under intense pressure toward fragmentation, in American popular culture James saw "an intense desire among people to bring the separate facets of human experience into an active relationship, to express their full and free individuality within new and expanded conceptions of social life." This he called "the struggle for happiness."[53]

Whitman, in the effort to follow out a new ethos and theory of democratic culture, seeking a new synthesis of individuality and community independent of past hierarchical structures, had revolutionized the methods of modern verse. In a different way, Melville, in addressing questions of why Ahab's crew in *Moby-Dick* did not rebel, was exploring far more important issues for the mid–twentieth century than Flaubert, Dostoevsky, or Rimbaud, the supposed fathers of "modernism," according to Eurocentric accounts. The creation of Ahab "is a masterpiece, perhaps so far the only serious study in fiction of the type which has reached its climax in the modern totalitarian dictator."[54] Melville was not writing a political tract; he was instead doing what novelists do—witnessing, limning the characteristic types of his time—but because of his social and temporal location at a historical turning point he could imagine a previously unimaginable type of the period to come. Whaling was a global corporate enterprise, with floating factories on seven seas. Ahab, the leader of men in pursuit of his object, knows how to manipulate their desires to coincide with his own.

James went on from Whitman and Melville to argue that their intellectual grasp of the contradictions between democracy and the rising capitalist system was matched by an activist engagement with those contradictions in the abolitionist movement, beginning with the enslaved. "Without this constant contact with the mass, Abolitionism would have been nothing, and none knew this and admitted it more freely than the Abolitionists themselves. They had found what both Whitman and Melville had failed to find." Without help from any "alien tradition but from the very genius of the country," the abolitionists replicated the spirit of the early Christians, the Puritan revolution in England, and the early Bolsheviks, "types which have appeared only when fundamental changes are shaking a society to its depths."[55]

Contemporary popular culture in the United States is their true successor, not T. S. Eliot or Ernest Hemingway. The fundamental ideas that Whitman, Melville, and the abolitionists stood for in America's coming of age as a modern nation "are now placed in an entirely different setting." Popular media like paperbacks (Yerby's novels), *Life*, and comics now embody "the clearest ideological expression of the sentiments and deepest feelings of the American people and a great window into the future of America and the modern world." Behind the label of "entertainment," in comics and film is hidden a major manifestation of social rebellion, "the bitterness, the violence, the brutality, the sadism simmering in the population, the desire to revenge themselves with their own hands, to get some release for what society had done to them since 1929."[56]

This appeal to popular resentment was filled by the market ethos itself. The detective story had been around since Poe, but its efflorescence in the 1930s in the gangster-detective novel was a response to popular desire: "the producer of the film or the newspaper publisher of a strip aims at *millions of people*, practically the whole population, and *must satisfy them*." One might suspect that the owners of the publishing and movie houses and record labels disseminating jazz had an ideological agenda, feeding pablum to the people to distract them from their real problems, but James emphasizes that the writers themselves sensed a mood in the public and answered it. The popularity of these forms indicates "a mass response to society, crises, and *the nature and limitations of that response*."[57] The great movie magnates might be antiunion, but they dare not make an anti-CIO movie. Dangerous political content is left out of popular media because of a state of armed neutrality, so to speak, agreeing to leave dangerous content alone: hence the limitations of popular media for either revolutionary or reactionary propaganda.

The movie studios put enormous resources into trying to gauge mass demand, not into thinking about how to sustain capitalist society. They just want to make money on each film, which is the opposite of what one finds in a totalitarian society. As a result, films represent "some of the deepest feelings of the masses, but represent them within the common agreement—no serious political or social questions which would cause explosions."[58]

Yet in the comics and detective novels and films, both the outlaw and the detective have become popular mirror images, both scorning the police as agents of "official" society. They follow a personal ethic that is oblique to bureaucratic order and implicitly undermining its pretensions, suspicious of its allegiance to entrenched power and its professed rationality. James refers to Chandler's Philip Marlowe and Hammett's Sam Spade, but he might just as well be pointing to Batman.

Simultaneously with James's striking analysis (and McLuhan's ruminations on the "folklore of industrial man"), John A. Kouwenhoven's *Made in America: The Arts in American Civilization* (1949) analyzed the relationship between technology, engineering, architecture, jazz music, and literature as expressions of a vernacular culture developing along indigenous lines in tension with inherited, primarily European artistic forms, primarily in the nineteenth century. Central to his argument was the fact that American culture since the Revolution, unlike any other, had developed in relationship to modern technology and the new modes of production, including serial manufacture, which themselves were "vernacular" cultural products of the American social (and indirectly physical) environment. Kouwenhoven limned a "democratic-technological vernacular" through patterns that *"comprise the folk arts of the first people in history who, disinherited of a great cultural tradition, found themselves living under democratic institutions in an expanding machine economy."*[59]

The United States was the only major power whose culture had not developed from preindustrial, inherited racial or ethnic patterns but rather within and in association with modern technology itself and often in response to distinct geographical challenges: hence the "American" style of axe, the American-style locomotive and riverboat, balloon-frame home construction, the steel suspension bridge, the Model T, the first skyscraper. In all of these achievements, form followed function (as Louis Sullivan asserted) and resulted in new forms of aesthetic pleasure that were both popular and modern. Literature and visual arts lagged behind because of the hold of traditional aesthetic hierarchies.

Kouwenhoven takes offense at the opposition between the "practical" and the "aesthetic" in the Western tradition of art appreciation, which removes the aesthetic from everyday life and makes it a marker of class and exclusivity—"cultivation." He shows greater respect for the elements of design and form that develop as people create satisfying patterns in response to the new social and physical environment. The widespread neglect, if not dismissal, of this tradition marks a lack of self-confidence in the realm of aesthetics, a dependence upon those who "know better." "It was only in areas from which the propaganda of culture was completely excluded that the vernacular aesthetic of the machine was wholeheartedly accepted."[60] Le Corbusier had a similar complaint about the "cultivated" view of the arts in New York, decrying, "Caravaggio in university studies, surrealism in collections and museums, the inferiority complex which obsesses those who wish to break away from the simple arithmetic of numbers . . . the funereal spirit which appears in the hours of spiritual creation."[61]

To Kouwenhoven, literature had fallen behind architecture and engineering in the rise of vernacular culture, burdened by academicism, except in a few bold exceptions considered subliterary by the professors of their day—notably Whitman, Melville, Poe, and Twain. Moreover, the vernacular literary forms developed along with new techniques of distribution, such as cheap newspapers (featuring human-interest stories) and subscription publishing, in which traveling sales agents took orders for books to be mailed later to individual homes—ancestors, by the way, of the paperbacks. Even Emerson had developed his distinctive essay style addressing lyceum audiences in far-flung towns and cities, audiences whose attention he had to learn to retain by any means necessary. In short, the distinctive literary inventions of the United States had been provoked by the challenges peculiar to a "democratic" society in particular geographical circumstances and in association with machine technology.

In music, there was jazz, which Kouwenhoven treated as one of the distinctive artistic manifestations of a popular, and modern, American culture—a position that Ralph Ellison, an admirer of Kouwenhoven's work, would further develop in now classic essays. A "performer's art," jazz was also "inextricably bound up with such technological advances as phonograph recording and radio broadcasting" (which is part of what Adorno held against it, incidentally). The microphone also affected the contemporary sound of jazz in both vocal performance and instrumentation. In its combination of syncopation and polyrhythms, jazz was fundamentally distinct from European concert music, even though it borrowed harmonic and scalar qualities from that tradition. The rhythmic structure of jazz, including its use of the "break" (performers breaking off from the dominant rhythm to improvise but ultimately return to it), reconciled the "the demands of group performance (the arrangement) and individual expression (the solos)." An art form resolving the fundamental conflict of modern society that such earlier writers as Emerson and Whitman had emphasized, jazz thus had less in common with what is traditionally emphasized in American art criticism (individual genius *or* "tradition") than with what the modern world demands, a kind of flexible cooperation that allows the free expression of individuality and impulsive adjustments to changing rhythmic situations, suitable in its fundamental simplicity and adaptability for "mass participation and enjoyment." These were the qualities—not its "American" birth—that made it of such importance worldwide. Le Corbusier called Manhattan skyscrapers "hot jazz in stone and steel."[62] He, too, recognized both forms as achievements tuned to the most dynamic forces of modernity. *This* was the avant-garde.

3

LABOR, POLITICS, AND THE ARTS

···

From 1917 through the mid-1930s, the success of the Russian Revolution gave communism, and Marxism in general, an imposing prestige in American intellectual circles. During the rise of fascism in Europe, antifascism was often associated with communism and various "progressive" groups more or less associated with it, and the Popular Front policy of broadening the communist tent outside of Russia succeeded in replacing or co-opting other left-oriented alternatives, expanding the Party's reach and influence. Mary McCarthy would remember that the Party had a "virtual monopoly on the thought of the left" until 1937–1938.[1] In "The Legacy of the Thirties" (1947), Robert Warshow outlined how "the Communist movement of the 1930s was a crucial experience" for most American intellectuals. It "was a time when virtually all intellectual vitality was derived in one way or another from the Communist party."[2] Even among Southern, politically conservative white writers, Marxist terms inflected a longstanding argument against industrial capitalism derived from very different bases. Marxism was not and never had been the only anticapitalist alternative in American intellectual life, but in the late 1920s and throughout the 1930s it had pride of place, especially in the North, and it inspired many writers, absorbing or overcoming the more independent radicalisms of the 1910s and early 1920s.

A series of well-known events—the Moscow Trials, the Ribbentrop-Molotov Pact, the assassination of Trotsky—came as a shock to many erstwhile Party members and their sympathizers. But for many creative writers, the turn away from communism in the 1940s came as a result of neither Stalin's perfidy nor Cold War repression but because of both communists' treatment of artists and the scientistic nature of Marxist historicism itself.[3] To attribute the turn against communism tout court to "Cold War liberalism" obfuscates the problems in Marxist communities of the time and oversimplifies a complex process of disengagement.

Daniel Aaron's description is still the best, stressing that writers were never fully trusted by the American communist leaders and that even writers closest to the Party "refused to shut up or to take discipline." They discovered that one could not be both a good communist and a good writer. Yet they did not abandon the Party because of being persecuted: "Rather, it seems to have been boredom that repelled them and that killed their zeal."[4] Writers and other creative artists had begun to rethink the nature and social role of their work. They increasingly stressed the *process* of artistic production and reception over predetermined aims.

As committed leftists in the arts turned away from communism, they often did so through questions of labor—their own labor. Neither did all of them put Marx aside. A need to recapture the meaning of personal experience characterized the late 1940s especially. Speaking from a perspective common to many leftists of the immediate postwar years, Warshow wrote, "The most important effect of the intellectual life of the 30s and the culture that grew out of it has been to distort and eventually to destroy the emotional and moral content of experience, putting in its place a system of conventionalized 'responses.'" This effect corresponded to the effects of mass culture, the chief function of which "is to relieve one of the necessity of experiencing one's life directly."[5]

It has been argued that Richard Wright and Ralph Ellison renounced communism because of the Communist Party's retreat from its 1930s advocacy of revolutionary Negro nationalism and the "Black nation" thesis, which held that African Americans should have an autonomous country in the Southern Black Belt.[6] Before Hitler broke his nonaggression pact (1939) with the Soviet Union, the Communist Party fought against American intervention in the "imperialist" war and stressed the battle for black civil rights and self-determination, but after Hitler's invasion of Russia in June 1941, the Party sidelined the battle against racism in favor of a unified push for the United States to open a "second front" against Germany. The move disillusioned many and convinced some of the bad faith of white communists on issues of race. But this is a smaller part of the story than one would expect.

Richard Wright did observe that the Communist Party had regressed from its "position on the American Negro" between 1936 and 1944, regretting that "militancy on the Negro question has passed into the hands of right-wing Negroes" (by which he probably meant the anticommunist NAACP leadership), but he blamed the communists' obtuseness to people's needs for his disaffection, not the policies of the Party as such. Like many other lapsed American communists of his day, he quit because of its members' narrow-mindedness, intolerance, and "an imperious way of working," which would require him to sacrifice his intellectual and artistic integrity.[7] "Must I discard my plot-ideas and seek new ones? No. I could not. My writing was my way of seeing, my way of living, my way of feeling; and who could change his sight, his sense of direction, his senses?"[8] Wright split with the Communist Party over a question of labor—his labor.

In *Native Son*, as sympathetic a character as Boris Max has less interest in Bigger's individual life than in making a point about communism, racism, and the American socioeconomic order. Indeed, he takes on Bigger's case only because District Attorney Buckley has brought the Communist Party into it by blaming the Party for radicalizing Bigger. Max builds a passionate, brilliant, exhaustive critique of American racism and capitalism as an indictment of the society that has formed Bigger Thomas, but he remains blind to Bigger's struggle for meaning. Wright literalizes this blindness when, after his final talk with his client, appalled by Bigger's assertion of his individual integrity, "Max groped for his hat like a blind man, he found it and jammed it on his head. He felt for the door, keeping his face averted. He poked his arm through and signaled for the guard. When he was let out he stood for a moment, his back to the steel door."[9] The scene is all the more tragic because of how committed Max has been to Bigger and the heroic effort he has put into the case. But when the case is lost, he turns his back on the boy.

Much as Bigger Thomas's search escapes the understanding of Boris Max, Wright's struggle for expression of African American experience escaped his communist comrades' comprehension. Taking notes on the lives and vigorous speech of the "black boys" of the South Side, Wright observed,

> These boys did not fear people to the extent that every man looked like a spy. The Communists who doubted my motives did not know these boys, their twisted dreams, their all-to-clear destinies; and I doubted if I would ever be able to convey to them the tragedy I saw here.
>
> Wrestling with words gave me my moments of deepest meaning.

Such wrestling, for Wright, meant allowing images to take shape "out of the depths of me . . . feeling my way, trying to find the answer to my question," as opposed to beginning with an answer.[10] For this he was suspected of Trotskyism.

The job of the novelist was not to prosecute a case, justify a position, present or revise a "doctrine." Even if the doctrine was sound, it was irrelevant because the artist's responsibility was to be true to the complexity of *experience*, not thoughts about experience, not a philosophical or political position. It was, in Warshow's words, "to create what seems (at least to him) an adequate emotional and moral response to experience, a response that is 'objectively' valid in the sense that it seems to inhere in the experience itself and to come into being automatically, so to speak, with the re-creation of the experience." This is, moreover, for Warshow as for Wright, the path to "universality" in fiction: "The novel as an art form rests on particularity: the particular becomes universal without losing its particularity—that is the wonder." One can get closer to the "essence" of an experience if he is "willing to see it as the experience of particular human beings in a specific situation."[11] It also entails facing one's own relation to that situation. If the consciousness of difference is there, so is the possibility of change.

Young James Baldwin, seeking his way as a writer, accused Richard Wright of falling down on the job along just such lines, succumbing to the demand for "protest" literature. He needed to distance himself from Wright at this time to find himself as a writer, most notably in "Everybody's Protest Novel" (1949), even though he found Wright's literary celebrity and unflinching honesty inspirational. Yet his model was more Henry James than Wright's Theodore Dreiser or H. L. Mencken, and he was too young to have fully matured in the atmosphere of Marxism, which Wright himself had abandoned by the time he took Baldwin under his wing. The distinction between Dreiser and Henry James is particularly noteworthy. Baldwin, a Trostkyite briefly in the mid-1940s, cut his teeth in the left-wing anti-Stalinist journals that chastised what they considered the vulgar Marxism and Popular Front liberalism of the 1930s, epitomized by the work of figures like Vernon Parrington and Granville Hicks, who championed Dreiser and disdained James as an effete Anglophile.

James, often dismissed in the 1920s and 1930s as a writer who had abandoned America to write about rich people in Europe, rose in stature throughout the 1940s, thanks in part to anti-Stalinist *Partisan Review* critics, particularly Lionel Trilling. Trilling had warned,

> Dreiser and James: with that juxtaposition we are immediately at the dark and bloody crossroads where literature and politics meet. One does not go there gladly, but nowadays it is not exactly a matter of free choice whether one does or does not go. . . . The liberal judgment of Dreiser and James goes back of politics, goes back to the cultural assumptions that make politics.[12]

Trilling's approach to criticism—in which the sensitive experience of a novel is a battle of heroic proportions, a test of one's moral imagination even deeper than surface "politics"—is everywhere evident in Baldwin's early essays. This returns us to the issue of the open-endedness of artistic creation in relation to political formulae and Baldwin's impatience with "propaganda." If art is supposed to serve a direction already known, then the kind of artistic integrity to which he (like Wright, ironically) was committed was out of bounds.

One can thus fully agree with recent arguments against reductive views of the so-called social realism of the Popular Front, many of which (including Warshow's) date to the 1940s, while nonetheless perceiving how artists came to feel a conflict between communism and the *work* of the creative imagination.[13] This feeling had consequences for their views of the relationship between art and the *polis*—that Greek root from which Western views of politics derive, meaning *community* or *city*.

The historical desiderata of Western history have shaped our notion of politics into categories distinct from aesthetics, and thus we come to think in terms of how this or that "aesthetic" comports with this or that "politics." Trotsky allowed that art should be exempted from propagandizing for political programs, which made him attractive to some Marxists affiliated with the arts, but his position implies that art is marginally relevant to the locus of ultimacy for the *polis*, for to Trotsky what still really counted was the "political" direction of history (detached from aesthetics) as charted by Marx and Engels, in which art had a negligible role to play.

What if one began to wonder about the possibility of not simply reversing the hierarchy between aesthetics and politics but reorienting the relationship as such? This is what was happening in the 1940s—no more emphasis on "base" and "superstructure" assuming a causal relationship between economics and culture in human history but a curiosity about human "nature" and about what people want or need. And a curiosity about rethinking the genesis and goals of creative expression as inherent in human nature. There was a growing tendency to see art ecologically or, as the poet Muriel Rukeyser said of poetry, as a "transfer of human energy" (thus anticipating Charles Olson's manifesto "Projective Verse").[14]

Rukeyser did not regard such a view as apolitical, but neither did she *define* it *as* political; she thought in more adaptive terms about

> the moving relation between the individual consciousness and the world. . . . I think human energy may be defined as consciousness, the capacity to make change in existing conditions. It appears to me that to accept poetry in these meanings would make it possible for people to use it as an "exercise," an enjoyment of the possibility of dealing with the meanings in the world and in their lives.[15]

Her language shades into that of the American pragmatist philosophers. Pragmatists did not regard aesthetics as secondary to politics or cognition. Charles Sanders Peirce had argued that even logic was dependent on ethics and ethics dependent on aesthetics. John Dewey regarded aesthetic experience as the "primary instance of meaning," in relation to which "affairs of knowing and action" are determined.[16] Only by means of freedom and development in the aesthetic realm, he thought, through the growth of a truly democratic culture, would political freedom finally emerge. Such a view had implications even for organizing labor.

Questions very similar to Wright's about trying to understand the "black boys" of Chicago's South Side independent of Party formulae surface in Carlos Bulosan's *America Is in the Heart*, a classic of Asian American (and specifically Filipino American) literature that draws inspiration from Wright's example and his autobiography, *Black Boy*. The sort of search for answers that guides Wright's writing process guides Bulosan's search for the best way to organize Filipino workers. Bulosan's favored term for progressive political organizations is "democratic." Thus the CIO is more "democratic" than the AFL, for example. And while Bulosan is clearly a writer of the Popular Front, he ultimately realizes that the Communist Party is not democratic; it uses underhanded strategies to try to gain control over the labor movement rather than letting workers make up their own minds about tactics and ideology.

When he attempts to organize Filipino workers into a union in Stockton, California, Carlos comes up against demands that any attempt at organizing come under Party leadership. Carlos feels he should first determine how the workers themselves feel about giving leadership to the communists. For this he is accused of "intellectualism." Bulosan concludes, "I was naïve. I wanted to be sure that communism was what Filipinos needed. I felt somehow that I needed it too. What was the nemesis of communism? Was it Trotskyism? Whatever it was that seemed relevant to the needs of the Filipinos in California, I knew that I must assimilate it."[17] Here, for all of Bulosan's Marxism (he specifies a commitment to dialectical materialism),[18] his attitude is akin to Wright's about getting at the truth of his people's lives, connecting his explicitly political project with the growth of his ambition to write creatively: "Yes, I will be a writer and make all of you live again in my words."[19] But his writing puts him under suspicion.

In the second part of *Black Boy*, Wright relates how he was told, when questioning antidemocratic tactics, "Intellectuals don't fit well into the Party, Wright."[20] He found himself suspected of Trotskyism, although he knew nothing about Trotsky's intellectual work.[21] In the end, it is his writing that gets Wright in trouble, as he interviews black communists in order to write stories based on their lives. "Why was it that I was a suspected man," he asks, "because I wanted to reveal the vast physical and spiritual ravages of Negro life. . . . What was the danger in showing the kinship between the sufferings of the Negro and the sufferings of other people?"[22] Like Bulosan, Wright depicts himself as naïve, unable to grasp the Party's animus against anyone expressing themselves outside the auspices of an autocratic structure.

In *Lonely Crusade* (1947), Chester Himes gave a long thick cry of defiance against what he perceived as Communist Party manipulation and deceit in the field of organized labor. Lee Gordon, the protagonist, has been tasked with convincing Negroes to join a striking aircraft workers' union in Los Angeles. Near the beginning of the novel, the union leader Joe Ptak warns him that the communists will try to recruit and control him. Joe says they have good contacts and can help but not to let them "run the show": "'Watch out they don't undermine you or double-cross you. And don't you fight 'em for God's sake. Let me do that.'"[23] Through the body of the novel we are never sure who is a communist and who is not, including Ptak, because of the intricate machinations of the Party puppeteers, who perpetually turn people against one another in a cynical strategy for taking over the union—or destroying it if they cannot gain control. Rising conflict throughout the novel is attributed, above all, to the attempts of the communists to manipulate and eventually to frame Lee Gordon, nearly getting him executed for a murder he did not commit.

From the start, Lee is suspicious of communists, including an African American named Luther McGregor who befriends him, doing the bidding of the Party on one hand and lining his own pockets on the other. The way the Party has changed course concerning the war and the Negro, Lee believes, is only a symptom of a deeper flaw in which the ends justify the means. Communists turn friend against friend in a fog of never-ending schemes to gain power over the union, framing even their own to achieve set purposes. The most sympathetic communist character, Abe Rosenberg ("Rosie"), befriends Lee, defends him against false charges, and is expelled from the Party for doing so. Rosie's continued commitment to communism comes across as naïve, fulfilling a psychological need for a deterministic historical vision to replace Jewish messianic thought, but he joins his faith in Marxism with a belief (equally "Jewish") in the importance of each life on its own terms. Rosie's principled resistance to Party demands, deriving from his Jewish heritage, redeems him as a man.

Lee comes to trust and admire the white union leaders Smitty and Joe Ptak, who maintain faith in the union. They work to overcome all attempts—by both the Communist Party and the owner-capitalist Louis Foster—to turn black and white workers against each other, and they come to Gordon's aid when he seems almost certain to be headed for death row. Himes condemns the Communist Party for its unconcern for individuals, its willingness to sacrifice virtually anyone for the "cause" (also a central theme of Lionel Trilling's *The Middle of the Journey*, published in the same year), but he does not attack collectivism as such. The union ethos embodied in Smitty, Joe Ptak, and ultimately Lee Gordon epitomizes how a collective anticapitalist labor effort can not only countenance but inspire belief in personal integrity. Smitty remains personally loyal to Lee Gordon and brings to his side Joe Ptak, who is willing to sacrifice himself for the cause, and a lawyer who risks disbarment for taking on Lee Gordon's case. Smitty and Ptak are canny organizers bent on achieving the union's ends, but not at the cost of self-integrity.

On the other hand, Bart, the African American West Coast chairman of the Communist Party, follows directives from the national committee of the CPUSA ordering the state committee to kill any rumors of betrayal of the union, once it becomes known that one of their own had taken money from the capitalist Louis Foster. As a good Marxist, Bart knows the end justifies the means: "Therefore guilt and innocence were inapplicable in the moral sense. Revolutionary tactics were not to be interpreted in the light of bourgeois concepts, or defined by bourgeois terminology, but considered only in terms of preparation for the coming battle." He quotes Marx: "Law, morality, religion, are . . . so many bourgeois prejudices, behind which lurk just as many bourgeois interests." Bart tells himself that the "guilty" were simply "those who hindered, obstructed, opposed, or were indifferent to the rise of the proletariat," and "no individual was beyond sacrifice for the ultimate aim." (Again, an identical theme emerges in Trilling's novel of 1947.) But Bart finds himself more "Negro" and more "American" than communist: "His American instincts were diametrically opposed to the ruthless nonconformity of revolutionary maneuvering." Bart follows orders anyway, with the result that despite his rise from black laborer to high position, and despite the respect he has earned from Party members, he feels no pride in his accomplishments. His labor for the Party is meaningless to him. He has done too many things as a communist official "against his innate convictions." Too often, he had had to deny there was any such thing as "integrity" in order to sustain his communist faith. "It was not that the Communist Party lacked integrity; it simply did not recognize it."[24]

This is a devastating indictment, for Lee Gordon's struggle through-out the novel is for integrity and self-respect—which he equates with "manhood." Honesty and meaning, in *Lonely Crusade*, are not equivalent to pure individualism but rather requirements for human solidarity and love of another. In his lowest moment, drowning in the cynicism sur-rounding him, Gordon concludes that

> the one rigid rule in human behavior was to be for yourself and to hell with everyone else . . . ; that honor never was and never would be for the Negro, and integrity was only for a fool; that from then on he would believe in the almighty dollar, the cowardice of Negroes, and the hy-pocrisy of whites, and he would never go wrong.
>
> And because all these fine conclusions were so dissatisfying, he arose and went to bed with Ruth. And she could have been any woman with two legs and a stomach.[25]

In the climax and denouement of the novel, picking up the union banner from the fallen Joe Ptak during a pitched battle at the factory gates, Lee Gordon regains his sense of integrity, a belief that not all whites are hypocrites nor all Negroes cowards, and reverent love for his wife.

Himes did not get here by way of hanging out in New York literary circles and reading *Partisan Review*; he had worked in the LA shipyards. The novel's anticommunism is not simply "Cold War liberalism" but an argument about the role of personal integrity in the battle for organized labor. Himes extended this to an argument about the importance of per-sonal integrity to the novelist, knowing full well how former allies would attack him. (They did.)

Richard Wright made a similar indictment in "The Horror and the Glory," the second half of *Black Boy* (which was dropped from the book at the urging of the Book-of-the-Month Club). As leader of the South Side John Reed Club of Chicago, he had to battle Party members "for a more liberal program for the club," allowing the development of writers and artists, yet this led to continual tensions, coming to a head by charges against an artist named Swann of being a police collaborator and

Trotskyist: "We all liked Swann, did not believe him guilty of any misconduct; but we did not want to offend the party." Ultimately, it is discovered that the accuser had escaped from a mental institution and that the charges against Swann were baseless. He was apprehended and returned to the hospital, but when asked by club members what had happened to him, Wright wrote, "I could but lie."[26] To preserve the dignity of the club's leadership, he could not admit that they had all been duped by a "madman."

In *For Whom the Bell Tolls*, Hemingway (who in the mid-thirties had addressed the League of American Writers, a Stalinist-led group) similarly critiques communist leadership on the Republican side of the Spanish Civil War as self-interested and unconcerned with the lives of the peasant Loyalists, whose labor of death it cynically manipulates. Robert Jordan, in contrast, acts by a personal code of conduct keyed to performing his duty while remaining "honest" about what he observes and experiences in relation to the peasants with whom he works. His integrity is thoroughly bound up with his sense of solidarity with the antifascist peasants and his capacity for love. This emphasis on recovering an authentic relationship to experience (the keynote of all of Hemingway's work at a time when he was at the peak of his fame) and the connection of personal meaning to collective struggle (a new note struck in this novel) had consequences for the honest labor of writing.

This point of view inhered in the practice of the abstract expressionists, some of whom were or had recently been, like Wright, Marxists. In their "Editorial Preface" to the inaugural issue of the journal *possibilities*, Robert Motherwell and Harold Rosenberg identified the magazine with

artists and writers who "practice" in their work their own experience without seeking to transcend it in academic, group or political formulas.

Such practice implies the belief that through conversion of energy something valid may come out, whatever situation one is forced to begin with.

The question of what will emerge is left open. One functions in an attitude of expectancy. As Juan Gris said: You are lost the instant you know what the result will be. . . .

The temptation is to conclude that organized social thinking is "more serious" than the act that sets free in contemporary experience forms which that experience has made possible.

One who yields to this temptation makes a choice among various theories of manipulating the known elements of the so-called objective state of affairs. Once the political choice has been made, art and literature ought of course to be given up. . . .

If one is to continue to paint or write as the political trap seems to close upon him he must perhaps have the extremest faith in sheer possibility.

In his extremism he shows that he has recognized how drastic the political presence is.[27]

Obviously, then, artists like Motherwell remained leftist in political orientation even when that orientation was far from obvious in the visual vocabulary of their work.

To link Wright, most often termed a literary naturalist or "social realist," to abstract expressionism, is counterintuitive. Yet by the 1940s (unlike in 1937's "Blueprint for Negro Writing") Wright described his practice in terms much like those used by Motherwell and Rosenberg. The interest in "process" was pervasive.

Norman Lewis, an African American painter, explained his move from social realism to abstract expressionism in his "Thesis, 1946," identifying his turn away from "an over-emphasis on tradition" and "propaganda," as well as "Negro Idiom," to a concept that

treats art not as reproduction or as convenient but entirely secondary medium for propaganda but as the production of experiences which combine intellectual and emotional activities in a way that may conceivably add not only to the pleasure of the viewer and the satisfaction of the artist but to a universal knowledge of aesthetics and the creative faculty which I feel exists for one form of expression or another in all men.[28]

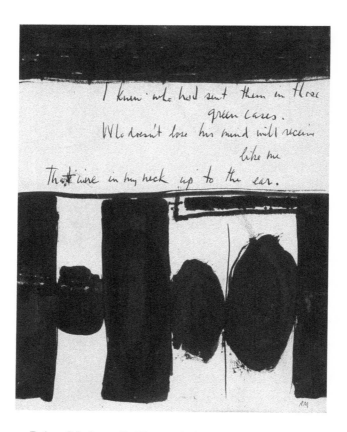

FIGURE 3.1 Robert Motherwell, *Elegy to the Spanish Republic No. 1*, 1948. 10 3/4" x 8 1/2" (27.3 x 21.8 cm), ink on paper. *Source*: Museum of Modern Art. Gift of the artist. Art © Dedalus Foundation Inc/Licensed by VAGA, New York, NY. Digital Image © The Museum of Modern Art/Licensed by SCALA / Art Resource, NY.

Lewis considered himself a Marxist, but his aesthetic philosophy was also pragmatist, marked by John Dewey's aesthetic theory. (He studied under Charles Alston, a pragmatist aesthetician who directed "306" in Harlem, and he was also an admirer of Dewey's protégé Albert Barnes, the millionaire creator of the Barnes Foundation.) As he grew disillusioned with what he considered a Marxist emphasis on art as illustration of social conflict, he came increasingly to believe in the experimental aspect of creation. Often inspired by jazz, Lewis explored the

FIGURE 3.2 Norman Lewis (1909–1979), *The Wanderer (Johnny)*, 1933, oil on canvas, 36" x 30", signed and dated. *Source*: © Estate of Norman W. Lewis; Courtesy of Michael Rosenfeld Gallery LLC, New York, NY.

possibilities of nonrepresentational visual rhythms, painting as "an activity of discovery in that it seeks to find hitherto ignored or unknown combinations of forms, colors, and textures and even psychological phenomena, and perhaps to cause new types of experience in the artist as well as the viewer."[29]

In his departure from social realism, Lewis was following a path not unrelated to Richard Wright's. After working in the Federal Arts Program of the WPA in the mid-1930s, when he was engaged in social realism and involved with the John Reed Club, Lewis became associated

FIGURE 3.3 Norman Lewis (1909–1979), *Crossing*, 1948. Oil on canvas. 25" x 54", signed. *Source*: © Estate of Norman W. Lewis; Courtesy of Michael Rosenfeld Gallery LLC, New York, NY.

with artists involved in the development of what came to be called abstract expressionism. He taught at the Jefferson School of Social Science from 1944 to 1949, which he likened to the New School for Social Research except that it was "much more revolutionary." But he was eventually asked to leave because of his refusal to teach "social realism" in painting. He and Ad Reinhardt (who also taught at the Jefferson School briefly) grew close and shared the same views about the "ineffectiveness of protest paintings," although they remained politically radical.[30] In 1947, Lewis wrote a friend about his disillusionment with the Party:

> After seriously painting and thinking scientifically I came to certain definite conclusions—which you will find yourself doing, if you approach painting as a true Marxist.
> Last Thursday the Party held a symposium at Manhattan Center—on Art & Propaganda. Joan, Alex, and I bought tickets—then I suddenly decided not to go—I imagined it would be on the same old questions and attitudes with no universal consideration. The following day I

met with one of Goodelman's students. . . . She said the meeting was dull,—This is no more than I expected—now I shall read what the D. W. [*Daily Worker*] or N. Masses [*New Masses*] has to say—

Now I am wondering will the *Daily Worker* or the *New Masses* sound like that record—"Daddy, you were so right" in their praise of Foster on art.[31]

Lewis's continued identification as a Marxist even as he drew away from communist organs comports with the way others of the period modified Marxist approaches to aesthetics in line with pragmatist orientations. This did not mean that Lewis was growing apolitical personally. He simply came to feel that explicitly "political" art was ineffective: "I don't think it helps the struggle. So later I became involved in unions; I felt that picketing and any kind of mass demonstration had more of an impression on people than painting pictures and trying to arrest that same audience."[32]

In 1943, Adolph Gottlieb and Mark Rothko wrote the critic Edward Alden Jewell that no set of notes could "explain" their paintings. "Their explanation must come out of a consummated experience between picture and onlooker."[33] This idea parallels the argument that, for example, the "point" of a lyric poem is not an interpretation in prose but an *experience* of the poem that is consummatory in itself yet never definitive of its "meaning." The attitude comports not only with that of the jazz musicians the abstract expressionists so admired but with that of the ecologically minded writers I will discuss in later chapters. One finds over and over again an emphasis on "experience" and "transfer of energy" in approaches to artistic creation—but not as something to be *represented*. No, the experience *is* the encounter between the artwork and its *experiencer*—whether artist or reader/viewer/listener. John Dewey had enunciated something very close to this conception in *Art as Experience* (1934).

Great art, Dewey had argued, is not something above the common life of a people "but something which should give the final touch of meaning, of consummation, to all the activities of life." In a defense of the New Criticism, René Wellek once accused Dewey of denying "all distinction between aesthetic and other experiences of heightened vitality,"[34] but in fact Dewey felt fine art performed a vital function both socially and individually, uniting process, product, and perception. The point of aesthetic creation, to Dewey, was to intensify living, to bring both artist and audience through conflict and tension to a new harmony. This, for Dewey, is what we mean when we speak of "*an* experience," one that conveys the impression of culmination, completeness in itself. In distinctively aesthetic experience such characteristics are controlling; in the dominantly aesthetic object "the factors that determine which can be called *an* experience are lifted high above the threshold of perception and are made manifest for their own sake."[35]

But what did "experience" mean to the pragmatists and those Marxists who were drawn to similar views of the relationship between art and social "reality"? Marxist critics often have a special animus against pragmatism because of what they understand as its naïve and vague deployment of "experience." Noting that the New York intellectuals of the 1940s, in their transition from revolutionary communism, began to see art as truer to life and experience than "theory," Alan Wald writes, "Underpinning their argument about the relationship between art and experience is a line of reasoning that engages rather simplistic, non-Marxist assumptions about ideology and epistemology that can only be called pragmatist."[36]

To some Marxists, pragmatism enshrines a concept of experience over against "ideology" that renders "aesthetic experience" as the paradigm of experience freed of any factors that would thwart its development. This is a fundamental misunderstanding of what pragmatists meant by "experience." Dewey himself came to regret titling his most important book *Experience and Nature* because of the common misunderstanding of his use of the term "experience," wishing he had used *Culture and Nature*. Culture, he believed, was the very form of human experience; this embraced social formations' effects but could not be reduced to them.[37] Experience, in pragmatist terms, was not independent of what Marxists called ideology, economics, or the habits and naturalized conceptions of any society: this is a fundamental pragmatist understanding going back to the most accessible essays of William James and arguably Ralph Waldo Emerson in such essays as "Experience" and "Fate." What pragmatism denied is that one can get "outside" of experience (which resides not in individual consciousness but between the self and all that exists outside of it) to an objective understanding of social "reality" and its ultimate trajectory.

Simplistic assumptions about pragmatist notions of experience and the role of art were rife in communist circles of the 1930s and 1940s and have not since retired. "For the Marxist," Alan Wald argues, "to settle on the terrain of experience is to submerge oneself in the unexamined stuff of ideology. This distinction between pragmatism and Marxism may help inform . . . the interpretation of literature produced by the New York intellectuals during the 1940s."[38] *Precisely.*

For some, like Wald and Terry Eagleton (who has also posed pragmatism as a bête noir), "experience is another word for everyday consciousness, imbued with the norms and values of class society and its rulers."[39] It is an understandable but faulty objection. Pragmatists took aim early on at class rule and its ideological supports through mass media. More to the point, Dewey had argued in the mid-1930s that historical developments including European nationalism, capitalism, and imperialism had compartmentalized art to "reflect and establish superior cultural status" until it no longer functioned as a *"part* of a native and spontaneous culture." To recover the continuity between the arts and normal processes of living must be the goal in a democratic culture, while nonetheless stressing art's *consummatory* function.[40] One does not set artistic values "with primary regard for moral effect," but all aesthetic experience ends up having a moral effect because it trains the sensibilities upon which ethical consciousness depends:

> While poetry is not a criticism of life in intent, it is in effect, and so is all art. For art fixes those standards of enjoyment and appreciation with which other things are compared; it selects the objects of future desires; it stimulates effort. . . . The level and style of the arts of literature,

poetry, ceremony, amusement, and recreation which obtain in a community, furnishing the staple objects of enjoyment in that community, do more than all else to determine the current direction of ideas and endeavors in the community. They supply the meanings in terms of which life is judged, esteemed, and criticized.[41]

Art was thus inherently critical. On the other hand, the false concept of "art for art's sake" was a logical consequence of the divorce in Western culture between "the consummatory" and "the instrumental," or between "culture" and labor.

In striving to distinguish the aesthetic qualities of capital-*A* "Art" from "every thing that is existential in nature" and from "all other forms of good," high-modernist critics and artists, in unconscious collusion with capitalist tendencies, had carried to conclusion "the isolation of fine art from the useful, of the final from the efficacious. They thus prove that the separation of the consummatory from the instrumental makes art wholly esoteric."[42] Fine art thus became a class marker and, thanks to its rarity, financially valuable, set apart in collections and museums to demonstrate the good taste of millionaires, national glory, and so on—removed, in short, from the common life of a community.

Dewey believed the best art was that which most fully conjoined creative process and product, or the recurrent and ordered with the incomplete, uncertain, spontaneous, and novel—views obviously germane to abstract expressionism but also to forms of poetry growing out of Whitman's, including William Carlos Williams's practice in the late 1940s.

The central problem with pragmatism is that it provided a powerful dialectical alternative to Marxism. (Some tried to conjoin them.) Pragmatists, as antifoundationalists, did not have the Marxist certitude about the objectively "real," nor could they see the reason for taking a theorem about universal history as a proof. Even more profoundly, from the standpoint of an artist, they did not identify, a priori, the locus of ultimacy in politics or economics as conventionally understood.

The pragmatist approach to the relationship between aesthetics, ethics, and politics was not limited to the New York intellectuals. This conclusion is somewhat surprising because, according to the common wisdom, the 1940s was the nadir of Deweyan pragmatism.[43] That was certainly true in some sectors of the intellectual universe. Dewey's optimism about human nature and his anti-interventionist stance in the period before Pearl Harbor were overshadowed by the rising influence of Reinhold Niebuhr and others who were convinced that radical evil had been underestimated. But Wald is right about pragmatism's influence in the realm of aesthetics for leftist writers working outside the universities.

This development represents a recurrence of the sort of "native" radicalism of the early twentieth century, which had its own antecedents in the mid-nineteenth-century radicalism of the transcendentalists and of Fuller, Whitman, and Melville (the latter two often being invoked by radicals in the 1940s). In the 1937 "Editorial Statement" inaugurating the reborn *Partisan Review* as dissociated from the Communist Party, the editors announced that they would model the journal after left-wing magazines of the 1910s and 1920s: "the forms of literary editorship, at once exciting and adventurous, which characterized the magazines of aesthetic revolt, were of definite cultural value; and these forms *Partisan Review* will wish to adopt to the literature of the new period."[44]

They had in mind magazines like *The Masses*. When the leaders of *The Masses* recruited Max Eastman in 1912 to take over as editor without pay, he turned it into a revolutionary bullhorn and venue for insurgent poetry and art of the Ashcan School. Yet Eastman, while inspired by Russian Bolshevism, was only marginally Marxist. Lenin he regarded as a "great man" of History, yet his mentor was John Dewey, who guided his studies and had him to dinner every Sunday during his graduate studies at Columbia. As of its 1913 editorial manifesto, *The Masses* was

a revolutionary and not a reform magazine; a magazine with no dividends to pay; a free magazine; frank, arrogant, impertinent, searching for the true causes; a magazine directed against rigidity and dogma wherever it is found; printing what is too naked or true for a moneymaking press; a magazine whose final policy is to do as it pleases and conciliate nobody, not even its readers.[45]

It was, in short, experimental. Eastman would be the first of the radical vanguard to attack Stalinism and defend Trotsky, well before it became acceptable, and as a result lapsed into obscurity. He ultimately recoiled from Trotsky and Marxism as such.

Paul Grimstad has recently demonstrated the centrality of literary pragmatism's uses of "experience" to experimental writing in the United States from Emerson to the James brothers. The process of composition for the writers he examines is in itself continuous with "experience" rather than an attempt to represent experience.[46] This argument holds true for such writing in the postwar period, as well. We will soon see how the emphasis on process distinguished Dewey's quasi-formalism from that of the more politically conservative, university-based New Critics and such poet-celebrities as T. S. Eliot and Ezra Pound.

Without referencing pragmatism, Lionel Trilling came to rest in something strongly resembling the pragmatist position after his formative attachment to Marxism. This outlook is as abundantly evident in his novel *The Middle of the Journey* (1947) as in his championing of Henry James. For what pervades his work is an aversion to absolutes or to knowing the laws determining any future. Instead, a constant moral attentiveness and aesthetic sensitivity to everyday experience as well as human connection emerge from the uncertainties of encounters with otherness, yet with a sense of the tragic too often disassociated with the pragmatists and their predecessors. The encounter with evil—ultimately, with death—requires a sense of tragedy that neither wallows in guilt nor extols purity and innocence and that accepts chance as an existential challenge to personal integrity.[47] Against it no ideological or religious certainty can guard.

In the mirror image of ideological certainty, this equals "shilly-shallying" liberalism. In the liberal imagination it amounts to an elemental, and natural, curiosity that all group projects suspect and punish even though they depend on it for their very life. It is, so to say, universal in its very contingency. In Lionel Trilling's novel, the alternatives are an easily corrupted idealism invested in a progressive "future"—that of the fellow-traveling Stalinists—and a recoil from communist commitment into conservative Christianity (based on the career of Whittaker Chambers). The weakness of this novel of ideas lies in the fact that, as Robert Warshow pointed out on its first appearance, its chief characters—a "liberal," two radicals who refuse to acknowledge communist perfidy, and an ex-Stalinist spy who has turned reactionary and Christian—stand for certain predetermined intellectual/moral positions. In fact, at a crucial moment, the main characters are starkly differentiated according to their different interpretations of a critical essay on a literary text—Melville's *Billy Budd, Sailor.* The novel, in short, dramatizes political positions in relation to literary interpretation and aesthetic sensibility, ultimately privileging a liberalism chastened by recognition of evil. It was the only novel Trilling, who aspired to be a novelist, would ever write. He thereafter traded that aspiration for a form of creative criticism and became one of the most-followed critics of an age when a work of literary criticism could sell over 100,000 copies in its first year.[48]

From the "New York intellectuals" one might well turn in contrast to the Southern Agrarians–become–New Critics whose interpretive practices took hold in the universities in the course of the 1940s. Their literary labor had specific institutional bearings. It can hardly be overemphasized that this was an academic development featured in college-supported literary reviews: *The Southern Review, Kenyon Review, Sewanee Review.* It began as an interacademic insurgency combating English departments' emphasis on bibliography, philology, textual criticism, and a literary historicism focused on "who, what, where." (They were still trying to imagine "why.") There was "scholarship," and there was "criticism"—one carried on in the colleges, the other in the New York literary reviews.

What held the New Critics together, as René Wellek asserted in a defense against harsh caricatures drawn in the 1960s, was their "reaction against the preceding or contemporary critical schools and views" ensconced in the MLA and the universities. "What in the American situation mattered most was that they were united in their opposition to the prevailing methods, doctrines, and views of academic English literary scholarship"—a scholarship "purely philological and historical" and with no relationship to contemporary literature. They were college teachers attempting to establish professional security "in an environment hostile to any and all criticism."[49] In arguing for the value of criticism, the New Critics insisted on separating aesthetic experience from practical concerns, rhetorical persuasion, political doctrine, or emotional effusion. They stressed the unity and coherence of a work of art and made aesthetic judgments based on such criteria—not only form (rhythm, rhyme, and stanza in poetry, for example) but tone, point of view, narrative structure, diction, and theme.

The route to this academic formalism came by way of specific engagements with the relationship between art and politics beginning in the 1930s—and the profession of teaching. In the 1940s the ostensibly "apolitical" approach to creative literature was defended on political grounds as befitting democracy versus totalitarianism, even as it was detached from the embarrassing Southern Agrarian ideology of its origins. Nonetheless, those origins have something to do with the utter disregard of African American–authored literature as the New Criticism took hold in the academy along with its brand of Anglo-American modernism. Notably, New Directions Press, which was closely associated with the New Critics and their favorite authors and which grew to prominence along with New Critical methods, did not publish a single black author in its first three decades, at least.

The Agrarians of the late 1920s and early 1930s, with essays collected in the book *I'll Take My Stand*, positioned the place-oriented, nonindustrial, "European," and even feudal ethos of the South against Northern industrialism, which they saw leading to the breakdown of community and the rise of communism.[50] They seem to have read Marx and Engels—and John C. Calhoun—positing that industrial capitalism would lead inevitably to communism. (The title Allen Tate, Robert Penn Warren, and Andrew Lytle favored for their agrarian manifesto was *Tracts Against Communism*.) Between 1933 and 1936 they even collaborated with the openly fascist Seward Collins and his journal *American Review*. But following a 1936 interview Grace Lumpkin conducted with Collins, which identified their aims with European fascism, the Agrarians immediately cut ties to Collins and shifted course, insisting that their political views were the lone bulwark in the United States against fascist tyranny, which the New Deal among other efforts portended.[51] Yet the erstwhile Agrarians' continued support of racial segregation in the South, antimodernism, and something close to "blood-and-soil" regionalism inevitably associated them with the specter of European fascism, and by the end of the 1930s they had disbanded, the most influential of them dissociating themselves from any overt politics while pursuing academic careers in creative writing and literary criticism.

This dissociation was itself "political." One critic has attributed John Crowe Ransom's retreat from agrarianism to his attempt to rebut essays by Theodor Adorno that Ransom had published in the *Kenyon Review*.[52] Ransom, Tate, and Warren found resistance to totalitarian uniformity in the sensibilities and values instilled by art and aesthetics developed free of other concerns. They came to the position that, as Robert H. Brinkmeyer writes, "art best manifested—and thus defended—democratic principles through its complicated interior dynamics."[53] But it would take a college education in what was termed, circa 1941, "The New Criticism" to appreciate such dynamics.

Several of the most important "New Critics" denied there was ever any such group. Robert Penn Warren put it most memorably in an interview conducted in Fanny and Ralph Ellison's Rome apartment in the late 1950s:

Let's name some of them—Richards, Eliot, Tate, Blackmur, Winters, Brooks, Leavis (I guess). How in God's name can you get that gang into the same bed? There's no bed big enough and no blanket would stay tucked. When Ransom wrote his book called the *New Criticism* he was pointing out the vindictive variety among the critics and saying that he didn't agree with any of them. The term is, in one sense, a term without any referent—or with too many referents. It is a term that belongs to the conspiracy theory of history. A lot of people—chiefly aging, conservative professors scared of losing prestige, or young instructors afraid of not getting promoted—middlebrow magazine editors—and the flotsam and jetsam of semi-Marxist social-significance criticism left stranded by history—they all had a communal nightmare called the New Criticism to explain their vague discomfort. I think it was something they ate.[54]

Nonetheless, Warren admitted that the "New Critics" had something in common: "a willingness to look long and hard at the literary object." Their emphasis on a work's internal dynamics, via "close reading," put them on a vector of partial convergence with the promodernist, anti-Stalinist *Partisan Review*.

Ransom presented this new trajectory in a 1940–1941 lecture series arguing for the role of art in society, equating poetry with a "democratic state" and prose discourse with the "totalitarian state." The totalitarian state, he posited, views its citizens as "functional members whose existence is totally defined by their allotted contributions to its ends," having no use for their individual character. In contrast, poetry or creative writing allows its citizens "the free exercise of their own private and independent characters."[55] The democratic character of poetry resided not in its theme or prose "meaning" but in the individuality yet interdependence of its parts. Having moved from Vanderbilt University to Kenyon College in northern Ohio to found the *Kenyon Review*, Ransom put his vision into effect in the composition of the journal, which became the most prestigious purely literary review of the decade. Ransom and Allen Tate, who moved with Ransom from Vanderbilt to Kenyon, attracted the ambitious young poets Robert Lowell, Peter Taylor, and Randall Jarrell—the latter to become a particularly influential critic and the former a major poet of the 1950s and 1960s. When the influential *Southern Review* (led by Agrarians Robert Penn Warren and Cleanth Brooks at Louisiana State University) folded for financial reasons, it was essentially merged into the *Kenyon Review*. Cleanth Brooks moved to Yale in 1947, and Warren joined him in 1950, signaling the centrality of the so-called New Criticism in the universities. Yale would continue its dominance in literary theory into the 1970s, when it became, with Cornell and Johns Hopkins, a nursery for poststructuralism.

In keeping with its aesthetic stance, the *Kenyon Review* condemned "patriotic" literature. Freeing the arts of propaganda and didacticism was the key to nourishing their democratic character. This put the journal at odds with such critics as Archibald MacLeish (Librarian of Congress and a well-known poet) as well as journals like the *Nation* and *New Republic*. While the editors themselves would answer any call to play a direct part in the war as citizens, Ransom asserted, the journal could by its very nature play no part in the "war effort."[56] Art's social function is inherent in its form rather than its explicit content.

By this time Ransom was repudiating his former Agrarian arguments, and so was Allen Tate. But Tate still saw a connection between what he regarded as the instrumentalism of pragmatism and the social sciences on the one hand and totalitarianism on the other:

> What we thought was to be a conditioning process in favor of a state planned by the Teachers College of Columbia University [which promoted John Dewey's progressive educational theories] will be a conditioning equally useful for Plato's tyrant state. . . . The actuality of tyranny we shall enthusiastically greet as the development of democracy, for the ringing of the democratic bell will make our political glands flow as freely for dictatorship as, hitherto, for monopoly capitalism.[57]

Tate foresaw fascism taking hold in the United States at the expense of the "critical spirit."

Thus, as early as 1940 one can anticipate the later argument in defense of awarding Ezra Pound the Bollingen Prize of the Library of Congress for his *Pisan Cantos*, despite the fact that the book virtually opens by mourning the "martyrdom" of Mussolini. To a majority of the judges (Tate being one of them), its overt politics was beside the point. What drove Tate to this extreme and partly motivated his work as editor of the *Sewanee Review* at the height of its influence in the 1940s were the demands of MacLeish, Van Wyck Brooks, and others (mostly outside academia) to make artists choose between art and patriotism during the early war years.[58] Robert Penn Warren shared this concern, although he was considerably less paranoid than Tate.

Warren always disliked political "right-thinking" as an approach to fiction or poetry. He condemned MacLeish and Brooks's position on formalist as well as moral grounds, arguing that the very form of poetry required tension, variety, complexity, paradox. Charging that "political didacticism came close to mirroring the censorship and conformity enforced by totalitarian states," he feared that independent artists who did not fall into line would be deemed treasonous.[59] The attempt to "purify" poetry of moral complexity and uncertainty forgets that "the hand-me-down faith, the hand-me-down ideals, no matter what the professed content, is in the end not only meaningless but vicious."[60]

Warren was always more an explorer of the moral complexity of human experience than a *moralizer*, and unlike the antipragmatist Allen Tate he greatly admired William James, an influence on his most "political" fiction, *All the King's Men*. Notably, Warren early on had been conditioned and weaned from hand-me-down ideals in the climate of the New York intellectuals, on visits to Manhattan while a student at Yale. It was Paul Rosenfeld—one of the first generation of New York intellectuals, along with Randolph Bourne and Van Wyck Brooks—who in the late 1920s had introduced Warren to modern art and its relationship to modern literature. And Rosenfeld first inspired him—really assigned him—to write fiction based on the sort of Southern tales he often recounted: "Rosenfeld was responsible not only for publishing my first fiction," wrote Warren in 1947, "but for its very existence."[61]

Based in part on the career of the populist Louisiana governor Huey Long and initially conceived as a play in 1939–1940, *All the King's Men*, as James H. Justus has pointed out, centers on "the theme of power, its distribution, ethics, and consequences."[62] Warren finished the verse play *Proud Flesh* while living in Rome on a Guggenheim Fellowship in 1939–1940, "to the tune of military boot-heels on the cobbles." As he later wrote, "the shadow of a European as well as a home-grown dictatorship lies over the composition."[63] Out of that play grew *All the King's Men*.

Fascism haunts Warren's novel in more interesting ways than if it were merely an exposé of a quasi-fascist in a one-party Southern state. It was, he said, about "the genesis and temptations of power," how "strong men" arise in a power vacuum to serve as a "fulfillment" for those who follow and support them. However, he characteristically wanted the story to be more "personal" than "political," "to show how the issues come to crisis in personal terms" and "to indicate some interplay . . . between the public, political story and the private, ethical one."[64] In a sense, the novel is about personal responsibility and balancing the importance of *process* with the importance of *aim*.[65] The ethical story involves Willie Stark's rise to power and his determination, once in power, to build a hospital to serve the poor—surely a laudable, not to mention progressive, aim. To this aim he manipulates the political and legal systems at every level through graft, blackmail, and bribery.

Willie Stark and his follower Jack Burden (the narrator and "chorus" of the novel) are characters in process, both being shaped by events and personal decisions the tragic effects of which they cannot know in advance. Through most of the novel, Burden absolves himself of responsibility in his service to Stark, much like the Nazi defendants at Nuremberg; he is merely following orders. By the end, the summer of 1939, he understands that he and many others share in the blame, that he must "go out of the house and go into the convulsions of the world, out of history into history and the awful responsibility of Time."[66]

Warren purposely made Willie Stark "more humanly acceptable" than either Huey Long or Mussolini in order to frustrate melodramatic readings, to force a more complicated moral response on the part of the reader, and he built this complexity into the form of the novel, especially through point of view. The focalization through Jack Burden, who is gradually drawn into Stark's web and even more gradually realizes how deeply he is implicated in its sticky weave, recalls Nick Carraway's narration of *The Great Gatsby*, but the size and social intricacy of the novel evokes the work of Henry James. Within the frame tale of Cass Mastern, which he relates from the vantage point of looking back, years after discovering it and after the death of Willie Stark, Jack Burden comes to perceive what Cass Mastern learned, "that the world is like an enormous spider web and if you touch it, however lightly, at any point, the vibration ripples to the remotest perimeter."[67] The oft-quoted description of the web here (which could easily be mistaken for something by William or Henry James) curiously, and no doubt inadvertently, mirrors the New Critics' view of the best works of poetry and fiction.

With the rise of the New Criticism, which gained its greatest institutional force in the course of the 1940s, the scholarly side of the literary field grew increasingly important to contemporary literature as universities became the major incubators and patrons of literary work and as college-based journals associated with the New Critics became major venues for contemporary literature. This profoundly altered the context of writers' labor. A professional competition developed between the independent critics and writers and those groomed by and for the academy—now tenured and tenure-track professors. As American taxpayers' cash flowed into universities through the G.I. Bill and college education became a middle-class expectation, the adaptable New York intellectuals were absorbed, often uncomfortably. Some threw darts. Critics like Edmund Wilson and Alfred Kazin attempted to halt the juggernaut, but they hardly stood a chance against expanding institutional pressures. What Mark McGurl calls "The Program Era" took off, hand-in-glove with (in William James's words) "the PhD octopus."

One can easily understand why the New Critics' emphasis on aesthetic form and craft lent itself to the teaching of creative writing. Much of the best writing occurred, however, between the camps of New York intellectuals and academics associated with the New Criticism or independent of both—Gwendolyn Brooks's work, for example, and Robert Hayden's, or for that matter Wallace Stevens's and William Carlos Williams's. Leroi Jones and Allen Ginsberg emerged in the 1950s, but not from university writers' workshops. Randall Jarrell and John Berryman owed as much to Marxism and the New York intellectual ambience as to the New Criticism in its *Kenyon Review* iteration, and Jarrell's poetry of the 1940s is inescapably "political."

In "The Emancipators" Jarrell answers Marx and his predecessor Rousseau, who had famously written, "Man is born free; and everywhere he is in chains. One thinks himself the master of others, and still remains a greater slave than they." Jarrell replies, "Man is born in chains, yet everywhere we see him dead." Marx had written: "Workers of the world unite! You have nothing to lose but your chains." To which Jarrell, addressing Western voyagers, explorers, and European capitalists, replies:

> On your earth they sell nothing but our lives.
> You knew that what you died for was our deaths?
> You learned, those years, that all men wish is Trade?
> It was you who understood. It is we who change.

The stanza signifies on Marx's theory of value and the commodification of labor, extending Marxist critique to ecological concerns:

> You guessed this? The earth's face altering with iron,
> The smoke ranged like a wall against the day?
> The equations metamorphose into use: the free
> Drag their slight bones from tenements to vote
> To die with their children in your factories.[68]

Jarrell was a true "post-Marxist"; he had thoroughly absorbed Marxian thought and never abandoned it, yet he ultimately found it insufficient to address the problem of meaning and the importance of individuality. Like many of his generation, he turned to psychoanalysis. It was precisely the war, and not just the Stalinist betrayal (a major factor for his fellow poet John Berryman, among many others), that accounts for this shift.

Berryman at this time was also an overtly political poet of the Left. "River Rouge, 1932" commemorates the killing of four young men leading a mass demonstration outside the River Rouge plant of the Ford

Motor company. "Thanksgiving: Detroit" similarly commemorates a strike and battle with police in Detroit:

Thanksgiving, and more than turkeys underground.
Opinion underground. Who shall be glad?
Finks and goons in the streets of the city, cops
Clubbing and watching the clubbing of men, men hide.[69]

On the other hand, the poem "Communist" speaks to the feeling of betrayal and shame young communists in the United States felt on learning of the nonaggression pact between Germany and Russia, the Russian invasion of Poland, and then the Russian invasion of Finland. Written in ballad form as a dialogue between a mother and her communist son, each stanza ends with the son evading his mother's questions about how he explains the actions of Russia: "'For I'm worn out with reading and want to lie down.'" The concluding stanza reads:

'O I fear for your future, Communist, my son!
I fear for your future, my honest young man!'
'I cannot speak or think, mother; let me alone,
For I'm sick at my heart and I want to lie down.'[70]

Berryman addresses the very problem Warshow emphasized: how communism interposed a set of stock responses between the individual and experience, making them "inauthentic." The view was common at the *Partisan Review*, where some of Berryman's first published poems appeared, and he was close friends, going back to college and graduate school, with Delmore Schwartz, who edited *Partisan Review* from 1943 to 1955. Yet Berryman was also a rigorous formalist critic deeply versed in Western prosody.

Toward the end of *The Dispossessed*, Berryman's second book, is a cluster called "The Nervous Songs," dedicated to his brother. There are nine of them, each composed of three sestets. Each includes the word "song" in its title—"Young Woman's Song," "A Professor's Song," "The Song of the Bridegroom," etc.—anticipating the "dream songs" that would come some years later and make Berryman famous.

These first two Berryman books have attracted little attention; virtually all of the scholarship focuses on his "breakthrough book," *Homage to Mistress Bradstreet*, and *The Dream Songs*. Yet the "confessional" mode for which those books are celebrated, and for which they are regarded as standard-bearers of postmodernism, is clearly evident in both *Poems* and *The Dispossessed* (which featured, for example, "The Ball Poem," one of his most anthologized). Berryman's turn against the "impersonality" preached by T. S. Eliot is already abundantly evident in poems written to friends named in the poems, in revelations of Berryman's spiritual and emotional torments, as well as in his overtly political poems and poems in which the personal and the political are thoroughly intertwined, as in "Rock-Study with Wanderer":

When shall the body of the State come near
The body's state stable & labile? When
Irriding & resisting rage & fear
Shall men in unison resemble men?

Detroit our heart   When terribly we move
The sea is ours   We walk upon the sea
The air is ours   Hegemony, my love,
The good life's founded upon LST.[71]

"LST" here refers to "Landing Ship, Tanks," for the vessels that landed tanks on the beaches of North Africa and Normandy.

Already, Berryman's work registers the intimate relationship between the most intimate details in one's life and public events or political realities for which the "Confessional Poets" would become famous in relation to the Cold War 1950s. He inverted the relationship between "politics" and personal history. Arthur Miller once made a related point concerning Tennessee Williams's plays:

Streetcar at the hour of its birth echoed the fate of the outsider in American society and raised the question of justice. But it did so from the inside out. Williams, in fact, had much earlier written what would have been labeled socially conscious plays with a distinct Leftist coloration, the hurt individual against a brutal society's injustices. . . . With *Streetcar* and in other, more recondite tonalities like those in *Glass Menagerie*, the individual and his inner life moved to the center and social conditions were symbolized, as in Stanley Kowalski and the disappeared father in *Menagerie*. Williams the poet was not as politically neutered as many assume, and some part of the immense wave of appreciation for *Streetcar* was a tribute to its social reality as well as its personal poetics.[72]

The inescapable yet ambivalent bond between the personal and the political became an emphasis of left-oriented writers still reeling from the betrayals of "official" communism and at the same time resistant to all that the left-wing critics of the thirties resisted in American society—the Ku Klux Klan, fascist sympathizers, union busters, laissez-faire capitalism.

Yet the relationship between the personal and the political could take other forms, even while pitted against the philistinism of "mainstream" American culture. Witness the case of Ezra Pound. While Gertrude Stein was patting hands with the GIs liberating her village in the south of France, Pound was penned in an open cage, guarded by GIs in the city of Pisa, on nineteen counts of treason. A plea of insanity saved him from execution and got him confined to St. Elizabeth's in Washington, D.C. Before long friends were hatching schemes to win his release.

One plan involved, according to Archibald MacLeish, giving him an award that would embarrass the government into setting him free, and what could serve better than one conferred by the Library of Congress? The battle of the Bollingen Prize, beginning in February 1949, pitted the Aesthetes against the Philistines, to invoke an ancient opposition appropriate to the moment.

The story has been told often so I will cut to the chase. The prize committee—the Fellows of the Library of Congress in American Letters—was packed with New Critics and their allies, including Conrad Aiken, Allen Tate, T. S. Eliot, W. H. Auden, Robert Lowell, Louise Bogan, Katherine Anne Porter, and Robert Penn Warren. Others not connected to the New Criticism included Karl Shapiro, Paul Green, and Katherine Garrison Chapin. Only Shapiro and Chapin voted against awarding the prize to Pound (although they voted him second of four finalists), Shapiro citing Pound's unrepentant and virulent anti-Semitism. Paul Green abstained.[73] Faced with the fact that Pound had clearly won the committee's vote, Shapiro felt the award should not be given without an accompanying denunciation of Pound's politics. Better yet, it should not be given at all.[74]

In "Treason's Strange Fruit" Robert Hillyer, the president of the Poetry Society of America, charged that Pound "served the enemy in direct poetical and propaganda activities against the United States."[75] Evoking the famous antilynching song, the title may be unintentionally ironic, because Hillyer's attack had the marks of a nationalist hanging party. That Pound should be awarded a prize connected with a national institution in the wake of the very war in which he took the anti-American side was clearly perverse. But Pound was merely a symbol, a goat. The problem, to Hillyer, was not Pound so much as the deracinated aestheticism of a rising "priesthood" of New Critics to whom T. S. Eliot (who had taken British citizenship) and Ezra Pound were gods and who had taken over English departments across the land.[76] The disconnection between aesthetic "modernists" and the common culture was clearly proven. Hillyer's position—cast in nationalist terms but also in the cause of a more old-fashioned and popular poetics—was shared by many, including the U.S. Congress, which promptly ordered the Library of Congress to cease sponsoring the Bollingen Prize.

The whole controversy—carried on extensively in *Saturday Review, Poetry, Partisan Review, Senior Scholastic, The Nation, Masses and Mainstream,* and other journals through the fall of 1949—quickly became less about Pound or his poetry than about the position of the New Criticism and modernist "difficulty" in American letters. What responsibility did poetry have to politics, to universal ethics, or to the culture shared by most Americans?

What is most astonishing about all of this today is how passionate and widespread the controversy became. Can one imagine a fight over a prize in poetry today bearing so much weight? Wai Chee Dimock has taken up Pound's case as an ironic yet instructive model of how aesthetic judgment as a universal human faculty undermines the case for seeking human rights via the political sovereignty of nation-states. The "aesthetic" of expatriate, avant-garde modernism in the context of the uproar over Pound's award became equated for some with anti-Americanism. "The idea that poetry might be written (or read) with an evaluative criterion other than its Americanness," Dimock asserts, "was treasonable in itself."[77]

This was not the case. Dimock's extrapolation from Pound's situation that the "aesthetic" equates in the 1940s with a betrayal of "Americanism" downplays what was most important to the editors of the *Saturday Review* and ignores the New Critics' arguments that their methods *were* "American." Pound's prosecutors agreed that positing political tests for poetry was "undemocratic" but felt that a poet "cannot shatter ethics and values and still be a good poet."[78] It was not a matter of "Americanness." The very "priesthood" of New Critics whom Robert Hillyer attacked—for "totalitarianism," no less—considered their aesthetic theory to align with "democracy" as opposed to the "totalitarianism" of Hillyer and his ilk, whom they accused of chaining aesthetic creation to political positions and threatening "intellectual standards" with appeals to "popular hysteria." Tate considered Pound a "fool" about politics, "but there is a principle at stake which transcends his idiocy and we have got to stand by it."[79] Of course, the statement implies that particular experts know what the standards are. Tate referred to them as "objective." Karl Shapiro had another notion, and he could not entirely dissociate the objectives of the Pound advocates from their gentile presumptions.

The fact that Dimock chooses this drama of 1949 for her emblematic case of the universality of aesthetic judgment (as opposed to nationalist politics) helps pinpoint the significance of that moment in history. It was the time of universals and aesthetics, when aesthetics invaded history in the old sense and attempted to enthrone itself relatively independent of "politics" or nationalism. Yet "democracy" remained a transcendent value to all parties in the debate.

It was the *process* of close reading, the appreciation of *how* poetry incorporated complexity and variety, tension and paradox, not the "theme" of any given work, that comported with democratic processes and served as training for democratically inclined personalities according to the so-called New Critics. The point was affirmed by Arthur Schlesinger Jr. in *The Vital Center*, which gives significant attention to the fate of the arts under the Soviets—spontaneity, creative independence, complexity, and even "anxiety" came under attack. Worst of all, too many artists accepted the charges against them and apologized for their sins. Like the Nazis (and Robert Hillyer), the Soviets took aim at "cosmopolitanism," "formalism," and "decadence."[80] No previous despotism, charged Schlesinger, had so brutally interfered with the liberty of writers and artists. Thus artistic freedom was fundamental to democracy—and to "Americanism," if, as Whitman had once asserted, "democracy" and "America" were convertible terms. So they seemed to many people in the aftermath of World War II.

Hillyer himself was called a traitor for his views—a traitor to the cause of art. In response to the controversy in the *Saturday Review*, Malcolm Cowley judged the *Pisan Cantos* an inferior book and Pound's weakest, but he criticized the attack on the judges as misleading and charged Hillyer with going over to the enemy, "like Pound in another war" and appealing "under false colors to the great hostile empire of the Philistines."[81]

One of the two members of the Bollingen Prize committee who voted against Pound agreed with Cowley on this score. Karl Shapiro recoiled against Pound's anti-Semitism, yet his objection to giving Pound the award was quite different from Hillyer's. While serving as consultant in poetry to the Library of Congress in 1946–1947, he wrote a long Greek-style drama in verse, "Trial of a Poet," which might well be taken as a commentary on the Bollingen Prize controversy if not for the fact that it preceded that event by two years. It opened with an epigraph drawn from the chorus of Milton's *Samson Agonistes*:

In seeking just occasion to provoke
The *Philistine*, thy Countries Enemy,
Thou never wast remiss, I bear thee witness:
Yet *Israel* still serves with all his Sons.

Shapiro opens with a heroic yet tragic portrait of the poet who had given American literature a cosmopolitan richness, "Sending us postcards and Catullian epigrams / In our own dialects." No traitor to "American" aesthetics, he had expanded the possibilities of American expression. He was indeed a heroic poet, according to the sympathetic Chorus in its opening strophe:

Great as an equal
He sat down with masters, he furthered them
In heroic efforts, indefatigably seeking
What the age demanded
And finding the forms that the age deserved.

Reduced to a "sad crumpled poet" at the present time, "he has found dignity and tragedy / In the failure of crime."[82]

Pound provoked and fought the Philistines, yet the poets (like the Israelites of old) remain bound to them. The Philistines remain in control— which Samson (in Milton's poem) says is not his fault but rather that of the leaders of Israel. Of course, in Milton's lines Samson has been betrayed by Dalila and shorn of his power. Shapiro's epigraph may suggest that Fascism has played her role to Pound's Samson and betrayed him to the Philistines. Shapiro implicitly defends Pound against them, arguing (as the defenders of the Bollingen Prize committee would) that his work should not be judged on the basis of patriotism versus treason. "There was no crime," we are told. "There was, however, a failure of the word."

Addressing Evil in the closing lines of the poem, the Chorus concludes, "The failure was to fall into your hands."[83]

Poets are not above other people, and, however brilliant, they can misuse their talent. The poet on trial accuses the Chorus of the play of an "underlying belief" that the Poet is "a better man, if a worse citizen, than all other men." Baffled by the possibility that a poet could "commit a substantial evil," they lay the blame on "the age and its officialdom . . . but not upon themselves." This is the Nuremberg defense avant la lettre. A hieratic sense of printed words leads the poet's sympathizers into error. On the other hand, the defendant passes sentence on himself—"to be known hereafter as a dull poet and the lapdog of his age"—not as a citizen but as an artist.[84] Shapiro anticipates by fourteen years Hannah Arendt's argument about Eichmann in Jerusalem and the "banality of evil." Yet the "dullness" here has also to do with how Pound's attempt to make his poetry a vehicle for his repellent political views had affected its quality as poetry.

The epigraph finally allows Pound a tragic character. The prisoner himself interprets the epigraph authoritatively: "Israel is poetry. Thy country is America. The Philistine is the enemy within. In destroying the works of the Philistine, the prisoner blindly destroyed himself."[85] Shapiro condemns Pound, the pedagogue who had never been a professor, but not with moralistic melodrama. Paradox, irony, tragedy—key terms of the aestheticians—infuse the drama. At its center is the mystery of evil, to which no one is immune—a human "universal," so to speak. "Politics" as foundational theme or intention had lost its power among poets as the forties came to a close. There were other rooms in the house.

4

THE WAR

· · · · · · · · · · · · · · · ·

n "Before Disaster," a poem in the 1943 volume *The Giant Weapon* and subtitled "Winter, 1932–33," Yvor Winters registers his unease while observing packed city traffic on a six-lane highway, a metaphor for a highly mechanized world order in which mass organization, minor but aggregating errors of judgment, and lots of steel can lead to catastrophe:

> Ranks of nations thus descend,
> Watchful to a stormy end.
> By a moment's calm beguiled,
> I have got a wife and child.
> Fool and scoundrel guide the State.
> Peace is whore to Greed and Hate.[1]

Many books of the 1940s feature such foreboding scenes set in the 1930s. Irwin Shaw's war novel *The Young Lions* begins on New Year's Eve in 1937, with alternate chapters introducing the book's three main protagonists in their home environments. In each there is a foreboding of war and an emphasis on the decadence of American and Austrian societies, along with fascist and anti-Semitic brutality in both Europe and the

United States. In the crucial moment of the Spanish Civil War, the British government has impounded all the Loyalist gold in London, and Washington is thought to be secretly favoring Franco. An American tourist's charmed holiday in the Austrian Alps turns to nightmare when her hosts and friends toast Hitler and she suddenly fears for the life of her Jewish fiancé. That night she is nearly raped by the son of her hotel-keeper, and Christian Diestl, the German ski instructor who has converted from communism to Nazism (and the German protagonist of the novel), warns that everyone knows the man is a rapist. Another protagonist, the playwright Michael Whitacre, muses simultaneously in New York on the decadence of Hollywood and Broadway denizens, disdains his cheating wife, and longs for a rigorous and ascetic existence. In Santa Monica, Noah Ackerman attends his dying father in a cheap hotel. After his father dies, dwelling on the persecution of his people, Noah discovers that no mortuary will bury him because they won't serve Jews.

From 1937 to 1939, the sense of coming cataclysm was inescapable. Only ignorance or cowardice could temporarily shield one from the truth. In the fall of 1938, Germany took over the Sudetenland after the Munich Agreement among the European powers, the most infamous act of appeasement in modern history. Further miscalculations would follow. Martha Gellhorn set her novel *A Stricken Field* (1940) in the months leading up to the German invasion and railed against the passivity of France, England, and America. Meanwhile Charles Lindbergh urged nonintervention in the war from 1940 through 1941 as celebrity spokesperson of the America First Committee. That position was embraced by many left-wing as well as right-wing writers and politicians until Pearl Harbor.

W. H. Auden's "September 1, 1939" is only the most famous of the poems reflecting on the prewar interregnum:

> I sit in one of the dives
> On Fifty-Second Street
> Uncertain and afraid
> As the clever hopes expire
> Of a low dishonest decade.[2]

John Berryman's first book of poetry, published by New Directions in 1942, begins with "The Dangerous Year," predating Auden's lament with a footnote: "New York, / 1 March 1939": "Slaughter goes on in China, refugees call / For aid; but these things are remote, they can / Touch us scarcely at all." Americans feel safe, guarded by the Atlantic and Pacific oceans. Yet the speaker distrusts this sense of security.

> *The car is still upon the road*, we say.
> What road? Where will you sleep tomorrow night?
> Where are the maps that you had yesterday?
> By whose direction are you moving now?
> The light is thin and grey.

It is time, the poet warns, to let go of the "crass hope of a world restored / To dignity and unearned dividends," to stop being willfully blind before "The midnight of the mind."[3]

At the threshold of the decade, Americans can no longer hide behind a fiction of being protected by oceans as apocalypse nears. The storm clouds kept massing over both oceans until December 11, 1941. Elizabeth Bishop's first book of poems, *North and South* (1946), specifies on the copyright page, "Most of these poems were written, or partly written, before 1942." For American writers of the World War II generations, December 7, 1941, divided their lives into before and after.

Dawn Powell's *A Time to Be Born* opens with what Gore Vidal considered the best rendering in contemporary fiction of the last months before Pearl Harbor:

> You woke in the morning with the weight of doom in your head. You lay with eyes shut wondering why you dreaded the day; was it a debt, was it a lost love?—and then you remembered the nightmare. It was a dream, you said, nothing but a dream, and the covers were thrown aside, the dream was over, now for the day. Then, fully awake, you remembered that it was no dream. Paris was gone, London was under fire, the Atlantic was now a drop of water between the flame on one side and the

waiting dynamite on the other. This was a time of waiting, of marking time till ready, of not knowing what to expect or what to want either for yourself or for the world. . . . Day's duties were performed to the metronome of Extras, radio broadcasts, committee conferences on war orphans, benefits for Britain. . . . There was no future; every one waited, marked time, waited. For what?[4]

After Pearl Harbor, a new phrase came into common use: *for the duration.* "It had a finality, a suggestion of everlastingness, out of all proportion to its literal sense," according to the narrator of Charles Jackson's *The Fall of Valor,* "and the worst of it was, no one needed to complete the phrase . . . as if, in these changing times, only one thing had 'duration.'"[5]

Many Americans still passionately opposed U.S. involvement in the wars against Germany and Japan and suspected the Roosevelt administration's intentions. Secretary of the Treasury Henry Morgenthau Jr. suggested two days after Pearl Harbor the formation of a propaganda agency of civilian writers to build public support for the war effort. The Writers' War Board was formed soon thereafter, with a board of forty writers in the New York area and ultimately drawing on the talents of nearly five thousand writers. Technically independent of the government but partially funded by it, it worked closely with the Office of War Information. It sent editorials and stories to newspapers and radio stations and placed stories by popular writers in magazines like the *Saturday Evening Post, Collier's,* and *Reader's Digest.* It started a "War Script of the Month" service, providing scripts of radio plays for local amateur performance to up to 825 radio stations. Most famous of these was Stephen Vincent Benet's *They Burned the Books,* about the Nazi book burnings. The board's propaganda focused on the savagery of the enemy, promoting racial tolerance and equality at home, and building support for international cooperation after the war.

To convince Americans of the malignancy of Germans, in 1942 the board focused on the razing of Lidice, Czechoslovakia, in retaliation for the murder of a notorious SS officer, Reinhard Heydrich, by a Czech and a Slovak soldier flown in from England. A Lidice Committee planned a multipronged propaganda campaign to burn the name of Lidice into American consciousness. A town in Illinois was renamed Lidice in a ceremony broadcast internationally, headlined by Wendell Willkie. A Lidice Lives Committee continued the campaign with other renamings and the creation of public sculptures. Edna St. Vincent Millay, once controversial but now a literary celebrity, contributed *The Murder of Lidice*, which was broadcast by NBC on October 19, 1942, and published simultaneously in *Life* and then in a longer pamphlet version by Harper & Brothers for mass distribution.

> Hear us speak; Oh, hear what we say,
> Who and where soever ye be . . .
> Unless ye would die as we!

> Dead mouths of men once happy as you
> As happy as you and as free!
> Till they entered our country and slaughtered and slew,
> And then,—oh, never forget the day!—
> On the tenth of June in '42
> They murdered the Village of Lidice!

> . . . .
> Careless America, crooning a tune:
> Catch him! Catch him and stop him soon!
> . . . .
> Or will you wait, and let him destroy
> The village of Lidice, Illinois?[6]

In one scene, a German officer brains a newborn baby against a bedroom wall while its mother is taken away to slavery. Evidently the play achieved its intended effect: the *Christian Science Monitor* called it "war propaganda of the right sort," and *Theater Arts* praised its "emotional impact on the audience."[7]

Unlike these deliberate propaganda efforts to inspire a spirit of vengeance, however, much of the literature of the war was introspective and
self-questioning rather than angry and triumphalist. Even *The Murder of
Lidice* begins in a self-questioning mood about the fate of the earth and
the nature of human beings:

> Ye martyred peoples of this maddened planet,
> This Earth, which like a moth about the sun
> Today does whirl, as if it would itself
> Its own destruction wreak, seeking to fall
> In flame from out its orbit, and between
> Its sister worlds be seen no more at all:
> Human disaster on so vast a scale
> The mind cannot conceive . . . [8]

The issue here is not who the bad guys are but human nature itself and
the fate of a planet gone mad. In *The Bewildered Planet* (1942), the émigré
surrealist Max Ernst made a related statement, using what he called an
"oscillation technique," a form of automatism, that has been called a pre-
cursor to Pollock's drip paintings (fig. 4.1). To create the random orbits of
the "planet" on the right half of the canvas, he punched a hole in the
bottom of a can tied to a string and filled the can with paint, then allowed it to swing over the yellow field in random loops. This motif of an
earth adrift from its moorings, its axial spin wobbling randomly and or-
bit thrown off a regular course, suggests temporal disorientation, which
became a major theme in the literature.

According to the most compelling literary works, even if—no, especially
if—one felt oneself to be in the maw of history, temporality had changed.
This abeyance of "normal" time, following immediately on the Great
Depression, which had destabilized the liberal-progressive view of history, rivets the postwar imagination to World War II. It would all later
be massaged into the progressive view of history and a Cold War return
to so-called normalcy, but a closer examination even today leads to inescapable doubts, beginning with the question of Time.

FIGURE 4.1 Max Ernst, *The Bewildered Planet*, 1942. Oil on canvas, 110 x 140 cm. *Source*: Collection of the Tel Aviv Museum of Art. Gift of the artist, 1955. © 1942 Artists Rights Society (ARS), New York / ADAGP, Paris.

Throughout the literature of the war one finds an attempt to capture the changing phenomenology of time. While reading became an important means through which soldiers "killed time" or took their minds off of paralyzing fears, acts of narration served as a means of humanizing time, making the experience of war comprehensible, forestalling a dissolution of the self. Yet in doing so they took one away from the whirling, chaotic center of it all. "It was strange to be so close to things and yet so far away," according to the narrator of *A Walk in the Sun*. "That was war. That was always war. It was confused and it was incoherent and it was unreasonable. Nothing ever happened quite on time, nothing ever happened exactly as was expected."[9]

Time also acquired spatial coordinates; one was closer to or more distant from the indefinable center at which time ceased to exist, the center of the vortex that would never get into the books. One waited, dread-fully, to see how things would play out. Or one was in the midst of things and out of it. The world "whirled." A very similar sensation in the experi-ence of a young girl approaching puberty is rendered in Carson McCull-ers's *A Member of the Wedding*, in which the timing of the war and of the girl's adolescence are intimately intermeshed:

> It was the year when Frankie thought about the world. And she did not see it as a round school globe, with the countries neat and different-colored. She thought of the world as huge and cracked and loose and turning a thousand miles an hour. The war and the world were too fast and big and strange. To think about the world for very long made her afraid. She was not afraid of Germans or bombs or Japanese. She was afraid because in the war they would not include her, and because the world seemed somehow separate from herself.[10]

This sense of separation, of loneliness and unreality, surfaces over and over again, in accounts of both the battlefront and the home front.

In the early 1940s, people were already wondering if the world after the war would be totally different from what preceded it. Everything, though moving fast, was on hold. (Hence the "whirling" metaphors.) Even after the summer of 1942 and winter of 1942–1943, when it seemed clear that the Allies would succeed, no one knew how long the war would last because the leaders of both Germany and Japan seemed bent on fighting a losing battle to the last ditch (and they did). How many people, and especially how many Americans, would die in the interim? For them, time would stop; and for their families? The war years were a period of holding one's imaginative breath, of waiting, on the one hand, or, on the other, of undergoing a trauma too difficult to absorb, out of time and out of mind. Thus Gwendolyn Brooks entitles one of her soldier poems, "my dreams, my works, must wait till after hell."

This was so on the home front as well as the battlefront. In Martha Gellhorn's *Liana*, set in the Caribbean, each evening the main charac-ters listen to the radio for news of the American landings in North

Africa (the forgotten first "D-Day"). "It was like getting ready to abandon a torpedoed ship, it was like waiting outside the operating room while a surgeon worked over someone you loved, it was anything helpless and terrible and suspended in time."[11] Eleanor Roosevelt, Gellhorn's friend and admirer, wrote in her column "My Day" for June 7, 1944,

> So at last we have come to D-Day, or rather, the news of it reached us over the radio in the early hours of the morning on June the 6th. . . . Curiously enough, I have no sense of excitement whatsoever. It seems as though we have been waiting for this day for weeks, and dreading it, and now all emotion is drained away. . . . The time is here, and in this country we live in safety and comfort and wait for victory. It is difficult to make life seem real. It is hard to believe that the beaches of France which we once knew are now places from which, in days to come, boys in hospitals over here will tell us that they have returned. They may never go beyond the water or the beach, but all their lives, perhaps, they will bear the marks of this day.[12]

All were preparing for the road ahead, to end the war: "That day is coming surely. It will be a happy and glorious day. How can we hasten it?"

As Anatole Broyard later remembered, the war broke "the rhythm of American life. . . . It was as if a great bomb, an explosion of consciousness, had gone off in American life, shattering everything. Before that we had been too busy just getting along, too conventional to be lonely. The world had been smaller and we had filled it."[13]

Saul Bellow's first novel, *Dangling Man* (1944), meditates on the sense of unreality experienced by a draftee as he awaits induction, with the sense of posthumous existence Karl Shapiro identified in the seventh poem of his series "Recapitulations." Shapiro refers to induction as "the summons to end time."

<blockquote>

The armory was cold,
But naked, shivering, and shocked he was enrolled.

It was the death he never quite forgot
Through the four years of death, and like as not

</blockquote>

The true death of the best in all of us
Whose present life is largely posthumous.[14]

In *The Fall of Valor*, traffic in midtown Manhattan comes to a halt for a ragtag procession of men and boys on their way to an induction center. Silent, the watching crowd wishes they could be elsewhere, not witnesses. The inductees themselves pass in embarrassed self-consciousness, "hangdog and silly": "for them, in short, this was The Day."[15]

Time peters out into nothingness at the edge of the war zones. Shapiro's poem speaks of all the movement caused by the war—of refugees, émigrés to London and New York, millionaires leaving their lands, citizens snatched out of quotidian life and sent who knows where:

And elsewhere, at the witless edge of time,
Millions went wandering on foot too far,
With no more voice, unhelmeted and pale,
Pursued in sleep their endless wanderjahr,
Down to the dark where heated winds prevail
And evil mates with evil in the slime.[16]

The poetry and fiction soon following the war, especially by veterans, suggests that only at the end of the war, and in its aftermath, did the Holocaust emerge as a worthy justification for what many soldiers (including Jewish American soldiers) experienced as an incomprehensible chaos.

All too common in the war novels are revelations of what a soldier or sailor did before joining the army or navy. The code was not to ask—something particularly emphasized in Gore Vidal's first novel—but it always came up. The point here is that the prior experience could be completely disconnected from the present. A hotel clerk might find himself leading a regiment as commissioned officers were picked off in combat, and then he might find himself dining with English royalty because of his rank, all the while wondering what would become of him after the war. An alternation between present action and memories of the past set the cadence of some novels. John Horne Burns uses the method to structure his novel *The Gallery*, alternating present-tense "Promenades" with retrospective "Portraits." The method is even more striking and effective in Mailer's *The Naked and the Dead*, which formalizes and highlights the alternation with interchapter "Time Machine" interludes (a technique tellingly adapted from Dos Passos's "Camera Eye" episodes in *U.S.A.* [1938]) reflecting on each character's past. Even in style, these interludes remind one of 1930s-era fiction as they describe mining families in Montana, company towns, hobo jungles, the Mexican quarter of San Antonio, a poor white hellraiser and horsebreaker from West Texas, the son of a Jewish shop owner from the Bronx, and so on. Since these are vignettes, biographies of young soldiers before the war, they are of course also about the 1930s as experienced by boys of eight to eighteen in that decade and implicitly meditations on the lives they may be going back to if they survive the war, a subject on which servicemen in all of the novels often speculate. Collectively, they present a collage of Depression-era America and a cross-section of society, interrupted repeatedly by the chapters dealing with the surreal present.

Related to this alternation between present and past is the function of letters from home that spark ruminations about the past, a crumbling marriage, a warm bed. These letters provide a fragmented narrative of the home front, but men have trouble conceiving that in between letters they anticipate moments that have already passed by the time a letter arrives. Gallagher in Mailer's novel learns from an officer that his wife died in childbirth immediately after it happens, but he continues to get letters from her for weeks thereafter, ending with one written the day she went to the hospital. He reads them knowing what the end will be in advance. In a related vein, Randall Jarrell's poem "Mail Call" speculates, "Surely the past from which the letters rise / Is waiting in the future, past the graves? / The soldiers are all haunted by their lives."[17]

Memories of one's activities before the war, however unhappy, are crucial to one's sanity. The present, as men await battle or even take part in it, is put on hold. In Harry Brown's *A Walk in the Sun*, the narrator ruminates,

The funny thing was that they were not very much concerned with what was facing them ahead. Each had his own problems, his own desires and wishes. They kept these personal things uppermost in their minds, as they had always done ever since they came into the Army. The war was incidental to a man's thoughts. It entered into them, of course, but it did not take them over bodily. There had been too many years of life, too many memories, before the war had come along. A man could exist on these memories, he could withdraw into them, he could construct them into an unpierceable shell. They were his defense against the violence of the world. Every man in the platoon had his own thoughts as he walked along, and they hovered unseen over the little group, an indefinable armor, a protection against fate, an indestructible essence.[18]

When that essence is taken away by panic, a man ceases to be human and is reduced to a quivering mass of flesh. Narrative brings form and meaning to experience; the two are inseparable, in dialectical relation, because "meaning" is not just intellectual, to be found at the end of a logical operation; it involves feeling and memory, the sense of past connection with others, and futurity. It is the humanization of raw experience without which one feels helpless and alone, reduced to bare life, exiled from the realm of the "human."

To render time comprehensible seemed somehow important to maintaining sanity, congruent with the great philosopher Paul Ricoeur's later argument in *Time and Narrative* that narrative is as crucial to the experience of time as temporality is to narrative.[19] This need to order temporal experience is reflected in the way a number of the best war novels are strictly delimited in time. A formal organization of time in the structure of the fictions serves to control the chaos within (as rhythm shapes time in musical forms); it is as if the authors need it to manage their material. Has this any relation to the fact that free verse declines in the early 1940s and more traditional forms dominate, that *The Waste Land* is answered by *Four Quartets* and H.D. writes her rather ceremonious *Trilogy*— entirely in couplets except for the opening poem, which is in tercets— while the "war poets" overwhelmingly opt for what would later be termed "closed form" and even William Carlos Williams starts pacing on the variable foot—his attempt at a regularization of a vernacular American measure?

Paul Fussell has argued that the narrative pacing required of a novel prevents the novels of the war from rendering the chaotic nature of battlefront experience; he privileges a few mostly recent memoirs. Yet the best of the novels experiment with ways of rendering the chaotic temporality of battle experience in ways no memoir, constrained by what is remembered and therefore ordered long after the fact, can. Some of them—scarcely novels at all—use the sheer abstraction of chronological time as a formal method of ordering episodic events in preference to novelistic emplotment. *Limit of Darkness* takes place in the course of twenty-four hours, beginning at dawn, five A.M., on Guadalcanal, and ending at the same time the next day. Each chapter covers exactly one hour and begins with a graphic image of the face of a watch indicating the hour beginning each chapter, which is also the key graphic design element chosen for the title page. James Gould Cozzens's Pulitzer Prize–winning novel *Guard of Honor* takes place in the course of precisely three days (a weekend) on an Air Force base in Florida. *A Walk in the Sun* takes place in the course of a single day. Burns's *The Gallery*, a book saturated with grief and disorientation, ends with the precise dates of its own composition, "18 June 1945–23 April 1946," and dates the events of which it speaks to the summer of 1944. Its symmetrical and alternating "Promenades" and "Portraits" are framed by an "Entrance" and "Exit"—suggesting not only a unit of time but an ordered movement, or rather an ordering of confusion. Each "Promenade," a quasi-autobiographical vignette, begins with the phrase "I remember."

In narrative descriptions of battle one frequently finds an emphasis on the mutability of time—it speeds up, it stops, it crawls. At the end of *A Walk in the Sun*, the character Tyne is the center of consciousness. As he and his squad crawl toward a farmhouse before a bridge is blown (a signal for them to charge the German-occupied house), he is thinking, "Nothing was slower than crawling, nothing in the world. How long would it take to crawl around the earth? A hundred years? A thousand years?"[20] A minute or so later, still crawling as machine-gun bullets whiz over his head, "Pictures flashed across his mind and were gone before he could grasp them. Everything speeded up; the world was moving at a dizzy pace. He could not keep up with it. It was going faster and faster. In a minute it would fly away." Then he hears explosions from the bridge,

> and then everything that had been moving so fast stopped dead. The world stopped. Time stopped. The war stopped. The German machine-gun stopped. What had spun so fast, what had nearly hurled Tyne among the stars was stopped dead, with such violence as to shake his body the way a woman shakes a mop from a window. His mind became clear as polished glass. Everything in his life had led up to this moment. It was his. Nothing could take it from him.
>
> Slowly, almost gravely, he rose to his feet and blew a blast on his whistle. Men rose all around him. He saw them sharply in the shimmering air. He broke into a run.[21]

In these closing paragraphs of *A Walk in the Sun*, the method turns surrealistic. Dream and reality interpenetrate, time stops, moments past become present, the farmhouse has eyes.

> He found himself reviewing the whole day in snatches. He saw Porter's face, twisted, and Hoskins's face, set. He saw Trasker with his jaw gone and McWilliams with his hands stretched out as though they would protect him from the plane. It seemed to him that McWilliams had been dead a very long time—that he had been dead for an eternity and that for eternity he was doomed to go through that same impotent action of stretching out his arms. Sometimes Tyne could not distinguish the living from the dead. Faces had a tendency to run together, to blur, to become indistinct. They became as confused and as difficult to explain as the battles they had been in. They ran together like letters in the rain. They had no real identity. They were swallowed up in a mist, in a vapor.
>
> And so were Tyne's thoughts. One moment he saw himself sitting by the fire at home; the next moment he saw himself, as though from

a great distance, crawling over a muddy plain. But the landscape was familiar for all that. It was the landscape of dream. He had been moving through it for years; he would probably never find his way out of it.[22]

In addition to these moments of transformation from the impressionistic naturalism of Stephen Crane into a more recognizably modernist, surrealistic method, in the poetry and fiction of the war one encounters attempts to conquer the mind's incompetence to encompass the vast machinery of war and its own subordination to that machinery, as expressed in the famous last quatrain of Richard Eberhart's "The Fury of Aerial Bombardment": "Of Van Wettering I speak, and Averill, / Names on a list, whose faces I do not recall / But they are gone to early death, who late in school / Distinguished the belt feed lever from the belt holding pawl."[23] This kind of deindividuation often finds its equivalent in a curious distancing of the soldier-speaker from the horrors in which he is enmeshed, accompanied by archaic poetic forms like the ballad, which have the effect of depersonalization.

This effect is best exemplified in Louis Simpson's "Carentan O Carentan" and "Arm in Arm." Simpson served mainly in the glider infantry from the invasion of Normandy through Belgium, the Netherlands, Bastogne, and Berchtesgaden, and the two ballads are based on terrifying experiences. A laconic tone, grimly humorous, pervades both. In "Carentan O Carentan," the speaker recounts walking at combat-interval over a romantic hay meadow near the sea on a glorious June morning, when

The watchers in their leopard suits
Waited till it was time,
And aimed between the belt and boot
And let the barrel climb.

I must lie down at once, there is
A hammer at my knee.
And call it death or cowardice,
Don't call again on me.

Everything's alright Mother,
Everyone gets the same
At one time or another.
It's all in the game.[24]

"Arm in Arm" recalls another actual battle in which Simpson's infantry unit was pinned down and bombed in a cemetery. Friend and enemy corpses mingle with unearthed skulls:

Which were the new, which the old dead
It was a sight to ask.
One private found a polished head
And took the skull to task . . . [25]

The bleak humor inheres in the distancing and irony, in the perfect rhymes, in simple diction, and in the evacuation of feeling—the poem's own "polish."

The defacement of the individual is a common motif in the literature of the war, a trope for utter depersonalization. In Irwin Shaw's *The Young Lions*, a German officer's face is obliterated, yet he lives on, eventually committing suicide after learning that his wife cannot bear to look at him. *A Walk in the Sun* opens with a young lieutenant (whom one expects to become the chief protagonist) having his face shot off during the beach landing in Normandy. He dies on the spot. Losing the memory of faces or losing one's own face is the ultimate trope for not just anonymity but disappearance. In Gellhorn's *A Stricken Field*, the protagonist flies out of Prague and toward the temporary safety of France, thinking she will never again see the brave leftists and Jews she had met: "She had already forgotten the names and remembered only the faces. All the faces blurred in the gleaming band of the propeller, the lined, intent, frightened, bewildered, despairing, angry, lonely; the faces of the lost. I will forget them too. There will be so many others."[26]

The theme of anonymity applied particularly well to "replacements"—new soldiers sent to replace those killed or wounded. Lacking friends or acquaintances in the patrols to which they were assigned, these men were the most expendable of all. Chapter 33 of *The Young Lions* begins in a "replacement depot." "We are all interchangeable parts," one man observes to a newcomer.[27] The plot pivots on Ackerman's determination to team up with Whitacre in a replacement camp to which he has been sent and get back to the platoon to which they had both earlier belonged, even though this risks court-martial and execution.

In Jarrell's poems of the 1940s, one finds a near obsession with the meaning of the individual life heightened by the fact of depersonalization in war. This is connected with a distrust of "theory," even though Jarrell's basic political orientation remains Marxist. His poems epitomize a general revulsion against the erasure of individuality by "the state" (a term Jarrell uses frequently in the 1940s), experienced by people on all sides of the war and of all ideologies. "The Lines" is Jarrell's most direct statement about soldiers' anonymity, which connects with their endless waiting—often as not waiting "To form a line to form a line to form a line": "After the things have learned that they are things, / Used up as things are, pieces of the plain / Flat object-language of a child or states." After they die, they "lie as numbers in the crosses' lines." In the hospital wards, the wounded lie in lines: "Some are salvaged for their state, but some / Remanded, useless, to the centers' files." Only at the end, when the men die, do "the lines break up, for good; and for a breath, / The longest of their lives, the men are free."[28]

Jarrell was deeply impressed by Marxism's theory of capitalism's revolutionary, global reach and role in the rise of modern states, which in turn lead inevitably to world war, in his thinking. The poems of *Little Friend, Little Friend* imply repeatedly that world wars are ultimately about Trade and Empire. At times, as in "The Emancipators," addressed to the Western voyagers, imperialists, and capitalists, he implies that World War II seals the trajectory of history since the rise of capitalism and ponders ecological catastrophe (a theory also endemic to Charles Olson's evocative study of Melville, *Call Me Ishmael*). The final stanza of "The

Wide Prospect," his most encompassing poetic statement on this theme, reads:

> All die for all. And the planes rise from the years:
> The years when, West or West, the cities burn,
> And Europe is the colony of colonies—
> When men see men once more the food of Man
> And their bare lives His last commodity.[29]

In "The Sick Nought," Jarrell questions the authority of histories and theories justifying any soldier's death and implicitly the origins of the sovereign power that sends one out to die. Addressing a soldier in a hospital, the speaker ruminates:

> I see you looking helplessly around, in histories,
> Bewildered with your terrible companions, Pain
> And Death and Empire: what have you understood, to die?
> Were you worth, soldiers, all that people said
> To be spent so willingly? Surely your one theory, to live,
> Is nonsense to the practice of the centuries.[30]

How can one ask a man to give up his life for a theory, a state, an economic wish? On what ethical basis does one owe the State one's very life? Has one not lost the most important battle when one loses one's bare life to the state?

> What is demanded in the trade of states
> But lives, but lives?—the one commodity.
> To sell the lives we were too poor to use,
> To lose the lives we were too weak to keep—
> This was our peace, this was our war.[31]

Elsewhere, Jarrell expanded on the point: "When one considers the mechanisms of the contemporary states—from the advertising agencies that turn out their principles to the aircraft factories that turn out their practice," one can only conclude, "it is we who wither away, not the state."[32] Jarrell was not the only one to ask such questions. They are implicit in much of the war fiction, in which individuals, platoons, entire companies are deliberately sent out to die in order to "buy time" for a larger maneuver. I hasten to add that his attitude shifts in Jarrell's next book, *Losses* (1948), in which the concentration camps emerge as a subject, an indication of how the Holocaust came to function as an ex post facto justification for the war.

"The Wide Prospect" is followed in *Little Friend, Little Friend* by Jarrell's most famous poem, "The Death of the Ball Turret Gunner," best remembered for its final line, "When I died they washed me out of the turret with a hose."[33] The poem's opening line, "From my mother's sleep I fell into the State," alludes to how the ventral ball turret of a B-17 flying Fortress required the diminutive gunner to crouch in the fetal position. The mention of the State has been criticized as arbitrary and off-key, a judgment impossible to sustain when the poem is read as a coda to the book. Indeed, the poem strikes all the chief notes of the book in a compellingly distilled monody: sleep, dream, the State, the evisceration and erasure of the individual, and a complete absence of a good-guy/bad-guy view of war (in short, of patriotism). It also bookends the volume in concert with the opener, "Second Air Force," which begins with a mother's perspective on the State's ability to take her son and put him in a Flying Fortress.

This sort of concern pervades Gwendolyn Brooks's brooding war poems that form the concluding sequence in *A Street in Bronzeville*. In "still do I keep my look, my identity . . ."—always left out of anthologies, including her own *Selected Poems*—she asserts, "Each body has its pose. No other stock / That is irrevocable, perpetual / And its to keep." In death even, however mangled, the body "Shows the old personal art, the look. Shows what / It showed at baseball. What it showed in school."[34] The poem is most likely left out of anthologies because it does not reference racial difference; in the context of war poetry, however, it resonates unmistakably with the resistance to disindividuation that war elicits in lyric, as in one of Western lyric's primal forms, the elegy.

Karl Shapiro, stationed on a destroyer in the Pacific, asserts in "Elegy for a Dead Soldier":

> We ask for no statistics of the killed,
> For nothing political impinges on
> This single casualty, or all those gone,
> Missing or healing, sinking or dispersed,
> Hundreds of thousands counted, millions lost.
> . . . .
> However others calculate the cost,
> To us the final aggregate is *one*.[35]

The abstractions that justify war lose all purchase when one focuses on the "final aggregate" of any man's or woman's life.

The incorporation of the individual into the war machine has its corollary in the inhuman aspect the new machinery of war takes on when viewed from outside by its victims. After an attack on his platoon by German fighter planes, described in *A Walk in the Sun*, the narrator tells us:

> Tyne sat stupefied. The attack had shocked him. Planes always did. They were an impossible, unimaginable force. He could understand men against men, and even men against tanks, but planes were something else again. He had once read a fantastic story about gigantic insects that turned against man; the planes were those insects. . . . It was impossible to conceive any human being, any human element, hidden in their bowels and controlling them. They had a life of their own, vindictive, murderous.[36]

It helps to remember that in World War I planes were used mainly for observation and tanks were slow, flimsy contraptions of little practical use.

The Great War was still a war of horse-drawn weaponry and infantry charges. World War II featured tank battles, aircraft carriers, carpet bombing from 15,000 feet. If trench warfare dominated the literature of World War I, the literature of the Second World War is dominated by fleets of bombers, cities of rubble, exploding ships, planes plummeting to earth and sea in flames. To capture the reality of "the war in the air" posed a new challenge to novelists and poets. Hemingway's treatment in *For Whom the Bell Tolls* of the use of planes in the Spanish Civil War (like Picasso's *Guernica*) anticipated what would become a main feature of novels to come.

In the novels of the air war, death and destruction can seem utterly abstract, just as the earth itself looks newly abstract from high in the air. A bomber crew takes off after breakfast, disappears over the horizon, and never comes back. Another crew bombs a city from thousands of feet up and watches puffs of smoke mushroom from the earth as the plane banks toward home through air criss-crossed by white tracers and pocked with black blossoms of antiaircraft fire to a safe base in England or the Solomon Islands. The next morning at mess, the men look around to see who didn't make it back.

Artistic abstraction came to seem realistic, as in Richard Eberhart's "Dam Neck, Virginia":

Anti-aircraft seen from a certain distance
On a steely blue night say a mile away
Flowers on the air absolutely dream-like,
The vision has no relation to the reality.

The floating balls of light are tossed easily
And float out into space without a care,
They the sailors of the gentlest parabolas
In a companionship and with a kind of stare.[37]

The journalist and novelist Vincent Sheean wrote of his awe of the air war–related inventions of radar, sonar, and high-altitude aerial photography, all miraculous methods of abstraction that signaled the new nature of war-fare.[38] Technology made possible mass murder at a distance.

In "Take-Off Over Kansas," John Ciardi describes the conversion of farmland into a "plaid abstraction" as the plane climbs and then the con-version of the flyer into a function of the plane as it reaches altitude, where "By mask and tube we suck our lives from tanks. / And gloves that were our hands touch steel":

> What shall the guns think when a shadow spans
> The digits of a sight, and triggers move?
> Was any human part in the machine
> That left its smoke to show which way it dove?
> You only see the first plume and first fall.
> You think, "It was not human after all."[39]

Recognition of this "conversion," as Ciardi termed it, of fighter pilot, gunner, navigator, or bombardier into a function of the plane itself (and then a smoky "plume") shaded into fears about human extinction as the abstract nature of advanced weapons systems "encouraged," as Dan Jaffe put it over forty years ago, "the elimination of human feeling."[40] Post-modernism, perhaps.

Yvor Winters's "By the Road to the Air-Base," opening his book of poems *The Giant Weapon*, registers some such recognition. Perhaps a riff on William Carlos Williams's "Spring and All," which began with "On the road to the contagious hospital," this short poem of four quatrains in iambic trimeter begins with descriptions of grass and salt marsh, tidal slime, shellfish and sea fowl and at the end of the third stanza unobtru-sively introduces a disturbing image:

> The highway, like a beach,
> Turns whiter, shadowy, dry:
> Loud, pale against the sky,
> The bombing planes hold speech.

Immediately the poem returns to pastoral, describing fruit growing in the orchard, scholars pausing to speak, and concludes, "Through gardens bare and Greek, / I hear my neighbor's bees."[41] The resonant image of the bees eerily echoes that of the bombers, and the abstraction of war for an English professor safe in Palo Alto haunts the imagination with a new dread of where it is all leading. "Summer Noon: 1941" augments the effect: "The sky, distended, bare / Now whispers like a shell / Of the increase of war. / Thus will man reach an end." Thus, too, will snakes and mice repossess the suburban garden. Living in fear of his own will, man will yet move where that will drives him, "With mind and word grown still."[42]

The sense of being caught in a military-industrial machine ("each specialist himself precision's instrument")[43] shades into renderings of a war-industrial sublime, its sublimity attributable to fear and awe no longer of nature's power but of human processes too complex to grasp in any single mind, perhaps already beyond human intelligence to control, and bending the powers of nature toward the destruction of the world upon which human beings depend. In "The Emancipators" Jarrell addresses the explorers, imperialists, and capitalists driven by the worship of Trade to bind the globe on a path of destruction, "You guessed this? / The earth's face altering with iron, / The smoke ranged like a wall against the day?"[44] (Early in the war many Marxists viewed it as a contest between imperial powers over spheres of trade—which indeed it partly was.) It is during World War II that Aldo Leopold, not coincidentally, writes *A Sand County Almanac* and his attendant essay on a "Land-Ethic," texts replete with war imagery, structured rhetorically by allusions to fascism and the futility of conquest and metaphorically by battle tropes.

One finds in the literature of the war no panegyric against the enemy but a questioning of the nature of humanity. "You would feel that after so many centuries," wrote Richard Eberhart (a mentor to both Robert Lowell and Harry Brown), "God would give man to repent; yet he can kill / As Cain could, but with multitudinous will, / No farther advanced than in his ancient furies."[45] Not all poets denied or downplayed the heroism of the Allied soldiers, however. Marianne Moore, for one, borrowed from a newspaper editorial the title "Keeping Their World Large" to stress the martyrdom of the American servicemen:

> Marching to death, marching to life?
> 'Keeping their world large,'
>   whose spirits and whose bodies
> all too literally were our shield,
>   are still our shield
>
>   They fought the enemy,
> We fight fat living and self-pity.
>   Shine, o shine,
>   Unfalsifying sun, on this sick scene.[46]

The poem eschews any patriotic idealization of the society the soldiers fight to protect (gesturing toward Robinson Jeffers's terse "Shine, oh Perishing Republic"), but this was not good enough for Jarrell, who attacked Moore's war poems for their celebration of soldiers' "heroism." Jarrell rejected any notion that the soldiers were martyrs, as if their deaths could be redeemed and sanctified under the banner of the nation, as if common soldiers could make choices. Jarrell critiques Moore's need to give meaning to soldiers' deaths:

> She does not understand that they are heroes in the sense that the chimney sweeps, the factory children in the blue books, were heroes: routine loss in the routine business of the world. She sees them (the recurring triplet in the major theme of the poem ["In Distrust of Merits"]) *fighting fighting fighting*; she does not remember that most of the people in a war never fight for even a minute—though they bear for years and die forever. They do not fight, but only starve, only suffer, only die: the sum of all this passive misery is that great activity, War.[47]

The same theme occurs in Harry Brown's play *A Sound of Hunting* (1945), in which enlisted men at the front chew out a famous journalist for making them seem like martyrs:

> And you can hardly wait to get out of here to make a martyr of Small. You'd probably like him to get knocked off, so you'd have a really good story. . . . Well, you're not going to write about Small, see? If his wife saw the story she wouldn't understand it. She'll feel we let Small down, and she'd hate us till the day she died.

Small's company is furious with Small for putting them in the quandary of either endangering themselves to save him or having his death on their conscience if they follow orders and leave him behind. In the closing line of act 1, Staff Sergeant Mooney, the one most intent on getting Small out alive as they are ordered to leave him, rants: "That stupid little bastard. Of all the days in the world." The men reject the idea that the war has some meaning that justifies either their pain or their guilt, in contrast to the journalist, Finley, who charges, "Some fellows have been close to the fighting so long they've forgotten what's behind the fighting."

> COLLUCCI: Mr. Finley, what kind of a story you going to write?
> FINLEY: The true story.
> SHAPIRO: That's the kind. Like it says in the *Soldier's Handbook*.
> FINLEY: What does it say in the *Soldier's Handbook*?
> SHAPIRO: All sorts of crap.
> COLLUCCI: If I was writing a story I'd say, "Willie Small sat on his tail because he was a dope. Willie Small caught a cold. That's all. I hope." Hey, a poem. Pretty good, huh? [*he shakes hands with Shapiro*][48]

Brown, who wrote for *Yank* in the army and created the comic character Artie Greengroin, honors the pain endured and courage required of these soldiers, but he objects to the gains accrued to the journalist, his employer, his audience—for that matter his country—by stories of martial heroism. Such stories only encourage more war. Louis Simpson, already fearing war with Russia in 1946, records a similar response to the martyrology that always follows war in the poem "Roll," addressed to the dead of Utah Beach in Normandy: "'Why am I here?' said one on the way to his death. / I would bring him a wreath, but fear / Rousing his wrath. I'd say more, but my tongue is no trumpet."[49]

World War II sent many soldiers, like Simpson, in the direction of writing after their service. They differentiated creative writing from other uses of language for its truth value. Good and great writers made a living in journalism and film during the 1940s. Many worked in the Office of War Information, a propaganda agency. Yet most attested to the superiority of fiction and poetry in getting at "the truth" of the experience of war, a truth inexpressible in journalism and other media. They needed to bring form to experiences that baffled comprehension and tested the limits of their humanity.

Novelists, poets, and playwrights took aim at journalism, movies, and the armed forces' public-relations work for conveying false images of war—hygienic, chaste, and patriotic. As James Dawes has written, "During war the effect of violence upon language is amplified and clarifies: language is censored, encrypted, and euphemized; imperatives replace dialogue, and nations communicate their intentions most dramatically through the use of injury rather than symbol."[50] Experienced writers who had worked in Hollywood, as journalists, or in the Office of War Information (OWI) knew firsthand the pervasive constraints on what could be reported. The OWI's Bureau of Motion Pictures, which attempted to produce at least moderately realistic films about the war, was defunded by a two-to-one vote in the House of Representatives over conservative distrust of the "communists" in the OWI.[51] Harry Brown was a Hollywood scriptwriter (and Oscar winner) on whose work *The Sands of Iwo Jima* (1949) was based. The film was nominated for five Academy Awards, including Best Writing in a Motion Picture Story and Best Actor, for John Wayne, yet in his fiction he satirized Hollywood movies of warfare.

The director John Huston, who entered the service with high hopes and attempted to create honest films about the war, came away disillusioned and dejected: "In the Second World War I had as high hopes as anybody. It looked to me as if we were on our way to some kind of understanding of life." But he came to feel that he had, as Mark Harris has put it, "colluded in a lie."[52] The army only "wanted to maintain the 'warrior' myth."[53]

Movies depended on levels of investment that only the promise of mass consumption could justify. Producers had to worry about regional and political attitudes affecting distribution and audience appeal. But precisely because of the mass consumption of movies, they threatened political elites. Both forces put a clamp on filmmakers in the 1940s. The impossibility of making an honest film about the war in Hollywood of the 1940s and 1950s has been well documented.[54]

James T. Farrell in 1946 pointed to the glaring "differences in treatment between films and novels, the greater freedom of the novelist over the scenarist." The novelist "may dare to say in public what even the most powerful motion picture magnate dares not whisper." The greatest danger zones were leftist politics and sex. A case in point is the contrast between Hemingway's novel *To Have and Have Not* and its Hollywood adaptation (with a script written by William Faulkner). As Farrell points out,

> The hero, in the novel, smuggled arms for Cuban revolutionists who were fighting the terroristic Battista regime; in the film, the hero helps to win the World War by putting himself in the service of anti-Vichyites. Cuba becomes Martinique. Changes of this kind were made not for any artistic reasons at all, but for purely immediate political ones. At the same time, the relationship between the hero and the heroine becomes utterly senseless.[55]

In the preface to a collection of his own wartime journalism, John Steinbeck bluntly called the book's contents "period pieces, fairy tales, half-meaningless memories of a time and of attitudes which have gone forever from the world, a sad and jocular recording of a little part of a war I saw and do not believe, unreal with trumped-up pageantry." Yet that is the war most Americans to this day believe in. Steinbeck emphasized the often misguided self-censorship of journalists. "And perhaps that is why," he added, "when the war was over, novels and stories by ex-soldiers, like *The Naked and the Dead*, proved so shocking to a public which had been carefully protected from contact with the crazy historical mess."[56] Norman Mailer observed that he "was enlisted . . . on my side of an undeclared war between these modes of perception called journalism and fiction. When it came to accuracy, I was on the side of fiction. I thought fiction could bring us closer to the truth than journalism."[57] It was a conviction he carried through the rest of a career that hovered on that boundary. Martha Gellhorn complained that she could not write the stories she wanted to as a journalist because editors either would not believe them or would censor them. Only through fiction could she approximate the truth of what she witnessed.[58]

Histories, dependent on official reports and journalism, and unduly influenced by officers, would be false, as well, written by victors, remote from the multidimensionality, and thus the form and meaning, of human experience, including its unconscious recesses, its dream-work. (Is it merely coincidental that the explosion of psychoanalysis in American intellectual life and literature followed the war?) Nor was memoir trustworthy. One theme that recurs in the writing of veterans is how quickly the soldiers' actual experiences came to seem unreal, irrecoverable, and how they rescripted traumatic, shameful, or humiliating experiences as they considered how reports of their actions would be received at home or how they themselves would tell their stories to loved ones. Many simply chose to remain silent—not just because their experiences were incommunicable to anyone who had not been through them but because their experiences made no sense even to themselves.

Literary treatments of the war hover around this incommunicability and crisis of meaning, but they have been vastly overshadowed by popular history books, documentaries, movies, and television shows that depend for their very production and distribution on an appeal to fantasies the contemporary war literature contradicts. The attempt to capture "the real war" inspired a range of poetic and fictional approaches, methods, and images. Yet books of the 1940s concerning the war have been largely ignored, and the notion has developed that no one could write articulately about it until the 1960s. A 2008 book on *The Poetry of War* has argued that "for many poets [of World War II], silence has seemed the only option."[59] Studies that discuss the poetry of the Second World War rarely focus on the poems written during the war or in the late 1940s.[60] In a chapter on "The American War Novel" in *The Cambridge Companion to World War II*, Norman Mailer and Martha Gellhorn are the only novelists of the 1940s given serious attention. Kurt Vonnegut's justly celebrated *Slaughterhouse-Five* is unique in form, tone, and style, but the themes are thoroughly congruent with the war novels and poems of the 1940s. Ignoring most of the novels published in the late 1940s helps support a characterization of the whole lot as looking back not to the "immediate precursors, Hemingway, Faulkner, and the modernists, but rather to an earlier patrimony represented by the work of writers like Dreiser."[61] Mailer's novel owes far more to John Dos Passos (and Herman Melville, a modernist hero revived in the 1920s) than to authors like Dreiser. Other novels show the impact of Hemingway, Joyce, and the surrealists.

So disorienting was the war that modernist techniques—albeit rendered more "accessible" to nonelite readers—were bent to new uses. One finds them, above all, in attempts to render ruptures in the sense of time and space and in the relationship between inner thinking (particularly memories that keep the self grounded) and outer event. These attempts hover around a moving void that evokes the mystery of experiences that are finally inexpressible, defying narrative order and language itself. Most of them question or directly attack routine attempts to give heroic meaning to a soldier's death. Not a few are existentialist/absurdist in orientation. The best of them, too, raise the taboo question of the difference between fascist, communist, and democratic exercises of sovereign power from the standpoint of the individual requisitioned to give up his life.[62] They broach the question of human rights.

One can only be startled today to find in the literature of the war, especially the poetry, a disinclination to blame the Nazis or Japan for the global apocalypse. Yes, Hitler is a monster, and yes, the United States had no choice but to enter the war, but this is not what writers focus on. More often, one finds doubts about the self, existential guilt, a probing for the disease in the human heart that causes war. Marianne Moore wrote,

> There never was a war that was
>   not inward; I must
> fight till I have conquered in myself what
> causes war, but I would not believe it.
>   I inwardly did nothing.
>   O Iscariot-like crime![63]

Moreover, the war brought a shameful self-consciousness about the fascist and racist qualities of Americans themselves, including those who were engaged in the fighting. Again, Marianne Moore provides an example:

> We
> vow, we make this promise
>
> to the fighting—it's a promise—"We'll
>   never hate black, white, red, yellow, Jew,
> Gentile, Untouchable." We are
>   Not competent to
> make our vows. With set jaw they are fighting,
> fighting, fighting,—some we love whom we know,
>   some we love but know not—that
>   hearts may feel and not be numb.
>   It cures me; or am I what
>   I can't believe in?[64]

Moore attempts to absolve the fighters of her sins. Alas, the literature of the war, particularly by combatants, reveals sickening levels of racism, anti-Semitism, and senseless brutality among the soldiers—and almost no suggestion of moral superiority of the Americans to their antagonists. War is a leveler, this writing tells us; it forces everyone into the slime.

Psychological researchers during the war found that American soldiers "had no meaningful understanding of why they were fighting or what the war was actually about. Worse, they did not seem to care."[65] Brown, among others, suggested that honoring the dead for their "sacrifice" was dishonest because it bought civilians and the state an undeserved peace of mind.

This point is made over and over again in the fiction. In Shaw's *The Young Lions*, anti-Semitic enlisted men are convinced that President Roosevelt is Jewish and had entered the war as part of an international conspiracy to enrich Jewish bankers while killing off gentiles. Even the Jewish protagonist in Gellhorn's *The Wine of Astonishment* cannot understand the reason for the war and blames European Jews for not emigrating—until the end of the novel, when his discovery of the death camps inspires a powerful rebirth of Jewish identity. In not a few of the novels, enlisted men blame Jews for the war against Germany, even if they understand the need to fight the "Japs" in revenge for Pearl Harbor. Many think the war against Japan justified but the fight against Germany only because of Germany's alliance with Japan.

In *The Young Lions*, new recruits are given an "orientation lecture" by a Lehigh University professor on "the Japan question." He tells them it is all a question of economics: "Japan needed to expand and take over the Asiatic and Pacific markets and we had to stop her and hold onto them ourselves. It was all according to the beliefs that Michael had had about the causes of war for the last fifteen years. And yet . . . he hated the professor. . . . He wanted to hear that he was fighting for liberty or morality or the freedom of subject peoples." The other men do not care one way or the other; they only want to go to sleep. The professor goes on: "It is absolutely imperative that we have . . . free and unhampered access to the wealth and buying power of China and Indonesia."[66] The chapter turns immediately after this to American anti-Semitism, as a landlady kicks Michael and his gentile wife out of her hotel upon learning he is Jewish.

The war allowed writers to present a cross-section of American life as it threw all manner of men together in platoons and squadrons, a point often made about idealized cross-ethnic bonding in Hollywood war films. The writers themselves are more of a cross-section of the American population than those of any preceding war. Harvey Shapiro (a veteran of the war) has pointed out that most of the significant poets of World War I were British and mostly officers. The American poets of World War II were diverse in background and position; many were enlisted men. Their poems "do not glory in brotherhood and they do not, as a rule, find nobility in one another. Quite the contrary, they often dislike one another or dislike being put cheek by jowl alongside one another. If they are in the infantry, they bear no love for their officers."[67] The comment is equally true of the fiction. Christian Diestl, the German protagonist in *The Young Lions*, is disgusted by "the whole myth of comradeship in war." He despises most of the men in his troop, hates his commanding officer "worse than Churchill, worse than Stalin."[68] Similarly, but from the American side, Howard Nemerov's late memoir-poem "IFF" begins,

Hate Hitler? No, I spared him hardly a thought.
But Corporal Irmin, first, and later on
The O.C. (Flying) Wing Commander Briggs,
And the station C.O. Group Captain Ormery—
Now there were men were objects fit to hate.[69]

Ethnic and class tensions, regional stereotypes, anti-Semitism, and anti-black racism play an enormous role in the writing about a war that few young men could escape even if they wanted to, even if they had children (and many did). The shift from civilian to soldier was often involuntary.

It has become popular to think of soldiers in World War II as a "band of brothers," and surely this was occasionally true in special volunteer units, but fiction and poetry by GIs soon returned more often tell a different story—of people who barely knew one another before getting killed and who, if they did survive more than a few months, did not get along, who often hated one another despite being thrown together in a platoon, a fighter-plane outfit, or a bombing crew. Howard Nemerov wrote a whole poem about such hatreds:

> Not to forget my navigator Bert,
> Who shyly explained to me that the Jews
> Were ruining England and Hitler might be wrong
> But he had the right idea . . . We were a crew,
> And went on so, the one pair left alive
> Of a dozen who chose each other flipping coins
> At the OTU but spoke no civil word
> Thereafter, beyond the words that had to do
> With the drill for going out and getting back.[70]

The title of Randall Jarrell's poem "O My Name It Is Sam Hall" alludes to one of the popular army songs of the day, the lyrics to which run like this:

> O my name it is Sam Hall
> And I hate you one and all—
> Yes, I hate you one and all,
> God damn your eyes.[71]

In war fiction by veterans, GIs most often detest their officers, at times murderously so. And the soldiers fight for no cause except to get home in one piece.

White racism is a common subject in writing about the war. It did not take the Cold War, as is often charged, to awaken white American writers to the viciousness of American racism; many of them were veterans of the antiracist struggles of the 1920s and 1930s, including Witter Bynner, whose poem "Defeat" asks the question, "Whom are we fighting this time, for God's sake?"

> On a train in Texas German prisoners eat
> With white American soldiers, seat by seat,

While black American soldiers sit apart,
The white men eating meat, the black men heart.

With the Civil War nearly eighty years in the past, it seems the South has ultimately won: "Mark well the token of the separate seat, / It is again ourselves whom we defeat."[72] Similar feelings inspired John Frederick Nims's "Race Riot," addressing the 1943 riots in Detroit, America's "arsenal of democracy":

On isle or desert, from grey ship or train
Your help, Detroit, in guarded crate arrives.
But what can the tall soldier think, who flings
His life away for rhetoric of freedom—
What think to see your guns, your perfect planes
Crusted with outrage of American blood?[73]

The battle against racism in the United States was part of the story of World War II in American literature. The ban on speaking out against American racism that applied to popular media—even jazz, which did speak out in highly ambiguous terms—did not hold in the realm of literature. In Gwendolyn Brooks's poetry concerned with the war one finds both outrage and a confidence that segregation's days are numbered. In "the white troops had their orders but the Negroes looked like men," white racial formulas come unfixed in the face of combat:

But when the Negroes came they were perplexed.
These Negroes looked like men. Besides, it taxed
Time and the temper to remember those
Congenital iniquities that cause
Disfavor of the darkness.[74]

In the context of war and dismemberment, attempts to keep black and white separate grow superfluous, even impossible. Brooks considers the difficulty of separating black from white in the context of war with a metaphor alluding to the challenge of properly identifying the shattered remains of bombed bodies for boxing and burial:

> Such as boxed
> Their feelings properly, complete to tags—
> A box for dark men and a box for Other—
> Would often find the contents had been scrambled.
> Or even switched. Who really gave two figs?[75]

If this poem expresses some hope that white soldiers themselves may be loosening the racial straightjacket of Jim Crow, another poem in the same collection, "Negro Hero," suggests something quite different.

Uncharacteristically direct and "unlyrical" for Brooks, this poem launches the rawest poetic attack on white racism of the time. Subtitled "to suggest Dorie Miller," the poem takes inspiration from the story of a mess attendant on the *USS West Virginia* (where he was also the heavyweight boxing champion) during the attack on Pearl Harbor. Miller won the Navy Cross in 1942 for his heroism that day, personally presented by Admiral Nimitz at a time when black sailors were not allowed to assume combat roles. He had been called from his battle station during the Japanese attack to carry wounded men to safety and then to attend the mortally wounded captain. Then he took over a machine gun and, untrained in its use, fired on the incoming planes until ordered to abandon ship. Brooks begins, "I had to kick their law into their teeth in order to save them." The poem speaks to the experiences and feelings of many black soldiers and sailors, who were assigned to servant roles throughout most of the war. Even when given combat duties, they were regularly humiliated while prevented by military rules from retaliation against white bullies. The speaker of "Negro Hero" abandons lyricism and poetic indirection in rhythms uncharacteristic of Brooks at the time:

> Naturally, the important thing is, I helped to save them, them and a
>   part of their democracy.

Even if I had to kick their law into their teeth in order to do that for
   them.
And I am feeling well and settled in myself because I believe it was a
   good job,
Despite this possible horror: that they might prefer the
Preservation of their law in all its sick dignity and their knives
To the continuation of their creed
And their lives.[76]

The final poem of *A Street in Bronzeville*, entitled "the progress," ends with the returning black soldiers' threat to the racial status quo ante: "How shall we smile, congratulate: and how / Settle in chairs? Listen, listen. The step / Of iron feet again. And again wild."[77]

Even the politically conservative novelist James Gould Cozzens, in his Pulitzer Prize–winning *Guard of Honor*, draws attention to the problem of racism in the military, only to suggest that, in the interests of military discipline, the battle against segregation will have to wait until after the war. The novel, considered by Bernard DeVoto one of the best of his era, centers around segregation and white animosity to black officers on a Southern air base. The white Southern racists are clearly in the wrong, but Cozzens (who worked in publicity during the war) ends up justifying the decision of the base's commanding officer to maintain "discipline" by punishing the black officers for insubordination. Cozzens admires the intelligence and self-discipline of the white leader who has to maintain order and lines of authority in ambiguous circumstances, but, even here, for segregation the writing is on the wall.

The artist Jacob Lawrence, serving in the Coast Guard on the service's first "integrated" ship, tended toward the hopeful view of how war was leading toward integration. Captain Charlton Skinner, who insisted on full integration aboard the *Sea Cloud*, had Lawrence's position reassigned from steward (a typical rating for black sailors) to public relations, so he could paint, and Lawrence started a series of works featuring the daily life of the ship and the progress of integration. In 1944, the

Museum of Modern Art held a second exhibit of his Migration Series along with a number of the new paintings. The MoMA's press release stresses that the new paintings

> suggest the gradual beginnings of a solution to the problem so mov-ingly portrayed in the Migration Series. . . . In Lawrence's Coast Guard pictures both races face the same fundamental problem—the war. Colored and white men mingle in recreational sports on deck, eat together, work together. Colored and white hands reach out with equal eagerness at mail call. Death and injury play no favorites, and all Uncle Sam's nephews rate the same pay in their non-racial classifications.[78]

A publicity photograph showed Lawrence with Captain Joseph Rosenthal and Carl Van Vechten in front of a painting of white and black sailors at mess together.

After the war, Lawrence completed a new series of paintings based on his experience, the War Series (1946–1947), which likewise stressed tendencies toward integration and the difficulty of separating black from white in war's whirlwind. In *Beach Head* (fig. 4.2), black and white are hard to distinguish, the postures of the bodies match, and white and black men share the burden of transporting the wounded on stretchers while others surge forward, grenade and rifle in hand. The image is perhaps less realistic than forward-thinking, in fact.

The best of the war novels sometimes characterize American officers as fascists. In John Hersey's Pulitzer Prize–winning *A Bell for Adano*, the hero is constantly challenged to counteract the effects produced by other officers, who are indistinguishable from fascists to the local Italian citizenry, particularly a General Marvin, who is popularly known in the United States as a hero. General Cummings in Mailer's *The Naked and the Dead* is a self-avowed fascist:

> The concept of fascism, far sounder than communism if you consider it, for it's grounded firmly in men's actual natures, merely started in the

FIGURE 4.2 Jacob Lawrence, *Beach Head*, from *The War Series*, 1946–1947. Tempera on composition board. 15 7/8" x 20 1/6". *Source*: Whitney Museum of American Art, New York; Gift of Mr. and Mrs. Roy R. Neuberger. © The Jacob and Gwendolyn Knight Lawrence Foundation, Seattle / Artists Rights Society (ARS), New York.

wrong country, in a country which did not have enough intrinsic potential power to develop completely. In Germany . . . there were bound to be excesses. But the dream, the concept was sound enough. . . . America is going to absorb that dream, it's in the business of doing it now. When you've created power, materials, armies, they don't wither of their own accord. Our vacuum as a nation is filled with released power, and I can tell you that we're out of the backwaters of history now. . . . Watch. After the war our foreign policy is going to be far more naked, far less hypocritical than it has ever been. We're no longer going to cover our eyes with our left hand while our right is extending an imperialist paw.[79]

I do not quote this as a historical prediction that proved prescient. What is astonishing today is that a novel with this message would have been a bestseller in 1948 and make its author famous overnight.

Equally corrosive of the providential mythology concerning American involvement in World War II is John Horne Burns's *The Gallery*, which Gore Vidal called the most "authentic" of the well-known books about the war, "the best book of World War II."[80] Anticipating Mailer's General Cummings, a spectral "parachute captain" confides in another soldier that the United States

is the only country that has enough food and gasoline and raw materials. So they're expending these like mad to wipe out the others in the world who'd like a cut of their riches. In order to preserve their standard of living for a few more years, they've dreamed up ideologies. Or their big business has. So they're at war with nearly everybody else in the world. . . . They will win this war. They'll reduce Europe to a state of fifteen hundred years ago. Then their businessmen and their alphabetical bureaucracies will go into the shambles of Milan, Berlin, and Tokyo and open up new plants. . . . We're destroying all the new ideas and all the little men of the world to make way for our mass production and our mass thinking and our mass entertainment. Then we can go back to our United States, that green little island in the midst of a smoking world. Then we can kill all the Negroes and the Jews. Then we'll start on Russia.[81]

The view of American soldiers we get in *The Gallery* could not be more contradictory of the images of them one finds in the media of film or journalism. Burns brings out their queerness, their frequent brutality toward the "Eyeties," their profiteering from the desperation of hungry Italians on the black market, and their sexual exploitation of desperate girls, women, and boys. *The Gallery* is, among other things, an extended indictment of American culture, in which the decadence of occupied Naples seems positively noble alongside the shallowness and rapacity of the conquerors, as suggested by the book's epigraph from *The Trojan Women*: "How are ye blind, ye treaders-down of cities?"

For most Americans of the postwar period, the nation's role in World War II has seemed a mighty confirmation of its providential role in world history. Not so to Burns. In the opening of the "Seventh Promenade" the narrator confides,

> I remember that my heart finally broke in Naples. Not over a girl or a thing, but over an idea. When I was little, they'd told me I should be proud to be an American. And I suppose I was, though I saw no reason I should applaud every time I saw the flag in a newsreel. But I did believe that the American way of life was an idea holy in itself, an idea of freedom bestowed by intelligent citizens on one another. Yet after a little while in Naples I found out that America was a country just like any other, except that she had more material wealth and more advanced plumbing. And I found that outside of the propaganda writers (who were making a handsome living from the deal) Americans were very poor spiritually. Their ideals were something to make dollars on. They had bankrupt souls. Perhaps this is true of most of the people of the twentieth century. Therefore my heart broke.
>
> I remember that this conceit came home to me in crudest black and white. In Naples of 1944 we Americans had everything. The Italians, having lost their war, had nothing. And what was this war really about? I decided that it was because most of the people of the world didn't have the cigarettes, the gasoline, and the food that we Americans had.[82]

Burns's one-hit wonder is as good as any with which to end this chapter. *The Gallery* expresses the most durable themes of American writing of World War II, in a form that bears the imprint of its time. It is a book betwixt and between, a threshold marker, in multiple dimensions, from its textual formatting to its generic indeterminacy and structure. "The Gallery" itself, the Galleria Umberto Primo, has the shape of an enormous cross, which the narrator tells us in the "Entrance" is "a cross between a railroad station and a church." And a crossroads: "Everybody in Naples came to the Galleria Umberto."[83]

The book's liminality shows up even in odd details: in the representation of dialogue, Burns does not use quotation marks for a character's speech but rather a dash at the start of a line, as in a French novel. And one can never determine the relationship between its chief center of consciousness—named "John"—and the author himself, a quality that will later show up in fiction called postmodern.

A seeming hybrid of fiction and nonfiction, the "Promenades" feature a first-person narrator named John and begin "I remember," a phrase liberally repeated from paragraph to paragraph, drawing attention to the subjective temporality of the text. The month of August 1944 gradually emerges as pivotal to the consciousness informing it all. The "Portraits," narrated in third person, are more likely fictional, although perhaps loosely based on actual persons and events, and a "pfc" (Private First Class) often serves as a curious observer of events, a minor character whom one suspects to be Burns himself. The term "Portrait" suggests fixity, while "Promenade" suggests passage from one place to another or, indeed, through the "gallery" of portraits. Yet Burns also blurs this distinction: the portraits are all short stories focusing on a particular character, and the promenades are entitled for fixed places—Casablanca, Fedhala, Algiers, and especially Naples. Yet throughout we move through liminal space and time. Even at the beginning and end, we are in two thresholds: the book is framed by an "Entrance" and "Exit," from which there is no before or after.

Although the book has an entrance and an exit, there is not exactly a beginning, middle, and end—it is not a novel, nor even a narrative exactly, but a promenade through a gallery. There is no central conflict leading to climax and resolution, although the book has a number of key themes. Like the "all-over paintings" of the abstract expressionists, it has no focal point.

Are the Americans liberators or conquerors and oppressors? Perhaps they are both. The "others" are not exactly enemies, although the most unattractive American soldiers think of them as such and extend their domestic racisms (antiblack and anti-Semitic) to the "lower races" they encounter in North Africa and Italy. The Italians are not like the Germans, however, who do appear briefly, near the end of the book, as enemies and oppressors of the Italians. Germans and Americans are the only characters whom we actually observe killing and being killed: they kill each other. The American assault on the Germans makes them liberators and not simply exploiters. Surrounded, as well, by former fascists suddenly claiming otherwise, they are "occupiers" in a nebulous position. The settings are not at the front—the front remains at an uncertain distance to the moving north, the site of an encounter with unimaginable and uncommunicable violence, a vortex of silence.

Some men are on respite from the front and will soon return. Yet most, true to the facts, have never been combat soldiers. One heads up a military-intelligence unit whose task is to censor outgoing mail (in a deeply ironic "portrait" that is surely based in part on Burns's own experiences in just such a unit). The officer, Major Motes, is presented first as a racist upper-class Southerner, whose first assignment was to head a Negro division in the United States before being reassigned to intelligence in North Africa. There he spends his time dreaming up ways of expanding his office with the help of various forms of publicity so effective that when a general visits from the Pentagon bent on forcing him to cut his staff so more replacements can be sent to the front, he succeeds in convincing the general that he needs even more men in his unit. The men, who have resented his dictatorial, quasi-fascist practices, suddenly come to his side in gratitude and in fear of being sent to war. He is ultimately relieved of his position in August 1944 but consoles himself that he is a man "out of [his] time," "a gentleman from Virginia," and begins making plans to "go to the Pentagon and sell them the idea of setting up censorship among civilians in the United States. Americans couldn't trust even one another in wartime."[84] In this portrait Burns was positively prophetic.

While there is considerable reference to remembering, the characters of the book seem uncertain of any future. They live in the present, intensely so, because the war has alienated them from any past and left them all in limbo: "I guess we're just bogged down in today, Moe said. You know how it is, boy. . . . The moment just seems there, that's all. . . . You don't feel you ever lived at any other time but now . . . not yesterday . . . not tomorrow."[85] Yet the *present* does not exist for the characters either: "I keep thinkin of myself like I'm a was . . . not a is," a corporal says to Moe—to which Moe responds,

> "I guess . . . the present doesn't exist for us. His tongue was pricked by the toothpick in his lips. Or we don't want to think about it."
>
> "—Well, that would be all right too, the corporal said. Except I can't think of the future either. . . . It's all past. Past tense like in grammar in school. Like an old man. An I'm just twenty-one. . . . Christ, lieutenant, I don't wanna have any memories yet . . . or be one."[86]

Partly for this reason, there is a lot of eroticism. The release from past and future allows a loosening of sexual norms and their containment of eros.

There are many scenes of sudden love and/or sex between strangers in the face of uncertainty and the intense sensation of life's brevity. The suspension of time, in which one seems to live in neither past, present, nor future intensifies erotic desire. "In a war one has to love, if only to reassert that he's very much alive in the face of destruction. Whoever has loved in wartime takes part in a passionate reaffirmation of his life."[87]

Yet in this interstice of time, the experience of erotic love can exceed any directed goal of orgasm, male or female. The most explicit statement of Burns's attitude to love and sex features a relationship (which may well last only one night) that could be either hetero- or homosexual and is worth quoting at length:

> For the act of love is only the continuation and the resolution of a desire and a mystery already set up in two minds. The blueprint becomes the working model, the raw stone the statue. I remember lying there, lost and wondering. I put my hand out to encounter another hand, already reaching for mine. My mouth went out exploring, only to meet another

mouth working toward mine in the darkness. In that kiss I felt as though my tongue had at last articulated a word I'd been striving to pronounce all my life long. In those long kisses there was nothing brutal, nothing rapacious, as mad love is said to be, so that the lovers lacerate one another's lips. I think we were both a little sad when we kissed. In those kisses we tried to heal each other's souls.

And I remember the sweet slowness of undressing one another, the longing and the languor. The clothes dropping whispering to the floor, the shadowy bodies gradually revealed, the secrets even more secret and removed that they lay under our hands. It seemed that in our lethargic and compassionate caresses we were trying to console each other for every hurt the world had ever inflicted: I am with you to comfort me, and I will comfort you. For I love you.

And I remember how exquisite was our leisure with one another. If there was passion—and indeed there must have been much—it only carried us slowly and steadily up to that place where there is understanding. Higher and higher. We didn't say much, only one another's names in a rising intensity of pain and delight. And for one instant we were in a place where there was no difference between us. We melted into all those who've ever loved and lived at all.[88]

The Italians are presented as a people more capable of love than Americans, and there is plenty of idealization and projection here. What stands out is nonetheless the liminality of Naples in every conceivable way—no doubt a reflection of Burns's passage from one phase of his own being to another. To overemphasize the sexual aspect of that passage seems wrong. Gore Vidal said of the scene from which I have just quoted that it reveals "a man discovering himself for the first time." In writing *The Gallery* Burns had "the luck to know, if only briefly, what it was to be alive with all senses responsive to all things, able to comprehend another person and to share that truth which is 'valid for everybody else.'"[89] Vidal was far from alone in considering *The Gallery* the best and most authentic "novel" of World War II. Hemingway, Gellhorn, Edmund Wilson, John Dos Passos—all major literary figures of the day—hailed Burns's work for its brilliance, authenticity, and audacity. A biography of Burns by David Margolick appeared in 2013, breaking a silence of six decades, but so far other scholars have ignored the novel.

It has been a long time since critics prized the Whitmanesque responsiveness to all things that Vidal praises, comprehending "others" (wherever the "I" resides) and sharing the "truth which is 'valid for everybody else.'" Yet this urge to universality, not nearly as simple as it is often presumed to be, permeated the literature of that liminal decade, as we will see in the cases of Jewish-authored, African American–authored, and gay or queer writing of the 1940s.

5

AMERICA! AMERICA!

....

A Jewish Renaissance?

In 1947, the British historian Cecil Roth published an essay in *Commentary* entitled "Jewish Culture: Renaissance or Ice Age?" He pointed out that before long, if not already, English-speaking Jews (5 million in North America, 750,000 in the British Empire) will comprise "by far the greatest homogeneous linguistic bloc in the Jewish world, as Yiddish-speaking Jewry was for so long"—in fact, "the greatest homogeneous linguistic bloc that has ever been in the Jewish world."[1] Would this not bode well for the evolution of a cultural renaissance led by English-speaking Jews, particularly in the United States? The potentialities were immense:

> The evolution of American Jewry during the past sixty years has been from some points of view the most important fact in Jewish history since the Middle Ages, because in it and through its instrumentality the future of Judaism has perhaps been secured. It would seem obvious that American Jewish history should have a tremendous significance in the eyes of the American Jew.[2]

The historian Salo Baron, also writing in 1947, saw

incontestable signs not only of a general cultural awakening, but of a certain eagerness of the Jewish public to pioneer in the unexplored realms of a modern culture which would be both Jewish and American, and to find some new and unprecedented spiritual and intellectual approaches to the Jewish position in the modern world.[3]

Ironically, however, in this "pioneering" the Jewish writers and intellectuals would be concerned less with advancing Jewish traditions or Jewish identity as such than with American culture more broadly construed and with the "human condition" in the modern world. Cecil Roth lamented, rightly or wrongly, that the Jewish public seemed indifferent to Jewish history and heritage. What was lacking for a Jewish renaissance was "popular interest and popular support."[4] He might have added that there was not much interest on the part of Jewish writers or publishers, either.

This fact seems counterintuitive, for the Holocaust and the founding of the state of Israel caused a powerful resurgence of Jewish self-consciousness in the immediate postwar period. Moreover, if the Holocaust came to function, after the fact, as a justification for American participation in World War II, it could do so only at the expense of American anti-Semitism, a common subject in the literature of the 1940s. Polls showed that between 1946 and 1950, the proportion of Americans who had heard any criticism of Jews in the past six months dropped from 64 percent to 24 percent.[5] In contrast, anti-Semitism had intensified during the war, when many blamed Jews for American entry into the war, as the literature attests. In *The Young Lions*, anti-Semitic gentiles blame the war on Jews. Noah Ackerman overhears one of them saying, "Hitler is probably wrong most of the time, but you've got to hand it to him, he knows what to do about the Jews."[6] The novel includes vicious episodes of Jew-baiting, as does Mailer's *The Naked and the Dead*. One theme of *The Young Lions*—a runaway bestseller and critical success—is a growth of Jewish self-consciousness on the part of Noah Ackerman, who starts out an assimilated Jew feeling little connection to his dying father's intense concerns for the Jewish people in 1937. The war precipitates Ackerman's identity *as* a Jew who values Jewishness.

By the early 1940s the destruction of European Jewry made the United States especially important to Jewish life globally. Almost no Jewish books were being published outside the United States by 1941. A Jewish book council, concerned about the survival of Jewish civilization, was founded in 1942 to spark "a Jewish renaissance in America," promoting books in English, Hebrew, and Yiddish. And, in fact, plenty of new books by Jewish authors or bearing on Jewish life came out.[7] At no time in history had Jewish publishing been so concentrated in one small place. And never had literary publishing in the United States been so concentrated in Jewish hands. Upstarts of the 1910s and 1920s were now captains of the industry. They had been influential in American publishing since the 1920s (Huebsch, Liveright, Guinzburg, Farrar, Knopf), but by now they were well ensconced in the New York publishing establishment and widely admired. They were joined by Jewish refugee publishers like the Germans Helen and Kurt Wolff, who founded Pantheon, and the Frenchman Jacques Schiffrin, editor of the famous Paris imprint Pléiade, who fled to New York in 1941 and joined the Wolffs at Pantheon as vice president.[8]

Salman Schocken, cofounder with Martin Buber of a Zionist journal in 1915 and later of a press, fled Germany in 1934 for Palestine, then moved to New York in 1940, where he continued strictly "Jewish" publishing. He had advocated against Jewish cultural assimilation in Germany since first reading Buber's Hasidic stories. In 1945, with the help of fellow refugee Hannah Arendt, he founded Schocken Books, the American publisher of Kafka's works in the very era when, as Anatole Broyard later put it, "Kafka was the rage."

But Kafka was not chiefly read as a Jewish writer at the time. In fact, he was "the first author of non-Jewish content" Schocken's firm brought out, doing so chiefly because the Nazis had proscribed it.[9] Rather, his work was embraced as "a complete description of the condition of man," to quote Isaac Rosenfeld's commentary of 1947: "Kafka begins, where he ends, with an understanding of the limitation of human freedom, and an effort to transcend that limitation to the achievement of as much peace as one can reach in mankind."[10]

Jewish cultures were highly diversified, and Jewish poets and fiction writers did not mostly focus on "Jewish" subjects. Lillian Hellman's and Arthur Miller's plays of the 1940s, for example, did not address specifically Jewish concerns and cannot be said to have any formally unique features attributable to their Jewish ethnicity. This is particularly notable in the case of Hellman's *The Watch on the Rhine* (1941), which concerned tensions surrounding a German family taking refuge with relatives in the United States. The husband and father is an anti-Nazi German resistance fighter married to an American woman, but at no point does the play even bring up the Nazi targeting of Jews, for Hellman was more interested in a message attacking all forms of fascist power and oppression of minorities. Jo Sinclair's *Wasteland*, which "pioneered the so-called Jewish novel" of the postwar period, according to one critic, was the only story or novel of hers that had a "Jewish" focus.[11] Of the novels about the war, the gentile Martha Gellhorn's *The Wine of Astonishment* (1948), which comes to focus on a Jewish soldier as protagonist, centered more on "Jewish" issues and anti-Semitism than any other of which I am aware—although plenty of other fiction and poetry addressed anti-Semitism, of course. And, as Werner Sollors has pointed out, the first novel to confront the Holocaust fully would be the gentile John Hersey's *The Wall* (1950),[12] although *The Wine of Astonishment*'s plot finally turns on Jacob Levy's discovery of the death camps.

The Holocaust brought home sharply to every American of Jewish origin an intense awareness of their Jewishness, yet this did not lead mainly in the direction of a consciously Jewish American cultural movement. Perhaps such energies were siphoned off to the birth of Israel, in which many Jews took vital interest. Even the American Jewish Committee's bimonthly magazine, *Contemporary Jewish Record*, founded in 1938, changed its name to *Commentary* when it became a monthly in 1945, aiming in its editor's words "to carry into larger fields the fine tradition established by this magazine since its founding seven years ago." Elliot E. Cohen's rhetoric reassures readers that the magazine will still be "Jewish"—"We shall have ampler opportunity to picture Jewish life in this country and abroad in its rich variety" while tracing "more fully the trends and patterns emerging in the postwar world." But instead of presenting Jewish life mainly in its own context, it would present it "in its inter-relations with those basic issues of thought, politics and culture that are the concern of all human-kind."[13] At *Partisan Review*, once the *Menorah Journal*, "Jewish" concerns became even more peripheral as the editors and contributors won fame and the sense of battling Philistines and Stalinists gave way, in Irving Howe's words, "to the feeling that 'we' were getting closer to the center of American cultural life, there to bedazzle, instruct, and punish, and to test our powers."[14]

Were Jewish intellectuals, in a period when anti-Semitism was still strong in the United States, keeping their heads low, attempting to "fit in" with the white Christian majority? This may have been true in some cases, but Jews had long been involved in unpopular civil-rights, left-wing, and revolutionary causes in numbers far above their proportion of the populace. They had played important roles in the cultural insurgencies of the 1920s and 1930s. The theories of Marx (a Jew) had provided a major path for the secularization and "assimilation" of first-generation Jewish American intellectuals, when Marxism was generally considered a threat to Americanism.

Many Jewish-authored books in the 1930s and 1940s came in the form of memoirs and semiautobiographical novels about the psychological journey from immigrant "ghetto" to multiethnic "America," frequently by way of leftist politics. Yet cultural-identity politics held little interest for them; they could not see it as relevant to their own needs or their intellectual development, nor to the world at large. Who, after all, were the greatest exponents of identity politics in the 1930s and early 1940s? Mussolini, Hirohito, Hitler. At home: Father Coughlin, the German *Bund*, Southern senators, nativists, racists, and anti-Semites.

In the 1940s Jewish public intellectuals came into their own. They were known to be Jewish, and their journals continued to attend to "Jewish" issues. But their effect was to shape the dominant interpretations of modern American culture rather than to effect a Jewish "renaissance." This trajectory had a past. Jews had been importing European modernism and Russian fiction to the United States since Alfred Knopf's desertion of Mitchell Kennerly to found his own firm in 1915 and the founding of the Modern Library by Horace Liveright shortly thereafter, making "modern" literature by other than English authors available for American consumption. They had also been the chief publishers of the "Little Renaissance" of the 1910s and 1920s and of the Negro Renaissance (now known as the Harlem Renaissance) of the 1920s and 1930s.[15] This tendency continued through the 1940s. Symptomatically, "Jewish" books were more often published by university presses and other "non-Jewish" houses than by Knopf, Liveright, and company.[16]

Yiddish literature had been central to Jewish publishing in Europe, and Yiddish remained the first language of many Jewish immigrants and their children in the first half of the twentieth century, but Yiddish book publishing never took off in the United States.[17] Yiddish fiction, popular in newspapers and magazines through the 1920s, trailed off in the course of the 1940s. Virtually all the major "American" Yiddish writers were born abroad before 1900 and published their important work before 1940, with the exception of Isaac Bashevis Singer, who continued to publish celebrated fiction into the 1960s, when it was read primarily in English.[18] Most American Jews felt no need to sustain Yiddish as a language. The story is similar for Hebrew literature. In 1927 there were 110 Hebrew authors in the United States, but American Hebrew literature met its demise by midcentury, leaving Israel "the sole flourishing center of Hebrew letters."[19] American writers in Hebrew themselves "shunned total allegiance to an Israel-centeredness or a set of literary themes or group behavior expected by the Zionist national agenda," willfully attempting an Americanization of Hebrew literature in part by treating specifically "American" subject matter—including most notably Native American and African American material. As a result they became of marginal importance to the Hebrew literary tradition, and the language died out completely as a factor in American literature by midcentury.[20]

What seems most extraordinary about Jewish writers', editors', and publishers' relation to American literary culture in the 1940s is the extent of leadership and almost total merging with other elements to form what would come to be called the "mainstream" in postwar America. Young

Jewish men raised on pulp fiction and the bodybuilding magazines and books of Bernarr McFadden invented the first American superheroes starting at the tail end of the 1930s—Superman and Batman, followed by Captain America during the war—and blasted the age of comic books wide open in time for the teenaged soldiers in basic training or camped in points unknown. While anti-Semitism gripped elite English departments, jousting Jewish critics such as Alfred Kazin, Lionel Trilling, Irving Howe, Philip Rahv, Clement Greenberg, and Harold Rosenberg helped define the terms with which modern American literature and art would be discussed. American studies in the academy, too, served in part as a mode of assimilation for Jewish scholars in the field, while their "outsider" perspective helped shape that emergent interdiscipline.

In his preface to *On Native Grounds*, Alfred Kazin wrote: "The greatest single fact about our modern American writing" is "our writers' absorption in every last detail of their American world together with their deep and subtle alienation from it." Such alienation, he added, might be widespread among modern writers everywhere, "But what interested me here was our alienation *on* native grounds—the interwoven story of our need to take up our life on our own grounds and the irony of our possession."[21] Notice the possessive pronoun. He might as well have been speaking of himself as of the *goyim* on whom his study focused. Reading *On Native Grounds* (1942) and Kazin's first memoir, *A Walker in the City* (1951, written from 1946 to 1950), in the reverse order of their publication makes both books more interesting today than they would be otherwise. The memoir explains a lot about the preface to *On Native Grounds* and its relationship to Kazin's (working-class Russian) Jewishness. The field-defining critical study (on the strength of which Kazin would be sent to Europe after the war to explain American culture) is an "assimilationist" book in a truer sense than what the term is generally taken to mean, for assimilation works in both directions. Kazin did not merely "assimilate" to some preexisting America; he took possession of it as an "alien" and assimilated its cultural heritage to his own needs, finding in the great American writers (all white, gentile, and male) aliens, "lonely Americans"—like him.[22] They were no more "insiders" to America than he. Their search took place within himself even as he searched for an American home. The final sentence of *A Walker in the City* could as well refer to the American authors he cherished as to the sights and sounds of the city and the girls he heard one evening laughing by the reservoir in Brooklyn's Highland Park: "it was hard to think of them as something apart, they were searching out so many new things in me."[23] Ultimately, the otherness of "America" itself—its elusiveness requiring of each generation and each individual, however identified, a remaking—is irresolvable. He came to realize that "America" (whatever it was) no more belonged to "them" (the gentiles, the "Americans") than to him. Again, in *On Native Grounds*, he asserts, "our modern writers have had to discover and rediscover and chart the country in every generation . . . but must still cry America! America! As if we had never known America. As perhaps we have not."[24]

Such discourse pervaded the environment in which the early work of James Baldwin and Ralph Ellison took shape, just as in their early reviews and essays one can feel the New York "literary temperament" of the 1940s that mostly Jewish critics promulgated: "the firm, terse, intellectually ambitious prose, the fluent, sophisticated breadth of reference, the concreteness of idea—political at the core—the taste for epigram."[25] As Irving Howe later put it, this new essayistic style "willfully called attention to itself as a token of bravura, a mixture of mandarin elegance and street outcry . . . the writer as skilled infighter juggling knives."[26] As often as not, they aimed the knives at one another. This powerful mode of criticism existed in tense competition with the "New Criticism" of university English departments, a mode largely developed by Southern Protestant Agrarians such as Cleanth Brooks, John Crowe Ransom, Allen Tate, and Robert Penn Warren. I do not mean to suggest, however, a Christian-Jewish divide. Edmund Wilson, nemesis of the New Critics, was a model for the "New York intellectuals," and the young James Baldwin a budding fellow traveler.

Kazin's representative figures take on the features of "aliens," like so many of the Jewish intellectuals of Kazin's generation: William Dean

Howells, of all people, who had fled his native Ohio Valley for Boston to make a career, becomes with his late-career move to New York Kazin's chosen symbol for the break that set off "modern" American prose from what preceded it. (American modernism in Kazin's telling derived from "the realization that the old formal culture—the 'New England idea'—could no longer serve.")[27] The influence of modern European literature—whether of the Russian realists or the French and Scandinavian naturalists—was ancillary to this realization, not its cause. Yet that New York was the major port of entry for such influences was certainly not lost on Kazin, who used as his frontispiece for *A Walker in the City* Alfred Stieglitz's iconic photograph *The Steerage*. There, too, was a modern (Jewish) American original whose gallery An American Place had helped shape Manhattan modernism and the emergent modernist idea of "Americanism."

Given the force of the Puritan heritage, as critics understood it in the early twentieth century, Christianity loomed large on the historical horizon of the "American" imagination. Not coincidentally, Jesus often shows up in Jewish-authored texts of the 1940s, particularly in works that concern Jewish identity. In Jo Sinclair's *Wasteland*, the expletive "Jesus Christ" comes out of the Jewish protagonist's mouth so often as to seem a verbal tic. Karl Shapiro's *V-Letter* (1944) has so many poems turning on Christian references that one might assume the poet to be a devout Christian. As a matter of fact, during the war Shapiro, who had dropped any religious identification in the 1930s, grew deeply interested in Christianity, in part by way of a Catholic correspondent who encouraged him to take instruction in the faith. Although he never converted to Christianity (he came close), it had a strong imprint on his poetry at the time, and his nonreligious Jewish identification had much to do with that. He later hypothesized that many Jews of his generation went through such a phase.[28] Shapiro was apparently right. As Lewis Fried has demonstrated in relation to Jewish fiction of Shapiro's generation, "The writer's deployment of Jewish and Christian symbols argued for the universality of the *situation* of faith. It also emphasized the limitations of a specific Jewish representation of experience." In novels of the 1930s and 1940s, "The

American-Jewish literary imagination began to depict its characters in and not necessarily apart from a Christian world-view."[29]

Shapiro's poetry certainly bears this out in a different genre. "Christmas Eve: Australia" meditates on the war in the Pacific and the meaning of Christmas: "I smoke and read my bible and chew gum / Thinking of Christ and Christmas of last year." Musing on what the "quizzical soldiers" near him are asking of the war and future Christmases, he grows "sick of causes and the tremendous blame / Curse lightly and pronounce your serious name."[30] Perhaps the quizzical soldiers are wondering why a Jew is reading the Christian Bible on Christmas Eve, particularly considering the "tremendous blame" Christians place on Jews for Jesus's death. Yet to this Jewish soldier, Jesus is "serious" business, and the Christian Bible a valued resource, as we learn from the next poem, "New Guinea," which begins with an epigraph from the Book of Revelation 6:6, as translated in the King James Version of the New Testament: "And see thou hurt not the oil and the wine."[31] This poem full of allusions to the sixth chapter of Revelation, which treats of the apocalypse, reflects on the catastrophic effects of the war on the native people of New Guinea, who need have taken no part in it but for the battle between foreign empires. What effect does it have on their faith and worship? "What happens to the dark primordial law / Of those whose home this is, happens to us." The speaker universalizes the meaning of the verse from Revelation to pray for continuance of the native culture:

Their desolation see us deeply trust
And never hurt their oil and their wine:
Peace to the science of these fevered woods,
Their attributes, their language and their gods.[32]

"Sunday, New Guinea" follows only two poems later, again universalizing the meaning of Christian worship:

From every side, singly, in groups, in pairs,
Each to his kind of service comes to worship Him.

Our faces washed, our hearts in the right place,
We kneel or stand or listen from our tents;
Half-naked natives with their kind of grace
Move down the road with balanced staff like mendicants.[33]

The war goes on over the hill, and the jungle encroaches on the soldiers' "sacred rites," while the speaker reminisces about Sundays at home reading the comics and the *New York Times*, long lounging afternoons, and his love.

But while Shapiro's book incorporates Christianity, the speaker is also explicitly Jewish, and one who meditates on the meaning of being Jewish. In "Jew," he writes: "The name is immortal but only the name, for the rest / Is a nose that can change in the weathers of time or persist / Or die out in confusion or model itself on the best." If Jewishness cannot always be "seen" in the physiognomy, it is *felt* as stigmatized otherness. The long heritage of anti-Semitic scapegoating inheres now in the very name, "Jew," ironically identifying that designation with Jesus/Yeshua himself: "Our name is impaled in the heart of the world on a hill / Where we suffer to die by the hands of ourselves, and to kill."[34] If in some sense the poem "Christianizes" Jews, it also re-Judaizes Christianity in terms of a universalist religiosity. In the same year that *V-Letter* came out, Waldo Frank published "The Jew in Our Day: Preface to a Program" in *Contemporary Jewish Record*, arguing that "The finest personal flower of Judaism is Jesus. Jesus was a man in whom the cosmic consciousness was so strong that its ecstasy became the norm of his life."[35]

When Shapiro returned from the war, the poetic vocation took the place that religious contemplation had held for him during the war. His poems, written in isolation and published while he was on duty, had made him famous and a spokesman of his generation. Upon his return, he was named poetry consultant to the Library of Congress. The draw of Christianity, of any religion, receded as his vocation as poet claimed him. Yet Shapiro drew a distinction between religious identity and ethnic identity and correlated the ethnos of poets with that of Jews. "Heritage" had little to do with it:

The poet is in exile whether he is or he is not [Jewish]. Because of what everybody knows about society's idea of the artist as a peripheral character and a potential bum. Or troublemaker. Well, the Jews began their career of troublemaking by inventing the God whom Wallace Stevens considers the ultimate poetic idea. And so I always thought of myself as being both in and out of society at the same time. Like the way most artists probably feel in order to survive—you have to at least pretend that you are "seriously" in the world. Or actually perform in it while you know that in your own soul you are not in it at all. You are outside observing it.[36]

Alfred Kazin made a nearly identical observation, and his journey also included a close brush with Jesus/Yeshua as he crossed the bridge to adulthood. An intense adulation of Yeshua caught hold of him when a Yiddish-speaking man, taking him to be Jewish, handed him a copy of the New Testament on the steps of the New York Public Library.

I could not read more than two or three pages at a time before turning away in excitement and shame. . . . I had known [Jesus] instantly. Surely I had been waiting for him all my life—our own Yeshua, misunderstood by his own, like me, but the very embodiment of everything I had waited so long to hear from a Jew—Yeshua, our own long-lost Jesus, speaking straight to the mind and heart at once.[37]

This Yeshua was Jewish, not an "escape" from Jewish ethnicity, yet the feeling of connection—accompanied by excitement and shame, transformation—altered the boundary between Jew and gentile at the same time that Kazin's exploration of New York outside of Brownsville and his reading tied him to a broader world. He began walking to a new public library in the "American" district, and an obsession with late-nineteenth-century American history took hold, "where, I thought, I would find my way to that fork in the road where all American lives cross."[38] At that crossroads he met all the "lonely Americans" like him—Whitman,

Dickinson, Eakins, Veblen: aliens (and non-Jews) all. The result was his breakthrough, field-defining book *On Native Grounds* (1942), which helped frame the understanding of modern American literature for years to come.

Sholem Asch has been called "the first Yiddish writer to become a prominent literary figure the world over." He had been writing and publishing fiction in Yiddish on Jewish life, history, and religious concerns since the turn of the century, when he lived in Poland. He moved to the United States in 1914 and eventually took American citizenship. But in 1939 he began a series of novels based on the life of Jesus, hoping to demonstrate that anti-Semites were false to "true" Christianity, the roots of which were profoundly Jewish. Probing the origins of Christianity in the life of Jesus and his apostles, between 1939 and 1949 he published the Christological series *The Nazarene* (1939), *The Apostle* (1943), and *Mary* (1949)—controversial among some Jewish readers used to his earlier work but popular internationally. And in the midst of this, he published a nonfiction statement of his beliefs, *One Destiny: An Epistle to Christians* (1945), to demonstrate that Judaism and Christianity were "inextricably interrelated." This was a direction specific to that ten-year span; in the 1950s he turned back to firmly "Jewish" historical fiction, beginning with *Moses* (1951).[39]

Poems in Muriel Rukeyser's *Beast in View* (1944) often allude to Christian themes as she meditates on the crisis of her times. "Holy Family," for example, figures "A man and woman riding. / Riding, the newborn child. / . . . They childless disappear / Among the fighting men. / Two thousand years until they come again."[40] In "Ninth Elegy: The Antagonists," she writes, "We are bound by the deepest feuds to unity, / To make the connections and be born again, / Create the creative, that will love the world."[41] The book is rife with references to children to be born and the world that must follow for them to populate in a new spirit of universal kinship. "A Translation: *from* 'To the Unborn Child' *by Hans Carossa*" was first printed, as Rukeyser's "Note" explains at the end of the book, as a Christmas poem to the critic Norman Holmes Pearson.[42] The lines opening the final stanza ask, "To whom do I speak today? Who shall tell us / that you are alive again? Who shall tell us today / that you will eat the bread of the earthly fields?"[43]

These Christian references and allusions are no attempt on Rukeyser's part to compromise her Jewish identity; they suggest instead how a Jewish woman can speak for Christians, for all humanity, in the midcentury crisis. The seventh section of "Letter to the Front" begins, "To be a Jew in the twentieth century / Is to be offered a gift. If you refuse, / Wishing to be invisible, you choose / death of spirit, the stone insanity." Rukeyser, perhaps too optimistically, identifies the "gift" with "torment" but also "the accepting wish, / The whole and fertile spirit as guarantee / For every human freedom, suffering to be free, / Daring to live for the impossible."[44] These lines can be interpreted as identifying the Jew of the twentieth century with Jesus of Nazareth. In a related way, Rukeyser opens her long poem "To the Soul and Body of John Brown" (a Christian martyr) with an epigraph from the Book of Joel, in the English of the King James Bible, "*Multitudes, multitudes in the valley of decision!*" Rukeyser's next book of poetry, *The Green Wave* (1948), features two "Christian/Jewish" poems: "Christmas Eve" and the long poem "Easter Eve 1945." Jewishness, in Rukeyser's view, is not a particularist identity but a pathway to a universal subject position, a crossroads, made ethically obligatory in an age of global catastrophe, in which the extermination of the Jews takes on planetary significance.

Leslie Fiedler made precisely this point in a *Commentary* essay in 1949 taking on the question of how to respond to the long history of literary anti-Semitism in the Western tradition, which showed itself even in the work of "modernists" much admired by contemporary Jewish authors—most notably and recently T. S. Eliot and Ezra Pound. Contemporary Jewish authors could not disown Eliot, for his work (published initially by Jews) had helped form their aesthetic sensibilities. Neither could Fiedler give up Ezra Pound's poems for their "evil doctrine"—"There is beauty and a degree of true vision that we cannot afford to sacrifice."[45] Instead, one must translate the evil qualities ascribed to the mythical Jew into more universal terms, for those qualities exist not in Jews as Jews but in all human beings. And the gentile must learn that he has projected onto the Jew the evil that haunts us all. Fiedler concludes on an upbeat note, observing that Jews have moved from the periphery to the center of American culture, and increasingly the images of the Jew are a common creation of Jews and of gentiles "whose sensibilities have been profoundly conditioned by ours":

> In this apocalyptic period of atomization and uprooting, of a catholic terror and a universal alienation, the image of the Jew tends to become the image of everyone and we are perhaps approaching the day when the Jew will come to seem the central symbol, the essential myth of the whole Western world.[46]

Fiedler would go on to author classic studies of American literature that have never gone out of print.

Fiction by Jewish American authors of the period reveals the same cast of mind. Just as African American writers of the time often rejected the notion of a separate "Negro literature," most Jewish critics and writers rejected the notion of a "Jewish American" literature. Philip Rahv, editor of *Partisan Review* in the 1940s, would write as late as 1967 that "the American-Jewish writers do not in the least make up a literary faction or school" and that "the homogenization resulting from speaking of them as if they comprised some kind of literary faction or school is bad critical practice in that it is based on simplistic assumptions concerning the literary process as a whole as well as the nature of American Jewry, which, all appearances to the contrary, is very far from constituting a unitary group in its cultural manifestation."[47] Similarly, Frederick R. Karl wrote that Jewish writers in the United States "are American writers, not Jewish writers, not members of a Jewish club, affiliated to each other not as Jews but as Americans." Even "to speak of them as 'Jewish American' is to homogenize what should be particularized."[48] As Alexander Bloom has argued in a study of the Jewish New York intellectuals, the idea of Jews' centrality to "the dilemmas of modern existence" was broadly accepted from the late 1940s through the 1950s; the more their views were accepted, the less peripheral and, in a sense, "Jewish" they became. Alienation was the common condition, and Jews were understood to have long experience with it.[49]

Moreover, the very feeling of being an "outsider" was thought to be an advantage in understanding the "center." Alfred Kazin confided to his journal, "I have never been able to take society for granted, and least of all my own place in it. That is one of my values: I am always concerned with the central situation, precisely because I have always felt myself on the periphery."[50] At the same time, Kazin rejected any special status as outsider or victim. He admired those, like Faulkner, who took full measure of any human being's potential for good and evil. Prompted by thoughts about *Intruder in the Dust*, Kazin wrote in his journal in September 1948 about what he called Faulkner's

> *sounding* of all our immense possibilities for good and evil—the haunted awareness by the American of his peculiar domain in the world. But Faulkner actually evokes something far more immediate; the relationship of the oppressor and the oppressed, seen from the point of view of the oppressor himself—the former master, the white man in the white-Negro relationship. Thus reminding us with full force what it is the Southern writer has that other Americans lack, what makes the others so thin, so morally coarse, so *unfounded* on anything but his discovery of himself, if that. It is the awareness, the Southern writer's, of the *relationship* between master and servant, between guilt and history, and the fact that this relationship is seen from above [that] is all the more significant to his own possession of the complexity of his experience.[51]

In contrast, Kazin believed,

> The Jewish writer thinks of himself as the oppressed, the alienated, the man things are done to. . . . The oppressor-class writer is often the greater, because he has not lost his dignity by abjection, and has even *added* to it by understanding of his guilt. The oppressed has the consciousness of his ethical superiority; the oppressor of his central place in the human domain.[52]

For Jewish critics, it was important to resist the tendency to embrace a historical "victim" mentality, an identity formed by victimization or in reaction against it.

Saul Bellow's *The Victim* follows the experiences of a Jewish man who has, in his own mind, narrowly avoided being one of "the lost, the outcast, the overcome, the effaced, the ruined."[53] Sensitive to anti-Semitic slights to the point of paranoia, he also has a tendency to self-defensiveness and uncertainty. The novel explores the ambiguities of Jewish identity in the United States—particularly male Jewish identity—assimilation, and the waning of anti-Semitism. Relationships between Jews and gentiles play the central role in the novel as Asa Leventhal negotiates his role in two separate plotlines. Throughout the novel, Asa's wife, Mary, significantly, is out of town, and he is living as a bachelor for several weeks.

The first plot concerns the illness and ultimate death of a young nephew, Mickey Leventhal, the son of Asa's absent brother Max and Max's Italian American wife, Elena, who is Catholic. The novel begins when Asa is summoned by Elena to help her with young Mickey, who has fallen ill. Leventhal at first questions how sick the boy really is and then tries to convince Elena that he should go to the hospital, but Elena will not hear of it. He brings in a doctor who ultimately convinces her to hospitalize the boy, but by then it is too late. Leventhal believes (wrongly, it turns out) that Elena blames him for the boy's death, ascribing this in part to her superstitious Catholicism. The plot is complicated by the fact that Elena's mother is on the scene, and Leventhal is convinced that, as a devout Catholic, she hates Jews. (This view is later briskly discredited by his brother.)

The second plot involves a gentile named Allbee who has lost his job and blames Leventhal for it. Allbee had helped Leventhal get an interview for a job at a magazine, during which Leventhal grew enraged at not being hired and insulted Allbee's boss. This argument contributed to Allbee's being fired (although we learn that there were other factors, as well). Allbee thus plays the role of "victim" in relation to Leventhal, while Leventhal struggles constantly with a tendency to see himself as a victim. The anti-Semitic Allbee is, in fact, an alter ego to Leventhal, a perfect example of the kind of "loser" and outcast Leventhal fears he might have become. Moreover, Allbee's anti-Semitic stereotypes about Jews match Leventhal's insecurities about stereotypically "Jewish" characteristics. As one of the earliest and most astute reviewers put it, "The anti-Semite is both a materialization of the real threats that surround Leventhal, and a negative, extreme inversion of himself. The relationship of both to each other has a kind of lopsided symmetry and ingenious duality."[54]

As in Poe's doppelganger tales, Leventhal's interactions with Allbee are strangely cut off from relationships with others. The man stalks Leventhal, looking for opportunities to interact with him, and ultimately persuades Leventhal to let him live in his apartment while his wife is away. The relationship between the two men is dreamlike, disconnected from public "reality." Allbee virtually takes over Leventhal's apartment, even sleeping with a prostitute in his bed. Near the end of the novel, Allbee attempts suicide by turning on the gas in the oven and sticking his head in it (while Leventhal is asleep and therefore also vulnerable). This finally enrages Leventhal enough to kick him out.

The two plotlines alternate throughout the novel. And just as Leventhal's wife is out of town throughout the main action concerning Allbee, so is Elena's husband (Asa's brother) throughout the illness of Mickey. Max arrives just after his son has died, and the novel ends quickly thereafter, with Asa Leventhal having one last interaction with Allbee years later. While out with his wife at a show, Leventhal spots Allbee with a well-known actress. Allbee has put himself back together and is successfully employed in radio advertising. He apologizes to Leventhal and says he "owes" him "something." He has made his peace "with things as they are," having learned that "The world wasn't made exactly for me."[55] (Perhaps a riff on the notion of a "chosen people" so dear to American ideology and Jewish covenantal theology.) The novel ends with Leventhal asking Allbee, "who runs things?" Is there a higher power? Is anyone in charge?

The reviewer for *Commentary* found Bellow's novel most notable for departing from Jewish fiction that focused on a self-enclosed Jewish world—the Lower East Side, Coney Island, the Bronx: "Saul Bellow's *The Victim* is, as far as I know, the first attempt in American literature to consider Jewishness not in its singularity, not as constitutive of a special world of experience, but as a quality that informs all of modern life, as the quality of modernity itself."[56]

As Leventhal's sense

> of having trespassed, of presuming, of not belonging, of not possessing, is plainly Jewish, of course—it is the psychology of the modern *galut*. But it is plainly something else too. It is an essential part of the sense of the city that is captured so well in this novel, it is the malaise of the megalopolis, it is the discomfiture and dispossession of everything human in face of the colossal indifference of modern metropolises. Not only the Jews are in *galut*.[57]

And not only is the Jew the "victim." In fact, the temptation of identifying as a victim—the one who is blamed—runs like a bright thread throughout the novel. That identity depends, one might say, on the idea that someone or something *is* in charge—God, for example. The young boy, Mickey, is the only one who dies in the novel, but he is never a *victim*, and Leventhal is held responsible for the death only in his own imagination, one that tends to position him as the one to be blamed.

Claiming to be Leventhal's victim, Allbee victimizes Leventhal. Yet, insofar as Allbee is Leventhal's alter ego, Leventhal is his own victim. Yet Allbee is, in part, a victim of Leventhal's disastrous attack on his former boss, an attack motivated by Leventhal's feeling that the boss had no right not to hire him. That attack led (in part) to Allbee's firing, which in turn helped lead to his divorce and overall disintegration. Taking on oneself the identity of alienated victim—as both Allbee and Leventhal do—becomes the prototype of the modern urban ethos of the deracinated individual perpetually uncertain of where he stands.

This is largely the way Martin Greenberg interpreted the novel in his review for *Commentary*, "Modern Man as Jew," and it still seems to me the most convincing way of understanding it. What is most striking, however, is how utterly foreign it is to the discourse of more recent interpretations, mostly under the auspices of literary and cultural studies devoted to constituting a Jewish American canon and academic field. For Greenberg most emphasizes the universality of the complex at the core of Bellow's novel. We will see parallels in African Americanist and "gay" literary criticism of the time. There is no erasure of the particularity of Jewish experience, but that particularity—even the extreme victimization of Jews—gets enfolded into a more universalist framework.

The record is clear that Bellow was highly sensitive to anti-Semitism in American intellectual life and in editorial offices. Disdaining "assimilation," he also disliked what he called "Ivy League kikes" who tried to "fit in" with the WASP-dominated academy. But he also rejected the tag "Jewish American writer."[58] Although he was proudly Jewish, and American, and a writer, he saw no value in stringing those terms together. Nor did he believe in later years that he and other renowned authors like Philip Roth and Bernard Malamud, with whom he was routinely identified, were aesthetically connected. To him, such "identity"-based groupings were usually wrongheaded and imposed from outside for questionable reasons, particularly "P.R." for American Jews who were pleased that Jewish writers were succeeding. He resented Jewish expectations that authors "represent" Jewish experience positively and regarded the Jewish American writer tag as untruthful and imposed by the media, marketers, and academics. It had, he thought, "a flavor of the ghetto about it."[59]

Such views were typical of authors of his generation, and they fly in the face of more recent efforts to constitute Jewish American literature as an academic field, emphasizing continuities between Jewish writers and their distinction from non-Jewish writers—often accompanied by an emphasis on the Protestant "literary establishment" that resented their incursions. (Less often acknowledged is the extent of Jewish leadership in the field of publishing.) I do not mean to question the legitimacy of such efforts but rather to point out how different was the cultural ecology of the 1940s.

Like Bellow, Arthur Miller did not consider himself a "Jewish writer"; he was "a Jew who writes."[60] In a March 1948 article for *Jewish Life*, reproducing a speech to the American Committee of Jewish Writers, Artists, and Scientists, he explained that "The cords which bind any people together to the degree that warrants their being called homogeneous nations or people have been so loosened and cut as to leave the Jewish writer with no other identity than his American identity."[61] And this speech was given not long after he had published a novel highlighting anti-Semitism. A biographer presents it as a peculiarly ambivalent self-presentation peculiar to Miller, but in fact the attitude was widely shared.

In February 1944, shortly before being incorporated into *Commentary*, the *Contemporary Jewish Record* published a "symposium" on the importance of specifically Jewish identity to the work of Jewish authors under age forty, with Muriel Rukeyser leading off. She began by recounting her family background, which did not hold to the typical pattern of recent immigration from Europe or Russia; her American-born parents were thoroughly assimilated, and she grew up with virtually no notion of Jewish difference. "I had no idea of what a Christian was. . . . I did not know what a Jew was, nor that the word could be used in contempt." Although her mother had suddenly become religious at one point, Rukeyser found more stimulation in the Bible than in the synagogue, and was mostly bored by the Reform Judaism she encountered. "I do not know how representative I am of any group in Jewish life. I was brought up without any reason to be proud of being Jewish, and then was told to be proud; without any reason for shame, and then saw that people were ashamed." While acknowledging her ethnic Jewishness, Rukeyser viewed it as relatively insignificant to her writing:

I have always accepted the fact that the treatment of minorities is a good test of democracy, or any other system. I do not believe that is a particularly Jewish idea. . . . On the way out of adolescence, I searched, as others do, for ancestors. I felt, then and now, that if one is free, that freedom can extend to a certain degree into the past, and one may choose one's ancestors, to go on with their wishes and their fight. But I do not think that Jews are any more responsive to any of these ideas than are Christians.[62]

Rukeyser concedes that with the rise of anti-Semitism, a Jew cannot help but think of the struggle of the Jews for life and freedom, or to establish a home in Palestine on socialist principles, but for her in this context Jewishness functions chiefly as a bulwark against any sort of chauvinism or ethnic narrowing of humanistic concern. Assuming rightly one's responsibility as a Jew means guaranteeing oneself "not only against fascism, but against many kinds of temptation to close the spirit."[63]

Alfred Kazin, of very different background from Rukeyser, came to similar conclusions. "I learned long ago to accept that fact that I was Jewish without being a part of any meaningful Jewish life or culture. . . . The writing I have been most deeply influenced by . . . has no direct associations in my mind with Jewish culture; it has every association, of course, with the fact that, like many another American, I have had to make my own culture."[64]

In *A Walker in the City* (1951), Kazin would approvingly cite Thorstein Veblen expressing "the hope that the Jews would never form a nationalistic movement of their own, since that would be a loss for world culture." In an essay of 1919 reprinted in *Contemporary Jewish Record* in 1944, Veblen had written (as Kazin quotes) that it is only when the gifted Jew escapes from his separate cultural environment and "falls into the alien lines of gentile inquiry and becomes a naturalized, though hyphenate, citizen in the republic of learning, that he comes into his own as a creative leader in the world's intellectual enterprise."[65] Alluring as it is in many ways, to Veblen (and apparently Kazin at that moment) the establishment of a separate Jewish nation along Zionist lines would be a loss for all; the greatness of the Jewish intellectuals derives not from an insular self-pride and nationalism but from their critical temperament, skepticism toward settled opinion, deriving in part from learning that Jewish traditions themselves have no grounding in absolute truth; they thus become skeptics of all absolutes more readily than others. Kazin considered this line of thinking a self-portrait on the part of Veblen, who was not Jewish, but he also knew it fit his own case perfectly.

(On a related note, in 1943, Daniel Aaron earned the first doctorate in Harvard's new History of American Civilization program,

> which signalized my merger with the USA and my dehyphenation. . . . I was now lumped with what the Frenchman Crevecoeur called [in 1782] "this promiscuous breed, that race now called American," and I was acting the role of licensed practitioner of American studies in the United States and elsewhere. But there was still something of the outside observer in my disposition, a felt affinity with Thorstein Veblen's "renegade Jew."[66]

He would be one of the founding figures of American studies and the founding president of the Library of America.)

Although Lionel Trilling grew up with a strong consciousness of being Jewish and was raised in an Orthodox household, he attested,

> I cannot discover anything in my professional intellectual life which I can trace back to my Jewish birth and rearing. I do not think of myself as a "Jewish writer." I do not have it in mind to serve by my writing any Jewish purpose. I should resent it if a critic of my work were to discover in it either faults or virtues which he called Jewish.[67]

In his role as citizen his Jewishness was "a point of honor," but not in the sense of pride in a great historical identity and tradition, only as a point of resistance to hatred and persecution. In the face of the decimation of Jews in Europe, Trilling acknowledges the "gracelessness" of such an admission, which he suspects he shares with most other Jewish American writers, but he cannot regret it. Having once served on a journal concerned with enhancing Jewish cultural self-consciousness that above all attacked "the sin of 'escaping' the Jewish heritage," he discovered that its effect was to foster "a willingness to be provincial and parochial," encouraging well-off Jews to become "one of the most self-indulgent and self-admiring groups it is possible to imagine."[68]

Louis Kronenberger, a drama critic for *PM* and *Time*, observed that the occasion of being asked to contribute to the symposium had made him realize that he "had never previously connected my race with my profession—that I had never thought of myself as a Jewish writer. . . . I have never regarded most other Jews who write as Jewish writers either." Racism or anti-Semitism has turned many Jewish writers into passionate liberals or radicals, "but by doing so it has made them the less Jewish in their approach. For they have seen anti-Semitism as merely one facet of intolerance, and discrimination as but one facet of injustice."[69] Overwhelmingly, even when contributors to the forum attributed a "difference" in their writing to Jewishness, it was not so much in reference to heritage, literary form, technique, language, or even history but rather as making them passionate defenders of freedom and "toleration." Yet Howard Fast, who said as much of himself, added that "too many Jews fall into a sort of soul-sickness, whereby they become the center of a universe—a dark universe where forces are pro-Jewish or anti-Jewish, where Jews are hated or persecuted or tolerated or loved—and so on, ad infinitum."[70] He could see no valid difference between the work of Jews and non-Jews. If Jews have been persecuted, so have other national minorities worldwide, notably Negroes in the United States, and Jewish writers should join hands with others who combat oppression everywhere.

Jo Sinclair's first novel, *Wasteland*, ends up making a nearly identical argument. It won the prestigious Harper's Prize for a first book and a rave review by her literary idol Richard Wright in *PM* as well as a fan letter: "I'm not one to write letters to other writers," he wrote.

> Usually, I never even feel the impulse to do so; but when I finished your "Wasteland" I thought that I ought to let you know that I think it great. Honesty such as you put into words is seldom seen. . . . You have said about the Jewish family what I've been trying to say about Negro families. And you said it well, poetically. I don't know what others will say to

you about what you've written; maybe you'll get some of the hot blasts I've gotten and grown used to. But that doesn't matter. You are right. . . . The kind of glory you are going to get will have in it the sting of bitterness. But keep on.[71]

Wasteland follows the struggle of a "passing" Jewish newspaper photographer for self-acceptance and escape from the "ghetto" of shame about his working-class Jewish family.

John Brown (born Jacob Brown, the surname being an Anglicization of Braunowitz, although "John Brown" also alludes to the abolitionist martyr) lacks "identity." All of the action is narrated in the context of Brown's sessions with a psychotherapist, chiefly by way of the therapist's record of their conversations. The narrative method subtly shifts within each episode, however, from the therapist's notes to a free indirect discourse hovering closer to the subjectivity of Brown himself.

Brown has undertaken therapy at the urging of his sister Deborah/ Debby, who has preceded John in overcoming shame not only about her family background but about her queer sexuality and former gender confusion. (She has always felt like a boy and dresses and wears her hair like one.) Debby functions as a kind of coach and role model who leads John to a Jewish "coming out" that ends up also being a resurgence of pride in his family coupled with full integration of his sense of Jewishness with Americanism.

What brought John to the therapist is his fear that his nephew Bernie will inherit the same "wasteland" he feels he inhabits because of what he perceives as the futility of his family members' lives. His role as youngest son in the yearly *seder* on Passover, which falls on his birthday, is central to this problem. It had been sacred to him growing up, but in adolescence he came to feel ashamed of his family at about the same time he began working at a newspaper, in an all-gentile environment. He had changed his name from Jake to John or Jack and began "passing." And then the *seder* had been spoiled for him when he realized one year that no one in the family was paying attention as he read from the Haggadah at his appointed time. A long period of shame about being Jewish followed, in which he perceived his working-class parents as "dirty Jews" and was embarrassed that his sister Roz worked as a nightclub waitress. He grew afraid that his nephew Bernie would be "wasted" like himself.

To overcome the "wasteland" within himself—a self-imposed "ghetto"—and help his nephew Bernie avoid a similar fate, John needs to gain pride in himself and his family. And this very journey to self-acceptance has the effect of integration with "American" society (*as* a Jew) and the world at large. John's conversion, which coincides with his coming out as Jewish at work, also coincides with his actively promoting racial integration between blacks and whites. When he takes Bernie to a boxing match after his conversion and hears Bernie making a racist comment, he immediately corrects him and counsels him to root for whichever fighter is most deserving regardless of race.

The plot builds toward its climax when he enlists in the armed forces on his birthday and participates once again in the Passover *seder* with his family. The psychiatrist writes in his journal that Jake had "begun to think in more universal patterns. The byplay at the fights concerning the Negro, and Bernie's attitude toward this subject, make a good beginning. S [Jake] has begun to see the larger ghettos of the world in relation to his own." For the resurrected Jacob Brown, serving in the armed forces amounts to joining others to "wipe out" ghettos everywhere. Proud of his enlistment, in the conclusion of the novel Debby tells him, "There are plenty of ghettos. . . . Anywhere you look you can see them. Maybe it takes a war to wipe them all out." And Jake replies, "I'd like to wipe them out, all right . . . Any kind. Every single one of them."[72]

Jacob's vocation as a photographer and Debby's as a writer are also central to the novel. While he climbs the ladder of success at work on the basis of his photographs for stories, Jacob privately takes photos for himself of scenes to which he finds himself viscerally drawn. This urge to a more self-expressive use of the camera parallels his internal transformation. A foreshadowing of his own "integration," for example, comes when he observes his mother and father in the kitchen reading the *Jewish World* and thinks of framing a shot with the Yiddish print in view and captioning it "AMERICANS, EVENING." Watching his mother pray on a Friday night, once again, he thinks of taking a portrait captioned "IN AMERICA THEY PRAY." One evening while his father is reading from the *Jewish World* about the Polish ghetto uprising and the massacre of the Jews, John's mother sighs, "To be a Jew today." The father replies, "Today, yesterday, tomorrow . . . what do they want of us!" The mother responds that she is glad to be a Jew but wants her children to live, and the father rebukes her: "They'll live, they'll live. Do you see one ghetto in America? A woman talks, as if to fools!" Jake wants suddenly to photograph them and make the caption, "AMERICA, AMERICA!"—which, by the way, was the title of the final chapter of Kazin's *On Native Grounds*, dealing with the documentary literature and photography of the 1930s.[73]

John has not been able to understand why Debby, whom he looks up to, would write on "Negro" subjects. Her first story (like Jo Sinclair's own) was about the lynching of a Negro and published in *New Masses*. Their family had never had much contact with Negroes. Yet Debby identifies with them and is drawn, she says, to "unfortunates . . . The strange people, the ones who are despised, or condemned, or lost." John's eyes drop "as if she had said 'people like me.'" John identifies with her as an artist, saying "That's just like me with my camera!" He describes the photos he takes for himself, about which he has never spoken before. "They're not like the stuff I take for the paper. Nothing at all like that. They're—queer. You know what I mean?"[74]

The conversation aids John's development, and he begins sharing his work. As he grows in understanding of himself and his family, Jake begins taking the photographs of his family he had once only dreamed of taking. One is of his parents in the kitchen, entitled "AMERICANS IN KITCHEN, EVENING." Another is of Debby with pen and paper, "YOUNG WRITER." The psychiatrist, with whom Jake shares this photo, says, "I'm glad you didn't title it differently" and points out that not long ago he would have captioned it "YOUNG LESBIAN" or "PORTRAIT OF A DEGENERATE." Jake says that he no longer thinks of her in terms of "man" or "woman"—he thinks of her as a writer first.[75]

In *Wasteland*, all "ghettos" interlock, and the goal is to "wipe them out," to create a common world. When Debby and Jake go to give blood together for the war effort, Debby says, "When I give blood I feel as if I'm giving it for Jews, too. Jews like Ma, who never had a break. Never. And I'm giving the pint for Negroes. . . . For people like me. . . . It's like giving your blood against any kind of segregation there is in the world." Noting that the authorities keep "Negro" and "white" blood separate, she seethes, "They make little ghettos for a thing like blood. When I give my pint, Jack, it's against that, too. Dead against it. Some day they'll know they can't do a thing like that."[76] After giving blood, they both feel "one with the world," and at the same time Jack asks Debby to call him "Jake" from now on. The psychiatrist notes in his journal:

> Not only has he, an individual, offered himself to a major thing and been accepted, but his family has offered itself to America and been encompassed. Jewish blood, in his mind not too long ago a despised thing, has been accepted and now flows in the mixture of American blood. S [Jake] has proved to himself, in a most obvious way, that he is a member of a group which is of value to the world. . . . S gave his blood . . . to break down the walls of ghetto. With him, however, the reason was not the universal one of Deborah's; with him it was his individual ghetto, and that of his family. Out of this small reason some day may come the greater issue; his thinking already has stretched to meet the horizons of his sister's.[77]

Psychic wholeness arrives by way of self-acceptance as a Jew (and as "queer") but does not stop there. It leads on to Jake's ability to give of himself as "Everyman." "His acceptance in this role proved of more importance than the Jew and patriot roles, though they stem directly from it. Everyman is alive. He is a member of society, a working part of it; he belongs. . . . Everyman is strong enough to say his right name out loud."[78] Such is the striving toward "universality" by way of self-acceptance in all of one's multidimensionality, a sameness that encompasses without erasing difference. The theme is common to much literature of the 1940s.

Debby's self-identification as a "writer"—not a "Jewish writer" nor a "Lesbian writer"—comports with Jo Sinclair's own self-identity but also with that of many other writers who were Jewish. It is not that she did not also identify as a Jew. Rather, these were two different dimensions of her personal identity. If her Jewishness, and queerness, inflected her writing and her choice of subject matter, it made her no different *as a writer* from others whose experience as gentile, as Negro, as straight, as male, inflected their work. This insistence, difficult and contradictory as it may seem, was ubiquitous and indicates a trajectory of shared aspirations, particularly among "minoritized" writers. The aspiration correlates with Berenice's lament, in *The Member of the Wedding*, that we are all "caught" within limiting social distinctions that are never adequate to our desires. The resulting feelings of alienation become a "universal" condition. This view was so common among secular Jewish writers as to be virtually an article of faith.

As in Robert Duncan's argument concerning "the homosexual in society," which I will discuss in chapter 7, for most Jewish writers one's "differences" are what join one to a shared human consciousness, and the "universal" is an aspiration that emerges at the crossroads of identities—one to be shared across physical and social differences. In Isaac Rosenfeld's *Passage from Home*, the young Jewish protagonist has an epiphany as he walks along a busy street in Chicago:

While I wondered over the diversity of the world as I watched the faces going by, knowing that no two were alike and that no two would ever be alike, I imagined that this fact imposed an extraordinary condition on life. Whatever happened to me, since it would always be different from what happened to another, and never exactly duplicated anywhere in time, had to happen; it was necessary because it was different. God, in whose existence I had profoundly believed as a child, again seemed to me a being I could believe in, at least on this basis. The world was absolutely endless and complex: this was God, the imagination that kept on creating differences, face from face and life from life.[79]

The gulf between persons—"differences so great that to breach them one would have to cross the world itself"—makes it seem impossible that one could strike up an acquaintance across gaps of race, physical condition, culture, social identity, yet, "Nevertheless, people did get to know one another with ease, it seemed a simple thing. But how in God's name was it possible?"[80] The awareness of these gaps derives in part from Bernard's sense of difference as a Jew, but he concludes that it would

> reveal itself to anyone who would inquire softly. I had come to know a certain homelessness in the world, and took it for granted as a part of nature. . . . The world is not entirely yours; and our reply is: very well then, not entirely. There were moments, however, when this minor world was more than universe enough; times such as when grandfather would be raised to nobility, or when the family, gathered of a holiday, would distil so rare and joyful a spirit that all the assurance which had been lacking would rush back in flood, and one could feel the presence of God in it, and one could cry, "This is reality, truth, beauty, freedom! What has the rest of the world to compare?" but then, this too would vanish, and I would ask, "What am I?"[81]

The specificity of his Jewishness—at key moments, Jewish ritual offers an ecstatic sense of connectedness, uniting mind, body, and spirit—becomes a passageway to an existential illumination about Bernard's connection with others in time and space and to wonder about what it means to *be* in any form, embodied, homeless, yet free in the presence of others. Jewishness as *separation* drops away.

For Rosenfeld, as for some African American authors of the time and for William and Henry James in an earlier generation, universals are always themselves in the making, so the universal (to the radical empiricist cosmopolitan) is not some fixed point to which particulars are reduced.[82] The universal remains "on the highway," to borrow Emerson's phrase, and one's own attempt to compose particulars into a particular order (what Stevens called a "rage to order"), or to finding a stopping place, is open to sudden transformation by ongoing experience.

Rosenfeld, considered by many of his cohort the wunderkind of the decade, made a specialty of alienation and the search for ecstasy, living an ultrabohemian life like none of the other New York intellectuals of his day, until he died at the age of thirty-eight in 1956. According to an oft-repeated story, when Saul Bellow learned he had won a Nobel Prize, the first thing he told a close friend was, "It should have been Isaac."[83] Rosenfeld called the 1940s "an age of enormity" and was thus, according to Theodore Solotaroff, a "deeply representative figure" of that decade.[84] His alienation was a kind of meta-Jewish one, the passage from home a necessary distancing from Jewish culture without any alternate harbor. In his one novel, the protagonist returns home at last to reconcile with his father and his heritage only to find it impossible. Steven J. Zipperstein judges *Passage from Home* "the most psychologically probing fictional analysis in English of the making of a Jewish intellectual" before the fiction of Philip Roth. "It is a study of what it feels like for a thinking person to come of age, to become aware of the grim cost of self-awareness: its erasure of childhood, the dismantling of the old-style Jewish patriarchy, the move into a life of freedom that is enticing and also, almost invariably, lonely."[85]

The young Trotskyist Irving Howe was so moved by it that it launched him into literary criticism. "The Lost Young Intellectual: A Marginal Man, Twice Alienated," sent unsolicited to *Commentary*, offered a passionate meditation on the novel and would be his first published critical essay.[86] To Diana Trilling, *Passage from Home* evaded the traps of the "Jewish genre novel" by treating Jewishness "as simply another facet of the already sufficiently complicated business of being a human being." In prior "Jewish fiction," Trilling charged, characters "are allowed only that kind of personal drama which reflects their drama as *a people*"—all difficulties are "assimilated to the parent problem of the relation of a subordinate social group to the dominant culture." In contrast, *Passage from Home* achieves a Jamesian complexity and universality in its exploration of the "moral nature of the early educative process."[87] There can be little doubt that Rosenfeld was striving for just such "universality" without in any way "assimilating" to WASP literary standards.

The lack of a strong sense of Jewish literary identity troubled later critics during the rise of identity politics in the academy, beginning with Leslie Fiedler, who in 1975 complained that the characters in Arthur Miller's *Death of a Salesman* are "crypto-Jewish"—"characters who are in habit, speech, and condition of life typically Jewish-American, but who are presented as something else—general Americans."[88] Regardless of whether one agrees with Fiedler's notion that the Lomans are "typically Jewish-American" rather than "general Americans," the observation has value in that *Death of a Salesman* has, since the night of its first performance, been regarded as a quintessentially "American" play. I should add that a similar critique was leveled in 1951 by an actor, George Ross, in *Commentary* while reviewing a Yiddish production/translation of the play in Brooklyn by Joseph Buloff entitled *Toyt fun a Salesman*. Fiedler may well have known of this production and/or the review. Ross felt the Yiddish version superior to Miller's play, even calling the Yiddish redaction the true "original" (which, of course, it was not).[89] Insofar as this judgment can be persuasive but has not gained traction, it indicates to what extent Jewish writers like Miller convincingly assimilated "American" culture to their own. Rather than effecting a "Jewish renaissance," Jewish writers and critics of the 1940s profoundly shaped conceptualizations of the "American-ness" of American literature.

Revealingly, at about the same time that scholars started critiquing playwrights like Arthur Miller for presenting Jewish characters in "general American disguise," others began viewing Tennessee Williams's plays as "closeted" gay dramas, and African Americanists began interpreting texts on nonblack or interracial subjects by African American authors as either bogus attempts at a "white" universalism or camouflaged treatments of African Americans. The evidence suggests a more interesting intellectual drama, mostly outside the academy, crossing many lines of social identity and hoisting a standard in which the freedom, security, and self-expression of "minorities" (including minorities within minorities) held the central place—at the crossroads, so to speak, of what might become a new planetary humanism, perceiving the sanctity of human beings not as abstract individuals but as inherently social, embodied and embedded in social relations, yet with passages toward "universality" nonetheless.

The critique of liberalism in terms of the "universal" (and therefore empty, nonexistent, or presumptively straight white male) subject, so common in our own time, was well known to writers of the forties, especially Jewish writers. It arrived on American shores in Sartre's series of three articles in *Commentary* in 1948, derived from his book *Réflexions sur la question juive* (published in English as *Anti-Semite and Jew*). The first essay opened with his attack on the "democrat," by which he had in mind the French liberal who adheres to Enlightenment ideals of universal human rights. Although, in actuality, presumptively Christian and "French," this liberal subject is theoretically stripped of all particular qualities, abstracted from his or her existential situation. That situation, for Sartre, is inextricable from the actual human subject. For contemporary Jews in France, according to Sartre, that situation is determined by anti-Semitism—not just the anti-Semitism of the anti-Semite but the *structural* anti-Semitism of French society, in which the "human" was presumptively Christian French, and Jews at best tolerated as long as they were not too Jewish. Thus French liberals of Christian background "accepted" Jews on the basis of a liberal humanism that ignored their Jewishness, despite the fact that their "Jewishness" was always on trial. The assimilation of Jews into liberal French society, in other words, was a play-act in bad faith. The Jew was still regarded and accepted *as a Jew*. And Jews who tried to play the role realized themselves at some level that this was the reality of their situation, making them inauthentic. Sartre argued that the situation of the Jew demanded open revolt as the only route to authenticity. This revolt would make the Jew authentically Jewish and at the same time authentic as a human being.

In 1949, *Commentary* published Harold Rosenberg's passionate reply, "Does the Jew Exist?" Rosenberg argued that the Jew *had a history* and stories deriving from that history, directly contradicting Sartre's argument. A Jew's identity as a Jew certainly was affected by a long history of anti-Semitism, yet the Christian anti-Semite did not define Jewish experience and consciousness. Rosenberg emphasized stories, historical consciousness, and family relations as the integuments of modern Jewish identity, not victimhood. He also objected to Sartre's dualistic division between the "authentic" and the "inauthentic" Jew. Sartre's argument, in fact, depended on an equation between being French and *not* being Jewish, an equation Rosenberg rejected—especially with respect to the American Jew's contemporary relationship to the United States, in which anti-Semitism hardly defined "American-ness" in the way it defined "French-ness." (Rosenberg allowed that Sartre's essay had some partial justification in the newly liberated but still highly anti-Semitic France of 1944, when he wrote it.) Thus Jews had many ways of being Jewish without being "inauthentic"; they had what one might call forms of "ontological resistance" deriving from their own history and varied ways of interpreting and sharing experience. At the same time, for writers like Rosenberg, or Isaac Rosenfeld, or Saul Bellow, to be "authentically" Jewish was no different from being "authentic," tout court. The issue of authenticity and the threat to authenticity by victimology applies to the gentile Kirby Allbee in *The Victim* as much as to Asa Leventhal.

The point of Sartre's analysis of Jewishness and anti-Semitism correlates with his statement in the introduction to the anthology *Orphée noir* (1948) that provoked Frantz Fanon's reply in *Black Skin, White Masks*, now foundational in black diaspora theory. There, as in his essays on the anti-Semite and the Jew, he asserted that the Negro as "other" was constituted by the objectification of their white oppressors, who presumed the *universal* human position as their own. In a similar spirit paralleling Rosenberg's, in the 1952 essay "L'expérience vécue du noir" (The lived experience of the black), translated into English as "The Fact of Blackness," Fanon would argue that the black man's existence was not entirely defined by others, by the whites' antiblackness. Sartre's argument ironically placed the white man at the center of the human situation:

> For not only must the black man be black; he must be black in relation to the white man. Some critics will take it on themselves to remind us that this proposition has a converse. I say that this is false. The black man has no ontological resistance in the eyes of the white man.

Overnight the Negro has been given two frames of reference within which he has had to place himself. His metaphysics, or, less pretentiously, his customs and the sources on which they were based, were wiped out because they were in conflict with a civilization that he did not know and that imposed itself on him.[90]

The black man's "ontological resistance" derives from his past, from his cultures (various as they in fact are), from the universally human desire to "find meaning in things" and "to attain to the source of the world," and from relationships that cannot be *defined* by white oppression—either negatively or positively—however extreme that oppression is.[91] That is, "black" identity is not entirely constituted in relation to that other abstraction, "whiteness," the presumptive equivalent of "antiblackness." (Rosenberg, in a related vein, critiqued Sartre's conception of the concentration camp as definitive of the relationship between anti-Semite and Jew.) But neither is the converse true: people termed "white" are not constituted entirely in relation to putative "blackness." Sartre's "two frames of reference" for the Negro are inadequate—just as, in Rosenberg's view, Sartre's absolutism about a choice between "authenticity" and "inauthenticity" for the Jew was wrongheaded, placing a presumptively and similarly reductive Christian "Frenchness" at the center.

Toward the conclusion of "The Fact of Blackness," Fanon relates his position to that of the Jew in relation to Sartre's *Anti-Semite and Jew*, having recognized in that book's description of anti-Semitism something relevant to antiblackness:

At first thought it may seem strange that the anti-Semite's outlook should be related to that of the Negro-phobe. It was my philosophy professor, a native of the Antilles, who recalled the fact to me one day: "Whenever you hear anyone abuse the Jews, pay attention, because he is talking about you." And I found that he was universally right—by which I meant that I was answerable in my body and in my heart for what was done to my brother. Later I realized that he meant, quite simply, an anti-Semite is inevitably anti-Negro.[92]

The relationship of Fanon's critique of Sartre to Rosenberg's is all the more significant for having not been a matter of "influence" between the two. In a 1966 interview, Saul Bellow took issue with Sartre's position in the same terms as Rosenberg and Fanon: "for Sartre, the Jew exists because he is hated, not because he has a history, not because he has origins of his own—but simply because he is designated, created, in his Jewishness by an outrageous evil."[93]

It is worthwhile in this context to look back at the opening essay of the first issue of *Commentary*. There, in 1945, John Dewey (a devout Protestant in his youth) replied to what he perceived as a dangerous separation of the "individual" from the "social" in the long history of the West, beginning with a division between "ends" and "means," favoring the former and associating it with "spirit," while "means" became associated with the material and the body. This division then became essential to a division in the notion of the human being, assigning ultimate value to a spirit independent of those social relations and material processes without which human beings simply cannot exist. Both laissez-faire capitalism and the "collectivist" reactions against it in the form of fascism and Soviet-style communism were practical symptoms of this separation of "the individual" from "the social" in Western humanism. In turn, the sudden conversion of many erstwhile communists, reacting against the betrayal of Stalinism, to a sanctification of "the individual" could only perpetuate the same disastrous division. (Thus began the rise of what came to be called neoconservatism.) No human being exists as an abstract individual—a fallacy that Western thought initiated by dividing "essential" spirit from "inessential" matter. Dewey countered that we are all what we are in relation to others, and as *embodied beings*. The "material," the "social," and the "individual" cannot be segregated from one another when taking into account the whole human being.[94]

Dewey's position comports with that of the Jewish writers of the day in their complex negotiations of the relationship between ethnic identity, religious identity, the ideal of universality or a planetary humanism, and aesthetics. Aesthetics do derive from heritage but also from exploration beyond the boundaries of the group and therefore constantly remake the relationship between individuality and social relations. This was, in fact, a pervasive narrative and thematic pattern in novels by Jewish Americans in the 1940s. It explains why they insisted that they must be free of the imposition of inherited "identity" even if they neither could nor would ever be independent of it. One could be American, and Jewish, and a writer—as so many insisted—without being a "Jewish American writer." There would be neither "renaissance" nor "ice age," but American literary culture would be, in part, Jewish through and through.

6

A RISING WIND

....

"Literature of the Negro" and Civil Rights

I n *After the Lost Generation* (1951), a critical study of fiction by authors who came of age in the 1940s, John W. Aldridge observed that the two "important new discoveries" of his generation in terms of subject matter were racial conflict and homosexuality. "Since the end of the war," he added, "there had been scarcely a serious novel produced which has not at least touched on the dilemma of the Negro or the Jew in modern society."[1] Aldridge charged that the subject was a "minor issue" for the culture at large and therefore inadequate; the writers of the 1940s had not "discovered the age" in which they lived. His remarks epitomize how much had changed that he and most of the scholarly community could not yet absorb.

American entry into the war brought the racial hypocrisy of the United States into bold relief, and antiracists were not about to let the opportunity pass. The NAACP, at the height of its power, with Walter White as president and the sympathetic ear of Eleanor Roosevelt, hammered at the ironies. A. Philip Randolph initiated the March on Washington Movement. When he pressed FDR for civil-rights legislation (with the first lady's support), the president, whose hold on power still depended on keeping the Democratic party from splintering between North and South, said, "Make me do it," and eventually the Fair

Employment Practices Committee (FEPC) was launched, along with a directive banning racial discrimination in the defense industries. But an executive order from the president could hardly change the hearts of white Americans and defense-plant employers. Even after FDR strengthened the FEPC in 1943 to help enforce its policies, it was never fully effective (as Chester Himes's *If He Hollers Let Him Go* attested). Nonetheless, there had never been such a ban on racial discrimination at the federal level, and by the end of the war the percentage of African Americans in defense-industry jobs had tripled, to 8 percent. Such efforts were soon to be rolled back. The FEPC was allowed by the Senate to die in 1946, and repeated efforts through 1950 to renew it would be rebuffed by an increasingly conservative congress. Meanwhile, other government programs such as the Federal Housing Authority had the effect of further entrenching residential segregation across the country.

The Civil Rights Movement of the 1950s and early 1960s had a prehistory as old as the American colonies, but most strategies of that movement, from sit-ins to consumer boycotts and integrated bus rides, were tested in the 1940s.[2] The Congress of Racial Equality was founded in 1942 by students in Chicago following Gandhi's principles of nonviolent direct action. Initially focused on challenging segregation in the North, they organized sit-ins and in 1947 sent a team of eight white and eight black men on a bus trip through the South to test a Supreme Court ruling against segregation in interstate travel. One of them later helped organize the "freedom rides" of 1961.

The battle for integration—not assimilation—set the keynote of the decade in black cultural politics, even when it was organized around black self-empowerment, through consumer boycotts and the like. A belief in the necessity of racial integration pervades the "literature of the Negro" by both black and white authors in the 1940s, pitted against the depth and breadth of American racism.

In *No Day of Triumph*, Saunders Redding relates his conversation with a couple of young men at Alcorn College in Mississippi who are trying to decide whether to enlist in the army or wait to be drafted. "They had been reading in the Negro papers of colored flying units. 'This war,' Ike said, is li'ble to open up things for the colored.' But Willie . . . said, 'It's a gawd-dawg shame it takes a war to do it.'" At Morehouse College, one of the race's finest, Redding finds only "spiritual decay" and thinks often of a Jewish friend's statement that everyone wants a place where they belong, where their spirit is free. Redding slowly realizes that his estrangement from others and theirs from him "was but a failure to realize that we were all estranged from something fundamentally ours. We were all withdrawn from the heady, brawling, lusty stream of culture which had nourished us and which was the stream by whose turbid waters all of America fed."[3]

At the end of the book, Redding's sense of alienation evaporates as he dances in rural Louisiana to Louis Armstrong's orchestra with a young woman named Mencia Melancon. The freedom and vitality in her dancing, and that of the others about them, "breathed the air of freedom . . . and they loved it." This could easily be an epiphany of racial pride and exclusive belonging; twenty years later it most likely would have been. Instead, Redding concludes that "the Negro is only an equation in a problem of many equations, an equally important one of which is the white man. To know and understand and love the Negro is not enough. One must know and understand and love the white man as well."[4]

The values and validities that Redding found "alive and solid" in American Negroes, he asserted, were held in common with others as "the highest common denominator of mankind. . . . They are, unmistakably, integrity of spirit, love of freedom, courage, patience, hope."[5] Freedom and democracy were not finished things, yet they appealed universally as aspirations. Redding's integrationism, finding inspiration in African American music and dance, in no way implies that African Americans must "assimilate" white American cultural values or fit into a predetermined structure, any more than did the work of a young Ralph Ellison as he emerged in the 1940s with a passionate belief in the resources of black vernacular tradition—featured in the best of his early stories, "Flying Home," which imagines a reconciliation between one of the Tuskegee airmen and an elderly black sharecropper who awakens him to the wisdom and dignity passed down through the black folk heritage. The idea was to transform American culture. One literary historian, while admitting that "a windfall of resources did open up and national public attitudes changed" for black writers in the 1940s, charges that "an assumption underlying the discussion about democratizing resources was that blacks would achieve full success when they had assimilated to white American values and cultural models."[6] This may have been true in the political realm, journalism, and popular culture, but it is hard to square with tendencies in the arts.

African American visual arts, nurtured by institutions going back to the 1920s such as the 135th Street branch of the New York Public Library and the Harmon Foundation, acquired a new level of prestige in the 1940s, with the career of the twenty-three-year-old Jacob Lawrence taking off when the Museum of Modern Art exhibited his Great Migration series (1941) and then purchased it jointly with the Phillips Collection in Washington, D.C. What made this historic is that the Phillips and the MoMA were not philanthropic or WPA organizations—they were established private institutions dedicated to modern art as such. Lawrence's paintings referenced the struggle against racism, black folk values and their transformation in the urban North, labor, and cultural resilience. Romare Bearden's first solo show also took place in 1940. While a few black artists of the 1920s and 1930s had enjoyed critical success, Lawrence's rise, at the age of twenty-three, had no precedent. By his early twenties, he had developed a distinctive style between figural composition and abstraction, "modernism" and "folk art," featuring recurring patterns of color and geometry across multiple panels to create sequential narratives drawn mainly from African American history.[7]

Meanwhile, in Chicago the South Side Community Art Center opened in late 1940 with exhibitions and classes. Gordon Parks had his studio in the basement. Eleanor Roosevelt spoke at the inauguration ceremony, and in its first year the center organized twenty-four exhibitions attended by 28,000 people. But there was tension between the black bourgeois trustees and the artists, whose work conflicted with their "uplift" ideology. Artists like Parks, Margaret Goss, and Elizabeth Catlett remembered that there was more cross-racial than cross-class solidarity, and a rebellion by the board, according to Parks, "was always at hand." It was a time, according to Goss, of "black and white unite and fight," or as Catlett recalled, "greater collaboration between Negro and white."[8] According to Goss, such collaborations ended in the 1950s because of anticommunism and the suspicion that any white person associating with black people was a communist.

This was also a dynamic era for black performance on stage. Between 1945 and 1950, according to Paul Nadler, "the American professional theater produced twenty shows on civil rights issues, nine of them on Broadway."[9] Paul Robeson, of the Harlem Renaissance generation, starred as Othello on Broadway in 1943–1944—the first black actor to play the role on the Great White Way. Eleanor Roosevelt attended and wrote about the performance in her newspaper column "My Day." *Variety* reported on the thunderous ovation as an indication "that these times are when the sweep and majesty of artistry and a democracy must encompass racial barriers."[10] The production set a record run for Shakespeare on Broadway that held to 1998; it was the pinnacle of a theater career that would be destroyed by McCarthyism.[11]

In May 1940 Abram Hill founded the Negro Playwrights Company, to be followed by the American Negro Theater, which has been called "the most important, self-contained black theater troupe between the demise of the African Company in 1823 and the birth of the Negro Ensemble Company in 1967."[12] It became a training ground for the likes of Sidney Poitier, Ossie Davis, Ruby Dee, Harry Belafonte, Ann Petry, and Alice Childress. For its first five years, its home was the basement of the 135th Street branch of the New York Public Library, like earlier such efforts going back to the earliest years of the Negro Renaissance.

Yet why should the basement theater of a branch library be a significant incubator of black arts in the United States? According to Langston Hughes, theater production depended on "connections," and these were hard to make for Negro playwrights, given the segregated social life of the United States and the financial resources required to mount professional theater productions, which in turn depended on ticket sales to fairly well-off, mostly white audiences.[13] Literature required a smaller investment, and the product sold at a modest price in cities across the country.

Events of the 1940s transformed the production and reception of African American literature and of "literature of the Negro" more generally. The sheer quantity of writing concerning civil rights and black life in America expanded, but recognition of its importance grew even more, in part because of a growing African American audience, epitomized by the birth of *Negro Digest* (1942), *Ebony* (1945), and *Jet* (1945) magazines as well as the more short-lived *Negro Story* (1944–1946) and *Negro Quarterly* (1942–1943). W. E. B. Du Bois founded the journal *Phylon* in 1940 as essentially the first black-studies journal. A growth in the number of black bookstores was "one of the healthiest developments" of the 1940s in the view of Langston Hughes.[14] By 1942, no serious white writer dealing with black characters wrote without an awareness of black readers.

In the 1940s, readers interested in black life made a distinction between black-authored and white-authored works, but the "literature of the Negro" was not generally understood to be "African American literature" as we think of it today.[15] *Phylon* carried an article stating optimistically that "Today it is true that the expression 'Negro literature' finds less acceptance among intellectual circles than ever before and that the Negro novelist, writing for both whites and Negroes, is realizing more and more that these two audiences are in actuality one."[16] There was no consensus about what "Negro literature" or "the literature of the Negro" signified. It could include works by black authors on any subject or works on African American subjects by authors of any race. In fact, the most distinguishing feature of "the Negro *in* literature" of the 1940s is the amount of writing by whites dealing centrally with African Americans and the amount of writing by African Americans dealing centrally with white people. For this reason, as a thought experiment against the grain of usual critical practice, and to emphasize the uniqueness of the 1940s, I will often focus in this chapter on such writing, while black-authored work on black subjects that is neglected here is treated throughout other chapters.

In 1949, Langston Hughes and Arna Bontemps published the anthology *The Poetry of the Negro*, made up of three sections, "Negro Poets of the U.S.A.," "Tributary Poems by Non-Negroes," and "The Caribbean." This last section made no distinction between the work of white and black poets, and with regard to the anthology's title, the editors explained that it referred more "to a theme and a point of view than to the racial identity of some of its contributors."[17] Many of the poems in the "Caribbean" section are unconcerned with racial subjects.[18] In contrast, when Bontemps brought out a new edition of the book in 1970, he radically revised the contents to make it more racially focused according to American racial definitions.

The decade of the 1940s saw a flood of fiction and poetry by both blacks and whites dealing with African American life and white racism, carrying on themes from the 1930s but more widely ranging and psychological in approach. Alain Locke wrote in 1939: "Today's literature and art, an art of searching social documentation and criticism, thus becomes a consistent development and matured expression of the trends that were seen and analyzed in 1925."[19] Locke, who had been comprehensively reviewing the "literature of the Negro" since the mid-1920s, had never considered the "Negro renaissance" a purely black enterprise, for he was interested both in the development of black authors and the transformative influence of black culture on American culture and world civilization generally.[20] After some disillusionment in the early 1930s with what today is usually called the "Harlem Renaissance," in the late 1930s and 1940s he was more prone to note continuities and to judge the early phase of the "long" New Negro movement positively.

The same was true of Langston Hughes, who wrote for *Phylon* in 1950:

> By focusing attention on Negro writers and on literature about Negroes, the Negro Renaissance provided a springboard for young Negro writers and for those who wanted to write about Negroes. . . . It can hardly be disputed that the "Renaissance" did a great deal to make possible a public willing to accept Negro problems and Negro art.

The field of magazine writing, in particular, had "opened up considerably" for black writers, and "in many major magazines articles and stories which take something other than the Octavus Roy Cohen line now appear frequently."[21] In fact, echoes of the Negro Renaissance pervade the 1940s, and younger authors like Chester Himes attested to its importance to them.

The 1940s witnessed a major expansion of literature by African Americans, including books that won major honors or were bestsellers. Richard Wright, as Sterling Brown pointed out in 1942, was the first black author to make a living off of writing alone. *Native Son* and *Black Boy* were both Book-of-the-Month Club selections. Ann Petry won the Houghton Mifflin Literary Fellowship for fiction to complete *The Street*, at 1.5 million copies the first bestseller by a black woman. Gwendolyn Brooks's *Annie Allen* (1949) won a Pulitzer Prize. Frank Yerby's *The Foxes of Harrow* was so popular that Blyden Jackson hailed "a great moment in American publishing for Negroes. It is likewise, one can say in all sincerity, an event in the fulfillment of American democracy."[22] Wright's *Black Boy*, even in its reduced state after Wright cut the second part of the story (about one-third of the original *American Hunger*), remained incendiary enough to provoke Senator Theodore Bilbo to rail in Congress: "It should be removed from the book stores; its sales should be stopped." Calling it "a damnable lie from beginning to end," he claimed the book aimed

> to plant the seeds of hate in every Negro in America against the white men of the South or against the white race anywhere, for that matter. That is the purpose. Its purpose is to plant the seeds of devilment and trouble-breeding in the days to come in the mind and heart of every American Negro. Read the book if you do not believe what I am telling you. It is the dirtiest, filthiest, lousiest, most obscene piece of writing that I have ever seen in print.[23]

That it had been chosen by the Book-of-the-Month Club made it all the more dangerous to the American public.

White authors' responses to black authors' works demonstrate the changing professional position and influence of African American writers. Startling new presentations of racial identity by white authors both new and old—most tellingly Lillian Smith, Carson McCullers, William Faulkner, Eudora Welty, and Howard Fast, along with work by the likes of Bucklin Moon as author and anthologist—radically redescribed the "Negro Problem." "Is there really a Negro problem," Bucklin Moon asked in the introduction to *A Primer for White Folks*, "or is it, as Lillian Smith recently suggested . . . actually a white problem?"[24] Smith's essay for the book, "Addressed to White Liberals," demands that white Americans

> look in a new direction for the source of our troubles. We have looked at the "Negro problem" long enough. Now the time has come for us to right-about-face and study the problem of the white man. . . . The white man himself is one of the world's most urgent problems today; not the Negro, not other colored races.[25]

White Southern writers were particularly sensitive to the resemblance of the racial dictatorship of the region to fascist thought and practice. W. J. Cash's *The Mind of the South* (1941) compared white Southern ideology to the fascism of Mussolini and Hitler.[26]

The publication of Richard Wright's *Native Son*, with its choice by the Book-of-the- Month Club, was one of the most consequential events in the history of American book publishing. "The day *Native Son* appeared," wrote the critic Irving Howe,

> American culture was changed forever. No matter how much qualifying the book might later need, it made impossible a repetition of the old lies. . . . Speaking from the black wrath of retribution, Wright insisted that history can be a punishment. He told us the one thing even the most liberal whites preferred not to hear: that Negroes were far from patient or forgiving, that they were scarred by fear, that they hated every moment of their suppression even when seeming most acquiescent, and

that often enough they hated us, the decent and cultivated white men who from complicity or neglect shared in the responsibility for their plight.[27]

Native Son, while fully expressing the nationalist aspirations of the black working class, was fundamentally integrationist. Hugh Gloster situated the novel in relationship to black-authored novels on non-Negro themes, quoting Wright's own statement that Bigger "was not always black": "More than anything else, as a writer, I was fascinated by the similarity of the emotional tensions of Bigger in America and Bigger in Nazi Germany and Bigger in old Russia. All Bigger Thomases, white and black, felt tense, afraid, nervous, hysterical, and restless." Gloster stressed the fact that "Wright's sympathies are comprehensive enough to include all exploited people; and *Native Son* illustrates, perhaps more effectively than any other novel by an American Negro, that it is possible to attack racial oppression and at the same time provide truthful implications for all mankind."[28]

At one point Bigger dreams of a movement led by a Negro Mussolini or Hitler, binding black people together into a powerful force, like the Japanese then conquering China. Yet ultimately Wright rejects this solution to Bigger's isolation, which stems from the way the white/black boundary dominates his relationship to his own feelings and all his human relationships, isolating him not only from others but from himself and his environment. Bigger's feelings of alienation, which helped make *Native Son* so compatible with French existentialism, are inseparable from the enclosure of race and are only overcome when Bigger and Jan Erlone come to *see* each other, in an intimate encounter recognizing each other's entrapment in identities that they cannot escape.

Jan tells Bigger that as he sat in jail for a crime he did not commit, put there because of Bigger's testimony, and grieving for Mary Dalton, "I thought of all the black men who've been killed, the black men who had to grieve when their people were snatched from them in slavery and since slavery. I thought that if they could stand it, then I ought to. . . . I said, 'I'm going to help that guy, if he lets me.'"[29] Jan Erlone sees his own suffering as ultimately deriving from the crimes of white supremacy. The effect on Bigger Thomas is transformative:

> Suddenly, this white man had come up to him, flung aside the curtain and walked into the room of his life. Jan had spoken a declaration of friendship that would make other white men hate him: a particle of white rock had detached itself from that looming mountain of white hate and had rolled down the slope, stopping still at his feet. The word had become flesh. For the first time in his life a white man became a human being to him; and the reality of Jan's humanity came in a stab of remorse: he had killed what this man loved and had hurt him. He saw Jan as though someone had performed an operation upon his eyes, or as though someone had snatched a deforming mask from Jan's face.[30]

Here begins Bigger's growth in consciousness about the meaning of his experience in the context of humanity as a whole.

Jan remains important for Bigger to the end. When Bigger says, "It's over for me," Jan asks, "Don't you believe in yourself?" When Bigger says, "Naw," Jan responds, "You believed enough to kill. You thought you were settling something, or you wouldn't have killed." Bigger thinks, "Did this man believe in him *that* much?"[31] Whereas Boris Max, Bigger's lawyer, delivers a brilliant courtroom speech on the history of white supremacy and capitalism as the contexts in which Bigger was made into who he was, he remains blind to Bigger's human need for meaning and his individual agency. Waiting on death row for his execution, Bigger (echoing Jan's earlier comments) shouts to Max:

> "What I killed for must've been good!" Bigger's voice was full of frenzied anguish. . . . "When a man kills, it's for something. . . . I didn't know I was really alive in this world until I felt things hard enough to kill for 'em. . . . It's the truth, Mr. Max. I can say it now, 'cause I'm going to die. I know what I'm saying real good and I know how it sounds. But I'm all right."[32]

They say goodbye to each other as "Max groped for his hat like a blind man." As Max walks away, Bigger calls after him:

> "Mr. Max!"
> Max paused, but did not look.
> "Tell. . . . Tell Mister. . . . Tell Jan hello. . . ."[33]

That dropping of the "Mister" signifies the uniqueness of his bond with Jan Erlone. Jan alone, Wright later said, really understood Bigger. Wright's next major project, *Twelve Million Black Voices* (1941), would be a collaboration with the white, Jewish photographer Edwin Rosskam, in which Wright wrote that the ties binding black and white Americans together

> are deeper than those that separate us. The common road of hope which we all have traveled has brought us into a stronger kinship than any words, laws, or legal claims. Look at us and know us and you will know yourselves, for *we* are *you*, looking back at you from the dark mirror of our lives.[34]

In the climactic sentence of "Everybody's Protest Novel" (1949), one of James Baldwin's most famous essays, he concludes,

> Bigger's tragedy is not that he is cold or black or hungry, not even that he is American, black; but that he has accepted a theology that denies him life, that he admits the possibility of his being sub-human and feels constrained, therefore, to battle for his humanity according to those brutal criteria bequeathed him at his birth. But our humanity is our burden, our life; we need not battle for it; we need only to do what is infinitely more difficult—that is, accept it. The failure of the protest novel lies in its rejection of life, the human being, the denial of his beauty, dread, power, in its insistence that it is his categorization alone which is real and which cannot be transcended.[35]

This can best be called a strong misreading. It is obtuse to the very burden of *Native Son*. Baldwin's differences from Wright lie not in his attitudes toward the relationship between blackness and humanity but in his aesthetic sensibilities and different views of the functions literature can serve. For Wright had been drawn to the art of fiction by those who used literature as a weapon, Baldwin by the likes of Henry James. As Baldwin later admitted of "Everybody's Protest Novel," his critique was less about Wright than an attempt to work some issues out in his own mind.

Baldwin's voice and emphases emerged in the reviews he wrote for *The Nation*, *New Leader*, *Commentary*, and *Partisan Review* in the late 1940s, in tune with attitudes often exemplified in those journals and partly in response to Wright's imposing example. Throughout the decade black critics had been decrying the "curse of propaganda" in fiction by Negroes. Baldwin—younger, more schooled in the fiction of Henry James and admiring of "high modernism" than most of them—ratcheted that critique up to a new and more furious level. In fiction he liked subtlety, psychological complexity, nuance; his own criticism, however, tended toward Olympian judgments, rhetorical extremes: "Perhaps the measure of the really stupendous inadequacy of the five novels under consideration," begins a review for *Commentary* in 1948, "is the fact that, of them all, the most impressive and the most valid is Millen Brand's quite unremarkable *Albert Sears*."[36] Chester Himes "seems capable of some of the worst writing on this side of the Atlantic."[37] Twenty-four years old and having scarcely published anything so far, Baldwin excoriates the "debasement of literary standards" in America, due in part to the wide gulf between the "personal or creative individual and that vast culture of the masses" that the writer cannot ignore.[38] To such conditions he attributes the ubiquity of the protest novel, his prime target in the years when his career began taking shape.

Baldwin's use of "we" can be as slippery (and prolific) as that of Lionel Trilling, whose essays in the same journals were earning him a central role in American literary culture. In *The New Leader*, critiquing Himes's *Lonely Crusade*, Baldwin concludes that in literature of the Negro even Bigger Thomas "is becoming irrelevant," for the black man is as many-faceted "as we ourselves are, as individual, with our ambivalences and insecurities, our struggles to be loved. He is now an American and we cannot change that; it is our attitudes which must change both towards ourselves and him."[39] Who is this "we"? Readers of journals like *The New Leader*? White Americans? Educated Americans in general?

Baldwin moved to Europe in 1948 on a Rosenwald Fellowship because he "wanted to find out in what way the *specialness* of my experience [as a Negro] could be made to connect me with other people instead of dividing me from them." In search of such connections, he discovered himself to be "as American as any Texas G.I. And I found my experience was shared by every American writer I knew in Paris."[40] As if in acknowledgment of his debt to Wright, the book in which he later reprinted "Everybody's Protest Novel" as the opening salvo bore the title *Notes of a Native Son*.

Wright's novel had an enormous impact on William Faulkner. It is impossible to read *Go Down, Moses*—especially the final story of the same title—hard upon *Native Son* and not feel the effect of that book. Samuel Beauchamp (Mollie's grandson) is a Bigger Thomas figure of the zoot-suit generation. Faulkner wrote Wright about *Black Boy* in the fall of 1945:

> I have just read *Black Boy*. It needed to be said, and you said it well . . . as well as it could have been said in this form. Because I think you said it much better in *Native Son*. I hope you will keep on saying it, but I hope you will say it as an artist, as in *Native Son*. I think you will agree that the good lasting stuff comes out of one individual's imagination and sensitivity to and comprehension of the suffering of Everyman, Anyman, not out of the memory of his own grief.[41]

In a 1957 lecture, Sterling A. Brown noticed the shift in Faulkner's novels of the forties, particularly in the treatment of Lucas Beauchamp, through whom Faulkner struggles to get at the interiority of a black character in a way he had never previously done.[42] White Southerners' denial of kinship across racial lines particularly drew Faulkner's attention as a betrayal of humanity. So-called miscegenation is no longer a "tragedy," although it is too much for even so idealized a character as Isaac McCaslin to deal with in *Go Down, Moses*. His attempts to keep himself pure by renouncing property are inadequate, and his inadequacy is nowhere more evident than when confronted by the mistress and child of Roth Edmonds, who lacks the courage to admit his love for her. Ike advises her to find a man of her own race in the North. "Go back North. Marry: a man in your own race. That's the only salvation for you—for a while yet, maybe a long while yet. We will have to wait." The most tortured moment in *Go Down, Moses* (the only book for which Faulkner took a title from black expressive tradition) comes when Ike, who has been built up as the conscience of the white South, simply breaks down in the face of this female descendant of the black and white lines of his family and the heritage of incest. "Old man," she replies, "have you lived so long and forgotten so much that you don't remember anything you ever knew or felt or even heard about love?"[43] This confrontation takes place in the very camp, in the last remnant of the deep woods, that Ike considers his refuge from moral contagion. Yet here his own white shame and guilt come dramatically to light as, in his own way, he pushes the woman out of his sight.

A quasi-parallel occurs in *Absalom, Absalom!* of 1936, but there, where the horror of interracial mixing exceeds that of incest in the mind of the white center of consciousness, one finds a suggestion that such mixing leads to idiocy and decadence. *Go Down, Moses* makes no such prophecy; it leaves the future wide open for the mixed-race child, if taken out of the South. Indeed, while Ike is childless and the "white" side of Carothers McCaslin's descendants headed for extinction in the male line, the "black" descendants survive. Ike says of the woman's child, "It's a boy I reckon. They usually are."[44] Mother and child, moreover, serve as moral judgment on the white father, who refuses to acknowledge them, even though we are given to believe he truly loves the mother. In his moral crisis, an intense misanthropy and self-hatred take hold of him, connected with the specter of German fascism and its American parallels.

In a 1943 letter to his stepson Malcolm Franklin, Faulkner wrote of some African American pilots

> who finally got congress to allow them to learn how to risk their lives in the air. They are in Africa now, under their own negro lt. colonel, did well at Pantelleria, on the same day a mob of white men and white policemen killed 20 negroes in Detroit. Suppose you and me and a few others of us lived in the Congo, freed seventy-seven years ago by ukase; of course we cant live in the same apartment hut with the black folks, nor always ride in the same car nor eat in the same restaurant, but we are free because the Great Black Father says so. Then the Congo is engaged in War with the Cameroon. At last we persuade the Great Black Father to let us fight too. You and Jim say are flyers. You have just spent the day trying to live long enough to learn how to do your part in saving the Congo. Then you come back down and are told that 20 of your people have just been killed by a mixed mob of civilians and cops at Little Poo Poo. What would you think?
>
> A change will come out of this war. If it doesn't, if the politicians and the people who run this country are not forced to make good the shibboleth they glibly talk about freedom, liberty, human rights, then you young men who live through it will have wasted your precious time, and those who don't live through it will have died in vain.[45]

Three key factors explain the increasing centrality of black characters to Faulkner's writing and their increasing complexity in the 1940s: the death of Caroline Barr ("Mammy Callie," as he called her) and his sudden awareness of her separate life and family, his reading of African American literature, and World War II, which struck him as a fundamental challenge to racial tyranny in the United States.

Joseph Blotner has pointed out that "Pantaloon in Black," finished in early 1940, "showed a very different perception of the inner lives of black people from that in the portrayal of Caspey and Simon Strother a dozen years earlier in *Sartoris*."[46] In this story, the white deputy at the end misinterprets all of the black protagonist Rider's actions because he cannot perceive them as motivated by grief over the death of his wife. Intriguingly, in a congratulatory letter to Eudora Welty of April 1943, Faulkner wrote (apparently while drunk): "You are doing all right. I read THE GILDED SIX BITS, a friend loaned me THE ROBBER BRIDEGROOM. I have just bought the collection named GREEN something, haven't read it yet expect nothing of it because I expect from you [*sic*]."[47] "The Gilded Six-Bits" (1933) is actually a story by Zora Neale Hurston, a climactic theme of which is whites' gross miscomprehension of black people and obliviousness to their grief—much as in "Pantaloon in Black."

Caroline Barr, to whom Faulkner would dedicate *Go Down, Moses*, died in January 1940. The phrasing of his eulogy for her matches that applied to Mollie Beauchamp in "The Fire and the Hearth."[48] The Faulkners took her to her cabin after she suffered a stroke, and her many children and grandchildren came to hold vigil until she died.[49] Faulkner seemed suddenly aware of how much of her life was outside his ken. His sermon for her funeral speaks eloquently and humbly of her importance to his life, yet with an awareness that this was not all her life meant in the larger scheme of things. Although Faulkner never fully outgrew his paternalistic racial attitudes, the shock of this recognition infuses his fiction after 1940. Blotner informs us that even toward the end of his life Faulkner "would talk of the difficulty of understanding Negroes' thoughts and feelings, compelled as they had been to develop patterns of concealment from white people."[50]

One detects Faulkner's awareness of an educated black readership in the portrayal of black characters throughout *Go Down, Moses, Intruder in the Dust*, and *Requiem for a Nun*. Indeed, one might call a number of these characters excellent "readers" of white character in a way far more complex than one finds in Faulkner's earlier fiction. The characters come in a greater variety; the stories convey more of a sense of the whites being watched and judged and manipulated by the black characters, which parallels the fact that white writers are more and more aware of black readers judging their work. The black characters withhold speech from the whites even as they claim agency and in various ways seek to manipulate or defeat the whites who subordinate, dominate, or oppose them.

Ralph Ellison, who was always highly critical of the racial ideology of Faulkner's early novels, had a very different opinion of *Intruder in the Dust* and the film inspired by it. *Intruder in the Dust*, he claimed in 1949, "is the only film [about black life by a white author] that could be shown in Harlem without arousing unintended laughter. For it is the only one . . . in which Negroes can make complete identification with their screen image. Interestingly, the factors that make this identification possible lie in its depiction not of racial but of human qualities."[51]

Human qualities? In recent years that phrase has come under suspicion in academic circles as a mask for a false, "liberal" universalism that keeps an unmarked whiteness at the center of the human. But Ellison was hardly the only African American author who embraced humanism as central to the project of black self-definition and liberation.[52] The equation worked the other way around as well, in terms of white writers as reviewed by black authors. When Richard Wright lauded Carson McCullers's *The Heart Is a Lonely Hunter*, he particularly marveled at "the astonishing humanity that enables a white writer, for the first time in Southern fiction, to handle Negro characters with as much ease and justice as those of her own race."[53] Gertrude Stein paid him a similar compliment after being loaned a copy of *Black Boy* out of an army library: "For the first time an American negro writing as a negro about negroes writes not as a negro but as a man. . . . It is the first really creative book written except my own in this period."[54] And to a reporter for the *Chicago Defender* she said, "The theme is the Negro but the treatment is that of a creative writer. . . . Wright's material doesn't dominate him. With most Negro writers the Negro is on top of the writer."[55] The highest praise Wright could heap on Theodore Dreiser for a luncheon in his honor was to call him "the greatest living humanist in America."[56] James Baldwin insisted, in a withering review of a novel by Shirley Graham, that "Relations between Negroes and whites, like any other province of human experience, demand honesty and insight; they must be based on the assumption that there is one race and that we are all part of it."[57] This notion of "humanism" does not entail the Renaissance and

Enlightenment concept that "man" (and, in particular, European "man") is the measure of all things; it is rather focused, in a more limited sense, on asserting a universal humanity, a potential for mutual understanding, and the ethical responsibility that persons have toward one another, regardless of race and nation.

A particularly telling case in point is Robert Hayden's great poem "Middle Passage." It first appeared in the fall 1945 issue of *Phylon*, but in a version that differs from the one we know today, because Hayden made extensive revisions for its publication seventeen years later in *A Ballad of Remembrance* (1962) and his *Collected Poems* (1985).[58] A major difference lies in the attention paid to the African kings who sold their captives to European traders. A key refrain of the original poem reads, "our gods false to us, our kings betraying us"—phrases that disappear in the later poem. An introductory section of five stanzas preceded what is now the beginning of the poem, and section 2 of the poem we know today, presenting the reminiscences of a white sailor in the slave trade, was introduced by the following:

Borne from that land—

    O Ancient mother made the whore of greed,
  of death the glittering concubine;
  O fiery kingdoms dazzling-dark with sun,
  thy smouldering riches cursing and consuming thee—

Our gods false to us, our kings betraying us
for rum and mirrors, muskets and a dream of power.

Rio Pongo   Gambia   Whydah   Calabar,
Gold Coast and Ivory Coast:
wound-vivid points upon the map of man's cruelty to man.[59]

Also missing from the second section in the later version is this concluding stanza:

Our gods false to us, our kings betraying us,
scattering us like seeds
to flower stubbornly in alien ground.[60]

These introductory and concluding stanzas framed the poem with a specifically African American narrator who was removed from the later version. They also framed the slave trade more comprehensively in the context of human greed—African kings' and European capitalists'. The first text emphasizes more than the later one both the kings' betrayals and the "flowering" of African Americans in the alien land. The missing lines resonate powerfully with one of the poem's key refrains in both versions: "Voyage through death, / Voyage whose chartings are unlove."

Hayden deleted or altered specifically the lines framing individual sections and framing the poem as a whole—making the poem less sermonic, more "modernist" and collage-like, and with no framing African American voice. Notice the difference in the conclusion of the poem. What we read today is the following:

The deep immortal human wish,
the timeless will.

Cinquez its deathless primaveral image,
life that transfigures many lives.

Voyage through death
to life upon these shores.[61]

In 1945 the conclusion read:

The deep immortal human wish,
the timeless will:

Cinquez its superb Homeric image,
life that transfigures many lives,

life that defines our history upon these shores.
Borne from that land—
           our gods false to us, our kings betraying us—
like seeds the storm winds carry
to flower stubbornly upon these shores.[62]

The poem is unquestionably more dramatic and striking in its leaner version, but it is also different in ideological terms, maybe owing to the context of decolonization in the early 1960s. Yet both versions center on a "deep immortal human wish." Hayden, who embraced the Ba'hai faith, always remained a "humanist" in this sense.

He would, on a different note, always emphasize the Americanness of African Americans and famously resisted being labeled a "Negro poet" in the late 1960s, when this was a much-reviled option. In 1945 the "American" emphasis was ubiquitous in African American writing (which did not imply patriotism). The related emphasis on the betrayal of African kings in the earlier poem also resonates more with the Marxist strains of the time, which emphasized class oppression. Cinquez is here a transfiguring rebel for defining black history in the United States as a new birth apart from "false gods" and feudal oppression *as well* as in resistance to racial slavery. Yet the "timeless will" of Cinquez is above all "the deep immortal human wish."

The belief in the universality of "human qualities"—in the years when the historic Universal Declaration of Human Rights was drafted and passed by the United Nations—lies behind the impulse of black authors to write texts that were not centered on "the black experience," texts that are rarely discussed in scholarship let alone reprinted or anthologized. Never before or since has this impulse been so common.[63] These novels tell us more about the new mood concerning literary engagement with race in the 1940s than any others. Since the Harlem Renaissance, many black authors had chafed against the expectation that they write exclusively on "Negro" subjects. But as Robert Bone pointed out in a 1958 study, "Thirteen of the thirty-three Negro novels written between 1945 and 1952 have a predominantly or exclusively white cast of characters."[64]

In a 1950 interview for the black journal *Phylon*, Langston Hughes was asked if he saw anything promising about the state of black letters: "The most heartening thing for me . . . is to see Negroes writing works in the general American field, rather than dwelling on Negro themes solely. Good writing can be done on almost any theme."[65] Hughes would include several tales of this sort in his long-lived anthology *Best Short Stories by Negro Writers* (1967). Willard Motley's *Knock on Any Door*, which centered on an Italian working-class family in Chicago's Near West Side (where Motley himself lived), became a bestseller and the basis of a hit film. Ann Petry's *Country Place* was about mainly white characters in a town based on Old Saybrook, Connecticut, where she had grown up and where for three generations her family had owned the village drugstore—as was true of her (white, male) observer-narrator. Black critics as of 1950 considered these novels by Motley and Petry among the most important literary achievements since 1935. Zora Neale Hurston published *Seraph on the Sewanee*, dealing with poor and working-class whites in Florida of the sort she had studied and observed at close hand in the turpentine camps.

These authors did not think that writing about white or otherwise nonblack characters was a prerequisite to treating "universal" themes, as has often been charged. In some cases, black writers wanted to reach a broader audience than "Negro fiction" generally attracted, which attests to the racist environment in which they worked. Yet writers also wanted to bring their work to bear on the full range of the world they knew. Hugh Gloster wrote in 1950, "To accept the principle that racial experience is the only natural province of the Negro writer is to approve an artistic double standard that is just as confining and demoralizing in American literature as is segregation in American life."[66] Those aspects of experience in which racial difference takes center stage should not be the sole province of black authors.[67]

Both black and white writers of the 1940s who addressed overtly "racial" subject matter knew that "white" experience was also racial. But not every story about white people by black authors is primarily "about" their race, nor is a racializing lens always the most productive one in approaching such stories. When a Trinity College professor sought to list Petry's *Country Place* among other novels about race, Petry rebuked him, citing Willard Motley's *Knock on Any Door*, Yerby's novels, and her own *Country Place* as works that "do not deal with racism in the United States."[68] Queer and Jewish authors were often every bit as resistant to being "confined" in their choice of subject matter and methods, and their treatment of "Jewish" or "homosexual" subjects often deliberately attacked minority-identitarian stances even as they attacked anti-Semitism, anti-black racism, and homophobia.

While novels by black authors and by white authors centered on white characters certainly *can* be primarily critiques of whiteness (Sinclair Lewis's *Kingsblood Royal* being a prime example), they often are not. Which social boundaries are most relevant to the conflicts of a work of literature cannot be adjudicated on the basis of an author's perceived race, and making "race" (of an author or a character) the determining aspect of any text can have the effect of suppressing other forms of recognition. The problem is analogous to the one Bigger must overcome in order to "see" Jan in *Native Son*. Neither character is "unraced" in this moment of recognition, yet they see each other for the first time in their particularity rather than through the "deforming masks" of racial abstraction, which is not the same as saying that they cease to be socially "black" and "white" or to perceive the existential reality of such definitions. It is an epiphanic moment for Bigger precisely because it is the first time he has ever felt a sense of human mutuality with a white person, making the boundary that has always oppressed him visible in a new way. In the same way, it is important to be able to put aside our irritable reaching after definitive racial meaning in every creative act by a black (or white) person.

Some black-authored novels not centered in "racial" themes were nonetheless understood to deal with struggles analogous to those of African Americans. Thus the critic Nick Aaron Ford wrote that Willard Motley, in following the life of an Italian American, "has symbolized the problems of all minorities, including his own race." But Ford considers Frank Yerby the chief "symbolist" among black authors, because he has

completely abandoned "racial material" and found "in the social rebels of
the white race" people who "have become pariahs among their own people, an archetype of racial rejection. But these white rejectees fight
back . . . and through them the rejected Negro can feel a sense of vicari-
ous triumph."[69] Yerby found his greatest commercial success and developed an enormous audience in this phase of his career.

The chances are that in many cases black writers simply found it hard
to sell what was called "racial" fiction, particularly in popular magazines,
which were most professional writers' bread and butter. Black authors,
no matter how briefly successful, faced nearly impossible odds for making
a living by writing. Editors' correspondence with Dorothy West's agent
make clear that *Good Housekeeping, Ladies' Home Companion*, and other
general-interest magazines she hoped to break into were constrained by
audience resistance to "depressing" stories about racism, although not
necessarily Negro fiction as such. The *Collier's* editor Elizabeth Boutelle
wrote West's agent in 1944,

> I notice that Miss West appears to be steering away from stories of col-
> ored people, and while this is easy to understand, I think it is regretta-
> ble. It does seem to me that there is a place for a warm human piece
> about Negroes, and, judging by what we have seen of Miss West's writ-
> ing, she is a person who could turn one out . . . *all* Negro stories don't
> have to be problem ones.[70]

West began planning a novel in which the "problem" is not directly one
of black versus white (although that conflict is ultimately foundational)
and landed an advance contract based on an outline alone in August
1945.[71] The ironical title was *The Living Is Easy*.

It is useful to understand how black authors and critics of the time
emphasized the "universal" significance of African American experience
because of the context of the immediate postwar world, in which striving
for a planetary humanism seemed the most urgent issue of the day. Writing about the specific struggles of African Americans could contribute
to that struggle. "Gwendolyn Brooks' Satin-Legs Smith," wrote Blyden

Jackson, "represents without apology the South Side of Chicago, but none of his unabashed local color prevents him from representing very well also the diminution of man as a romantic spirit in the machine-made monotony of the modern metropolis."[72]

Ann Petry, much admired for her acclaimed and influential Harlem-based novel *The Street* (which I will discuss in a later chapter), wrote *Country Place* the same year she moved back to her nearly all-white hometown, Old Saybrook, Connecticut, after nearly a decade away. She would stay there, in an old sea captain's house she bought with royalties from *The Street*, the rest of her life. Her family had run the town's only drugstore for three generations. They had lived in the same building as the pharmacy, and she knew well the vantage point on village life that social position allowed. Petry especially admired her aunt, who had run the store a generation before. She never married, and the family always called her "Miss James" in public out of fear that the white townspeople would begin calling her "Aunty." In Petry's telling, she was a remarkably self-sufficient woman who did her job professionally and kept her counsel to herself.

The sixty-year-old white male narrator of *Country Place* is also a druggist whose family has run the drug store of Lennox, Connecticut (transparently based on Old Saybrook), for three generations. He lives in the same building as the pharmacy. He has never married, and his only significant other is a female cat named Banana. He is called "Doc" by some in the town, "Pop" by others. Only one person refers to him as "Mr. Fraser": Mrs. Gramby, the wealthy white widow who lives in the town's most imposing house. "There is something very flattering about being called 'Mr. Fraser,'" he tells us, "in a town in which one is known as 'Pop.' I accept the latter title with what grace I can muster."[73] (I will refrain from speculating on how these parallels with Petry's own people have escaped critical notice.)

The story begins with Johnny, a white soldier, returning to the home of his parents and his wife, Glory, who has fallen in love with the town "bull," Ed Barrell, a married man whose wife is in a sanatorium and whose major preoccupation is seducing other married women. Glory's mother, Lillian, is a gold-digger who has married Mearns Gramby, the widow Gramby's son, and the two women long for the death of Mrs. Gramby so they can inherit her property and take over her house and servants. A ubiquitous, snooping taxi driver called "the Weasel" acts as a kind of voyeur and provocateur, needling Johnny about his wife's activities, exposing her adultery to Johnny's mother, and endlessly annoying "Doc" Fraser.

Mr. Fraser starts his story by informing us that no narrator of a tale can be objective and therefore he should give us information about himself, "For fat men do not write the same kind of books that thin men write; the point of view of tall men is unlike that of short men."[74] He does not specify his race, but eventually it becomes clear that he is white. He describes himself as a "medium kind of man" but also a misogynist.

> It is only fitting and proper that I should openly admit to having a prejudice against women—perhaps I should say a prejudice against the female of any species, human or animal; and yet, like most of the people who admit to being prejudiced, I am not consistent, for I own a female cat, named Banana. Though I am devoted to her, I am well aware that she is much closer to the primitive than a male cat.[75]

This information is significant, for two of the main villains of the story are women. Yet the most admirable characters in the story are also women: Mrs. Gramby, to whom the narrator says he is "devoted" and who wills her diamond ring (evidently her wedding ring) to him upon her death for being her "devoted admirer," and Neola, Mrs. Gramby's maid.

Recent critics have been keen to demonstrate how *Country Place* undermines the main narrator (for them the thematic center of the novel), but he is, on the whole, neither a paragon nor a recreant. The very method in which the narration shifts in *Country Place* reveals that Fraser's and the author's views of the chief characters are not far apart.

Frequently, as in much modernist narrative following Flaubert and James, Fraser is left behind as the narration shifts to free indirect discourse, viewing events from the perspective of characters in scenes he could not possibly inhabit. For example, when Johnny's wife, Glory, comes into Mrs. Gramby's home, the narration shifts to Glory's point of view:

> The old lady had made no effort to be friendly. She limped back to the living room, sat down in a wing chair, the same one she was sitting in now, picked up a book, and read it, turning the pages slowly, as completely absorbed as though she had been alone in the room.
>
> Where was Momma, anyway? This waiting was unbearable. The cats kept blinking their eyes, sneaking glances at her. No one save a horrible old woman like Mrs. Gramby would want to own three striped tiger cats and name all of them Leon.[76]

The point of view here is not that of Fraser, the novel's ostensible narrator; he does not introduce Glory's thoughts in the third person. The question "Where was Momma, anyway" is presented with no authorial flagging, as in "Glory wondered, 'Where was Momma, anyway?'" We are able to see more than Glory can see, even though we are looking through Glory's eyes, because of the distance between her evaluation of Mrs. Gramby and ours as readers. This narrative technique has an ironic effect: we can see that Glory is a hopelessly self-centered young woman who wants Mrs. Gramby to die so that she through her mother can inherit the Gramby mansion. Much of the novel moves in and out between third-person omniscient and free indirect style in this way, only occasionally (and noticeably) returning to Doc Fraser as a first-person narrator, as at the beginning of chapter 12: "That night the drugstore stayed empty, deserted. Finally I turned off most of the lights."[77]

We also know that Doc Fraser is fairly reliable because of the distance between his view of things and that of the village. Fraser attributes the village's views to those of the Weasel, one of the most distasteful characters. Just returned from the army, Johnny Roane, sharply reminded of all he disliked about his hometown, reflects that "The smile on the face of the little man driving the car was typical of the town's smugness, its satisfaction with itself, its sly poking fun at others."[78] The novel exudes a pervasively ironic viewpoint precisely because of Fraser's distance from the views of the town yet his refusal to meddle.

That the narrator, not just Mr. Fraser, finds Glory and Lillian despicable is abundantly evident from the entire structure of the novel, above all by Glory's racist attitude to Neola, Mrs. Gramby's black maid. Fraser is not presented as a racist but takes apparent satisfaction in the resolution, whereby Mrs. Gramby wills her house, along with money to maintain it, to Neola and the Portuguese gardener, newly married to each other. Fraser keeps his private life to himself and is more a servant to the town than a voice or leader of it. In this novel, as Mr. Fraser tells it, servants occupy the moral center. Except for them and the returning soldier, Johnny Roane, who wants to leave to pursue his dream of being an artist, the "town" is decadent and despicable.

We are tipped off to this in the first chapter, when Johnny, returning home after four years of service, notices for the first time how odd it is that the Catholic church is adjacent to the railroad while all the Protestant churches are on Main Street, something he had never noticed in all his years of growing up. The Weasel explains that "Lennox" doesn't much like Catholics, so the church is on the only piece of land they (the Irish who built the railroad) could buy. "It was like a faint cloud over the sun, so that you saw houses and trees in the distance, not clearly but blurred a little, darkened where they had been bright." Johnny is reminded of what he disliked about his hometown, "its sly poking fun at others." The first chapter ends with the observation that Sergeant Johnny Roane "was suddenly afraid. Because that rat-faced little man had managed to make him see that nothing ever was the same; nothing ever could be the same—either on the surface or deep underneath."[79] Johnny Roane's years away have alienated him from the classism and ethnocentrism of his hometown, and he wants to get away.

This framing of the story to come is complemented at the end of the novel, when Mrs. Gramby, in addition to willing her home to Neola and Portolucca and her diamond ring to Doc Fraser, gives her land on Main Street to St. Peter's Roman Catholic Church, "to be used in any way the church desires."[80] The novel is thus essentially a comedy in which a paro-chial, Anglo-centric, sexually perverted, and neurotically class-stratified New England village is reoriented toward a melting-pot future. But before it emerges into this sunny comic conclusion, the novel follows the conventions of New England gothic engulfed in the passage of a hurricane.

We learn of the sexual shenanigans early on, when introduced to the town "bull," Ed Barrell. Barrell is known to have carried on affairs with many of the married women of the town, to the knowledge of even their husbands—although this is never openly acknowledged—and Johnny Roane's wife has fallen in lust with him when the novel opens, to the extent that she cannot bear for her husband to touch her when he returns home. It is eventually revealed that Barrell has also laid her own mother.

The negative portrayals of Glory and her mother, Lillian, are modi-fied by the novel's reflections on their entrapment by class, race, and gen-der, an entrapment the war had briefly put on hiatus, giving Glory in particular a taste of freedom and self-sufficiency as she took a job in a store where she earned her own money and enjoyed social stimulation and male attention. Lillian, on the other hand, had married Mearns Gramby for his money because of her straitened circumstances as a seamstress and a single woman in a traditional, smug New England town. Both women are ethically deplorable—and pathetic—but, by way of Mrs. Gramby's self-critical reflections on Lillian, the novel ultimately attributes their moral error in great part to their entrapment by class, race, and gender. They are enticed by the culture to aspire to false ideals in pursuit of which they corrupt themselves, rather like the women in Fitzgerald's *The Great Gatsby*. Yet however much this may explain their weaknesses, it is insufficient to redeem them. Just after Mrs. Gramby reflects that she might be partly responsible for Lillian's hatred of her, she begins eating some chocolates Lillian has deliberately planted, knowing that Gramby is diabetic. When Mrs. Gramby opens the drawer in which she always keeps her insulin, she finds it unaccountably empty. But we know that it is empty because Lillian has taken the contents in a plan to murder her. Thus the reader feels satisfied when Lillian and Glory are left out of the will in favor of Neola and Portolucca. Their inheritance of the historic Mearns mansion seems emblematic of a postwar transformation as a decadent Anglocentric New England society is swept away. This is, then, fundamentally an integrationist novel, from the author's inhabitation of a white center of consciousness to the resolution in which an interracial couple inherit the village mansion and historic landmark.

While critics have largely ignored Petry's *Country Place*, the mere fact that Hurston focused *Seraph on the Suwanee*, her fourth and final novel, on white Southerners has often been disparaged as a betrayal of the source of her creativity in an attempt to appeal to white people (and Hollywood). Recent criticism sees it as either "a vacuous capitulation to white culture" or "a veiled critique that has been misinterpreted as selling-out."[81] In particular, some more recent scholars have argued that Hurston's characterization of Jim Meserve should be taken as purely ironic, that her novel is a subversive critique of how white liberal attitudes toward black people mask a manipulative exploitation. According to this view, which has merit regardless of Hurston's intentions, Meserve builds his success on black people's knowledge and labor while getting that knowledge and labor on the cheap by way of his apparent benevolence, benefiting from being white in his business transactions. Another critique has it that Hurston

> had to expose Jim's cruelty and the hollow center to his manly bearing, just as she had to divulge her revulsion for Arvay by not permitting her to escape the trap baited by her insecurity. Zora Neale Hurston demonstrates that both Arvay and Jim are captives of the sexual roles that afflict marriage, a social institution she eventually found unsuitable to her own life.

However, Robert E. Hemenway goes on to admit ruefully that such an interpretation "depends primarily on extratextual evidence."[82]

These judgments are difficult to maintain in the face of both the text and Hurston's correspondence while writing it. As John C. Charles has pointed out, Jim Meserve is partly based on the white man Hurston once described as the "one person who pleased me always. That was the robust, grey-haired, white man who had helped me get into the world." We learn in her autobiography that this man "took an active interest in her well-being until he died, when she was ten."[83]

> The hard-riding, hard-drinking, hard-cussing, but very successful man was thrown from his horse and died. . . . He was an accumulating man, a good provider, paid his debts and told the truth. . . . He was supposed to be so tough, it was said that once he was struck by lightning and was not even knocked off his feet, but that lightning went off through the woods limping. Nobody found any fault with a man like that in a country where personal strength and courage were the highest virtues. People were supposed to take care of themselves without whining.[84]

Compare this passage with the hard-drinking, hard-cussing, hard-fighting, and highly successful Jim Meserve's tall tale to Arvay when he is courting her:

> One time I was bossing a gang of lumberjacks and we was felling a big stand of cypress when a terrible thunderstorm come up all of a sudden. . . . Well, a great big bolt of that lightning, red-hot and gritting its teeth, took off and headed straight at me. It's a habit of mine, Miss Arvay, when I catch a streak of lightning aiming at me, to stand in my tracks and slap it right back where it come from. . . . But this here streak of lightning must of been even faster than it's supposed to be, because the next thing I knowed, it had done got past my hand and struck me. . . . All I could do to stay on my feet from that lick the lightning hit me. Man! But was I mad. . . . All them colored men that was working under me come running to see if I was killed. Outside of a slight headache, there was nothing wrong with me at all . . . but that sneaking bolt of lightning was done up pretty bad. Yes, Ma'am! Last I seen of it, it was going off through the woods a'limping.[85]

Hurston's characterization of Meserve reflects her interest in the art of the tall tale and the interest many American authors had in American folklore generally in the wake of the WPA Folklore Project. One lesson of that project (a subdivision of the Writers Project that Sterling Brown helped administer) had been the sharing of folk heroes, motifs, and narrative elements across racial lines. Hurston's characters in the 1940s epitomize her conviction that poor whites and poor blacks of the rural South, however segregated socially, shared a colorful way of "slinging words."

In much Hurston criticism, the mastery of image-making language and "signifying" is thought specific to African Americans, and her fiction is considered a glorification of black cultural specificity and racial tradition. Indeed Hurston herself considered it to be so until she spent time with poor whites in the turpentine camps of Florida. "About the idiom of the book," she wrote her friend and fellow author Marjorie Kinnan Rawlings (the author most famously of *The Yearling*), "I too thought that when I went out to dwell among the poor whites in Dixie County that they were copying us. But I found their colorful speech so general that I began to see that it belonged to them. . . . Just stand around where poor whites work, or around the village stores of Saturday nights & listen & you will hear something."[86] This discovery was a major inspiration for the novel. Throughout the South one found a "retention of old English beliefs and customs, songs and ballads and Elizabethan figures of speech. They go for the simile and especially the metaphor. . . . This is common to white and black. The invective is practiced from childhood." The whites, moreover, "did *not* get it from the Negroes. The Africans coming to America got it from them."[87] Even what Hurston calls "the double descriptive," "signifying," the art of the tall tale, and so on—all, in Hurston's view at this time, were shared across the color line.

Hurston said the novel focused on a common psychological complex epitomized by Meserve's wife, Arvay, whose feelings of inferiority undermine her personal relationships. Hurston claimed to have known such people, male and female, and had suffered from the same affliction in youth due to her self-described "homely" looks. She felt many marriages broke up over feelings of inferiority, and that was why she focused the book on the problem.[88] She did not think fulfillment meant the same thing for all women, and she was not at war with the institution of marriage. If Arvay found fulfillment in the role of traditional wife to Jim Meserve, that did not mean Hurston thought all women would find fulfillment in such a role. Hurston believed that she herself was a "strong" woman whose intelligence and independence of spirit put many men off and partly doomed her marriages. She did not think all women would, could, or should be like her.

Hurston's intentions have been so difficult to believe that, for those who have not read *Seraph* as a critique of Jim Meserve–like white liberals, it is instead a "whiteface novel": the characters are really black folk in white masks. These opposing interpretations share a commitment to separating "black" from "white" texts by any means necessary—a sign of how the critical imagination has shifted since the 1940s. We tie ourselves in rhetorical knots trying to avoid recognizing the consistency of her attack on our common wisdom and on Americans' belief "that people who do not look like them cannot possibly feel as they do."[89] In writing about the sort of whites she had met in Florida's small towns and turpentine camps, Hurston did not consider herself to be producing a more "universal" story, as sometimes charged, nor to be departing from the source of her creativity—the storytelling and word-slinging traditions of the rural South.[90]

We do not have to agree with her linguistic hypotheses. Dialectologists have abundantly disproven some of them, establishing distinct forms of Black English Vernacular. We all know that some forms of speech—words, pronunciations, accents, and so forth—are restricted based on our racial (and class) designations and on where and to whom we are speaking. They are part of the racial etiquette of American culture, derived from power dynamics with a history going back well before the founding of the United States. The point here is that in the 1940s Hurston was a contrarian to the mainstream of racial thinking in American culture. This is not so difficult to understand when we read her novel in relation to the American literature, music, and performance of the 1940s.

Hurston believed deeply that between the late 1920s and the mid-1940s, the United States had undergone a "revolution in national expression in music that is equivalent to Chaucer's use of the native idiom in

England. Gershwin's *Porgy and Bess* brought to a head that which had been in the making for at least a decade"—the displacement of Eurocentrism and the merging of "black" and "white" music into a new American sound. "What has evolved here is something American, and has come to be the national expression, and is as such influencing the music of the world." Hurston developed the character of Jim and Arvay's son, Kenny—a jazz musician—to make just this point. Late in the process of revision, Hurston added a chapter on his life in New York in order to "explain his success."[91]

In her essay "What White Publishers Won't Print," Hurston charges, "For the national welfare, it is urgent to realize that the minorities do think, and think about something other than the race problem. That they are very human, and internally . . . are just like everybody else." She urges publishers to recognize that Negroes and other minorities feel love, appreciate the beauty in nature, and are not defined by oppression. "As long as the majority cannot conceive of a Negro or Jew feeling and reacting inside just as they do, the majority will keep right on believing that people who do not look like them cannot possibly feel as they do."[92] Hurston believed the converse was also true.

Attempts to draw a bright line between the formal features of novels by African Americans and those by white Americans and to delineate an African American tradition through intertextual relationships among "black" texts can become tautological when categorization precedes interpretation. One begins by determining authors' racial identities and proceeds to sacrifice features and authors that do not line up, in order to confirm the division one started from. Thus one ends up finding what one set out wanting to find and missing a more interesting story. When asked what contemporary novelists most captivated her, Petry mentioned Faulkner and Bernard Malamud. This is not to impugn the reality of African American traditions in literature, regardless of racial antecedents; racism in the United States has inspired literary invention and ensures specificities in literary expression by all sorts of authors. Yet the need of scholars today always to presume the primacy of racial identity in literary labor reminds one of James Baldwin's complaint about racial-protest novels (whether by blacks or whites) as "fantasies, connecting nowhere with reality," because they worked strictly within the assumptions of racial categorization they purported to attack. Treating such categorizations as more real than the human beings to whom they are applied, they fell into sentimental traps, reproducing the very racial roles that immobilize us. "We take our shape, it is true, within and against that cage of reality bequeathed us at our birth; and yet it is precisely through our dependence on this reality that we are most endlessly betrayed."[93] The problem becomes most obvious when it turns out that a presumed African American author was actually "white," or vice versa, but it operates most often at a less embarrassing, unnoticed level in the way interpretation gets oriented by the categorizations adopted at the outset and deployed in opposition to each other.

Black characters show up often in fiction and poetry by whites not focused on racial issues in ways distinct from earlier literature of the 1920s and 1930s, and much of the work reflects the influence of African American literature. Just as importantly, the authors are self-conscious about their whiteness. They probe the psychology of racism and, as Lillian Smith put it, "the effect of segregation upon the human beings who segregate"—a major theme of her own novel *Strange Fruit*.[94]

Several of these novels could easily be read as responses to Richard Wright's suggestion that white authors should work against the racism of whites while black authors combat racial nationalism among blacks:

> Lillian Smith is one who sees this quite clearly and addresses her work to her own class. White writers should combat white chauvinism while Negro writers combat Negro nationalism, and chronic distrust of whites. Negro nationalism—the all-black community—spells social regression. . . . As I see it, integration—complete equality—is the only solution, and as an artist I want to bring out the oneness of human life.[95]

The influence of Wright's *Native Son* on white authors would be difficult to overestimate. The Jewish author Jo Sinclair called Wright "one of my library teachers in writing!"[96] In his letter to Sinclair following on his rave review of *Wasteland*, Wright wrote, "If you come to New York, I'll be happy and proud to meet you. And if there is any way in which I can be of service to you here in New York, I'd be more than glad to help."[97] Sinclair exclaimed to her intellectual mentor and confidante: "Oh, Helen. When I read *Native Son*, I—am I awake?"[98]

No exploration of America's "white problem" had a greater impact than Lillian Smith's novel *Strange Fruit*, taking its name from the song by Abel Meeropol, a Jewish man, and made famous by Billie Holiday. *Strange Fruit*'s setting in the aftermath of World War I resonates powerfully with the moment of its publication, 1944, when Allied victory was assured and everyone's mind began turning to what would happen after the war. The novel mentions the Great Migration of African Americans to the North, which had accelerated during World War II. Stationed in the Ruhr valley in the waning months of the "Great War," Tracy Deen, the white protagonist, grows reflective in conversations with other soldiers, particularly a radical from Newark:

> He thought the war was about democracy. Said he was fighting for that. Most thought he was nuts. Even after the armistice he kept talking. . . . This guy was always saying things about a new world where everybody would have food, and a job, where one man would be as good as another, and there'd be no more wars. That sounds good, you said, but you don't know the South, you don't understand us. We'd never let the Negro into that world and I'm not so sure you up in Newark would either. We'd never let the Jews in, a Swede from Chicago said, not in my town. We'd never let the Japs and Chinks in, somebody from California yelled . . . [99]

But Tracy begins increasingly to reflect on his life, past and future, inspired by the words of the man from Newark. These reflections ultimately begin to circle around Nonnie Anderson. He realizes that he is in love with her:

> She wasn't a Negro girl whom he had in a strange crazy way mixed his whole life up with. She was the woman he loved. And he saw her, tender

and beautiful, holding in her eyes, her pliant spirit, in the movement of her body, her easy right words, low, deep voice, all that gave his life its meaning.[100]

Yet the social codes of the South almost instantly reassert themselves when he returns home. As he passes a black preacher and his wife under a street lamp, the wife greets him with surprise. "Roseanna's voice curved to the ground as she spoke his name, though he heard, too, the razor edge of mockery that cut a swath through her humility. He had caught Roseanna without her white-folks manner, and it was as if she were hastily buttoning it on as she spoke to him." In the wake of this accidental meeting,

All he knew was, as he stood there looking at them, a door slammed in his mind, shutting out the new world, shutting out Nonnie with it. He was just there on the sidewalk, where he had always been, feeling the feelings he had always felt. He had been somewhere . . . in a dream maybe; maybe crazy. Maybe shell shock. . . . Maybe he'd lost, not his memory, but his white feelings.[101]

Tracy reacculturates himself to Southern white society.

The result will be his murder by Nonnie's brother and the lynching of an innocent man whom Tracy Deen considers his friend. Another irony in this brutal and tragic reassertion of white identity is that even as the KKK hunts down the family's servant to lynch him for Deen's death, people close to the Deen family (including Tracy's sister) suspect that Nonnie murdered him for abandoning her. But they don't speak up because they don't want anyone else to know of Tracy's love for Nonnie. At the heart of *Strange Fruit* from first to last is the White Problem.

The "White Problem" is also the chief theme of Sinclair Lewis's *Kingsblood Royal* (1947), which follows the transformation in a white man who discovers he is black. The chief theme of the novel is how, in adjusting to the social position of a Negro, the protagonist rises morally, becoming more human, more courageous, more intelligent, and more wise. In a subplot, his white wife stands by him and is also transformed from a typically racist white socialite to a brave and dignified woman. Fifty years before "whiteness studies" became fashionable in the academy, virtually all of its key themes and insights were in circulation. Charles Johnson writes that "after fifty-four years *Kingsblood Royal* reads as if it might have been written yesterday—and by someone with a master's degree in black studies" (a degree that did not exist in 1947).[102]

It is rather ironic that, at a time when black critics were frequently decrying the "curse of propaganda" in African American fiction (presenting impossibly good black characters, for example), the novels most deformed by deliberate propaganda and didacticism are those by whites excoriating or satirizing white racial neuroses while seeking to inform other white Americans of the existence of African American professionals educated at Harvard, Oxford, and the Sorbonne and fluent in several languages, with conversation more civilized and sophisticated than that found in any white social group, and women more intelligent, gentle, and beautiful than the most favored of the white gentry.

Bucklin Moon's *The Darker Brother* (1943) treats black working-class life between the wars. The book begins with a black family in the South and a boy's shock when his white playmate and best friend tells him on his birthday that from now on their relationship exists on a different basis, with the black boy subordinate. (This sort of childhood racial recognition scene is a staple of African American literature going back to the slave narratives.) Subsequently, Ben's father, Hezekiah, dies after falling from a deficient ladder while working in the orange groves of Florida. The mother moves with her two children to Harlem to live with her brother Lafe, a wealthy numbers king who is bent on giving Ben the best education possible and sending him to college. Harlem proves to be anything but the Promised Land, and the novel makes it clear that to survive at all blacks must often make difficult choices; to thrive, however briefly, usually means breaking the law, as Ben's uncle does. It highlights the criminalization of African Americans and the pervasive discrimination they face.

Essentially a proletarian novel with occasional echoes of the "hard-boiled" crime novel, *The Darker Brother* is a comprehensive exposé of American racism, South and North. At times it seems to parade the author's "insider" knowledge of black life in specific locales—for example, the "slave market" in the Bronx, where white women would daily bargain for black domestic workers, and the fact that domestic workers are not covered by Social Security (one feature of the structural racism further sedimented during the New Deal); discrimination in the defense industry despite federal prohibitions; and the intense racism faced by black soldiers insultingly stationed in the South.

It is also a hackneyed romance novel, ultimately focused on the love between the central characters, Ben and Birdie, which survives his flirtation with a life of crime, his service in the army, and her brief descent into prostitution out of pure desperation while he is away. In his emphasis on romantic love between black men and women, Moon could be responding to the very charge Hurston later made, in "What White Publishers Won't Print," that publishers would never publish a black love story. The novel is chiefly memorable for its subject matter, exposure of white racism in its many guises, and historical record of the Great Migration.

Zora Neale Hurston had befriended Moon when he was an undergraduate at Rollins College in the 1930s. His mentor, John Andrews Rice, frequently invited her to visit his classes, later moving on to found Black Mountain College, which incubated a postwar avant-garde. Moon had admired and learned from Hurston, although by the 1940s their paths had sharply diverged. Asked to endorse his first novel, she declined, later explaining in a letter to a friend that it focused too much on black suffering and failure—possibly a reflection of her intense anticommunism and objection to the vision of black life Richard Wright had implanted in the consciousness of white intellectuals: "I have wondered if I did right by not boosting Bucklin Moon. But the thing was so sordid it sort of went against the grain. Then too, it gives a falsely morbid picture of Negro life. . . . I wish him well, though. But that awful picture does Negroes in general more harm than good."[103]

In his next novel, *Without Magnolias*, Moon pivoted to make most of the major characters (all of them black) highly successful, including a wealthy doctor in Washington and his son, a Ph.D. in sociology from the University of Chicago and the president of a small black college in the South. A Hurston-like character makes an unflattering appearance in *Without Magnolias* as Laura Burroughs,

> a woman author whose earlier books had been considered quaint and charming but whose later ones, slightly repetitive, had for the most part been ignored. She had always written of her fellow Negroes on a patronizing level only a notch or two above the folkways patterns exploited by those white writers about whom she was most caustic. Yet she was still a name to be reckoned with.[104]

As Hurston had turned intensely anticommunist and Moon came under the influence of other black writers, his views of her had changed. He probably had been influenced by Richard Wright and by Sterling Brown, his main advisor for the anthology *Primer for White Folks*, whose poetry shows up in *Without Magnolias* in a highly flattering light. Yet the intertextual relations between Moon's novel and Hurston's work are pervasive, even in his use of vernacular speech and as the model of professional authorship she represented.

The character Eric, who had grown up in Washington, the lightskinned son of a wealthy doctor, had known Burroughs during her college days in Washington. (Hurston attended Howard University in the 1920s.) He had been in love with her at sixteen, when she was twentyone. "For that reason he would always have a deep affection for her in spite of the fact that he intensely disliked everything for which she stood—her studied scatterbrainedness, her profitable career as a 'professional' Negro, the fact that she made a living of singing for her supper." This characterization precisely fits the views some black male authors had of Hurston. "She affected a jive idiom that was always a little out of date; it eluded her somehow, changing so rapidly that she could never quite keep pace except by the standards of the white folks who considered her an authority whose word was as final as Webster's." While he didn't agree with Hurston's politics and considered her a sly compromiser of racial reality for personal gain, Moon captured her charisma and vitality. He paid tribute to her "sophistication that was only a little short of breathtaking."[105] No black intellectual of the time would have trouble recognizing the model for Laura Burroughs, nor that Moon was aligning himself with the Popular Front politics of Sterling Brown, Richard Wright, and perhaps Chester Himes.

In fact, like Himes and Himes's protagonist in *If He Hollers Let Him Go*, the chief working-class protagonist of *Without Magnolias*, Luther Mathews, gets a job in the defense industry working in a shipyard, which allows Moon to hype the CIO and the importance of working-class alliance across the color line and to dramatize the red-baiting that threatened any move toward such collaboration in the labor movement. As we will see, Himes was hardly so enamored of the CIO in his first novel, acquired by Moon, but his next novel, *Lonely Crusade*, was pro-CIO.

Burning with impatience over the stalled prospects of integration in the late 1940s and the endless compromises with Southern segregationists, Moon gave *Without Magnolias* an epigraph out of *Through the Looking Glass* by Lewis Carroll: "'A slow sort of country!' said the Queen. 'Now, *here*, you see, it takes all the running *you* can do, to keep in the same place.'"[106]

Early in the novel, Ezekiel Rogers, the president of a black college, is on a train bound for a meeting in Georgia and pulls out a new book by a prominent Negro author that he had gotten through "one of the book clubs":

He read until it was almost dark, then put the book aside angrily. The man could write, of that there was little doubt, but he did not see things as they really were. His vision was clouded by his bitterness, so distorted that he ignored completely the progress many Negroes in the South had made. Besides, it was a dangerous book, a book that the white South would resent. Now was not the time for resentment; rather it was the time for even closer co-operation, to gain concessions and then nail them down solidly against the storm that was certain to come after the war.[107]

Rogers makes a note to himself to ask the liberal editor of the local newspaper to let him write a review of the book.

By the time he reaches his hotel room in Georgia, however, he is so incensed by the indignities he has suffered on the trip that he instead writes a fiery essay pulling no punches, calling for a "dual pressure, the militancy of the Northern Negro working closely with Negroes in the South going as fast and as hard as they were able to, short only of actual danger from the violent mores of the region," and he plans to send it off to a periodical (apparently black owned) called the *New National*. The essay is "perhaps the most effective answer to his own [usually moderate] position that had ever been stated." The next morning, however, he suffers a failure of nerve and tears up the envelope, "almost hating himself."[108]

Showing all the ways in which black and "liberal" white Southerners fear frontal assaults on segregation—and routinely adhere to the mores that sustain and naturalize it—*Without Magnolias* emphasizes a new spirit among African Americans in the South, particularly among those coming of age during the war. Key characters, including Ezekiel Rogers's son George (a veteran of the war who returns home after losing an arm) and Eric Gardner, are unwilling to continue in the old compromising ways of their elders. The old mores of avoiding friction out of fear of violence are losing their hold, not only on such "educated" Negroes but on working-class young people. Esther Matthews, a working-class woman of the older generation, feels this shift whenever she boards a bus to visit her son and daughter-in-law, who live in government housing for defense-industry workers in the shipyard:

In the crowded bus she could feel the tension that existed, for tempers were short when everyone was jammed up into so small a space. It even seemed to her as though people themselves had changed.

In all her lifetime she had had no trouble with white folks. She had gone her way and they had gone theirs. . . . But now when she got onto a bus it seemed to her that every white person resented her . . . Nor, she admitted, did it stop there. Once she was in the rear of the bus among her own, she felt hate and bitterness all around her. Usually it was unspoken, remaining a kind of inner muttering and mumbling, but at times she saw Negroes who were almost as overt about it as whites . . . They were most often young, both men and women, and they carried themselves as though they were as good as anyone else and out to prove it. . . . There was no trouble, though often everyone in the bus seemed on the verge of it. All that was needed, it seemed to her, was a spark. When that happened there was bound to be an explosion.[109]

The main drama of the book derives precisely from this "new mood," the very mood that Ralph Ellison would speak of in his essays of and about the 1940s in the South.

The black intellectual representative of the new mood, Eric Gardner, confronts segregation directly and rejects the accommodations of his boss, President Rogers, to segregationist mores in order to protect his livelihood and the college he has built with the aid of white philanthropy. He boldly confronts one of the white trustees of the school, and Rogers's closest ally, in the trustee's home over cocktails. This trustee, Calvin Thornton, is a "liberal" newspaper editor who disagrees with segregation but believes in a "go-slow" approach much like William Faulkner. He feels certain that overt attacks on segregation and for complete racial equality will lead to massive white resistance and violence, including the destruction of his own press. He tells Gardner he is trying to change the mores of the white South, "but I've got to have time. It's got to come from the white Southerner. Every time a Northerner comes down here and tells us what to do it sets us back just that much further, makes our job that much harder."[110]

Gardner accuses him of being more concerned about the reputation of so-called enlightened white Southerners than the equality of the Negro, predicting, "Either you solve the Negro problem or others are going to solve it for you, and that time may be nearer than you think."[111] Thornton listens to the critique respectfully and wishes Gardner well, but immediately after he leaves, he calls Rogers to say he is too "dangerous" and must not have his contract renewed—a judgment with which Rogers agrees.

Thornton and Rogers have both been corrupted by their constant compromises with Southern custom to avoid violence and destruction of what they have built up (a college, a liberal newspaper). Both suffer from bad conscience and from emasculation in their miserable marriages, symbolic of their emasculation in general. (The gender politics of the novel are notably patriarchal.) George Rogers and Eric Gardner represent an emergent, more militant Negro leadership that will not compromise its ideals.

Ultimately, Ezekiel Rogers himself feels a bitter hatred not only for himself but for the "good and true" white man who had taken him under his wing as a youth and made his career possible. He had sacrificed his personal integrity to get ahead in a racist system.[112] Yet, at the very moment he feels ready to chuck everything and tell the truth in a climactic commencement speech, he buckles once again. The novel concludes with the implication that a new leadership is needed and makes clear where that leadership will come from.

Moon's novel enunciates the thoughts a young Ralph Ellison had at the time. In a 1961 interview, he related that when he started writing *Invisible Man* in the late 1940s,

> I got to thinking about the ambiguity of Negro leadership during that period. This was the late forties and I kept trying to account for the fact that when the chips were down, Negro leaders did not represent the Negro community.
>
> Beyond their own special interests they represented white philanthropy, white politicians, business interests, and so on. This was an unfair way of looking at it, perhaps, but there was something missing, something which is only now being corrected. . . . Implicit in their roles were constant acts of betrayal . . . the predicament of the Negroes in the United States rendered these leaders automatically impotent, until they recognized their true source of power—which lies, as Martin Luther

King perceived, in the Negro's ability to suffer even death for the attainment of our beliefs.[113]

Similarly, in a 1945 review of Richard Wright's *Black Boy*, Ellison concluded that Wright "has converted the Negro impulse toward self-annihilation and 'going-underground' into a will to confront the world, to evaluate his experience honestly and throw his findings unashamedly into the guilty conscience of America"[114]—exactly what Ezekiel Rogers dreams of doing in Moon's novel but cannot.

Ellison considered Moon's project consonant with his own. He favorably reviewed *The Darker Brother* for *Tomorrow* magazine, and in a 1945 review of Moon's edited volume, *Primer for White Folks*, he singled out the third section of the book, presenting the thought of contemporary writers

> on the "Negro question" and their recommendations for its solution. This section is especially valuable and will bear repeated reference as the tense period we have just entered unfolds. Here are the most democratically informed discussions of the racial situation to appear in print since Pearl Harbor.[115]

Ellison finds it significant that the contributors are mostly young, emerging after the Depression.

> As arranged here, [the contributions] offer a vivid statement of the strengths and weaknesses of the new mood born in the hearts of Americans during the war, a mood more precise in its fears (of racial bloodshed) than definite in its hopes . . . ; but more significant than their obvious fears and vacillations, they are valuable for something practically missing from American writing since *Huckleberry Finn*: a search for images of black and white fraternity.[116]

A distinguished scholar of Southern literature, under the impression that Moon was black, has recently used Moon's *Without Magnolias* to advance his argument that black and white Southern authors cannot fit under the same umbrella of "southern literature," pointing out that both *Without Magnolias* and *Primer for White Folks* aim "to subvert or negate white southern reality"—making them texts in a separate African American tradition. The novel, Michael Kreyling continues,

> makes the same point in editorializing fiction set in a southern milieu strongly foreshadowing Ellison's *Invisible Man* (1952). *Without Magnolias*, in other words, serves as a transition text from the so-called propaganda fiction of Wright to the so-called modern literature of Ellison. Ellison, indeed, knew Moon's novel and used it as an example in ongoing controversies he waged with Stanley Edgar Hyman and Irving Howe on the nature and meaning of African-American experience and literature. The purport of Ellison's two-front debate with Howe and Hyman, like the diptych of *Without Magnolias* and *Invisible Man*, is that a theory of literature and southern identity that claims to have black and white under the awning of "southern" merely draws a curtain over the problem of race and literature.[117]

A contemporary review of *Invisible Man* for the *New Republic* also grouped it with the work of Moon for avoiding "the bane of the problem novel," in which artistic sensibility is sacrificed to subject matter and racial and political clichés.[118] Nothing could be more ironic than Kreyling's use of Moon to buttress his argument against "integrating" black and white authors in the frame of "southern literature"—an integration that he calls "an enforced intertextuality that serves as a kind of symbolic bondage."[119]

Another sympathetic scholar, on the other hand, knowing that Moon was actually white, has charged that, however genuine and necessary his work was, he usurped space that should have been reserved for black authors. He should have devoted himself to getting black editors hired (assuming this was in his power) rather than presuming to attack racism with novels centering on black characters. The prominence of Moon and another white author/editor, Thomas Sancton, contributed to "the erasure of a competent and hungry black intelligentsia."[120] Compare this to the black reviewer for *Phylon* in 1949, who wrote that *Without Magnolias* "should . . . help many Negroes approach a better understanding of themselves."[121] In the *Journal of Negro Education*, Marion T. Wright lauded Moon's novel as "one of the best of the era."[122] Today it is almost totally ignored.

As an author and editor at Doubleday Doran, Moon was not standing in the way of his black compatriots. He was taking up space formerly occupied by the likes of Octavus Roy Cohen and helping change the context in which African American writing was received. When Moon left Doubleday to focus on his own writing, Chester Himes was left without a champion at Doubleday and had to seek a new publisher.[123] In 1953, Moon's writing career ended after he was fired from his job as associate fiction editor at *Collier's* over accusations that he was a communist (which he was not).[124] The mere fact that *Without Magnolias* had been positively reviewed in the communist-run *Daily Worker* was enough to put him under suspicion. He was ruined both financially and personally: as he fought the accusation, his marriage fell apart. Then he attempted suicide. The incident drew the attention of both *Time* and *Commonweal*, which compared him to Kafka's character Joseph K in *The Trial*.[125]

More radical than Moon's novel, however, was Howard Fast's fictional account of the restitution of white supremacy in the South after 1876, the subject of his prescient novel *Freedom Road* (1944), which can also be seen as a warning about the forces of reaction rising in America as the Second World War approached its end. W. E. B. Du Bois wrote of Fast's novel when it was reissued in 1952: "His story is fiction, but his basic historical accuracy is indisputable; its psychological insight is profound; . . . I am glad to commend it to all people who want to know the Truth and be free."[126] Fast was clearly a student of Du Bois's classic studies *The Souls of Black Folk* (1903) and *Black Reconstruction in America, 1860–1880* (1935), the influence of which can be found throughout this novel of Reconstruction in South Carolina, many of its characters and incidents based on actual events.

The novel's "psychological insight" derives from Fast's knowledge of African American literature going back to the 1846 *Narrative of the Life of Frederick Douglass, an American Slave*. This is most evident in the treatment of the central character, Gideon Jackson, who as a slave at the age of six experienced what scholars refer to as a racial "recognition scene," what Frederick Douglass referred to as the "blood-stained gate" through which as a child of nearly the same age he realized what it meant to be a slave. In Douglass's narrative, conversely, the final release from the feeling of being a slave comes when he speaks up in an antislavery convention, addressing whites as well as blacks. In *Freedom Road*, when Gideon is about to present himself as a representative to the state constitutional convention in Charleston, he initially feels afraid and inadequate, remembering the pivotal experience of his boyhood:

> He was a small black animal [in white men's eyes], and he knew it then, and even as a six-year-old child the terror was complete, awful, aching loneliness; hope that should be a part of every living thing was denied him. The white man, thereafter, was in a sense a locked gate, and though he had come very close to that gate since, he had never actually opened it.[127]

In part the novel follows Gideon's psychological transformation as he educates himself and gains the confidence to lead and to serve in the U.S. Senate before fighting to the death against the reimposition of white supremacy and the massacre of his people, black and white, in the town of Carwell.

Though it is melodramatic and didactic, no previous book by a white author can compare to this one in its combined racial politics, attention to black psychology, and popularity. (Incidentally, it was turned into a 1979 television miniseries starring Muhammad Ali.) Its history lesson about Reconstruction comprehensively counters the dominant view of historians at the time, who had been maintaining since the early years of the century that Reconstruction had been a vicious imposition by radical

Republicans seeking vengeance on "the South," aided by corrupt carpet-baggers who took advantage of ignorant, semisavage former slaves to foist a black tyranny on prostrate white Southerners.

Fast uses the fictional town of Carwell, South Carolina, and the career of Gideon Jackson as a microcosm of Southern history between the Civil War and the restoration of white supremacy by the old aristocracy. By the mid-1870s, led by Jackson, Carwell is a quasi-socialistic community of former slaves and poor whites who trust and care for one another, recognizing their common interests, governing themselves democratically, each giving to the community as they are able. Class divisions are nonexistent, and both former slaves and "white trash" gain in knowledge and dignity as they work together: "All the long centuries between feudalism and democracy, they had crossed over in one long step."[128] But the dethroned planters plot to win sympathy in the North and co-opt the KKK, to divide poor whites from blacks by playing up the value of white skin and thus restoring the old order. Fast features a few educated whites committed to equality as radical democrats and poor whites who ally with the freed slaves initially out of self-interest, which grows into a sense of loyalty and community over time and trials.

Freedom Road is also a patriotic book by an author who wrote for the Voice of America during the war. It fits into a line of American radicalism that goes back to the abolitionists. Under duress to stop the rolling back of freedom, Gideon Jackson attempts to send telegrams to Emerson and Douglass (the messages are intercepted and the messenger, Jackson's son, murdered). One of the poor white stalwarts in the last stand against the Klan is a great-grandson of Daniel Boone. Jackson's supporters include people who were friends and supporters of John Brown, Douglass, and Charles Sumner. Black heroes bear names like Zeke Hale (referencing Nathan Hale) and Hannibal Washington. A white New England schoolteacher named Benjamin Winthrope who has joined the community to teach the black and white children together is a descendant of John Winthrop. Another black hero is named Lacy Douglass. And of course there's a Lincoln—first name Ferdinand. There is also a war veteran named Leslie Carson (alluding to Kit Carson). And Gideon's chosen surname, Jackson, would seem to allude to the president of the "common man." Through the KKK, the ruling class assassinates a Winthrop, a Hale, a Washington, a Jackson, a Boone, a Lincoln, a Carson, and a Douglass. Coming on the heels of the WPA Projects' folklore, writers', and related programs, this is a roll call of national heroes, sacrificing their lives for democracy against the entrenched elites—fascists—who have never believed in democracy or equality, who have fought against the country's principles at every stage in its history.

Fast dedicated the novel "To the men and women, black and white, yellow and brown, who have laid down their lives in the struggle against fascism." Seemingly driven by a premonition of the assault on the New Deal and the rise of reaction following the Second World War, the novel deals with the triumphs and promise of Reconstruction and then its brutal dismantling by "fascists" after 1876.

Fast also addresses the way the interests of the powerful have shaped national memory. "You may ask," begins his afterword, "and with justice, is there any truth in this tale? And if there is, why has it not been told before?" He explains, "There was not one Carwell in the south at that period, but a thousand, both larger and smaller. . . . White men and black men lived together, worked together, and built together. . . . In many, many places they died together, in defense of what they had built." He cites his sources. Why has this been forgotten? Because

the memory was expunged. Powerful forces did not hold it to be a good thing for the American people to know that once there had been such an experiment—and that the experiment had worked. That the Negro had been given the right to exist in this nation as a free man, a man who stood on equal ground with his neighbor, that he had been given the right to work out his own destiny in conjunction with the southern poor whites, and that in an eight-year period of working out that destiny he had created a fine, a just, and a truly democratic civilization.[129]

As a leader of the Joint Anti-Fascist Refugee Committee, in 1949 Fast was sentenced to prison for contempt of Congress, having refused the

House Un-American Activities Committee's demand that he name contributors to a fund for orphans of Spanish Civil War veterans.[130] (One contributor was Eleanor Roosevelt.) In prison he began writing *Spartacus*, about an uprising by Roman slaves. Blacklisted after his release, he founded his own publishing company to publish it in 1951; the film version of 1960, in the midst of the Civil Rights Movement, was so successful it helped break the Hollywood blacklist.

Blood on the Forge (1941), by the African American author William Attaway (later a lyricist in collaboration with Harry Belafonte), similarly shows how Southern landowners and Northern capitalists turn workers against one another along racial and ethnic lines to prevent them organizing and gaining control over land and capital. It focuses on three black men from Kentucky in 1919, the year of the "Red Summer."

Working the land in Kentucky, the Moss brothers feel intuitively that land should be held in common. As Melody says to his brother Mat, "I got a big feelin' like the ground don't belong to the white boss—not to nobody."[131] Mr. Johnston, the white landowner, brutally exploits his black tenant farmers and will not hire white tenant farmers because they demand better pay and treatment, but he hires a poor white man as his "riding boss" to keep the blacks "in their place." Mat ends up killing the riding boss, whose background is nearly as humble as his own.

Much later in the novel, racial positions are reversed: Mat is deputized in a steel-mill town to attack white union men on strike and comes to see himself as the "riding boss," wielding power over the workers. He feels compensated in this role for years of racist humiliation. While many of the immigrant laborers hate most African Americans, Attaway attributes their hatred not to an inheritance of American-style racism but to the uses of blacks to weaken and destroy unions. In fact, "The union organizers made desperate efforts to induce the black men to join the movement toward a strike. But the steel interests had bought the black leaders."[132] Black politicians are brought in to tell the black workers to remember that the white workingmen who now want them in the union are the very people who used to spit on them and call them "nigger."

Mat agrees to become a deputy for the pay, but in the midst of fighting the striking whites he undergoes an epiphany. When he is clubbed on the back of the head with a pickax handle, he recalls the moment he killed Mr. Johnston's riding boss. As the blows continue to fall, he sees the action as from a distance, with "all the objectivity of a man who is closer to death than life. From that dark place he looked back at the world." And what he saw was

> a young Slav frantic because he was killing a man. A good face, a little crazy and twisted with repugnance for the blows he must deal.
>
> He, Mat, was the riding boss, and hate would give this club hand the strength it needed.
>
> His vision faded. He was confused. It seemed to him that he had been through all of this once before. Only at that far time he had been the arm strong with hate. . . . Big Mat went further away and no longer could distinguish himself from these other figures. They were all one and all the same. In that confusion he sensed something true. Maybe somewhere in these mills a new Mr. Johnston was creating riding bosses, making a difference where none existed.[133]

Attaway's idealism about the possibilities of interracial collaboration connected with that of Howard Fast and Bucklin Moon and with Marxist analyses of the racial situation. What is striking about the 1940s is that this idealism could be shared by authors, including African American authors like Zora Neale Hurston, who had radically different attitudes to communism.

Chester Himes's *If He Hollers Let Him Go* (1945) offers a biting antithesis to the idealization of the CIO that one finds in the novels of Moon and Attaway and to the Marxist interracialism of *Freedom Road*. (On the other hand, his next novel, *Lonely Crusade* [1947], which I will treat in a later chapter, would be extremely pro-CIO.) Here, the union recruits African Americans but still segregates and disempowers them. Most white workers are vicious racists, and Himes delivers the most comprehensive and detailed description of everyday workplace racism in twentieth-century literature. He had worked in the shipyards of Los Angeles and knew the drills. Union leaders, even when sympathetic, are timid about upsetting white workers, many of whom come from the Deep South. Emphasizing the need for unity against fascism, they refuse to battle the racism of the union's own white members. The call for "unity" amounts to telling black workers not to press their claims for equality too far. Bob Jones, Himes's protagonist, also disdains the communists for abandoning the fight specifically against racism. Jones dismisses liberal integrationism as his girlfriend Alice Harrison and her wealthy parents promote it. Yet he is no black nationalist, either. He is a revolutionist: "the only solution to the Negro problem is a revolution. We've got to make white people respect us and the only thing white people have ever respected is force."[134] When asked if he thinks a revolution by Negroes could be successful, he replies that it would be if they had enough white people on their side. In fact, the ultimate target, for Bob Jones, is racialization as such. He hates whites for their racism, but what he wants is not a separate sphere for blacks. The boundary between white and black is his ultimate antagonist, an affront to his manhood. He does not pose as a black man fighting for his people but as a humanist at odds with racial identity.

Alice argues that he should learn to thrive within the racial strictures of American society, which were not likely to disappear soon. In the vision that she and her family presented,

> You simply had to accept being black as a condition over which you had no control, then go on from there. Glorify your black heritage, revere your black heroes, laud your black leaders, cheat your black brothers, worship your white fathers (be sure and do that), segregate yourself; then make yourself believe that you had made great progress, that you would continue to make great progress, that in time the white folks would appreciate all of this and pat you on the head and say, "You been a good nigger for a long time. Now we're going to let you in."[135]

But to give up on forcing the issue of integration would make him the equivalent of a collaborator. He knows that no matter how successful he might be, "I didn't want to be the biggest Negro who ever lived, neither Toussaint L'Ouverture nor Walter White." Jones asserts that he could settle for any job,

> If I could be a man, defined by Webster as a male human being. That's all I'd ever wanted—just to be accepted as a man—without ambition, without distinction, either of race, creed, or colour; just a simple Joe walking down an American street, going my simple way, without any other identifying characteristics but weight, height, and gender.[136]

To Jones, and to Himes, the ultimate power of whites to racialize and delimit black people came in the realm of sexuality, where dwelled the deepest fears and fantasies that sustained the color line. For that reason, Jones's rebellion against the reign of whiteness and his own emasculation comes to a point in power fantasies of "having" and degrading a white, Southern, racist woman. We will deal later with issues of women and power in the literature of the 1940s, particularly by women. Here, what concerns me is the attack on the color line as such.

Himes resented any enclosure of his imagination and desires within the barriers of American racial common sense and the effect of these barriers on African Americans' own mentalities and personal relationships. He found little to love about American culture, including African American culture. The American color line provoked, repelled, and fascinated him. One can see this on the very surface of his novels in the 1940s. The most unique feature of those novels is not just how unflinchingly he bares his hatred but how fundamental it is to the very form and style of his writing, so that his novels have the effect of telling it like it is.

For this, the most infamous white provocateur of the Harlem Renaissance admired him and boosted his career: "People say bad things about him," wrote Carl Van Vechten to Himes's friend John A. Williams, "because he doesn't like most people and shows it. I admire his books."[137]

Himes credited prison with turning him toward fiction writing. His prison experience—and his ex-convict *identity*—help account for his liminal relationship to the established canon of African American literature. His obsession with issues of masculinity derives not only from the commonly cited emasculation of black men in the United States but from his prison experience in Ohio at the very origin of his aspiration to write, when he was in love with a fellow male prisoner.[138] The book he wrote partly based on this experience, *Yesterday Will Make You Cry*, his most personal, initially featured a semiautobiographical protagonist who was white and in love with another man.

I end this chapter with Chester Himes in part because he epitomized some of the most important tendencies and contradictions in "the literature of the Negro" in the 1940s, when he came of age artistically, and because he became important to authors of the Black Power era, when his career gained a second life with novels that were adapted into blaxploitation films. Several of the leaders of the Black Arts movement were gay or what today we might term queer, but they remained closeted (in contrast to the veteran civil-rights organizer Bayard Rustin, an integrationist and pacifist whose career began in the early 1940s). Modern racial nationalism has generally suppressed queer sexuality, as reproductive futurity demands heterosexual coupling, with women, particularly, assigned to reproduce the race. The resistance to racial nationalism as well as homophobia in the 1940s points to a conjuncture between various forms of oppression, including anti-Semitism, to which authors of the forties were peculiarly sensitive. Conscious of the global crisis of World War II, however, instead of developing a particularist identity politics, they responded to those forms of oppression by asserting their relevance to the project of a new kind of planetary humanism.

7

QUEER HORIZONS

....

Writing in 1951, John W. Aldridge, in addition to drawing attention to the pervasiveness of fiction dealing with African American and Jewish experience in the 1940s, contended that "a strong preoccupation with homosexuality as a literary theme runs through nearly all the novels the young writers have produced, and it has become one of their most distinguishing characteristics as well as the most curious."[1] Leslie Fiedler opened his famous essay "Come Back to the Raft Ag'n, Huck Honey" (1948) with the statement, "It is perhaps to be expected that the Negro and the homosexual should become stock literary themes in a period when the exploration of responsibility and failure has become again a primary concern of our literature."[2]

A pervasive and extraordinarily frank treatment of sex and, especially, non-normative sexuality comes into focus when reading the 1940s, often in connection with the heritage and continuing practices of racial oppression. This conjuncture is puzzling: is it because one's race and sex (today we might say gender and sexual orientation) were the two primary aspects of identity no one was allowed to choose? Both were starkly bifurcated in absolute terms within the discourses and social norms of the time. In the "queer" time of World War II—"the duration"—such norms were destabilized in the American literary imagination.

John Costello, who came to the topic after writing a bestselling book about the war, pointed out: "Sex and sexuality in all its guises and complexities played an extensive role in the war experience. . . . It enhanced intimacy and the expression of love that liberated many people from traditional inhibitions."[3] Freud had observed that in societies at war the usual repressions of the sex drive are partially lifted. The fear of death, the general social upheaval and rearrangements associated with the draft, and widespread physical uprooting from people's normal environments all contributed to a loosening of sexual mores.

While a kind of "war aphrodisia" (and mass rape) had long been associated with battle and its aftermath, in the period of "total war" the boundaries of normative sexuality lost their purchase on a much broader scale. The time was queer. A gay journalist in Gore Vidal's novel *The City and the Pillar* observes that "The war has caused a great change. Inhibitions have broken down. All sorts of young men are trying out all sorts of new things, away from home and familiar taboos."[4] Costello, a historian, echoes this opinion: "The mobilization, disruption, and excitement of so many lives was not only a catalyst of social change, but it also sowed the seeds of a far-reaching shift in private and public sexual attitudes."[5] In literature, explicit treatments of sexuality became commonplace in the same years that Alfred Kinsey collected and reported the controversial results of his research on the sexual behavior of the human male.

According to John d'Emilio and Estelle B. Freedman, "World War II could be considered the birth moment of modern gay and lesbian history."[6] This is not to say that homosexuality was "accepted"—not by a long shot. Antigay violence was common, and "coming out" was always dangerous both personally and professionally. Alfred Kazin, who shared the almost universal belief that homosexuality was "degenerate," noted in his journal of December 29, 1941:

Homosexuality as a fact in contemporary art and literature. We were talking the other night about the flood of homos in high places. Names: I've already, as I seem to every day, added a dozen to my list. For me it is a fact of social interest—horrifying, yet curiously illustrative of my perpetual growl about the quality of contemporary degeneration— worse, *passivity*.[7]

While the passage indicates the attitudes of a young, straight, "liberal" critic of the time, it also suggests how much more open homosexuality in literary circles was becoming. Discovering one's sexuality or new dimensions of it is a common theme in the fiction, poetry, and drama of the 1940s, including literature of the war. Homosexual tensions arise and fundamentally affect the plot of Mailer's *The Naked and the Dead*. Rumors of homosexuality abound in even the conservative James Gould Cozzens's *Guard of Honor*, and *The Gallery* opens every closet.

Championing gay or lesbian identity as such, however, was rarely the point of the work of gay, lesbian, or "queer"-oriented writers; they attacked homophobia and the need to "label" people according to their desires or sexual practices. And this critique, surprisingly often, connected with related, explicit critiques of racism and anti-Semitism. Identity politics is what fascists and anti-Semites practice, what homophobes practice, what white supremacists and segregationists practice. Again and again the intersection of such attitudes—how they "interlock," as James Baldwin would put it in 1949—emerges in the work of the 1940s. Representative of this point is Robert Duncan's celebrated essay "The Homosexual in Society" (1944). The essay was inspired, Duncan attests, by James Agee's "recent approach to the Negro pseudo-folk" in *Partisan Review*. Duncan addresses himself to

another group whose only salvation is in the struggle of all humanity for freedom and individual integrity, who have suffered in modern society persecution, excommunication; and whose "intellectuals," whose most articulate members, have been willing to desert that primary struggle, to beg, to gain at the price if need be of any sort of prostitution, privilege for themselves, however ephemeral; who have been willing rather than to struggle toward self-recognition, to sell their product, to convert their deepest feelings into marketable oddities and sentimentalities.[8]

Duncan presents as a model "Negroes who have joined openly in the struggle for human freedom, made articulate that their struggle against racial prejudice is part of the struggle for all; while there are Jews who have sought no special privilege of recognition for themselves as Jews but have fought for *human* recognition and rights."[9]

In contrast, Duncan could think of no homosexual willing to connect his own self-defense with a "battlefront toward human freedom." Instead, a cult of homosexual superiority and in-group sarcasm toward nonhomosexuals had taken root, "the cultivation of a secret language, the *camp*, a tone and a vocabulary that is loaded with contempt for the human." Among the most enlightened "queer" (*sic*) circles, fear and hostility toward outsiders, exclusion and blindness are the rule. Rather than battling fear and ignorance, they have sought to profit by it, enjoying the drama of their outsider status. In doing so, they have obscured the lessons of predecessors like Melville, Proust, and Hart Crane, "who have viewed homosexuality as one of many facets, one of the many eyes through which the human being may see and who, admitting through which eye they saw, have had primarily in mind . . . mankind and its liberation. For these great early artists their humanity was the source, the sole source, of their work."[10]

To understand the purchase of Duncan's argument requires understanding how he understands "universality" in, for example, Melville's and Hart Crane's work:

> Thus in Melville, though in *Billy Budd* it is clear that the conflict is homosexual, the forces that make for that conflict, the guilt in passion, the hostility rising from subconscious sources, and the sudden recognition of these forces as it comes to Vere in that story, these are forces which are universal, which rise in other contexts, which in Melville's work have risen in other contexts.[11]

Hart Crane is Duncan's ultimate model, one whose "visionary company of love" he feels later gay writers have traduced:

Where the Zionists of homosexuality have laid claim to a Palestine of their own, asserting in their miseries their nationality; Crane's suffering, his rebellion, and his love are sources of poetry for him not because they are what make him different from, superior to, mankind, but because he saw in them his link with mankind; he saw in them his sharing in universal human experience.[12]

Suffering, rebellion against persecution, love: these are not the special attributes of any group, to be rated on a scale of virtue and blame, but perennial attributes of human existence across all social differences.

Duncan is not naïve. The universal does not reside in what is stripped of all existential distinction—not gay, not Jewish, not Negro—nor is it implicitly straight or white, not straight or not white. It is not emptied of what makes people "who they are," as many critiques of liberalism hold, including that of Jean-Paul Sartre in the 1940s. No, one's "differences" are what join one to a shared human consciousness, and the "universal" is an aspiration that emerges at the crossroads of identities—one to be shared across social differences and inherent in freedom struggles past and, above all, present. Nothing is more indicative of the age.

Feeling "special" in one's difference, to Duncan, entails a "hypotrophy of feeling," setting boundaries on empathy and redirecting one's emotions toward campy self-ridicule and its accompanying narcissism. Duncan deliberately targets "camp"—"this gaiety (it is significant that the homosexual's word for his own kind is 'gay'), a wave surging forward, breaking into laughter and then receding, leaving a wake of disillusionment, a disbelief that extended to oneself, to life itself." The antidote to such disbelief is devotion to human freedom, "toward the liberation of human love" and the disowning of "*all* the special groups (nations, religions, sexes, races) that would claim allegiance."[13] The lure of one's fears and one's special status, the moral superiority of the victim, the protective associations of one's own kind will always be there, "offering for a surrender of one's humanity congratulations upon one's special nature and value," but it must be always recognized that the others, those who have surrendered their humanity, are not less than oneself. It must be always remembered that one's own honesty, one's battle against the inhumanity of his own group (be it against patriotism, against bigotry, against, in this specific case, the homosexual cult) is a battle that cannot be won in the immediate scene.[14]

Only continued resistance will make a better order possible. The battle against homophobia cannot be made into a special case, nor does Duncan leave much space for pride in a gay "identity" as such.

As if in affirmation of such a vision, "queer" sexuality appears frequently in novels chiefly focused on other issues, and not infrequently in ways intended to critique homophobia in the general society. Thus, as we have seen, the protagonist of Jo Sinclair's *Wasteland*, which focuses on issues of Jewish self-hatred, is guided to self-liberation by his lesbian sister, who functions as a model of integrity and commitment to human liberation after her own struggle for self-acceptance. (She is also committed to black civil rights.) The novel concerns overcoming shame about one's difference not through pride in one's special identity as a lesbian or a Jew but by thinking in more "universal patterns," recognizing "the larger ghettos of the world" in relation to one's own, overcoming one's own ghettoization through self-acceptance and commitment to human liberation everywhere.[15] In the *Gay/Lesbian Almanac*, Jonathan Katz ranked *Wasteland* one of three "major documents of homosexual resistance" (the others being Duncan's essay and Baldwin's "Preservation of Innocence: Studies for a New Morality") and judged Deborah Brown "probably the most complex, human, and affirmative portrait of a homosexual (male or female) to appear in American fiction before the publication in 1964 of Christopher Isherwood's *A Single Man*."[16]

In Willard Motley's *Knock on Any Door*, a bestseller by a black author that inspired a well-known film, Nick Romano, the delinquent, Italian American protagonist, and his friend Vito develop a scam in which Nick seduces older gay men into making passes at him, and then the two boys "roll" their target. They call it "playing the phoneys." Not long after they have started this racket, a middle-aged man named Barney befriends Nick at the pool hall, treats him to free games, and finally persuades Nick to come to his apartment with a promise of money for sex. Nick accepts the "trade" and is ashamed afterward, but he nonetheless continues "playing the phoneys." Rich businessmen will meet him at a bar on skid row and then take him to a downtown hotel, registering him as a son or brother. When he runs away from home, to "play the queers for money" becomes one of his standard modes of survival.

This exploitation of the "queers" opens into uncharted territory, however, when Owen, a young man who befriends, helps, and encourages Nick, turns out to be gay. Learning that Owen is queer, Nick tells him, "You're all right. I don't care what you are."[17] They become close friends and occasionally sleep together, although neither of them considers Nick to be gay.

Throughout the novel, Motley presents queer sexuality realistically and sympathetically, as "natural" although unjustly suppressed. Nick's relationship with Owen is the healthiest, most intimate, and supportive relationship he ever has. When Nick eventually does get married, he goes beforehand to visit Owen, and they reminisce about their friendship. Feeling their relationship will end, Owen asks Nick to come back the next day. At that meeting, he presents Nick with two gifts: a wedding present and a package to open on his first anniversary. The gifts prove to be an electric clock and a set of baby clothes. Throughout the novel, Owen is a paragon of kindness, love, and generosity. The relationship serves the novel as an open critique of homophobia. Indeed, Nick's relationship with his wife proves to be far more problematic than that with Owen, and he finds himself impotent in the marriage. This leads eventually to her suicide after Nick reveals to her that since the age of sixteen he has had sex with prostitutes and with gay men—"lots of them."[18] After her funeral, Nick goes to stay with Owen for several weeks in an attempt to recover from his guilt and grief.

In a related subplot, Nick's sister Ang (who had introduced Nick to his wife) falls in love with a Jewish man named Abe, but she cannot marry him out of concern for her mother, a devout Catholic. When Ang becomes pregnant, she asks Nick to find an abortionist. She barely survives the abortion but never marries. Thus the critique of homophobia parallels a more general critique of sexual, religious, and ethnic barriers to love and "natural" human desires. That Willard Motley was a black gay man centering a novel on an Italian American juvenile delinquent on the Near West Side of Chicago cannot be irrelevant to such overarching themes. His novel is queer itself in relationship to the various categorizations Motley had to negotiate, including that of "Negro writer."

Which might well help provoke a return to Lillian Smith's "Negro novel," *Strange Fruit* (1944). Tracy Deen's love for Nonnie Anderson, as we have seen, contradicts Southern norms. As Tracy readjusts to the white position he has inherited, he views his love for Nonnie as sinful, joins the church during a revival, and proposes to a white girl his parents want him to marry. He attempts to convince himself that he never loved Nonnie but merely used her according to the customs of the white South. He tries with all his might to "go straight," as he puts it. Yet the reader knows that his engagement to the white girl is a form of "passing." Here interracial love is "queer" (a term used in the text itself), and Tracy's attempt to "go straight" can only end tragically. Nonnie's brother, who interprets their relationship according to the usual mores of the South, murders him, and all knowledge of the love between Tracy and Nonnie—an embarrassment to his family—is buried.

Parallel to the major action is the queer story of Tracy's sister Laura. Their mother finds the figure of a woman's torso hidden in her dresser drawer. She discovers by reading Laura's letters that Laura sculpted it out of clay on the model of Jane Hardy, an older woman on whom Laura has a crush. "There're women, Laura, who aren't safe for young girls to be with. . . . There're women who are—unnatural. They're like vultures—women like that. . . . They do—terrible things to young girls."[19] Immediately following this conversation, unable to sleep, Laura begins musing on her brother Tracy. He had just joined the church and given Dorothy Pusey a ring, but Laura knows that

He didn't have it in him to go straight. Always he would be doing things—like this [sneaking out to see Nonnie]. It was as if he had to fail—as she had to succeed [in going straight]. Or was she succeeding? And now he would fail with Dorothy. Poor Dottie. She would never understand him. Who did? Always she would worry over him and try to reform him, pushing him further from her with each reformation, for he'd hate her for it.[20]

Laura's situation clearly corresponds to Tracy's.

Coming in late one night from a meeting with Nonnie, Tracy sees Laura reading in bed and stops to say, "There're other things in the world, Sis, but maybe you don't want them." "Maybe I would want them—if I knew what they are," she replies.[21] But she knows that he is hinting that she would be "going with" men and thinking of marriage. Still a college girl, Laura is dealing with confusion about her sexual orientation and the fear of being "queer." When she asks what he means, he responds:

"You aren't asking me to tell you are you?" And he had thrown back his head and laughed softly, and his teeth had flashed in the lamplight. She realized this was the Tracy that Negro girl knew. He had come so quickly from her that he had not had time to take on the protective coloring he wore in the Deen family. "Well . . . good night," he had said, and had limped quietly down the hall to his room, leaving her feeling deprived and restless. This was the Tracy Nonnie Anderson knew. The Tracy women loved.[22]

It is a two-way scene of recognition, in which the "queerness" of each remains unspoken.

Subsequently, Laura begins reflecting on her feelings for Jane, a solitary, bookish girl who kept to herself until the two found each other through mutual interests and freedom from fear about seeming odd:

And soon you were feeling with her a security that you had not felt since you were a little girl with your Mother. And you loved her. Yes, you loved her and wanted to be with her. And now Mother was labeling it with those names that the dean of women at college had warned you about. Yes, you knew. You knew and you did not know. Your mother knew and did not know. The dean of women knew and did not know. But you also knew if Mother made an issue, if she labeled this feeling for Jane with those names, there'd be no more feeling . . . [23]

This sacrifice of feeling demanded by custom and the need for "labels" extends to the feelings across racial lines, including those of a white child for a black nurse or playmate, and Laura knows that it will extend to her relationship to Jane Hardy. "You wouldn't want your relationship with Jane when Mother finished with it. You wouldn't want anything."[24] This "queer" interlude in the narrative—disconnected from the main storyline—reveals the psychosexual crux of *Strange Fruit*, which has to do with the power of desire and the power of social custom to thwart it, to twist it into literally torturous configurations, self-hatred, death, and disaster.

The passage also exemplifies the novel's most unusual narrative feature—a frequent shift to a second-person point of view. The "you" who does the thinking and the feeling shifts from one person to another, across racial and gender lines. While most of the narrative uses the third person, it repeatedly shifts through free indirect discourse to the second person, which "queers" the position of the uncategorized reader. "You" are Tracy, Nonnie, or Laura at various moments throughout the novel—one example of how form follows function in the art of the 1940s.

The first postwar novel to center on a gay male protagonist was Charles Jackson's *The Fall of Valor* (1946). Set in 1943, with pervasive references to the war and the fate of young soldiers, it initiated a series of novels of the immediate postwar period that treated male homosexuality as a "natural" although frighteningly stigmatized orientation—not necessarily exclusive of other forms of love. Homophobia, much more than homosexuality, emerges as a neurosis—and one to which gay men themselves are tragically susceptible. The novel does not directly counter the diagnosis of homosexuality as neurotic, but its protagonist has none of the features stereotypically attributed to gay men. Jackson (who had many of the characteristics of his protagonist) evidently accepted a Freudian association of homosexuality with the death drive. But *The Fall of Valor* treats homosexual desire as an orientation among others—a flaw, perhaps, but not a "perversion"—while targeting the perverse and tragic consequences of the homophobia pervading American society.

John Grandin, an English professor, loves his wife, Ellen, but after fifteen years of marriage feels a growing sense of inadequacy as a husband. His career is going well, and he has a book in press at Scribner's—*The Tragic Ideal*, appropriately enough—that is likely to make his reputation. Yet he feels vaguely that a blow is about to fall, some terrible personal catastrophe. He attributes it to the war, the foreboding and sense of suspension in time that permeates society. At the same time, however, he is deeply troubled about the state of his marriage. He knows that his wife feels unloved and desires greater intimacy, but John finds himself always avoiding it, despite his genuine love for her. Leaving their young sons with her parents in Maine, the two go on a romantic vacation on Nantucket to rekindle their relationship.

On the way they meet a younger just-married couple, Cliff and Billie Hauman, and John Grandin finds himself strangely captivated by Cliff, a marine captain of striking physique and boundless good spirits. Cliff takes to him immediately, calling him "Johnnie," and soon Cliff and Billie become part of the small group with whom John and Ellen sunbathe and socialize on the island. John finds Cliff's friendly overtures both welcome and oddly disturbing until, at the end of the second part of the novel—well over two-thirds of the way into it—he suddenly realizes that he is both in love with and sexually attracted to Cliff. Never having considered the possibility that he was sexually attracted to men, Grandin is profoundly shocked, worried, and determined to allow his friendship with Cliff to end. However, his wife simultaneously figures out what has happened and confronts him, and he admits that he fell in love with Cliff without even knowing it but that he still loves her and that their relationship is more important to him than Cliff can ever be. She initially recoils against his "perversion," to which he replies, "You'll only be sorry later, Ethel, if you begin to use words like that. . . . There's no such thing as perversion . . . everything is either normal, hypo, or hyper. If I've learned anything at all through this, I've learned that much."[25] He adds that his love for Cliff is not his "fault"—it was involuntary, something of which he was unconscious until he caught himself fantasizing about Cliff on the beach.

Feeling humiliated, hating John, Ethel leaves the island immediately and retreats to her parents' home, but while there with her two sons she realizes that she still loves John and that the infatuation with Cliff Hauman is of little importance compared to their marriage. She comes to accept it as a brief infatuation with no future consequences and writes John a letter, addressed to their apartment in New York, expressing her continuing devotion. John returns to New York but perversely leaves a letter for Cliff at the hotel expressing his fondness for him and inviting him to visit him in his apartment, where he will be alone for the near future. Cliff takes him up on the invitation, against John's expectations yet very much in line with his irrepressible desire. During their meeting alone in the apartment, John becomes convinced that Cliff is "playing" him—drawing out his desire only to humiliate him—yet he can't help declaring his love. When he approaches Cliff and passionately embraces him, reaching toward his waist front, Cliff explodes in rage. He grabs the fireplace tongs and beats John senseless. It seems that Cliff too is homosexually inclined at some level—he has been drawing John Grandin out from their first meeting—but he hates the inclination, and he acts out of panic.

The following chapter returns to Ellen in Maine, realizing (on the very day Cliff visits John in New York) that one reason she loved John so much is precisely that he had a partially "feminine" nature: "Had John Grandin been all male, they would not have met on common ground ever."[26] Assuming that he will never see Cliff again (as he promised he would not), she feels relieved that the marriage will survive and that she now has a greater understanding of and love for her husband. The tragedy, of course, is that at this very moment the hopes of both Ellen and John have been blasted. John, in the final moments of the novel, comes to on the floor of the apartment, thinking of the turn of events which had reduced him to a beaten man bleeding here on the floor. He had paid for an old flaw or error, paid twice over, far beyond his deserts; and in all justice, everything was as it should be. Luckily Ethel and the children had been spared the knowledge of the sight of this. But only for the time being. Like the students [at the college], they were certain to find out.

Certain that he will lose everything—his career, his reputation, his wife, and his sons—he drags himself to the door, where Ellen's letter has been delivered. In the novel's final line, as he reads the letter, "his sole emotion was a passionate regret that Cliff had not finished the job."[27]

The critical reception of *The Fall of Valor* was oddly split between respect for Jackson's courage in taking on such an explosive topic and regret that he had not advanced the understanding of male homosexuality beyond what could be found in the clinical literature. Prominent critics, including Edmund Wilson and Diana Trilling, were critical of Jackson's unorthodox treatment of John Grandin not as a neurotic but as a tragic figure. Trilling complained that

> scientific literature is full of psychologically sound records of the homosexual neurosis, and if we are to read Mr. Jackson's novel rather than a textbook, it must be because its study of disease will tell us about more than disease, enlarging beyond the usual limits of a case history our understanding of the world in which illness exists. *The Fall of Valor*, however, seems to me to miss fire on both these counts.[28]

Edmund Wilson in the *New Yorker* wrote a more illuminating review, focusing on the difficulty of treating homosexuality sympathetically and realistically yet producing a novel "which shall not prove repulsive to the novel-reading general public, and perhaps provoke attempts to suppress it." For Wilson, John Grandin is unrealistically ignorant of his sexual orientation—after all, he is a forty-four-year-old English professor—because of the author's need to make him "acceptable to the ordinary reader. . . . A true story of the marriage relation of a homosexual man with a heterosexual woman might reveal a long, messy ordeal or a practicable *modus vivendi*, but, in either case, it would be harder to put over as a novel for the general reader."[29] Jackson, however, had accomplished something unique in making homosexuality "middle class" and thus removing it from the more privileged and effete spheres treated by Proust and Gide. Wilson's diagnosis reminds us of the courage it took to broach homosexuality sympathetically even in the later 1940s, when Jackson's reputation was riding high on the success of his novel *The Lost Weekend* (about alcoholism) and its popular screen adaptation. As the sole recent critic of the novel has written, for the first time a popular American writer had openly centered a novel on the love of an older man for a man half his age, neither of whom displayed mannerisms that most contemporaries considered "queer."[30]

In the following year Gore Vidal's *The City and the Pillar* (1948) attempted deliberately to move beyond *The Fall of Valor*. Vidal would later boast that his was the first novel centered upon the love of an apparently "normal," "masculine," and athletic young man for another of the same type. If Jackson's *The Fall of Valor* had already opened this door, *The City and the Pillar* removed the locks and unpinned the hinges. And like Jackson's move to "gay" fiction in a cresting career, it was a particularly bold move.

Vidal had made his reputation with *Williwaw*, as one of the youngest of the young lions coming out of the war with stories to tell. His literary career was on an upward path and his famous grandfather trying to smooth the way for a career in politics for him when he sent the manuscript of his third novel to his publisher, a year after Jackson's novel appeared. Dutton hated it, but Vidal was their author, so they published it anyway. One editor assured Vidal that the book would ruin his career. Some newspapers refused to advertise it, others to review it. Two weeks after publication it was a bestseller.

The novel features Jim Willard's dawning awareness of his sexual orientation in late adolescence, his first sexual experiences, his denial of his homosexuality out of fear and shame, and then his gradual coming to self-acceptance through a series of short-term relationships, which present a thorough introduction to the ways of "queers" (as they were usually called) in the 1940s—how they find each other, how they make passes, how they respond to unwanted advances by men or women, how they use each other, how they suffer from self-hatred and self-pity—all the ways in which homophobic suppression of desire warps, condemns, and kills people.

Vidal aimed to shock readers with the amount and variety of homosexual activity going on between men who appear to be "normal": "I knew that my description of the love affair between two 'normal' all-American boys of the sort that I had spent three years with in the war-time army would challenge every superstition about sex in my native land. . . . Until then, American novels of 'inversion' dealt with transvestites or with lonely bookish boys who married unhappily and pined for Marines"—the latter a nod to *The Fall of Valor*. "I broke that mold."[31]

The story is all a flashback framed by brief opening and closing chapters that feature the same scene: the protagonist, Jim Willard, in a New York gay bar just after the end of the war in Europe, drinking himself into oblivion. The opening draws attention to a change in temporality: "The moment was strange. . . . Time had stopped." Further on, "Time collapsed. Years passed before he could bring the drink to his mouth."[32] Between these moments the story shifts back to June 1939 (a significant date in the war literature, as we have seen) and then works forward to the stalled moment of the opening, just after V-E Day in 1945. In the final chapter we return to Jim Willard in the bar where the novel opened, but we know now that he has just sexually assaulted and murdered his best friend and truest love from childhood, Bob Ford, because Ford has furiously rejected him. Ford did not just repel Jim's sexual advance but Jim as a person, as a "queer." The temporal form of the novel comports with that of the "war novels" and of Carson McCullers's *The Member of the Wedding*. "Normal time" frames the "queer" interim that coincides with the war.

The "story" starts at high-school commencement in a northeastern Virginia town in 1939, when Jim, always shy with girls and curiously disinterested in them sexually, feels an insatiable love for his friend Bob. Bob, who lusts after girls, has no sexual interest in boys, but the intimacy between them tortures Jim with longing, and during a drunken night away from home, he manages to make love with Bob at the site of an old slave cabin by the Potomac River. They already know that Bob is going away to sea. For the rest of the story, Jim dreams of resuming the love affair he has fantasized but that Bob considers "awful kid stuff" and buries in an unmarked grave. The story then follows Jim's dawning, conflicted awareness of "what he is" and his initiation into the many worlds of gay male experience in various American cities: Seattle, Los Angeles, New Orleans, and especially New York. We thus get a guided tour of white gay male experience in the midcentury United States, through all its nooks, crannies, mansions, and hotel rooms.

We also learn the most current vocabulary:

> The words *fairy* and *pansy* were considered to be in bad taste [in New York]. They preferred to say that a man was *gay*, while someone quite effeminate was a *queen*. As for those manly youths who offered themselves for seduction while proclaiming their heterosexuality, they were known as *trade*, since they usually wanted money.[33]

By the end of the war, Jim has finally come not only to acknowledge his homosexuality but to view it as "natural" and healthy. This is a gay bildungsroman in that it chronicles the development of a gay identity and Jim's achievement of self-knowledge before the final catastrophe. Returning to his hometown after years away, Jim has to manage his mother's and sister's questions and advice about marrying and settling down. His "masquerade" annoys and saddens him:

> He wondered suddenly what would happen if every man like himself were to be natural and honest. Life would certainly be better for everyone in a world where sex was thought of as something natural and not fearsome, and men could love men naturally, in the way they were meant to, as well as to love women naturally, as they were meant to. But even as he sat at the table, pondering freedom, he knew that it was a dangerous thing to be an honest man; finally, he lacked the courage.[34]

Pondering freedom. This phrase reveals the narrative logic by which Jim and Bob's one rendezvous took place at an "old slave cabin" in the woods by the Potomac, the place to which Jim mentally returns over and over during their separation. "Was it still there?" Jim wonders, as he fantasizes about renewing his relationship with Bob, even though Jim knows that Bob is married and feels no "lust for the male."[35] In this as in other white-authored novels of the 1940s dealing with queer sexuality, black experience and antiracist themes surface at pivotal moments. The dominant society has buried the history of slavery in the past, hidden it from view. But the reality of black experience, the need to bear witness, surfaces, in a kind of homology to the need for gay liberation and a questioning of the very categories that people must internalize to live. Queer love takes place in a disavowed location that everyone knows about.

Vidal was well known for resisting the notion of homosexual *identity*; he long insisted that there are no homosexuals, only homosexual acts. It is therefore somewhat ironic that in one of his earliest essay-reviews, a young James Baldwin took the publication of Vidal's *The City and the Pillar* and Charles Jackson's *The Fall of Valor* as the occasion for making his first public statement against homophobia and insisting on the fluidity of gender and sexuality, linking homophobia to the rigid boundary set between masculinity and femininity in American culture. The essay appeared in *Zero*, a little magazine published in Tangier in 1949; Baldwin would not include it in later collections of his essays. He critiques views of homosexual acts as unnatural (it is obvious that *nature* does not prohibit them) or ungodly ("God" is "man's most intense creation," so if He condemns so many people to "something less than life" we are limiting ourselves in our conception of the divine).[36] He then takes aim at the rigid demarcation of "masculine" and "feminine" attributes, particularly in noir fiction by the likes of James M. Cain and Raymond Chandler. Americans have created and perfected the "tough guy" to avoid the complexity of gender and thus adulthood itself. (Hence the essay's title, "Preservation of Innocence.") He then reads recent "gay" novels—particularly Jackson's and Vidal's—as following the "hard-boiled" masculinist style of Cain and Chandler and denouncing homosexuality.

The interpretation is understandable but misdirected. Jackson and Vidal had put in question the routine identification of male homosexuality with "effeminacy." They destabilized binary conceptions of gender and sexuality as well as the notion of homosexuality as unnatural. Because the novels both end in tragic acts of homophobic rage, Baldwin interprets them as homophobic themselves, concerned with "the ever-present danger of sexual activity between men."[37] Yet Baldwin's concluding thesis coincides with Vidal's views. Human beings, Baldwin writes,

> cannot ever be labeled. Once the novelist has created a human being he has shattered the label and, in transcending the subject matter, is able, for the first time, to tell us something about it and to reveal how profoundly all things involving human beings interlock. Without this passion we may all smother to death, locked in those airless, labeled cells, which isolate us from each other and separate us from ourselves; and without this passion when we have discovered the connection between that Boy-Scout who smiles from the subway poster and that underworld to be found all over America, vengeful time will be upon us.[38]

Vidal's point was, in part, precisely to make that connection.

Almost simultaneously with Vidal's novel, Truman Capote (whom Baldwin would meet in Paris about the time "Preservation of Innocence" came out, beginning a long friendship) published his first novel, *Other Voices, Other Rooms*—also overtly "queer" and publicized as such by Random House. The back of the dust jacket featured the young author in a flagrantly sultry pose, complemented by the publishers' claim on the front flap that the novel was "one of the leading incidents in the emergence of a new mode in American fiction."[39] The novel quickly moved up the bestseller lists. For all the fanfare, however, it has been largely ignored, only recently drawing increasing attention from scholars of queer fiction. I find it one of the most intricate, sensitive, and extraordinary of American novels.

Categorized as a novel of ambivalently expressed homosexual identity, it can only fall short, as some critics have argued. Yet to categorize it as a gay-affirmative novel, as some have attempted to do, raises even greater challenges. Read as a novel about the violence of categorization as such, however, it has few equals. Joseph Valente has argued recently that it anticipates twenty-first-century queer theory, departing from gay identity politics to offer "identity critique"—that is, taking a position that refuses to be identified on one side or the other of the homo/hetero boundary.[40] One result of this resistance to categorization is that the primary adult gay man is ultimately rejected as a model or mentor for the queer male protagonist. Yet Valente, who brilliantly notes the importance of physical "deformity" to the novel's critique, never mentions the centrality of race to Joel's disidentification. Racism is a main target of the novel. Racial segregation structures the narrative in both its plot and the rhythms of its symbolic form. The protagonist's rejection of his presumed white mentor, on a razor's edge as the novel ends, signals his turn away from "whiteness" as he has come to know it. Joel Knox's maturation depends on leaving behind the rotting palace of the Snow Queen.

Like key aspects of *Go Down, Moses* and all of *The Member of the Wedding*, the novel is ultimately as much about a white child's developing racialization on the brink of adulthood as about homosexuality, although the "queer" trajectory intersects with that subject matter, making for a rich treatment of the drama of race, sex, and gender realizations during the passage from childhood to adulthood. The novel queers racial identity just as it queers gender and sexual identity, as well as the physical categorizations that separate "midgets" from others, ultimately opposing all categories with the demands of eros.[41] Here again, Hart Crane's visionary company beckons just beyond the horizon visible from the "broken tower."

As the novel opens we meet Joel Knox, age thirteen, white, of New Orleans, the son of divorced parents, raised by his mother with no memory of his father and taken in by an aunt after his mother's death. Joel's father has sent for him from Skully's Landing, outside Noon City, Alabama. Bedridden and on the verge of death, he lives in a crumbling plantation house with his second wife, Amy, and his "queer" and decadent cousin Randolph. They are served by an ancient wizened black man named Jesus Fever and his twenty-one-year-old granddaughter, Missouri Fever, known as "Zoo." Like a long-stemmed rose, her most prominent feature is a very long neck. Joel arrives with a valise inherited from his grandfather, a well-known Confederate officer, looking forward to meeting his father.

That meeting is long delayed, and in the meantime Joel gets to know two local girls, twins named Florabel and Idabel. Florabel is normatively "girly"; Idabel is a tomboy who wishes to be a boy, and it is to her that Joel, an "effeminate" boy, is most attracted. They have various adventures (with much reversal of conventional gender position), but Joel quickly grows even closer to Zoo. They come to love each other, but not in a romantic or sexual way. Neither does Zoo serve as a "Mammy." Zoo has come from St. Louis to care for her grandfather and plans to move to the North whenever Jesus Fever dies. Mentored alternately by Randolph and Zoo, who present different alternatives of ethical orientation, Joel attempts to figure just where he fits, who he "is." The alternation structures the novel and sets up its central conflict.

The novel begins with an apocalyptic epigraph from Jeremiah 17:9: "The heart is deceitful above all things, and desperately wicked. Who can know it?" It is a key to Joel's struggle to know his own heart in a very confusing world. An African American spiritual gives the novel its other key allusion, reinforced throughout the story: "God gave Noah the rainbow sign, / No more water, the fire next time." Jesus Fever explicitly alludes to the spiritual when he, Zoo, and Joel are together in front of a fire one night, fantasizing about a future in which Joel and Zoo would stay together and he would buy her gifts with money earned from singing in vaudeville. A fireplace log falls and sends up sparks, which causes a nest of chimney swifts to fall into the fire and burn up. Jesus speaks up, ominously: "In fire . . . first comes water, and last comes the fire. Don't say no place in the Good Book why we's in tween. Do it? . . . You, . . . you-all! It's gettin powerful warm, it's gettin fire!"[42] To be 'tween is the burden of all, caught between the water and the fire.

Fundamental to the novel's narrative structure, and explaining the book's title, is Joel's alternation between rooms inhabited by Randolph and/or Amy and/or his father and rooms inhabited by Zoo and/or Jesus Fever. The alternation often defines the progression of chapters, moving from one group to the other. It suggests a division in Joel's loyalties, the pull of either small community. With Zoo and Jesus in chapter 9, Joel asks Zoo if she knows who Alcibiades was, for Randolph had said Joel resembled him. Zoo apparently does not know and says that Joel must have heard wrong; the name Randolph "most likely said" is Alicaster, the name of a choir boy in the town of Paradise Chapel who is so pretty he has the preacher and all sorts of "mens and ladies lovin him up." Alcibiades, in contrast, was a Greek general who repeatedly switched sides between the Athenians, Spartans, and Persians in the Peloponnesian wars before finally being done in by his enemies. Joel's relatives, particularly his cousin Randolph, draw him in, but so do Zoo and Jesus. From Randolph and Amy he absorbs condescending attitudes toward black servants that, when he finds himself with Zoo again, he imitatively expresses, only to be rebuffed by Zoo and made to feel ashamed. Zoo also tells Joel not to ask her about his father: "Don't never ax me nothin' bout Mister Sansom. Miss Amy the one take care of him. Ax her. Ax Mister Randolph. I ain't in noways messed up with Mister Sansom; don't even fix him his vittels. Me and Papadaddy, us got our own troubles."[43]

It is only because Joel is a thirteen-year-old boy that he (like Frankie in *The Member of the Wedding*) can shuttle back and forth between the two groups. Zoo seems aware, like Berenice Brown in McCullers's queer novel, that eventually he will have to "grow up" into his prescribed identity.

The novel moves on a pattern of dominant images: sun, snow, fire, water, clouds, thunder, rosebush, and a cracked bell. In Noon City and environs, the sun is oppressive and associated with white patriarchy—in fact, with Joel's father. Zoo, above all, feels oppressed by the sun and longs to move to a place with snow. Zoo and Joel both fantasize about snow, associating it with a relief from their circumstances. Zoo dreams of escaping Noon City for the North: "I wants to be where they got snow, and not all this sunshine." When she asks Joel if he has seen snow, he lies, "for he had a great yearning to see bona fide snow: next to owning

the Koh-i-noor diamond, that was his ultimate secret wish." He improvises a tale, apparently influenced by "The Snow Queen," about how he
and his mother got lost in the snow in Canada, ending up in an ice-cold
cave, and were finally rescued by a Canadian mountie—"only me, really:
Mama had already frozen to death."[44]

Snow proves dangerously seductive, as in the legend of the Snow
Queen, which Joel's Aunt Ellen read to him one night before he left New
Orleans:

> Listening to it, it came to Joel that he had a lot in common with Little
> Kay, whose outlook was twisted when a splinter from the Sprite's evil
> mirror infected his eye, changing his heart into a lump of bitter ice . . .
> suppose, like Little Kay, he also were spirited off to the Snow Queen's
> frozen palace? What living soul would then brave robber barons for his
> rescue? And there was no one, really no one.[45]

The danger shadowing Joel's transition to adulthood is that his heart
will turn to ice. Nowhere is this danger greater than in his relationship to
his would-be guardian, Randolph, the Snow Queen himself. Zoo—who
may be the very rescuer he needs—shares his dream of snow. In her attempt to move to a place with snow, she will find herself stranded on the
roadside and gang-raped at gunpoint. Asked by Joel if she had seen snow
on her journey to Washington, D.C., near the end of the novel, Zoo
replies:

> "Did I see snow!" and she broke into a kind of scary giggle, and threw
> back her head, lips apart, like an open-mouthed child hoping to catch
> rain. "There ain't none," she said, violently shaking her head, her black
> greased hair waving with a windy rasp like scorched grass. "Hit's all a
> lotta foolery, snow and such: that sun! it's everywhere."[46]

"Like Mr. Sansom's eyes," Joel says to himself—like whiteness.

The rose has a peculiar presence in the novel. In the final scene, it is a
bloomless stalk throwing a shadow like a sundial, keeping time as some

sort of apotheosis nears. Earlier in the novel, it centers a prayer meeting over which Zoo presides in the house behind the garden she shares with Jesus—most likely a former slave cabin. The meeting serves as a kind of initiation of Joel into the world—or "room"—she shares with Jesus. Zoo plays accordion while chanting prayers and dancing: "Listen oh Lord when us pray, kindly hear what us has to say." She chants and stamps the ground as clouds cover the sun and then lightning cuts the sky. As thunder rolls, Jesus grows cold and worries about the storm descending. "Then an unusual thing occurred: as if following the directions of a treasure map, Zoo took three measured paces toward a dingy little rose bush, and, frowning up at the sky, discarded the red ribbon binding her throat. A narrow scar circled her neck like a necklace of purple wire; she traced a finger over it lightly." In contrast with Zoo's kinship to the rose—in Christian iconography, a symbol of the blood of martyrs and the wounds of Christ—Randolph prefers "the solitary mole: he is no rose dependent upon thorn and root . . . : sightless, he goes his separate way, knowing truth and freedom are attitudes of the spirit."[47]

For Zoo truth and freedom are not matters of the solitary spirit. They have more to do with love—another meaning of the rose. Randolph's nihilistic solipsism reveals itself elsewhere, as well, in his love of mirrors and his attachment to "identity":

> They can romanticize us so, mirrors, and that is their secret: what a subtle torture it would be to destroy all the mirrors in the world: where then could we look for reassurance of our identities? I tell you, my dear, Narcissus was no egotist . . . he was merely another of us who, in our unshatterable isolation, recognized, on seeing his reflection, the one beautiful comrade, the only inseparable love . . . poor Narcissus, possibly the only human who was ever honest on this point.[48]

Zoo and Randolph serve as opposing mentors on Joel's journey toward selfhood, in which narcissistic "identity" is a primary obstacle.

Some warning of which of the two will win out is given in the midst of the prayer meeting in the home of Zoo and Jesus. After Zoo paces toward the rosebush and reveals her scar, Joel panics: "It was as though a brutal hawk had soared down and clawed away Joel's eyelids, forcing him to gape at her throat. Zoo. Maybe she was like him, and the world had a grudge against her, too. But christamighty he didn't want to end up with a scar like that."[49]

At this key moment, horrified by the scar revealing where Zoo's husband had slit her throat (like the stem of a rose), Joel recoils from his connection with her. Thunder booms, the earth shakes, and Joel flees the cabin for the big house. In his panic, he "pitched headlong into a briar patch. This was a kind of freak accident. He'd seen the patch, known it for an obstacle, and yet, as though deliberately, he'd thrown himself upon it."[50]

The event recalls one of the most famous Brer Rabbit tales, in which Brer Fox, attempting to catch and eat Brer Rabbit, fashions a tar baby and places it in the road. Brer Rabbit tries to engage it in polite greetings, but when the tar baby fails to respond, he gets angry and punches it, getting a paw stuck in the tar. He then strikes with his other paw and gets it stuck, as well. Trying to come unstuck from the tar baby, Brer Rabbit gets thoroughly tarred—blackened, so to speak. Fox laughs, thinking he has Brer Rabbit dead to rights. The rabbit asks Fox to throw him into a briar patch, which Fox does, thinking Brer Rabbit will be torn to pieces and die. Instead the rabbit escapes, announcing that he was born and bred in the briar patch.

Joel's leap into the briar patch to escape his predicament serves "to cleanse him of bewilderment and misery, just as the devil, in fanatic cults, is supposedly, through self-imposed pain, driven from the soul." Having escaped the tar in this act of disidentification with Zoo and Jesus, Joel recalls Zoo's concern for him and feels foolish: "She was, after all, his friend, and there was no need to be afraid." Zoo plucks the briars from him and asks why he acts "so ugly? Huh, hurt me and Papadaddy's feelins." It is not the last time he will do so. Yet Zoo forgives him and asks him to join in a final, silent prayer. When Joel bows his head the words will not come, because he is used to praying for simple things—a pocket knife, a bicycle. "Only how, how, could you say something so indefinite, so meaningless as this: God, let me be loved."[51] As if finishing the same prayer, Zoo whispers "Amen." And then the rain descends.

One is reminded of the spiritual: "No more water, the fire next time." Joel's betrayal of Zoo and Jesus, as if in fear of the stigmata of their blackness, anchors one of the novel's chief themes, the betrayal of a common humanity and of that humanity's dependence on love. We discover in the next chapter that such betrayal is inherent in the assertion of racial difference as much as in absolute gender distinction.

When Joel tells Randolph and Amy about Zoo's scar, Randolph wearily and sarcastically tells about the night Zoo's husband tried to kill her. He and Amy had lent her a room for their honeymoon. Sitting in the parlor with Amy, he had heard Zoo scream:

> "And I said: it's the wind. Of course I knew it wasn't." He paused, and sucked in his cheeks, as though the memory proved too exquisitely humorous for him to maintain a straight face. He aimed a gun-like finger at Joel, and cocked his thumb: "So I put a roller in the pianola, and it played the Indian Love Call."
>
> "Such a sweet song," said Amy. "So sad. I don't know why you never let me play the pianola any more."[52]

When Joel observes, in a panic, that Keg had cut Zoo's throat, Randolph replies with shocking unconcern, "Uh yes, absolutely." Amy then begins humming the "Indian Love Call." Randolph adds: "from ear to ear: ruined a roseleaf quilt my great-great aunt in Tennessee lost her eyesight stitching," while Amy keeps trying to remember the tune.[53] It becomes increasingly clear that the "big house" is the Ice Palace in Capote's gothic tale.

Randolph proves the antithesis of another white man whose memory is honored in the name of Jesus Fever's mule. In his address to the court before sentencing, the "real" John Brown famously said, "Now, if it be deemed necessary that I should forfeit my life, for the furtherance of the ends of justice, and mingle my blood further with the blood of my children, and with the blood of millions in this Slave country, whose rights are disregarded by wicked, cruel, and unjust enactments,—I say, LET

IT BE DONE." John Brown haunts *Other Voices, Other Rooms* from the moment Jesus picks Joel up in a wagon drawn by the mule at the beginning of the story to the final chapter. It makes sense to reflect on his connection with the apocalyptic strain in the novel.

Union folklore during the Civil War identified John Brown with John the Baptist. In Luke 3:15, John the Baptist says, as he begins baptizing people in the river Jordan, "I baptize with water, but there cometh one after me, the latchet of whose shoes I am not worthy to stoop down and unloose. He will baptize you with fire and with the Holy Spirit." Inspiration for the Negro spiritual, this passage also lies behind a popular version of "John Brown's Body," a well-known Union marching song during the Civil War:

John Brown was John the Baptist of the Christ we are to see,
Christ who of the bondsman shall the Liberator be,
And soon throughout the Sunny South the slaves shall all be free,
For his soul is marching on.[54]

The lines resonate in Zoo's "Sunny South" overseen by Joel's dying father. Brown's hanging came to be widely regarded as a portent of the war. In Capote's novel, John Brown dramatically reappears, hanged to death, in the final chapter.

The motifs structuring the novel—cloud, thunder, sun, rosebush, snow, bell, and John Brown—reappear in a complex narrative pattern in the climactic closing chapter. When Joel awakens in sickbed after his adventure at the circus with Idabell and Wisteria, he is back at Skully's Landing attended by Randolph, with whom he feels a strong bond of dependency and love. Randolph informs him that Zoo has returned. But when Zoo comes into the room, she seems far away, traumatized by the gang rape she has just survived. When she tells the story of her ordeal, Joel cannot bear it and plugs his ears: "what Zoo said was ugly, he was sick-sorry she'd ever come back, she ought to be punished, 'Stop that, Zoo,' he said, 'I won't listen, I won't.'" But Zoo takes on the look of Jesus in the ecstasy of his passion: "wide swung her arms embracing the eternal: she was a cross, she was crucified."[55] Through it all, Joel keeps his fingers in his ears in denial of her. It seems that he has, after all, chosen Randolph over Zoo.

The next day, he and Randolph set out for the Cloud Hotel next to the Drownin Pool, in a wagon drawn by John Brown. The purpose of the trip is not clear, for although Randolph says that Little Sunshine has sent for Joel, this turns out to be false. (It will turn out that the point of the trip is to have Joel away from the house when Aunt Ellen, his former guardian, comes to see him. She arrives while they are away, and Amy, following orders from Randolph, tells her Joel and his father have left. What Joel also does not realize is that, contrary to his belief that Ellen has never replied to his letters, Randolph has been intercepting all attempted correspondence between them.) Randolph himself has not been to visit the Cloud Hotel since he was a child. In fact, Randolph tells Little Sunshine that most of him never left the Cloud Hotel after his childhood visits. Joel seems entranced meanwhile and hallucinates the presence of many people out of the past. He looks into the fire in the fireplace and sees a vacillating shape of a face: "his eyes burned tar-hot as he brought them nearer: tell me, tell me, who are you? are you someone I know? are you dead? are you my friend? do you love me? But the painted, disembodied head remained unborn beyond its mask, and gave no clue. Are you someone I am looking for?"[56] Afraid of finding out who that might be, Joel draws back, thinking it would be better not to know the figure in the fire.

It turns out to be none other than John Brown. Joel, Randolph, and Little Sunshine hear a great clamor outside the room and go to investigate. Having climbed to the top of the stairs, the mule is on the balcony overlooking the lobby; he leaps when Little Sunshine orders him to come down and is hanged by the rope-reins about his neck, "his big lamplike eyes, lit by the torch's blaze . . . golden with death's impossible face, the figure in the fire."[57]

When they awaken in the morning, Randolph and Joel creep out of the hotel, Joel averting his eyes so as not to see the mule. He and Randolph make no mention of the accident, in effect disavowing John

Brown, "as if from the outset they'd planned to return to the Landing on foot." The effect on Joel is curiously liberating and confers on him the identity he has been seeking; he feels free of the past. "The morning was like a slate clean for any future, and it was as though an end had come." He cries to Randolph, "I am me . . . I am Joel, we are the same people."[58] He sees Randolph walking blindly in a circle, but Joel feels strong and self-confident, believing he finally knows who he is.

However, when they return to the Landing, they come upon Zoo trying to uproot the "slave bell" and Amy seeming to direct her. When Amy and Randolph go into the house, Zoo spits vindictively on the bell and kicks it over, saying, "Ain't nobody gonna pay cash-money for that piece-a mess. She plumb outa sense, the one done told Miss Amy any such of a thing."[59] As if to crown the corruption of a slave-owning legacy, Amy hopes to sell the bell—and, irony of ironies, expects Zoo to uproot it for her.

The scene harkens back to Joel's first discovery of the garden, at the end of chapter 2. He was playing "soldier" alone in back of the house and had charged toward the broken porch columns when he "discovered the bell. It was a bell like those used in slave-days to summon fieldhands from work." Joel had poked his head inside and, feeling the eyes of a lizard on him, withdrawn in fear. He then had looked up at the windows of the house, wondering which belonged to the rooms of his father and Randolph. "It was at this point that he saw the queer lady. She was holding aside the curtains of the left corner window, and smiling and nodding at him, as if in greeting or approval." We are told that she looked like a figure out of history in a white wig with a high pompadour and dribbling curls—perhaps a plantation mistress of antebellum times. (It later becomes clear that the "queer lady" is Randolph.) When she dropped the curtain, Joel, reawakening from a trance, "took a backward step and stumbled against the bell: one raucous, cracked note rang out, shattering the hot stillness."[60]

The novel's final paragraphs present an apotheosis of its interlocking motifs and themes. Zoo has retreated from Joel, leaving him alone in the garden behind the house known as "Skulls" (for Skully's Landing).

Clouds move in, becoming "thunder-dark" and "John Brown," and "when they were gone, Mr. Sansom was the sun." Joel waits apprehensively for something about to happen. A rose stalk throws a "shadow like a sundial," and the time of transformation arrives. He feels someone watching him from the windows of the house:

> All of him was dumb except his eyes. They knew. And it was Randolph's window. Gradually the blinding sunset drained from the glass, darkened, and it was as if snow were falling there, flakes shaping snow-eyes, hair: a face trembled like a white beautiful moth, smiled. She beckoned to him, shining and silver, and he knew he must go: unafraid, not hesitating, he paused only at the garden's edge where, as though he'd forgotten something, he stopped and looked back at the bloomless, descending blue, at the boy he had left behind.[61]

If this novel is a bildungsroman, it is the tale of a snowy bildung toward a heart of ice, narrowly averted as Joel turns away from Randolph and his father to take another path. Like the slave bell, the heritage of slavery and whites' disavowal of the humanity of African Americans resounds throughout the novel so insistently it is amazing how little attention has been paid to that theme and, for that matter, to the novel itself. Perhaps our categorizations are at fault.

Carson McCullers levels a related attack on the interrelationships between racism, racial binarism, and gender/sexual normativity in the South in virtually all of her fiction. Like Capote's, her hatred of racism went back to her Southern childhood and was the main reason for what she called her feelings of the "horror" of the South.[62] Connected with "abnormal" gender and sexual attributes is an interest in "freaks" more generally (particularly overt in *The Member of the Wedding*), similar to Capote's. Rachel Adams, in one of the best analyses of McCullers's fiction (specifically, *The Member of the Wedding* and *Clock Without Hands*), has observed that "freakish characters point to the untenability of normative concepts of gender and race" in McCullers's fiction. Adams sees this fiction as responding to the "paranoia and conformity that characterized the onset of the Cold War," but it can also be understood in the context of other queer fiction of its time—particularly that of Burns, Capote, Vidal, and Tennessee Williams—and the upwelling of "non-normative" sexuality during the war itself.[63]

It is not insignificant that *The Member of the Wedding* is set near a military base in the South and that its prepubescent protagonist gets involved with a soldier on leave, nor that the crisis of "belonging" occurs for Frankie when her brother returns from the army to get married just as she is making the transition between childhood and adulthood. There is a utopian moment when the black nanny Berenice Brown, the white "tween" F. Jasmine, and the very young white John Henry commune in the kitchen the last evening before the wedding, sharing their notions of a perfect world. It is a "queer" time at twilight, and after sharing their ideas of perfect worlds—Frankie's being one in which "people could instantly change back and forth from boys to girls," Berenice's one without war and in which "all human beings would be light brown color with blue eyes and black hair . . . all human men and ladies and children as one loving family on the earth."[64] This is followed by a "queer conversation" about love, which in turn leads to a conversation about being "caught" in separate identities in time and a sudden tearful moment of ecstatic communion as consciousness of their existential entrapment brings them together, as if feeling that such a moment may never come again:

> The three of them sat silent, close together, and they could feel and hear each other's breaths. Then suddenly it started, though why and how they did not know; the three of them began to cry. They started at exactly the same moment, in the way that often on these summer evenings they would suddenly start a song. . . . Often they would sing like this and their tunes were sweet and queer in the August kitchen after it was dark. But never before had they suddenly begun to cry; and though their reasons were three different reasons, yet they started at the same instant as though they had agreed together. . . . They cried in the dark for about a minute. Then they stopped as suddenly as they had begun.[65]

Thus ends their "final kitchen afternoon." The key here is that though their reasons for crying were different, they cried at the same time, unpremeditated but "as though they had agreed together." Hold that thought: it will appear again and again in the guise of the desire for universality.

The next day, the circle will be broken: the soldier will marry his bride, and F. Jasmine, her name changed to Frances, will begin to take on her adult identity as a white woman. The "queer" time of the novel coincides with the war years and connects this novel of 1946 with other "queer" texts of the late 1940s. José Esteban Muñoz's argument concerning a queer utopianism and its relationship to ecstasy and queer temporality is apt with respect to the horizon of the 1940s: "To see queerness as horizon is to perceive it as a modality of ecstatic time in which the temporal stranglehold that I describe as straight time is interrupted or stepped out of."[66] Here again we see how the tendency to divide the century at 1945 and read what comes after in relation to the Cold War screens out an important aspect of what made the social context and the literary expression of the 1940s so generative. Incidentally, during part of the time that McCullers wrote this novel, she was living in the same house as Richard and Ellen Wright in Brooklyn; he was starting his autobiography *American Hunger* (published in 1945 as *Black Boy*).[67] They were great admirers of each other's work.

McCullers's earlier *Reflections in a Golden Eye* (1941), a novella set on a military base in the South (what could be more patriarchal and heteronormative?), centers on "abnormal" emotions and inchoate erotic drives. It unsettles the homo/hetero boundary with characters who have both "masculine" and "feminine" qualities as well as erotic urges that cannot be easily pigeonholed. The central character, Captain Penderton, knows that his wife is carrying on a long-term affair with a neighbor and friend, Major Morris Langdon, but cannot decide whether he is more jealous of Langdon or of his wife. She was a virgin when they married, and "Four nights after her wedding she was still a virgin, and on the fifth night her status was changed only enough to leave her somewhat puzzled." Thereafter she has indulged in numerous affairs, which she "would probably have reckoned . . . according to a system of her own." As for the Captain, "he had a sad penchant for becoming enamored of her lovers."[68] In addition to being in love with Major Langdon (something he cannot admit to himself), in the course of the story he becomes obsessed with a Private Williams, although he does not know the basis of his obsession. Increasingly disturbed by his feelings for Williams, because of his own homophobia the captain develops an animus against him (much as the master-at-arms John Claggart in Melville's *Billy Budd* is in love with and "down on" the titular character). He begins by harassing the private in petty ways and ends by murdering him with a bullet to the head.

Private Williams himself has some unusual ways for getting off. He occasionally takes a horse from the post's stable and rides to a secluded clearing in the woods, where he unsaddles the horse and lets it run free. Then he strips off his clothes and lies down on a large flat rock in the middle of the clearing to soak up the sun.

> Sometimes, still naked, he stood on the rock and slipped upon the horse's bare back. His horse was an ordinary army plug which, with anyone but Private Williams, could sustain only two gaits. . . . But with the soldier a marvelous change came over the animal; he cantered or single-footed with proud, stiff elegance. The soldier's body was of a pale golden brown and he held himself erect. Without his clothes he was so slim that the pure, curved outlines of his ribs could be seen. As he cantered about in the sunlight, there was a sensual, savage smile on his lips that would have surprised his barrack mates. After such outings he came back weary to the stables and spoke to no one.[69]

Williams gains the same sort of satisfaction, oddly enough, by sneaking into Leonora Penderton's bedroom at night and staring at her as she sleeps.

McCullers at no point aligns such erotic encounters with definable sexual "identities" or even definable sexual practices. Private Williams's outings with the horse are not instances of "bestiality" any more than Captain Penderton's obsession with Williams can be called simply "homosexual." Similarly, Major Langdon's wife, who knows all about her husband's affair with her friend Leonora Pemberton, is in love with her "effeminate" Filipino servant, Anacleto, but there is no "sex" between them. It is Anacleto, who loves to paint with watercolors, who gives the story its title. He and Alison Langdon are planning to go away to live together one afternoon while he is painting in his room. Suddenly he crumples up the paper he has been painting on and stares into the fire, saying "Look! . . . A peacock of a sort of ghastly green. With one immense golden eye. And in it these reflections of something tiny and—"; Alison finishes for him: "Grotesque."[70]

All of the characters—"two officers, a soldier, two women, a Filipino, and a horse," whom the narrator identifies in the opening paragraph of the novella as "the participants of this tragedy"—are such reflections. All are, in other words, grotesques—indeed, made grotesque (like Sherwood Anderson's "grotesques" in *Winesburg, Ohio* [1919]) by their inability to voice or even acknowledge their actual desires—and the novel seems to have little in the way of an identifiable point other than to flaunt sexual "abnormality" without the narrative benefit of actual sex. (This no doubt bears some relationship to McCullers's own "queer" yet sexless relationships as well as her preference for triangulated ones.) As Melissa Free has aptly stated, "the grotesque, without the presence of the normal, is disorienting to the reader who expects, on the spectrum of deviancy, to be able to locate (him- or herself through) the ordinary."[71] Society's need to "know" and to identify sexual norms is completely frustrated here. Considering the role of sex in the history of the novel, this makes *Reflections in a Golden Eye* a queer novel, indeed.

Tennessee Williams, who had written the introduction to the first edition of *Reflections in a Golden Eye*, after reading *The Member of the Wedding* in 1946 thought McCullers "perhaps the greatest novelist then alive in America" and wrote her a letter to tell her so.[72] Their subsequent friendship grew precious and inspirational to both writers, who even worked across a kitchen table from each other, each on his/her own play, for several weeks in the summer of 1946 on Nantucket Island—McCullers on the play version of *The Member of the Wedding*, which Williams would bring to the attention of James Laughlin of New Directions Press, his own publisher.[73] Wishing they could be together again to write in each other's company, McCullers wrote Williams in February 1948, "Without my imaginary life—in which you play a leading part, *I would go crazy*."[74] Williams shared his thoughts about other gay writers, including the young Gore Vidal just after the publication of *The City and the Pillar*:

> Vidal is 23 and a real beauty. His new book "The City and the Pillar" I have just read and while it is not a good book it is absorbing. There is not a really distinguished line in the book and yet a great deal of it has a curiously life-like quality. The end is trashy, alas, murder and suicide both. But you would like the boy as I do: his eyes remind me of yours![75]

Part of what makes this correspondence significant is its indication of a growing self-identified (and at times competitive and rebarbative) community of gay/lesbian or queer writers.

Thus, for example, Capote had dedicated *Other Voices, Other Rooms* to the gay critic Newton Arvin, whom he regarded as a mentor. McCullers was also close friends with Arvin, and McCullers and Capote would develop a rather intense relationship/rivalry one critic has termed "tumultuous."[76] McCullers even thought he had plagiarized her own work for part of *Other Voices, Other Rooms*.[77] Confirming the perceived close relationship between Capote's treatment of his material and McCullers's work, Williams wrote her that he saw Capote as "a derivative writer whose tiny feet have attempted to fit the ten-league boots of Carson McCullers and succeeded only in tripping him up absurdly."[78]

McCullers disapproved of Gore Vidal, who, for his part, reportedly said of her that "an hour with a dentist without Novocain was like a minute with Carson McCullers."[79] Williams, in 1948, wrote disapprovingly of Gore Vidal's competitiveness toward Capote (which never really faded):

> He is interesting but is infected with that awful competitive spirit and seems to be continually haunted over the successes or achievements of other writers such as Truman Capote. He is positively obsessed with poor little Truman Capote. You would think they were running neck

and neck for some fabulous gold prize! I don't like that attitude and spirit in young writers. But of course it is a result of insecurity.[80]

Vidal would later lament Williams's self-hatred as a gay man and claim that he tried to point out to him that the ruling class used taboos, punishing people who broke them while, "best of all, creating an ongoing highly exploitable sense of guilt in just about everyone."[81] As important as the antagonisms in their friendship is the fact that they considered themselves part of a literary insurgency that was making a huge mark on the literary landscape of the late 1940s.

Among the most powerful works making that mark were Williams's *The Glass Menagerie* (1944) and *A Streetcar Named Desire* (1947). Considering the relationship between McCullers and Williams and the latter's opinion of *Reflections in a Golden Eye*, it seems worth quoting a close student of both on reasons for Williams's partiality for *Reflections*:

> I believe, thinking of his family, that [Williams] sees the struggle between the characters in *Reflections*, perhaps, as reflecting some of the dynamics in his family with his father's, I think, ambivalence and sexuality in that family and this sort of strange dynamics at work, with the Pendertons especially. With the Marlon Brando character in the film and how he was this sort of hyper-masculine figure, which was, of course, masking his repressed homosexuality, and the devastating effect that it has on everyone around them. And I think Williams may have responded to that. I think it is very similar to the way I've always thought of Captain Penderton, and it's great that Brando played them both, Captain Penderton and Stanley Kowalski. It's ideal that they were played by the same actor. They really are very similar portrayals of masculinity.[82]

In relation to the literature immediately following the war, Pemberton joins a number of previous hypermasculine figures masking their homosexuality. Moreover, Blanche DuBois's hypersexuality matches a general concern about women's sexuality during the war years and immediately after.

The tumultuous relationship between Stanley Kowalski and his wife and sister-in-law, along with a common accusation that Williams was himself homophobic at worst and conflicted about his own homosexuality at best, has tended to distract attention from the play's central and not-so-subtle attack on homophobia, its defense of love and critique of the "straight."[83] *Streetcar* has often been characterized as a "closeted gay play," with Blanche a stand-in for Williams, a gay man in drag, so to speak.[84] Certainly Williams had reason to fear being widely known as a homosexual playwright, but critics have been too interested in whether he presents "positive images" of gay men and in the possible autobiographical sources for characters—Blanche as either Williams or his sister Rose, Stanley as his father. Such strains of criticism tend toward reductive moralizing that takes us away from the play to questions of whether (or to what extent) Williams was self-hating, misogynistic, antimisogynistic, too caught up in contemporary psychoanalytic theories of homosexuality, and so on. I would like to emphasize that, regardless of Williams's self-understanding, the play gravitates around the violence of heteronormative discipline because of its pivotal role in Blanche's personal history. Homophobia—hers and her society's—is the central reason for her catastrophe.

Drawn to Stanley's friend Mitch—unlike Stanley, a gentle man insecure in his "masculinity"—and hoping to build a relationship with him, Blanche is struck by his love and care for his mother, who wants him to be "settled" before she dies. He has a great "capacity for devotion," as Blanche says, and he is lonely like her. His love for his mother reminds her of the love of her life, whom she lost. She had fallen deeply in love with a boy named Allan Grey as a sixteen-year-old girl but was "unlucky," as she put it. "There was something different about the boy, a nervousness, a softness and tenderness which wasn't like a man's, although he wasn't the least bit effeminate looking—still—that thing was there." She did not understand that he needed her "help"—whether to mask his sexual orientation or to "cure" him of his homosexuality is unclear. She only knew that on their honeymoon she had "failed him in some mysterious way and wasn't able to give the help he needed but couldn't speak of! . . . Then I found out. In the worst of all possible ways." She had walked into a room in which he was making love with an older man. Afterward, they had pretended nothing had happened and drove to a casino, where they danced to a polka song, the "Varsouviana." As Blanche tells the story initially, she says the boy suddenly broke away from her and ran out; then there was a shot. She ran outside with the rest of the crowd and learned that Allan had shot himself: "It was because— on the dance-floor—unable to stop myself—I'd suddenly said—'I saw! I know! You disgust me . . .' And then the searchlight which had been turned on the world was turned off again and never for one moment since has there been any light that's stronger than this—kitchen—candle." Blaming herself for her husband's suicide—her delay in telling Mitch of her outburst measures the degree of her guilt and shame—Blanche em- phasizes the nearly involuntary nature of her actions. Williams presents the event as a tragedy hinging on the social proscriptions against homo- sexuality, which have victimized both Blanche and her husband. Her telling the story to Mitch, and his sympathetic reaction, functions as an initial climax to the play. As Mitch draws her into his arms, saying, "You need somebody. And I need somebody, too," the polka tune that has been playing in the background through the conversation fades out, and Stella famously exclaims, "Sometimes—there's God—so quickly!"[85]

But of course there is more to come, another tragedy to follow, and in that tragedy, Blanche's reaction to her husband's death plays a central role. In the next scene, Stanley informs Stella that he has learned about Blanche's infamous sexual affairs, for which she was driven out of their home town, the very reason she has come to stay with Stella and Stanley. This information proves, of course, the undoing of Mitch's plans to marry Blanche, but what is interesting in the way Williams presents the breakup is how Mitch resents Stanley and seems to mourn the end of his romantic hopes. When he comes to confront Blanche about her past, he refuses to drink Stanley's liquor. His language in accusing Blanche is also illuminating: "Oh, I knew you weren't sixteen any more. But I was a fool enough to believe you was straight."[86] The word is repeated in Blanche's reply, "Who told you I wasn't—'straight'?" In other words, in her own way Blanche is "queer." And what made her "queer" was the death of her husband, as she finally tells Mitch:

> Yes, I had many intimacies with strangers. After the death of Allan—intimacies with strangers was all I seemed able to fill my empty heart with. . . . I think it was panic, just panic, that drove me from one to another, hunting for some protection—here and there, in the most—unlikely places—even, at last, in a seventeen-year-old boy but—somebody wrote the superintendent about it—"This woman is morally unfit for her position!" . . . True? Yes, I suppose—unfit somehow—anyway. . . . So I came here. There was nowhere else I could go.[87]

Blanche's "intimacies with strangers" will be echoed in her famous final line, "I have always depended on the kindness of strangers." It is all a tragedy of love in a "broken world"—the tragedy of Blanche's loss of her husband, and her loss of Mitch, and finally even her sister's betrayal of her. One is brought back to the epigraph of the play from Hart Crane's "The Broken Tower," rarely mentioned in criticism of the play:

> And so it was I entered the broken world
> To trace the visionary company of love, its voice
> An instant in the wind (I know not whither hurled)
> But not for long to hold each desperate choice.

Mitch also belongs in this tragic company. Echoing Blanche's accusation against Allan, he tells her he doesn't think he wants to marry her any-more, adding, "You're not clean enough to bring in the house with my mother."[88] In other words, she disgusts him.

Mitch apparently still loves Blanche and cannot forgive Stanley for telling him about her transgressions; nor can he forgive himself for his part in her demise. In the final scene, his feelings of remorse are clear. Mitch agonizes over Blanche's fate and eventually gets up from the poker table to comfort or protect her while she tries to fight off the matron; the stage directions say that as Mitch starts toward the bedroom to which

Blanche has retreated, "*Stanley crosses to block him. Stanley pushes him aside. Mitch lunges and strikes at Stanley. Stanley pushes Mitch back. Mitch collapses at the table, sobbing.*"[89]

As for Stella, she is having Blanche committed because she would not be able to go on living with Stanley if she were to accept Blanche's story that he has raped her. The disciplines of the "straight" triumph over love as the matron asks if she should put Blanche in a straightjacket. Although the doctor says it will not be necessary, he works up a "straight" performance of courtly behavior into which Blanche seamlessly inserts herself as they lead her to the asylum. While the doctor and matron lead Blanche away, Eunice "*descends to Stella and places the child in her arms. It is wrapped in a pale blue blanket. Stella accepts the child, sobbingly.*" Stella weeps "*with inhuman abandon. There is something luxurious in her complete surrender to crying now that her sister is gone.*" Meanwhile, Stanley croons, "*voluptuously, soothingly,*" "Now, honey. Now, love. Now, now, love. [*He kneels beside her and his fingers find the opening of her blouse*] now, now, love. Now love."[90] With Blanche gone, and a conspiracy of denial about the causes of her eviction, harmony is restored.

While the play is punctuated repeatedly by music—usually blues—the "Varsouviana," or "polka tune," has a special dramatic function, accompanying key moments in which Blanche's marriage is alluded to or in which she is imperiled. This dramaturgical detail is another indication of the centrality of Allan Grey's suicide—and the sacrifice of the un-"straight"—to the action of the play. If Stanley Kowalski is the dominating character of *Streetcar*—particularly in performance—Blanche is its tragic heroine.

It is important to note how important sexuality was to the very production of Williams's play under the direction of Elia Kazan. The critic and Williams biographer John Lahr reports Kazan's statement, "We were both freaks. . . . He was, as I was, a disappearer." Lahr continues,

They shared a profound curiosity about the vagaries of the human heart; in Kazan's case, since Williams was the first homosexual to whom Kazan had ever been close, this included the two of them going on double dates and sharing the same hotel bedroom for their homosexual/heterosexual couplings—after which, Kazan wrote, "My curiosity was satisfied."[91]

Williams's exploration of sexual desire, deriving from his own impulses and tortured relationships, may have been impossible without the destabilization of male-female relationships set off by the Depression and then conscription for World War II—yet even more by the suspension of "normal" time beginning in 1939. The "duration" soon entailed the imposition of rationing and all sorts of new directives in some spheres, while suspending previously accepted norms in others. It is no accident that Williams's personal initiation to the gay world and his coming out coincided with the advent of World War II. In turn, his exploration of queer horizons would spark the mid-twentieth-century renaissance of American drama.

The first production of *Streetcar* is now recognized as a turning point of American theater. Kazan insisted on a reconfiguration of the director's role that put the producer on the sidelines and the director in the driver's seat, in close collaboration with the actors and the playwright. The casting of twenty-three-year-old Marlon Brando, after attempts to bring in a big-name star, is now legendary. Lahr has compared Brando's acting at the time with the performance of a contemporary jazz musician: "The notes were there, but Brando played them in a way that was uniquely personal to him." His approach might be equally compared with that of an abstract-expressionist painter, going on instinct and pure nerve. "Instead of making everything learned and clear, Brando let the lines play on him and rode his emotions wherever they led him."[92] Kazan later described what it was like to direct Brando: "He even listened experientially . . . He was tuned in to you without listening to you intellectually or mentally. It was a mysterious process. . . . There was always an element of surprise in what he did." Relying on impulse, Brando's acting style on his first read-through for Williams in a Provincetown cottage augured a new kind of artistry, consonant with its moment. Williams intuitively connected it with the war generation in a letter to his agent immediately after the fact: "A new value came out of Brando's reading. . . . He seemed to have already created a dimensional character, of the sort that the war has produced among young veterans."[93] Williams's personal knowledge of such young veterans came chiefly from his sexual cruising, particularly in New York, where he might alternately succeed in attracting "rough trade" for a rendezvous or be beaten up.[94]

Elia Kazan felt right away that Blanche DuBois was based on Williams and Stanley Kowalski on his lover at the time, Pancho Rodriguez. He wrote in his autobiography that Williams was "attracted to the Stanleys of the world"—sailors, rough trade, violent men who titillated and frightened him (much like John Grandin in *The Fall of Valor*). "Blanche wants the very thing that's going to crush her. . . . That's the way Williams was. He was attracted to trash—rough, male homosexuals who were threatening him. . . . Part of the sexuality that Williams wrote into the play is the menace of it."[95]

Although the first-night performance won thunderous applause with multiple curtain calls, the sexuality in *Streetcar* was not, at first, to everyone's liking. George Jean Nathan's review called Williams "a Southern genital-man" and quipped that the play might as well be called "The Glans Menagerie."[96] Nathan, born in 1882 and one of the most influential drama critics going back to the early 1920s, was of a generation being displaced by the spectacle he had observed. *Streetcar* shook the ground beneath a declining American theater, and soon everything would be rearranged, from the role of directors to the styles of acting and the place of sexuality on the stage.

One month after *Streetcar*'s Broadway opening, Alfred Kinsey's *Sexual Behavior in the Human Male* was published and became "an instant bestseller."[97] Kinsey, a zoologist at Indiana University, reported that half of the men he had interviewed had felt erotically attracted to another man, and more than a third had sexually climaxed in an encounter with another grown man. His study also revealed the prevalence of many other sorts of proscribed sexual behavior, from masturbation to sex with animals. There was no such thing, he concluded, as "innate perversity," and he could find nothing "unnatural" about homosexuality: "it is difficult to maintain the view that psychosexual reactions between individuals of the same sex are rare and therefore abnormal or unnatural, or that they constitute within themselves evidence of neuroses or even psychoses."[98] According to the historian John D'Emilio, "Kinsey's work gave an added push at a crucial time to the emergence of an urban gay subculture. Kinsey also provided ideological ammunition that lesbians and homosexuals might use once they began to fight for equality."[99] As I have tried to show, this fight had already begun in the literature of the 1940s.

However, in the broader society a paranoid attack on homosexuality intensified in the wake of the Kinsey Report. In December 1950, the Senate Committee on Expenditures in the Executive Department issued its report, "Employment of Homosexuals and Other Sex Perverts in Government," the beginning of a purge involving the FBI and other federal agencies. In the resolution of *Streetcar*, as we have seen, the heteronormative nuclear family is restored at the expense of purging society of the un-"straight"—and disavowing the violence of that action. The scene is prophetic of what would happen in Cold War America.

8

WOMEN AND POWER

....

I n her book *Of Men and Women* (1941), Pearl S. Buck, one of only
three women Nobel laureates in literature before 1945, warned that
"psychologically and emotionally, war sets women back both in
man's mind and in their own."[1] As Elizabeth Bishop's poem of the same
year "Roosters" sarcastically carped, war is a time of prancing cocks. In
the "gun-metal blue dark" of crepuscular dawn they begin to crow, "brace
their cruel feet and glare / with stupid eyes":

> Deep from protruding chests
> in green-gold medals dressed,
> planned to command and terrorize the rest,
>
> the many wives
> who lead hens' lives
> of being courted and despised.[2]

The poem, written before Pearl Harbor, would prove prophetic, as a wave
of misogyny gained volume while men grew fearful and vulnerable.
Bishop never thought of this as a "feminist" poem until a generation
later. In a 1977 interview, she recalled, "Some friends asked me to read it

a year or so ago, and I suddenly realized it sounded like a feminist tract, which it wasn't meant to sound like at all to begin with. So you never know how things are going to get changed around for you by the times." Bishop refused early in her career to be included in "women's anthologies" or "all-women issues of magazines. . . . I felt it was a lot of nonsense, separating the sexes"—a feeling she later attributed to "feminist principles" stronger than she would have then been aware of. She described how college-educated women of her generation responded to being discounted intellectually: "One gets so used, very young, to being 'put down' that if you have normal intelligence and have any sense of humor you very early develop a tough, ironic attitude."[3] That sort of attitude pervades much of the best women's writing of the time.

Nonetheless, during the war, many women gained increasing power over their personal lives, as much of the literature suggests. It was the birth time, after all, of the Amazon superhero Wonder Woman, created by a male feminist who thought women should rule the earth. Farah Jasmine Griffin emphasizes the special quality of the 1940s for progressive black women artists in Harlem, due to the continued influence of the Popular Front and the progressive institutions that opened opportunities. Toward the end of the decade, however, "the venues and organizations that had supported them closed or were transformed. Cultural tastes changed. . . . Women who had filled factories and offices during the war were asked to return home."[4] Women's temporary and very partial empowerment caused men to respond in fear. We have seen literary reflections on or *of* this fear in male-authored war novels. Anxiety about what women might do in the sexually chaotic years of the war, especially while men were away, took on outsized proportions, following on the blows to male potency of the Great Depression.

The warrior myth celebrates masculine toughness and potency, necessities for men going to war, but war can be humbling and emasculating—one loses control over one's own life, not to mention bladder and bowels. Men's exclusive "possession" of women was imperiled, and popular culture focused on women's sexuality as a form of power or, alternatively, on their domesticity. Both alternatives expressed male fear and anxiety, expressed often in the war fiction. One of the nonfiction bestsellers of 1942, *A Generation of Vipers*, even took aim at "Momism" in openly misogynistic fashion.[5] Pin-ups festooned the bulkheads of ships and barracks lockers; they were painted on flying superfortresses. In Vidal's *Williwaw*, the protagonist wonders at the pervasiveness of pin-up pictures: "Occasionally there was no radio but the pictures were always there: half-dressed girls, in mysteriously lighted bedclothes, promising sex."[6] Yet this was also when the "women's film" grew popular, when, as Griffin writes, "women's narratives first hit the silver screen."[7]

After the war, the expected return to supposed normalcy brought a hypersexualization of female images at the same time that sexual activity was publicly reined in and women urged back into the home. "When a girl took off her underpants in 1947," Anatole Broyard later reminisced,

> she was more naked than any woman before her had ever been. . . . The men of my generation had thought obsessively about her body, had been elaborately prepared for it, led up to it by the great curve of civilization. Her body was on the tip of our minds, a pinup on the brink of our progress, our freedom. We'd carried it, like a gun, all through the war. The nakedness of women was such an anticipated object that it was out in front of American culture, like the radiator ornament on the hood of a car. We were at that point in our social evolution where we had taken in as much awareness of women's bodies as we could stand without going mad.[8]

Men were seemingly helpless before the draw of female sexuality, which only fed the hypersexualization and objectification of women. Fear of women's power over men by way of "sex" and "motherhood" inspired both the "femme fatale" of film noir and psychologists' worries about smothering mothers raising "momma's boys."[9]

Steven Dillon, in *Wolf-Women and Phantom Ladies*, has recently addressed female desire in pop culture, movies, comics, and pulp fiction, coming to the overall conclusion that misogyny, and specifically a fear of women's sexual desire, pervades the culture of the 1940s.[10] When women express desire, they are "wolf-women"; otherwise their desire seems spectral or nonexistent. But reading the most compelling literary representations focusing on the relationship of women to power, which is the central issue, one finds them refracting rather than merely reflecting the concerns in popular culture.

"Refraction" refers to how a wave of light coming at an angle to a boundary between two media bends as it passes from one to the other. A change in density at the boundary alters the wave's velocity and wavelength, much as literature's intensification of language refracts experience. We might go further and term its means *prosthetic*, the process of artistic work being a form of prosthesis that changes the boundaries of experience, that shapes and potentially alters how we see, hear, smell, feel, and even taste whatever we encounter.

Consider, as a prelude to what follows, Eudora Welty's 1939 photograph *Hypnotized, State Fair* (fig. 8.1). Welty's lens, and her angular positioning of the lens—where she stands—*refracts* the drama being photographed and thus profoundly alters it. Her handling of the artistic medium slows down and adds density to the visual experience in comparison with a straight-on viewing of the spectacle.

The angle from which the photo is taken captures a group of preadolescent boys observing what is to them a puzzling spectacle of female sexual objectification. From the camera's angle of vision, they are the ones being hypnotized. Posters in the background emphasize eroticization and exoticism, with lightly clad women posed on stage, capturing the boys' attention, while the man at the microphone manages the performance the boys are witnessing.[11] Yet what the photographer brings most to our attention are the boys, one of whom looks back toward his friends, and toward the camera, with a gleeful look. Welty stages *their* process of being interpellated into the position of the male gaze, being hypnotized like the man lying suspended above them, his head pointing toward the women's breasts. Welty takes the spectacle out of the carnival barker's control, layering it with dramatic irony, giving it new meaning and bitter humor.

FIGURE 8.1 Eudora Welty, *Hypnotized, State Fair*. *Source*: Reprinted courtesy of the Eudora Welty Collection, Mississippi Department of Archives and History, and Russell & Volkening as agents for the author's estate. Copyright © 1980 Eudora Welty, LLC.

Yet in the midst of widespread misogyny, the 1940s was an unusually significant decade for women's emergence in the literary field. Freda Kirchwey owned, edited, and published one of the most influential of the left-leaning weeklies, *The Nation*, having taken it over in 1937, and Mary McCarthy, Dorothy Parker, and Diana Trilling were significant presences in the New York literary world. Somewhat of a literary figure herself, Eleanor Roosevelt wielded political influence like no first lady before and befriended women writers. Her friend Martha Gellhorn occasionally preempted even Ernest Hemingway (whom Gellhorn married in 1940 and divorced in 1945) as a war correspondent. Feminist consciousness was strong in some literary quarters. Ann Petry attributed her emergence as an author to an English professor at Columbia University, Mabel Louise Robinson, who accepted her into her creative-writing course along with four other women students—all the men being gone to war: "She was truly interested in us, truly committed to our becoming writers."[12] As I have mentioned earlier, the "out" lesbian Gertrude Stein was also a celebrity worthy of the picture magazines even as the pin-up girl had become ubiquitous. The era was ripe for irony, paradox, and satire on the part of women writers. As Sandra Gilbert and Susan Gubar have written, "the blitz on women during World War II contributed to the formation of a female literary tradition which mourns the demise of Herland even as it documents female artistic survival behind a mask, a survival achieved only with the rictus of a grin set in place."[13]

The hoary opposition of the virgin and the whore, rare in fiction by women of the 1940s, looms large in male-authored novels, yet it is not always simple. In Hemingway's *For Whom the Bell Tolls*, the contrast between the half-gypsy, female guerrilla fighter Pilar and the innocent, "virginal" Maria could hardly be more stark, yet Pilar is heroic. The first thing Robert Jordan learns about Pilar is that "If you think Pablo is ugly you should see his woman. But brave. A hundred times braver than Pablo. But something barbarous."[14] Pablo was once brave, but now he is "very flaccid." He is afraid to die, whereas Pilar later proves herself the aficionado of what the Spanish call *duende*, an eloquent poet on the subject and smell of death.

Pilar's protectiveness of Maria and hints of a sexual attraction to the girl have the effect of "masculinizing" the elder woman, who dominates Pablo and verbally castrates him in front of his own band. Similarly, her previous lover, the bullfighter Finito, is feminized in comparison to Pilar. Though courageous, he was slight of build, emotionally fragile, and tubercular. Remembering his broken condition after one bullfight, when she massaged and washed him, she recalls his ironic comment, "'Thou art much woman, Pilar.' It was the nearest to a joke he ever made." Despite his vocation as matador, the relationship between them inverts traditionally masculine and feminine positions: he is "weak," she "strong." And in a loving relationship of five years ending with his death, "She . . . never was unfaithful to him, that is almost never." Finito's own chastity, on the other hand, is unquestioned, and she immediately takes up with Pablo after his death. She reflects on the death of Finito and the broken strength of Pablo only to conclude, "neither bull force nor bull courage lasted . . . and what did last? I last, she thought. Yes, I have lasted."[15]

When Pablo's own men are openly urging Robert Jordan to kill him, calling him a coward, even punching out his teeth to force him to fight so they will have an excuse to shoot him, Pablo calls them an "illusioned people . . . led by a woman with her brains between her thighs and a foreigner who comes to destroy you."[16] After this, Pilar urges Robert to kill him and becomes the leader of the group. Later, Pablo changes course and essentially saves the band in order to save his own self-respect, but Pilar remains the moral arbiter, accepting him back as a flawed but necessary ally. This is only one example of a powerful, emasculating, sexually uninhibited female figure in forties fiction. There are many more, not to mention the femmes fatales of film noir.

In *A Streetcar Named Desire*, Blanche might seem a delicate and tragic lady of the South on hard times, but Stanley sees her as a castrating nymphomaniac taking over his wife and home. He convinces the virginal "mama's boy" Mitch to drop her when he is on the verge of proposing and maneuvers his wife into committing Blanche (whom he has raped) to an asylum to save his own masculine priority. Even the major white female characters in Ann Petry's *Country Place* are powerful—and unfaithful—in comparison to the returned soldier-husband (whose wife has been cheating on him) and the faithful but impotent son of the village matriarch. She is ultimately the most powerful person in the town.

Chester Himes's furious bestseller *If He Hollers Let Him Go* features a protagonist obsessing over fear of being "un-manned" by women. The protagonist, Bob Jones, is a college dropout working in a Los Angeles shipyard during the war, a "leaderman" over a group of welders and the like. He is also all but engaged to a beautiful, professional black woman from a wealthy and well-connected family. A central conflict throughout is between, on the one hand, the appeal of going back to college, marrying his girlfriend, and working within the system as allowed to educated Negroes and, on the other, asserting his full "manhood" by refusing anything short of full equality with white men. The constant crisis of his manhood takes a critical form in a twisted sexual/power struggle with a blond, Southern white woman welder who works under him. Immediately before describing his first sight of this woman (Madge), he tells us that he has no sexual interest in white women: "Now I had Alice and the white chicks didn't interest me: I thought Alice was better than any white woman who ever lived."[17] The battle with Madge is not about sex but about power.

At first sight of Madge, Jones becomes a man possessed. Her appeal is not conventionally sexual nor that of the white woman on a pedestal. Quite the opposite:

> She was a peroxide blonde with a large-featured, overly made-up face, and she had a large, bright-painted, fleshy mouth, kidney-shaped, thinner in the middle than at the ends. Her big blue babyish eyes were mascaraed like a burlesque queen's and there were tiny wrinkles in their corners and about the flare of her nostrils, calipering down about the edges of her mouth. She looked thirty and well sexed, rife but not quite rotten. She looked as if she might have worked half those years in a cat house, and if she hadn't she must have given a lot of it away.[18]

Yet Madge's and Jones's eyes lock immediately in a charged moment of mutual recognition. He is quite used to white women's sexual games and has dated "nice" white women in the past, but something in Madge draws him irresistibly in rage and lust. Their first eye contact builds to a turgid consummation:

> Blood rushed to my head like gales of rain and I felt my face burn white-hot. It came up in my eyes and burned at her; she caught it and kept staring at me with that wide-eyed phoney look. Something about her mouth touched it off, a quirk made the curves change as if she got a sexual thrill, and her mascaraed eyelashes fluttered.
>
> Lust shook me like an electric shock; it came up in my mouth, filling it with tongue, and drained my whole stomach down into my groin. And it poured out of my eyes in a sticky rush and spurted over her from head to foot.

The frightened look went out of her eyes and she blushed right down her face and out of sight beneath the collar of her leather jacket, and I could imagine it going down over her over-ripe breasts and spreading out over her milk-white stomach. When she turned out of my stare I went sick to the stomach and felt like vomiting.[19]

A sadistic pas-de-deux ensues in which a dialectic between hatred and inexplicable lust plays out until, ultimately, Madge traps Jones in a locked room he stumbles into by accident, gets into a fight with him, and cries rape. His ensuing beating, arrest, hospitalization, and attempted escape end his relationship with Alice, to whom he had just proposed. To avoid a thirty-year prison sentence, Jones enlists in the army, and the novel ends.

Jones's bursts of lust for Madge, continually imperiling his future and his idyllic relationship with Alice, have all to do with his need to get even with the white world—the more so because Madge is an unreconstructed racist who seems to be drawn to him largely because of her hatred of black men. Sadism exists on both sides.

Meanwhile, the relationship with Alice threatens Bob's manhood because it requires "getting along" with what the white world will tolerate in a black gentleman. On top of this, after attending a party at the home of a black lesbian with whom Alice is close, he comes to believe that Alice is a lesbian. (This suspicion is finally laid to rest just before the novel's climax, in the same scene in which Alice accepts Bob's marriage proposal.) Why did Himes feel the need to introduce, midway through the novel, a black lesbian party scene in which Jones witnesses Alice apparently being "picked up" by an open lesbian? And allow the possibility of Alice's "queerness" to drift through the rest of the novel until just before the climax?

It has all to do with Jones's fear of women's power and with the fact that he cannot recognize women outside of their relationship to his own self-image as a "man." A major aspect of Madge's lust for Jones is her knowledge that she can get a black man lynched. She is sexually intoxicated by the power of her whiteness when she has Jones in her sights. By the same token, Jones's lust for her has to do with exerting masculine power over her "whiteness." Whenever he feels a white person humiliating or emasculating him, he wants to dominate a white woman sexually or else kill a white man.

When white men humiliate Jones on the job—for example, by deliberately telling racist jokes in his hearing—he feels the need to humiliate Madge:

> I felt low, dispirited, black as I've ever felt. Really a black boy now.
>
> But I knew I was going to have to say something to Madge if I got shot on the spot. Not to rack her back or cuss her out. That wasn't going to be enough. Not now. Not after having been tricked into listening to that bastard tell that joke. I was going to have to have her. I was going to have to make her as low as a white whore in a Negro slum—a scrummy two-dollar whore. . . . I was going to have to so I could keep looking the white folks in the face . . . all I could see was her standing there between me and my manhood.[20]

Madge has an uncanny insight into Jones's psychology. They are a match as bad as Batman and the Joker. "I was going to say," Jones tells us at one point, "'Look, bitch, let's stop all this jive and get together like we want.'" Later, after Madge humiliates him, he suddenly rushes off to murder his "white boy"—"I was going to walk up and beat out his brains."[21]

At the very time when Jones seems serenely on his road to marriage with Alice and a secure future, and after Alice has convinced him that she hasn't the slightest queer sexual orientation, Jones is caught by pure accident in the sex/power vortex with Madge that leads to military induction. This is a dreaded threat to his agency insofar as he sees it as a capitulation to white male power. It is probably significant that both Madge and Alice are financially independent. Although Alice still lives with her parents, she is a secure urban professional in social work and has no need for a man to support her. Madge, a single woman, is a skilled laborer in the high-paying war industry, Rosie the Riveter with a welding torch. As in so many novels of the 1940s, women's independence of men both financially and sexually inspires male insecurity and misogyny, foreshadowing the intensive effort to move women out of "male" occupations, to reconstitute and buttress the middle-class ideal of a nuclear family with a male breadwinner and a woman at home.

Some of the great novels and short stories of the 1940s depend structurally and stylistically on the gendered structure of power, and they are often by women with a wicked wit. Humor and satire depend on upsetting power. The monkey outsmarts the lion, the roadrunner outsmarts the coyote, Bugs Bunny outsmarts Elmer Fudd, the emperor has no clothes. In a pun, the "serious" meaning of a word gets upended by its vulgar twin. Some of the best writing by women in the 1940s, a "serious" and male-centered decade if ever there was one, took the form of arch humor and satirical invective often aimed at the scripts of gender in an era of total war. Yet dark-comic endings short-circuited the humor with ingenious twists indicating the limits of women's power.

Dawn Powell set *A Time to Be Born* in the weeks immediately before and after the American entry into the war. The novelist Amanda Evans (based on Clare Boothe Luce) is a transplant to New York who through beauty, ambition, and a keen sense of where power resides has vaulted from obscure Midwestern origins to marriage with a media tycoon and celebrity status, not to mention glamour, when a "mousy" friend of her past shows up on the scene needing a new start after a failed relationship. Recovering from having lost her husband to a friend and business partner, Vicky Havens, once Amanda's social superior, feels the full brunt of her own insignificance in New York. Powell's arch ironic tone, along with the pacing of the syllables in every sentence, the build-up of each paragraph, the laugh-out-loud effects on page after page, leave one helpless before her humor.

Throughout the novel, needing the help or simply empathy of another is the very definition of powerlessness. And power is everyone's goal. Amanda Keeler's secretary, for example, who researches, coauthors, and edits her work,

was allowed to insult at least a dozen people a day, and to enjoy immeasurably the spectacle of her superiors fawning over her as

representative of a great name. Boys having left her strictly alone during the formative years, she had been permitted leisure to acquire an
excellent education and to develop her brain to a point where its out-
come was well worthy of Amanda Keeler Evans' signature. . . . To have
confessed to being more than Amanda's patient secretary would have
lowered Amanda's prestige, and would have done herself no good. So
Miss Bemel gloried in Amanda's insolence and multiplied it, herself,
by a hundred.[22]

To command not love but envy is the commonsense understanding of
"success." Thus friendships wither before they can be born.

Attachments to old friends can bring only embarrassment, unless
those friends have the right pedigree. To Amanda Keeler, one of the privileges of adulthood was "to drop your childhood into a wastebasket, forget
it, burn it, destroy all evidence of past weakness. Another privilege—and
this, she arrogantly felt, was her special right—was unlimited power. To
deny the first was to forego the latter."[23] Yet, for women, power ultimately derives from men.

"Power" is the novel's keyword. When a former lover angrily accuses
Keeler of using him merely because he was "fool enough" to love her
even knowing what "a five letter woman" (w-h-o-r-e) she would always
be, Amanda is hardly offended:

Amanda did not hush him now, for this soothed her, brought back her
power, reminded her that she was Amanda, the Amanda that nothing
could hurt except anonymity. She was soothed, but she was curious, too,
that anyone should care so much about anyone, and be so affected physically by any other human being. She looked at his face surprised and
gratified that it should show pain, because this was a tribute to her of a
sort she could not understand.[24]

Women achieve power through sexual allure, glamour, and the "conquest" of powerful men. Thus Amanda has managed to win Julian Evans
away from his first wife through her sexuality. By marriage to the right

man she has attained celebrity and social power. Yet as the novel opens she feels restless:

> It was not that she wanted an affair for lust's sake, for she had a genuine distaste for sexual intimacy and hated to sacrifice a facial appointment for a mere frolic in bed; but there were so many things to be gained by trading on sex and she thought so little of the process that she itched to use it as currency once again, trading a half-hour in bed for a flattering friendship, a royal invitation; power of whatever sort appealed to her.[25]

In this world, any genuine emotion is a sign of vulnerability to be exploited by one's acquaintances. And power—the ability to use others without being used—is its own reward.

Ironically, therefore, the most positive characters in *A Time to Be Born* are those who allow themselves to feel; they are also most in danger of that most dreadful of American sins—"failure." Such are Vicky Havens and Ken Saunders. Vicky leaves Lakeville, Ohio, for New York after the humiliating demise of a relationship when her boyfriend elopes with her business partner. "Losing a lover," according to the narrator, "does to a woman what losing a job does to a man; all confidence in self vanishes. There is the overwhelming conviction that you alone are singled out as unfit for the simplest privileges of life, and the days are filled with tiny testimony to this."[26] Still in love with Tom Turner, despite his alcoholism, she hopes to build a new life in Manhattan. Amanda Keeler takes her under her wing, using Havens as an excuse to rent a studio apartment where she can carry on affairs without arousing the suspicion of her husband.

Ken Saunders, a failure of the male variety, is an aspiring novelist yet to publish a successful book. Amanda Evans abandoned him for Julian Evans and promptly had a bestseller, thanks mainly to Julian's power in the publishing world.

> Then Ken lost his job on a morning paper. Then he tried in vain to sell his old stories. Then he wrote a play that did not sell. Then he wrote a

series of articles for a magazine that promptly went bankrupt. Then he looked out his hotel window and saw, as the final blow, that there was no use jumping, because a bare ten feet below was a roof for sunbathers from MacKinney's Turkish Bath House.[27]

Of course it will turn out that Vicky and Ken—both struggling urban professionals seeking love and intimacy with another—are made for each other in the novel's comic denouement. Neither one holds an upper hand in their happy relationship, nor cares to.

Powell's Menippean satire, playing havoc with typical expectations of novelistic plotting, moves from scene to scene without a strong narrative pattern of rising conflict, climax, and resolution.[28] Its barbs spare no one, including the most sympathetic characters. As a "low" form, this kind of satire is typically judged inferior to "serious" fiction and drama. Powell's view was the opposite: "The only record of a civilization is satire— Petronius, Aristophanes, Flaubert. . . . These are so valuable that they are timeless."[29]

Like the *Satyricon*, *A Time to Be Born* includes brilliant set-pieces, often crafted around episodes of eating and drinking, in which a motley collection of characters jockey for attention and respect. A carnival atmosphere is given form by the brilliant pacing of the prose and the joy in wacky juxtapositions—for example, in this account of an after-dinner party at Vicky Havens's Greenwich Village apartment:

Even if Tom Turner [Vicky's former lover, now married to her former business partner, Eudora] had not been there the little group would have been a difficult one for any hostess to organize. Ethel carried on a constant flow of gossip about characters Uncle Rockman and Ken did not know, Vicky ate sandwiches and tried to avoid Tom Turner's urgent, curious gaze, Eudora drank and made sardonic exclamations, and Uncle Rockman and Ken talked feverishly of the atom. In occasional efforts at general conversation Tom Turner described the Lakeville Country club inner politics to Uncle Rockman, who vanquished him with learned commentary on the splendid work on the Soul being done at the Yale

Institute of Human Relations by somebody named Burr. Swinging lightly out of this, Uncle Rockman dealt with the Inverse Square Law, and finding his audience quite crushed he was able to take up the atom again, of which he spoke fondly as if it was a dear little Cupid flying through space making statistics for every good child. Ken Saunders eagerly encouraged this monologue as a means of freezing out Tom Turner, and Uncle had somehow gotten into quantum this and quantum that when a final sip at his drink made him slide farther down into the corner of the cushioned sofa and fall asleep.

Ethel Carey nudged Vicky.

"Is he keeping you?" she whispered. "I mean I don't see how anybody would let him go on like that unless he paid the rent."[30]

This scene does nothing to advance the plot; it exists for its own sake, but throughout is the basic idea behind the novel—people's often absurd maneuvering for attention and social position, which is all the more laughable in the context of the winter of 1941–1942.

Powell has been suspected of misogyny because of her sardonic treatment of women writers such as Amanda Keeler,[31] but this is merely a tribute to her mastery of a satirical mode that spares no one. The novels derive humor from exposing the pervasive gendering of power relations and how male supremacy constantly asserts itself despite the bumbling of the men who wield it over more intelligent, scheming women.

Although she owes her position to her media-tycoon husband, Amanda Keeler seems all-powerful socially. She even dominates her husband, who fears her putting "horns" on his head as a cuckold. Yet Amanda becomes irrelevant when the United States declares war. Social power shifts from New York to Washington, and social power is the only form available to ambitious women. In a bid to recapture her relevance, she reverses course, publicly revealing her plebeian immigrant origins, which infuriates her husband by threatening his aristocratic image. At the same time, he suspects her of an affair with one of his top foreign correspondents, Andrew Callingham—whom, in fact, she plans to seduce.

Simultaneously, and mysteriously, Amanda becomes pregnant and undergoes an abortion arranged by none other than Vicky Haven. For a brief moment she collapses into helplessness and apparently genuine vulnerability, but upon learning that Callingham (a character apparently based on Powell's friend Ernest Hemingway) wants to meet with her, she vaults into her former self within minutes after an incapacitating abortion. "With mingled relief and alarm Vicky saw the pale, wan creature of a moment before suddenly transformed into the brittle, competent woman she was supposed to be. . . . It was incredible, Vicky thought, bewildered. The woman was indestructible."[32] Amanda turns every reverse into an opportunity, yet all her strategies are dependent on the power invested in rich men.

Amanda figures that an affair with Callingham will burnish her image anew, á la Martha Gellhorn, perhaps: "They would do brave things together, sweeping through India and Africa, on just such intrepid adventures as had characterized his life before, nonetheless daring for their wire net precautions of money, prestige, and unlimited political protection."[33] Amanda's hopes are dashed by the fact that Callingham has no romantic interest in her; he is in love with another woman and hoping to marry. Moreover, she has miscalculated the importance of her marriage to Julian Evans, upon whose power her own depends. Callingham, far from being the independent he-man of the Hemingway stereotype, has no intention of imperiling his reputation and income by crossing her husband. Julian remains in control.

The novel satirizes the frivolousness of women's power as dependent on a man's power. As a result, most relationships are fraught with insincerity. Women jockey among one another for a "power" that is always dependent, the ability to command the envy of other women, directly or indirectly, by way of their relationships to men.

Powell's postwar novel *The Locusts Have No King* amplifies the point, again with arch humor:

If another woman is beautiful these eyes grudgingly admit that she is not ugly, no more than that; if she displays wit the eyes significantly find a wine stain on her dress. But when the other's toilette reveals free access to a fat purse, then the eyes are unmasked and flash with righteous indignation; this is the end for which a woman is a woman. Beauty, brains, position are enviable, not in themselves, but for their purchasing power; if crutches won masculine rewards these women would break their own legs. Flaunting of luxuries was testimony to superior power over men, medals of practical victories.[34]

The power of those men, in turn, depends upon an institutionalized performance of WASP ethnicity, haute-bourgeois class identity, and virile masculinity. Male sexual desire is relatively simple, a matter of lust for youthful, attractive women; female desire, because of male domination, is rarely so "authentic" or direct because of its elaborate subordination to phallocentric power. Powell has been accused of misogyny, but she is better understood as a second-wave feminist before the label and as the only satirist of the time who can still make one laugh out loud until it hurts. Fully of its moment and its place, the humor of her novels is nonetheless as timeless as Aristophanes's *Lysistrata*—of which it can be read as an ironic inversion.

Mary McCarthy's *The Company She Keeps* is equally peppered with arch humor deriving from power dynamics in male-female relationships and ubiquitous sexual affairs. As in Powell's novel, a key aspect of a married woman's power over her husband is the ability to "put horns on his head"—phrasing that confers agency on the woman, in this case the unnamed protagonist of "Cruel and Barbarous Treatment," the first chapter of the novel (originally a short story). "It was as if by the mere act of betraying her husband, she had adequately bested him." The chief satisfaction of the heroine's affair with an unmarried "Young Man" is to confer a feeling of superiority over both her husband and her lover: "These superiority feelings were fattening not only on the gullibility of her friends, but also on the comic flaws of her lover's character, and on the vulnerability of her lover's position. In this particular hive she was undoubtedly queen bee."[35]

Even her strategy for revealing the affair to her husband is a sadomasochistic bid for power, "for, as she was the weapon that dealt the wound,

she was also the balm that could assuage it," wooing him "to an uncondi-
tional surrender" by offering her sympathy for his suffering.[36] In the wake
of this exercise, however, her power immediately dissipates. The husband
quickly moves on, and with the excitement of the Secret gone, the Young
Man seems suddenly a bore. The fear of spinsterhood rises on the horizon. McCarthy pointedly satirizes her protagonist, but the ultimate target is the situation of women as the "second sex."

> Almost all women, she thought, when they are girls never believe that
> they will get married. The terror of spinsterhood hangs over them from
> adolescence on. Even if they are popular they think that no one really
> interesting will want them enough to marry them. Even if they get en-
> gaged they are afraid that something will go wrong, something will
> intervene. When they do get married it seems to them a sort of miracle,
> and after they have been married for a time, though in retrospect the
> whole process looks perfectly natural and inevitable, they retain a cer-
> tain unarticulated pride in the wonder they have performed. Finally,
> however, the terror of spinsterhood has been so thoroughly exorcised
> that they forget ever having been haunted by it, and it is at this stage that
> they contemplate divorce. "How could I have forgotten?" she said to
> herself and began to wonder what she would do.[37]

She imagines dreary dinners in tearooms with other spinsters, avoiding
the nicer restaurants because lone women in them appear conspicuously
forlorn. As in Powell's novel, the question of appearances haunts the protagonist as if she perceives herself as an actress in a Hollywood film. To
banish her fear and regain her feeling of power, the heroine reimagines
herself as a femme fatale, one for whom considerations of safety are irrelevant: "She was, or soon would be, a Young Divorcee, and the term
still carried glamour."[38]

"Glamour" is a key term for McCarthy as for Powell, that mysterious
"reformulation of the sublime," as Judith Brown brilliantly calls it, coex-
tensive with literary modernism as much as Hollywood stars or Chanel
No. 5. It involves an apparent absence of feeling, a cool surface—not

warm and fuzzy but artificial and distant. It awakens the "ache for the beautiful thing just out of reach," like Daisy Buchanan in *The Great Gatsby*.[39] Also associated with a deracinated cosmopolitanism, disconnection from familial origins, it requires reticence, "a barrier of impeccable reserve," to quote McCarthy.[40] A suspicion of emptiness behind the gorgeous surface often inheres in it, as if the obverse of its peculiar power.

The association of glamour with feminine power may, then, be a mirage. The hypereroticization of the surface and evisceration of feeling turns the glamorous woman into a statue too easily shattered when tragedy intervenes. In Powell's novel, Amanda Evans undergoes that transformation when she learns of her unwanted pregnancy: "Some persons were suited only to triumph and they existed only in a blaze of glory; in descent they were not the same people. . . . So Amanda, broken with her little misfortune, was not Amanda to Vicky but the curious awful spectacle of a statue in fragments."[41] In the humanization of the glamorous icon lies its destruction. It is therefore a dangerous goal for girls and women, a *fata morgana*.

Like Dawn Powell, too, McCarthy locates the performance of power in a particular type of WASP male, encapsulated in the title of one of her central chapters, "The Man in the Brooks Brothers Suit." The Man in question manages to seduce on a train—or perhaps rape—a younger "bohemian" woman of the sophisticated Greenwich Village sort despite her disdain for Midwestern "businessmen." Her stereotypes about such men fall apart in the initial encounter. His apparent naïveté draws her in, coupled with his wealth, his expressed infatuation, and his whiskey. His sudden confession of a desire to get a divorce and marry her ultimately "disarms" her, and she is, to put it indelicately, fucked. She is not, however, "ruined" nor wailing with misery in the aftermath. McCarthy treats all of this humorously and ironically; the protagonist is no shy maiden seduced by a cad but a grown woman with desires and intellect and prone to adventure while on the road.

In Petry's *The Street* a black woman's sexual "power" over men contributes to an overwhelming and terrifying level of powerlessness. Lutie

Johnson's physical attractiveness makes men "weak" in their desire for her—and thus in their need to dominate her—while her race and class make her vulnerable to sexual predation and ultimately powerless to protect her young son. *The Street* provides therefore an instructive contrast with Powell's and McCarthy's fiction while treating related geometries of power. Evie Shockley has pointed out Petry's use of the gothic mode.[42] It distinguishes Petry's work from some of her cohort while nonetheless connecting with respect to gender critique.

From the start, Lutie is presented in a nearly powerless position. The wind of "the street"

> lifted Lutie Johnson's hair away from the back of her neck so that she felt suddenly naked and bald. . . . She shivered as the cold fingers of the wind touched the back of her neck, explored the sides of her head. It even blew her eyelashes away from her eyes so that her eyeballs were bathed in a rush of coldness and she had to blink in order to read the words on the sign swaying back and forth over her head.[43]

The description presages feelings of being stripped and appraised as a sex object. The first person she meets in the building that she will ultimately move into—a madam named Mrs. Hedges—has eyes "as still and as malignant as the eyes of a snake . . . wandering over her body, inspecting and appraising her from head to foot." Next she meets the building supervisor, who "towered in the doorway, looking at her," his eyes quickly filling "with a hunger so urgent that she was instantly afraid of him and afraid to show her fear"—like a rabbit frozen by the gaze of a snake. On the stairs to the apartment, he stays behind her, and she can feel his eyes on "her back, her legs, her thighs. She could feel his eyes traveling over her—estimating her, summing her up, wondering about her."[44]

These images, while easily found in fiction about white women, too, evoke the heritage of the auction block. Lutie encounters a not-unrelated "wondering" about her and sexualization in the home of her suburban white employers, who assume that young black women are always sexually available and white men "weak" before their charms: "these people took one look at her and immediately got that now-I-wonder look." Male "weakness" is, however, the obverse of male power. Lutie's black apartment-building supervisor "radiated such desire for her that she could feel it. She told herself she was a fool an idiot, drunk on fear, on fatigue and gnawing worry. Even while she thought it, the hot, choking awfulness of his desire for her pinioned her there so that she couldn't move." At the same time, when Lutie finds herself desperate for money in order to get a divorce (after her husband has rejected her and taken another woman), her chief alternative is the one Mrs. Hedges, the brothel madam in her building, offers: "a nice white gentleman." While white and black sexual objectifications of her are not identical, they operate within the same network of power relations that tend to render black working-class women defenseless (unless, like Mrs. Hedges, they pander black girls to men). This is as true of Min, the woman who lives with the superintendent and fears his attraction to Lutie, as it is of Lutie: "a woman by herself didn't stand much chance."[45]

Even when Lutie achieves a modicum of glamour as a singer, she is completely in the power of her manager and his boss and in constant danger of sexual assault. When she first meets Boots Smith, who offers her a job singing, "his eyes on her face were so knowing, so hard, that she thought instantly of the robins she had seen on the Chandlers' lawn in Lyme, and the cat, lean, stretched out full length, drawing itself along on its belly, intent on its prey."[46]

In the black man's need for "possessing" a woman, however, is his need for a sense of power and self-worth. Petry repeatedly stresses white supremacy's and capitalism's "emasculation" of black men—the assault on manhood as aligned with power and ultimately the power to "possess" a black woman. Thus Boots Jackson drives his car recklessly, frightening her, as an expression of potency, and Lutie's husband picks up another woman because her desire for him restores his self-respect. At the most basic level, when he has little else, a man's "power" is coincident with "having" a woman. To Boots Smith, the years he had spent as a Pullman porter choking on the "Yes sirs" and "No sirs" endemic to the job translate into his need to own a woman or else feel "less than half a man, because he didn't even have a woman of his own, because he not only had to say 'Yes sir,' he had to stand by and take it while some white man grabbed off what belonged to him."[47] He would rather murder "his" woman than let a white man have her.

Similarly, Jones, the building supervisor, has been led to believe that Lutie rejects him as a black man and loves the white pub owner, Junto. Lutie, he concludes, is one of those women with "No use for men their own color. Well, he'd fix her. He'd fix her good. . . . She belonged to a white man. Well, he would get back at both of them." He will lure Lutie's son into crime so he will be taken away from her. Again, his obsession has to do with wielding power: "He could fix the kid and none of them could stop him. They would never know who was responsible."[48] Jones is thus part of the whole web of power that renders Lutie impotent (a term normally gendered male, because "potency" is presumptively masculine). Lutie cannot even save what is most precious to her, her own child. It is all about power, to which sex itself is subordinate in the end.[49]

At the center of the web of power in *The Street* is Junto. Yet he is ultimately a proxy. At the end of the book, when Lutie returns to her apartment knowing that both Boots Smith and Mrs. Hedges have been working for Junto, entrapping her, she senses a spiderlike presence in the room:

> The creeping, silent thing that she had sensed in the theater, in the beauty parlor, was here in her living room. It was sitting on the lumpy studio couch. . . . It was Junto. Gray hair, gray skin, short body, thick shoulders. He was sitting on the studio couch. . . . His feet were resting, squarely, firmly, on the congoleum rug. . . . She looked away and then looked back again. Sometimes he was there when she looked and sometimes he wasn't.[50]

This proves to be a kind of hallucination, but a prophetic one. And it has to do with the phantom nature of white, male power as well as the way it spins a wide web.

Lutie bathes and dresses, then goes to meet Boots in his apartment. Junto is there, and Boots is effectively pimping for him. But he is determined to "have" Lutie first, and when he attempts to subdue her she kills him, seeing in him all the powers arrayed against her, including, ultimately, "the white world which thrust black people into a walled enclosure from which there was no escape. . . . She saw the face and head of the man on the sofa through waves of anger in which he represented all these things and she was destroying them."[51] This is an image of Lutie exercising elemental power, overturning her subjection to others. That it is a black man who ironically represents "the white world" to her at this moment indicates the pervasiveness of white power. And her killing of him is, of course, a Pyrrhic victory: the upshot is that she will never see her son again.

Worse than that, to save her son from knowing his mother is a murderer, she flees the city without explanation; he will never know why she abandoned him. As in the work of Powell and McCarthy, the power of women's sexuality is ultimately used against them, in this case because its power over men incites their need to dominate and possess, and the woman has no other access to power except through her relationship to men. Yet the power of the color line fundamentally distinguishes Petry's novel from Powell's and McCarthy's. This is true in not only thematic but formal and stylistic ways, specifically its gothic aspects.

The most peculiar and haunting figures in the book are Mrs. Hedges and Junto, an interdependent pair of powerful yet socially abject persons who at a psychological level blur the boundaries between black and white, male and female. Junto is childless, seemingly sexless, and hardly "phallic" in appearance or manner, being grotesquely short and squat, and the black people of the street do not think of him as exactly "white," because he never makes them feel "black." Boots Smith

> didn't feel the same toward him as he did toward most white men. There was never anything in Junto's manner, no intonation in his voice, no expression that crept into his eyes, and never had been during the whole time he had known him, nothing that he had ever said or done that indicated he was aware that Boots was a black man.

He had watched him warily, unbelieving, suspicious. Junto was always the same, and he treated the white men who worked for him exactly the same way he treated the black ones.[52]

Similarly, Mrs. Hedges tells Junto, "I put up with you because you don't ever stop to think whether folks are white or black and you don't really care. That sort of takes you out of the white folks class."[53] In fact, the very invention of whiteness was and is dependent on caring about, defining arbitrarily, who was or is white and black, and Junto's skin is described as gray.

Mrs. Hedges is bald, burnt, and powerful. Once nearly incinerated in an apartment-house fire, she is permanently hairless and covered with terrible scars from head to foot. When the building superintendant is on the verge of dragging Lutie into the cellar to rape her, a superior force intervenes that one assumes to be masculine: "A pair of powerful hands gripped her by the shoulders, wrenched her violently out of the Super's arms, flung her back against the wall. . . . The same powerful hands shot out and thrust the Super hard against the cellar door." It turns out to be Mrs. Hedges, and at this moment Lutie gets her first good look at her: "looked at closely she was awe-inspiring. She was almost as tall as the Super, but where he was thin, gaunt, she was all hard, firm flesh—a mountain of a woman."[54] Mrs. Hedges is a monstrous and insidious figure, paired with Junto as a sort of invisible force on the Street, yet here, midway in the novel, she becomes a sympathetic figure with a paradoxically "rich, pleasant voice." She understands how Jones has been stunted by his environment, and we learn of her past suffering, which wins our admiration while also enhancing the character of Junto. As in some gothic classics, the monsters are humanized. Yet they also remain monstrous, shaped by and for the powers that confine Lutie Johnson and her son.

The relationship between Junto and Mrs. Hedges is queer—she will not agree to a romantic relationship with him, but as Boots recognizes, Junto is

nuts about that black woman on 116th Street, talked about her all the time. He had never forgotten the shock he got when he first saw

Mrs. Hedges. He hadn't really known what to expect the night he went there with Junto, but he was totally unprepared for that hulk of a woman. He could have sworn from the way Junto looked at her that he was in love with her and that he had never been able to get past some obstacle that prevented him from sleeping with her—some obstacle the woman erected.[55]

In fact, Mrs. Hedges refuses any overtures toward a romantic relationship with Junto—not because he is "white," despite her hatred of white people, but because her body has been so grotesquely scarred by fire that she never wants anyone, not even him, to see her unclothed. Yet it is precisely her scars that draw Junto to her.

After Mrs. Hedges saves Lutie, the narrator fills in the background of her present condition, as she remembers the fire and how it led to her partnership with Junto. During her first months in New York, she had been unemployed, destitute, incapable of attracting male attention, so "huge" and black that people were repelled by her. One night while gnawing on a chicken bone plucked from a garbage can, she finds a short, squat white man staring at her, a man with a pushcart collecting junk from the street. They strike a deal to help each other out, with Junto paying her to help collect bottles and scrap metal for him. She then suggests he get more pushcarts and hire others to work for him; then he starts buying real estate and makes her his janitor and rent collector. Their relationship grows from there.

After a house fire engulfs her in flames, she is left grossly disfigured and gives up hope of ever finding a man for love and protection. Yet Junto only admires her the more, "marveling at the indomitable urge to live, the absolutely incredible will to live," that had saved her:

She looked steadily at Junto, her eyes unwinking. He would probably be the only man who would ever admire her. He was squat. His shoulders were too big for his body. His neck was set on them like a turtle's neck. His skin was as gray in color as his eyes. And he was white. She shifted her eyes so that she could no longer see him.

"You're a wonderful woman," he was saying softly.

And even he would never want her as a woman. He had the kind of forthright admiration for her that he would have for another man—a man he regarded as his equal. Scarred like this, hair burned off her head like this, she would never have any man's love.[56]

As a result, Mrs. Hedges gives up on any thought of marriage and, with the protection of Junto from the police, starts a brothel in one of his buildings. The two look out for each other. She saves Lutie from Jones because Junto wants her, even though the sense one gets of Junto is that he is practically sexless and that his one true love is Mrs. Hedges.

Boots Smith also wonders why Junto wants Lutie, because he has never shown any sexual interest in women, despite all the young women who have been in his "joints." With a "sudden desire to see his face go soft and queer," Boots asks Junto how Mrs. Hedges is doing, as if asking about his wife, to which Junto, his face "melting" into a smile, replies "Fine . . . She's a wonderful woman. A wonderful woman."[57]

It is never clear that Junto wants to have sex with Lutie Johnson. We know only that he wants to "have" her. Boots thinks he wants her because she is "young and extraordinarily good-looking," but what may be equally as important is what Lutie represents to Mrs. Hedges, a "femininity" she envies as the obverse of her own "monstrosity." The scene in which Mrs. Hedges recalls the fire immediately follows on her saving Lutie from the building "Super." Spending time afterward close to Lutie,

studying her as she drank the hot tea and seeing the way her hair went softly up from her forehead, looking at her smooth, unscarred skin, and then watching her walk out through the door with the long skirt gently flowing in back of her, had made her think about it again—the smoke, the flame, the heat.[58]

Mrs. Hedges does think Junto wants Lutie for himself but also that he "would be willing to pay very high for her. Very, very high, because when he got tired of her himself he could put her in one of those places he ran on Sugar Hill."[59] Yet Junto knows that Mrs. Hedges refuses to "sell" black girls to white men and has no reason to believe that she would change this policy for him. We are therefore left in uncertainty about his motivation in wanting to "possess" Lutie, but what we do know is that both Mrs. Hedges and Boots Smith work to steer her into Junto's web.

Mrs. Hedges and Junto are the Street's queer power couple. They are functions of the entire society's race and gender oppositions even as they suggest the potential instability of those oppositions. Here we get to an elemental aspect of the gothic mode, its representation of the uncanny, the disavowed and abjected elements underlying the parceled surfaces of social order. While the mainstream culture maintains a strict division between black space and white space, Miss Hedges's relationship with Junto is "interracial" and at the same time hidden from view. If the "Super," Jones, is subterranean, they are potentially subversive, existing *on* the boundary yet serving to maintain it. Inevitably, systems of power require such boundary figures to maintain the distinction between order and chaos, yet for this very reason they threaten the distinction precisely because they exist between what must be kept apart. The system needs such figures at the boundary and produces them out of the flotsam and jetsam of its refuse.

This geometry comports with what might be called the hidden reality (as deconstructive criticism argues) that all binary oppositions contain within themselves their own unmaking, as each opposing term contains within itself the trace of the "other" against which it is defined, yet this reality must be obscured, sequestered, to sustain the difference. This is not to suggest that "black" and "white" or "male" and "female" are equal and opposed terms but that the entire structure depends upon an impossible and ecologically unstable separation. Only perverse machinations of power can maintain it, and somewhere, however hidden in plain sight, its incapacity will appear, often as an evanescent haunting in the personage of strange or monstrous characters.

Junto and Mrs. Hedges affect us as more dreamlike than naturalistic, surreal, because they are ghosts in the machine—yet at the same time sociologically true. Junto does not *represent* whiteness or patriarchy, nor does Mrs. Hedges represent blackness or femininity. Rather, poverty, patriarchy, and racism form them to the system's purposes—the white slumlord and the black madam. Petry develops them in elaborate detail as abstract yet legible characters of contemporary Harlem. That the "madam" side of this pair hovers over women's sexuality clearly indicates how central women's sexuality is to everything concerned with power. That she needs Junto, and he her, suggests how power is always ecological.

This brings me to the crucial point, on which I will conclude this chapter, that women authors' keen attention to the paradoxes of power applied not only to their treatment of female subjects. In "Powerhouse" (1941), inspired by a Fats Waller performance in her hometown, Eudora Welty notes a related dynamic in the eponymous character's relationship to the white audience. Welty had first heard and seen Waller in New York, probably Harlem. Her story brilliantly hovers between a focalization through the white townspeople, devastating in its precision about their racist fascination with and revulsion toward Powerhouse, and a very different one between Powerhouse and his band members, as they negotiate the racist context of their performance. That context includes the segregated audience and the need during the intermission to find a "black" haven (the World Café) in which to rest, which turns out to have only white covers of black music on the jukebox. By her own account, Welty wrote the story as a tour de force immediately after the performance— although to get it published she had to alter the conclusion, which featured lyrics from the song "Hold Tight" (referring to cunnilingus). As an exploration of white psychology absorbing black performance and of the black performer's negotiation of that enclosure, to this day there are few better in the American canon.

Recall how in Welty's photograph *Hypnotized, State Fair* we view the stage spectacle from the midst of the audience, observing how the young boys are hypnotized into the "othering" of women as objects of sexual fantasy. Here the storytelling strategy corresponds to that photographic positioning.[60] Powerhouse mesmerizes his white audience, which perceives him through demeaning stereotypes, as if at a carnival freak show:

There's no one in the world like him. You can't tell what he is. "Nigger man"?—he looks more Asiatic, monkey, Jewish, Babylonian, Peruvian, fanatic, devil. He has pale gray eyes, heavy lids, maybe horny like a lizard's, but big glowing eyes when they're open. . . . Is it possible that he could be this! When you have him there performing for you, that's what you feel. You know people on a stage—and people of a darker race—so likely to be marvelous, frightening.[61]

His very "power" as a staged spectacle is bound to his hyper-racialized and exoticized position, which he exploits even while detesting it. "Powerhouse is so monstrous he sends everybody into oblivion."[62]

Indeed he does. Powerhouse signifies relentlessly on the white audience's oppressive spectatorship, improvising on his objectification and on their appropriations of black musical culture. The whites find him apelike, and, as Kenneth Bearden has argued, he is a "signifying monkey" besting the lion with his tricks.[63] While the band plays "Pagan Love Song," "the one waltz they will ever consent to play—by request," Powerhouse begins a dialogue with the band musicians nearest him that presents a bitter commentary on the sappy primitivist love songs performed by many popular performers of the time, from the Andrews Sisters to Dorothy Lamour and Frank Sinatra.[64]

Native hills are calling
To them we belong
And we'll cheer each other
With the pagan love song.[65]

In ironic contrast to the tune he plays, Powerhouse improvises a story of his wife committing suicide while he is on tour, beginning, "I got a telegram my wife is dead." The telegram is from Uranus Knockwood—a parodic name for white society and the grim reaper. To get the message, he had to "go way downstairs along a long cor-ri-dor to where they puts us," and there Knockwood stepped out to hand him the telegram. While Powerhouse and the band members improvise the story for their own amusement, they complete the "Pagan Love Song" for the audience, looking forward to intermission. When intermission comes, they race for the door and head straight for "Negrotown," the only place they can be served—"where they puts us."

At the World Café, they order beer and check out the nickelodeon, chock-full of "white" covers of black-composed songs even in this "black" space.

> "Whose 'Tuxedo Junction'?" asks Powerhouse.
>
> "You know whose."
>
> "Nickelodeon, I request you please to play 'Empty Bed Blues' and let Bessie Smith sing."
>
> Silence: they hold it like a measure.
>
> "Bring me all those nickels on back here," says Powerhouse. "Look at that! What you tell me the name of this place?"
>
> "White dance, week night, raining, Alligator, Mississippi, long ways from home."[66]

Such are the blues.

Black people, recognizing Powerhouse, squeeze into the café to "enclose" him, and Powerhouse "affectionately" resumes the story about his wife. When she leaps to her death, Uranus Knockwood finds her: "That no-good pussyfooted crooning creeper, that creeper that follow around after me, coming up like weeds behind me, following around after me everything I do and messing around on the trail I leave. Bets my numbers, sings my songs, gets close to my agent like a Betsy-bug; when I going out he just coming in."[67] Knockwood bears a mighty resemblance to white crooners feeding off black artists—like those on the jukebox in the aptly named World Café—as he picks up the remains of Powerhouse's wife and carries them off.

The audience laughs—they are blues people, after all—and joins in a call-and-response:

> "Oh Powerhouse!"
>
> "You know him."

"Uranus Knockwood!"
"Yeahh!"
"He take our wives when we gone!"
"He come in when we goes out!"
"Uh-huh!"
"He go out when we comes in!"
"Yeahhh!"
"He standing behind the door!"
"Old Uranus Knockwood."[68]

Powerhouse takes imaginative control over his (and their) relationship with the ubiquitous Knockwood, the personification of white power and perhaps death itself. "You got him now," his band members say, as they head back to the white dance hall, intermission over.

Back at the piano, Powerhouse plays "for a few minutes with outrageous force and got it under his power—a bass deep and coarse as a sea net." The narrator, oblivious to his fury, remarks, "who could ever remember any of the things he says? They are just inspired remarks that roll out of his mouth like smoke"—primitive evocations of spontaneous nonsense. When the crowd requests "Somebody Loves Me," a Tin Pan Alley song by two white composers, Powerhouse erupts, piling up chorus after furious chorus until "His mouth gets to be nothing but a volcano."[69] Welty's framing drips with irony as she ends the tale. "'Somebody loves me,'" Powerhouse wails, "and looks out upon the place where he is [white dance, Alligator, Mississippi]. A vast impersonal and yet furious grimace transfigures his wet face," and then he finishes, "'Maybe it's you!'"

You might love me, he seems to be thinking, but I'll be damned if I love you. The fury of the black entertainer forced to "clown" for white folks redoubles the performance beyond their ken as a self-affirming act of defiance.

9

ECOLOGY AND CULTURE

··

I n one of the defining books of Cold War liberalism, *The Vital Center: The Politics of Freedom* (1949), Arthur Schlesinger Jr. attempted to define a political direction to defend against the threats of totalitarianism, on the one hand, and conservative reaction, on the other. Near the end of the book he came to the main reason that a new global political consensus must be reached:

> We have raped the earth too long, and we are paying the price today in the decline of fertility. Industrial society has disturbed the balance of nature, and no one can estimate the consequences. "Mankind," writes William Vogt, "has backed itself into an ecological trap." . . . In the light of this epic struggle to restore man to his foundations in nature, the political conflicts which obsess us today seem puny and flickering. Unless we are soon able to make the world safe for democracy, we may commit ourselves too late to the great and final struggle to make the world safe for humanity.[1]

Schlesinger put the onus on an ethical transformation of human beings en masse. In doing so, he cited Whitman's "Democratic Vistas," which had claimed the central role of literary expression in human history. To Whitman, literature written on new principles, through new processes, would bring into being cultures reconciling humans with one another across differences and with the nature of which they were a part.

In the 1940s, literature came to be not just a vehicle for delivering environmentalist or conservationist messages. Its relationship to the environment might be ontological, the processes of its utterance those of nature itself, forces in the ecosystem. Inherent in such a notion is the inextricable relationship between nature and culture, that nature is not culture's "other"—nor, say, its romantic origin. Culture may be a natural product of human beings, but it also has effects in the natural world— that is to say, it is part of the ecology of a place.

Rachel Carson, famous today for *Silent Spring* (1962), started out as a marine biologist with literary aspirations. Her book *Under the Sea-Wind* came out in 1941, the first of a now-classic trilogy on ocean ecology.[2] No scientific treatise, it tries to awaken its readers to a greater aesthetic and ethical connection to what goes on at and beneath the waterline. Carson knew that to make people care about the health of the oceans required overcoming the fact that human beings were not made to survive in them and, before the invention of the aqualung, had limited knowledge of the life therein. Even fishermen knew little of what lay or moved beneath the surface or of the complex interdependencies supporting their own ways of life. The challenge was, simply put, to overturn your point of view—to get you to think, as Susan Power Bratton has put it, "like a mackerel." Carson treated sea creatures as characters (some of them bearing their scientific names) and experimented with point of view in order to help the human imagination traverse, with the guidance of a nonhuman animal, the boundary between what lies above and below the ocean surface, inspiring wonder before the complexity of ecological processes in a foreign realm.[3]

Under the Sea-Wind encouraged what Bratton terms a "transboundary imagination" and in the process anticipated, indirectly, the land ethic of Aldo Leopold's *A Sand County Almanac* (1949). It also curiously correlates with the transboundary texts featured earlier in this book. However, despite positive reviews, it had little impact and sold poorly, for the Japanese attacked Pearl Harbor just as it appeared—Pearl Harbor, known today as a saltwater tomb.

In the same year as *Under the Sea-Wind*, a collaboration between John Steinbeck and the biologist Edward F. Ricketts appeared: *Sea of Cortez: A Leisurely Journal of Travel and Research* (1941). At the heart of the book's method is an understanding of their own expression as part of nature itself, scientifically precise yet not an "objective" scientific work—even though it included painstaking results of their collecting methods along with a "phyletic catalogue." "Let's go wide open. Let's see what we see, record what we find, and not fool ourselves with conventional scientific strictures. We could not observe a completely objective Sea of Cortez anyway, for in that lonely and uninhabited Gulf our boat and ourselves would change it the moment we entered"; they would become, willy nilly, "truly and permanently a factor in the ecology of the region."[4] No creature is autonomous, no species disconnected from the whole. The book critiques academic specialists who go into the field to find what they are looking for. Steinbeck and Ricketts emphasize what they call nonteleological thinking—avoiding the presumption that things are headed toward determinable destinations, whether heaven, hell, or progressively improved circumstances. There may be no waves of the future, only waves.

The expedition began about the time Germany invaded Denmark. The report of their own activities is shadowed by ruminations on the nature of *Homo sapiens*, a species with a "murder trait . . . as regular and observable as our various sexual habits." To be sure, they remark also on the effects of Japanese overfishing off the Baja peninsula. But just as importantly, they consider their relationship to their boat and how the human psyche has been shaped in relation to this ancient tool, acquiring a "boat-shaped mind" and the boat a "man-shaped soul." They meditate elsewhere on the "harvest of symbols" acquired over the ages of human interaction with other beings, which have grown into transcultural archetypes, a particular fascination of their friend Joseph Campbell.[5] In short, during their journey in the Sea of Cortez, the boundary between "nature," "science," and "culture" dissolved. Culture (including science) was a human function of nature.

Within the conservation movement, in the midst of the war, concern for wilderness, not to mention ocean ecology, receded. Aldo Leopold, now famous for the environmentalist classic *A Sand County Almanac*, was a specialist in game management with longstanding concerns for preserving wilderness. He helped found the Wilderness Society in 1935. He wrote a friend and colleague, however, that one neither could nor should expect much concern for wilderness in the United States in the midst of the war. The importance of ecology, on the other hand, only grew. The human-engineered ecological threat accelerated, and a multidisciplinary intellectual current stressed the enormous impact of human activity on the environment, at a planetary level. As Leopold's biographer has written, "conservation was now a global issue."[6]

Ecological threat pervades much of the decade's literature. Ivor Winters spoke for many in his starkly titled poem, "An Elegy":

Who will believe this thing in time to come?
I was a witness. I beheld the age
That seized upon a planet's heritage
Of steel and oil, the mind's viaticum:

Crowded the world with strong ingenious things,
Used the provision it could not replace,
To leave but Cretan myths, a sandy trace
Through the last stone age, for the pastoral kings.[7]

Faulkner's *Go Down, Moses* also sings an elegy for wilderness as the "big woods" of Ike McCaslin's youth shrink and the habitat for wild game disappears.[8] Robert Lowell's Pulitzer Prize–winning *Lord Weary's Castle* (1947) is packed with ecological fears expressed with images and metaphors derived from modern war machinery—steel ships and oil slicks (rather than wood and sail), sewage that sickens the "rebellious seas" in Salem harbor. Much of the book is a meditation on American history,

Lowell's perennial subject. In Concord, "Ten thousand Fords are idle . . . in search / Of a tradition"; the monuments are "dry sticks" commemorating "The Minute Man, the Irish Catholics, / The ruined bridge and Walden's fished-out perch." The Mammonism of "unbridled industry" overwhelms the power of the crucifix.

> This church is Concord—Concord where Thoreau
> Named all the birds without a gun to probe
> Through darkness to the painted man and bow:
> The death-dance of King Philip and his scream
> Whose echo girdled this imperfect globe.[9]

Lowell contemplates the threat of white Americans to human survival itself.

Wilderness will always be important to environmentalists, but the intuitive connection between "wilderness" and "ecology" that we find in much environmental "nature writing," and to which Leopold's book may have inadvertently contributed, is misleading. In fact, at the time his book was being written and published, ecology had been a growing subject in scientific circles since about 1911, when the term began to gain currency among botanists and the like. But the term was still uncommon even among Leopold's colleagues in conservation in the late 1930s, when he began using it in lectures and essays.[10] In the course of the 1940s it entered the general American vocabulary. A newspaper editorial of 1948 pointed out that "Citizens everywhere have been consulting dictionaries to learn the meaning of such words as ecology."[11]

One main incubator and distributor of the concept earlier in the century was the University of Chicago, where biology-based ecologists were allied with the intellectual orientation of the Chicago School of Sociology (which focused on urban ecology) and the pragmatist philosophy of John Dewey and George Herbert Mead. Between 1919 and 1922 Ed Ricketts studied there under the ecologist W. C. Allee, who stressed the biological benefits of aggregation and cooperation among animals. He became a disciple of that legendary teacher, passing his wisdom on to Steinbeck in the 1930s and 1940s.[12]

The development of ecology between biological and social sciences at the University of Chicago was dialectical and informed in both cases by pragmatist philosophy. The term "ecology" replaced the earlier term "nature's economy." Dealing with the interaction of organisms with one another as well as the nonorganic environment, it depended on social-scientific metaphors about "communities" and "populations." A two-way thoroughfare ran between sociology and biology- and botany-based studies of ecology. Aldo Leopold's approach to ecology and conservation bears the impress of these currents of thought as surely as Richard Wright's *Native Son*. Leopold refers pervasively to "biotic communities." In the development of theories of biotic interdependence, social-science terminology became a major resource for biologists, game-management scholars, and other science-based ecologists. On the other hand, sociologists drew pervasively on ecological concepts from biologists for metaphors with which to explain urban "zones," "succession," and social "metabolism."[13]

In a 1925 research plan, Ernest W. Burgess had explicitly adopted the term and concept of "succession" from the field of plant ecology to speak of the processes of urban expansion and "the tendency of each inner zone to extend its area by the invasion of the next outer zone," a process that Chicago plant ecologists had studied in the Indiana Dunes.

This aspect of expansion may be called *succession*, a process which has been studied in detail in plant ecology. If this chart is applied to Chicago, all four of these zones were in its early history included in the circumference of the inner zone, the present business district. The present boundaries of the area of deterioration were not many years ago those of the zone now inhabited by independent wage-earners, and within the memories of thousands of Chicagoans contained the residences of the "best families." It hardly needs to be added that neither Chicago nor any other city fits perfectly into this ideal scheme.

Complications are introduced by the lake front, the Chicago River, railroad lines, historical factors in the location of industry, the relative degree of the resistance of communities to invasion, etc.[14]

Burgess went on to speak of urban transformation in biological terms of "metabolism," adopting then-current tendencies of plant and animal ecologists to think of biotic zones as organisms. (Later "organism" was rethought as "community" and eventually "ecosystem," beginning in the 1940s.) Chicago sociologists applied such thinking to the various neighborhoods of Chicago and their interactions, including the Black Belt, and helped catalyze Richard Wright's thinking well before he wrote the introduction to Horace Cayton's sociological study *Black Metropolis* (1945). Notably, too, the urban ecology of the Chicago School—particularly that of Robert Park—drew inspiration from the fiction of American literary naturalists, particularly Dreiser, one of Wright's models.

It is well known that Wright was deeply impressed by the work of the Chicago sociologists as he wrote *Native Son*, and in a landmark study of environmental literature Lawrence Buell has usefully interpreted the novel in the context of environmental determinism, in a line with literary naturalists and "urban fiction" going back to Dickens.[15] However, the specifically ecological discourse in its very language commands attention. Boris Max's speech in court attempting to save Bigger Thomas from execution is primarily structured with ecological metaphors emphasizing the interconnection of life forms and the potentially catastrophic consequences of attempting to segregate one form of life from others, creating what had become "our whole sick social organism."[16] While presenting a Marxist analysis of the relationship between his client and the state, Max refers to Bigger's crimes as "instinctive," the natural results of a human being surviving physically and psychologically in an environment made hostile by others that do not realize how their hopes, fears, and actions are leading to their own doom.

I plead with you to see a mode of *life* in our midst, a mode of life stunted and distorted, but possessing its own laws and claims, an existence of men growing out of the soil prepared by the collective but blind will of a hundred million people. I beg you to recognize human life draped in a form and guise alien to ours, but springing from a soil plowed and sown by all our hands. I ask you to recognize the laws and processes flowing from such a condition, understand them, seek to change them. If we do none of these, then we should not pretend horror or surprise when thwarted life expresses itself in fear and hate and crime.[17]

This new life form, Max asserts, expresses itself in terms of its own fulfillment, not in terms of white society's "good" and "bad."

Scientists of ecology emphasized the process of "succession," by which the organisms in any space often prepared the ground for the nourishment of other species that would in turn alter the local biota, such that the place would be taken over by new life forms, the soil altered by these, and so on. Human interventions only moved the biotic developments in new directions. Max continues in terms deriving from the ecological notion of succession:

injustice blots out one form of life, but another grows up in its place with its own rights, needs, and aspirations. What is happening here today is not injustice, but *oppression*, an attempt to throttle or stamp out a new form of life . . . that expresses itself, like a weed growing from under a stone, in terms we call crime.

White men in power have attempted to prevent this form of life from spreading into their own habitat, have "marked up the earth and said, 'Stay there!' But life is not stationary."[18]

Attempts to fix problems with local remediation, such as Mr. Dalton's donation of ping-pong tables to the local boys' club, do nothing to solve the underlying problems, which require attention to the entire ecosystem. (In fact, Bigger notes that his gang used the boys' club as a meeting place to plan their "jobs.") Max uses biological terms metaphorically at times, but his argument is explicitly ecological throughout. To refer to Bigger's as a new form of life is not merely a metaphor. And a city is not defined as what "nature" is not but rather as one of the kinds of habitats that human animals, inspired by hopes and dreams, build—in part through the exploitation of other humans as well as other natural resources at hand. These habitats can become death traps, like Bigger's apartment for the rat he kills at the opening of the novel, for all life within them is interconnected. Only by understanding how strongly Bigger's life and fate are linked to everyone else's in the society can "we" find "the key to our future, that rare vantage point upon which every man and woman in this nation can stand and view how inextricably our hopes and fears of today create the exultation and doom of tomorrow."[19]

Significantly, as Wright presents it, the Marxist explanation of history, which also pervades Max's speech, has much to recommend it but fails to address Bigger's most fundamental need. Bigger's cry for understanding to Max in their final conversation, "what I killed for I *am!*"— which repels even Max—makes complete sense from an ecological point of view.[20] Wright affirms the import of Bigger's search for *meaning*, a value that is essential to human life but that historical materialism fails to encompass. As the philosopher Thomas Alexander has recently put it in *The Human Eros: Eco-ontology and the Aesthetics of Existence*, "human beings seek to live with a concrete, embodied experience of meaning and value in the world. We *need* to feel that our own lives are meaningful and have value. This is a biological claim insofar as if this need is denied we either die or become filled with destructive rage."[21] To Wright himself, writing came from a visceral need to wring meaning out of what he called "deadlocking tensions," and it was thus a key to survival. This would be the central theme of his autobiography, *Black Boy* (1945).

Ralph Ellison later took Wright to task for environmental determinism, to which Wright replied:

> I don't mean to say that I think that environment *makes* consciousness . . .
> but I do say that I felt and still feel that the environment supplies the instrumentalities through which the organism expresses itself, and if that
> environment is warped . . . the mode and manner of behavior will be
> affected toward deadlocking tensions.[22]

Wright's reasoning is exactly consonant with that of the Chicago ecologists—and, for that matter, the reasoning of Lewis Mumford (the predominant theorist of urban and regional planning) and Aldo Leopold (a major voice in conservation and wilderness preservation).

A similar reasoning underlies Ann Petry's novel *The Street* (1946), which is replete with ecological motifs. Petry characterizes the Street—116th Street in Harlem—as a segregated, hemmed-in microenvironment that stunts the lives of its inhabitants as it stunts their dreams:

> She stopped her slow examination of him [her building supervisor] long enough to wonder if a creature like this was the result of electric light instead of hot, strong sunlight; the result of breathing soot-filled air instead of air filled with the smell of warm earth and green growing plants and pulling elevators and sweeping floors instead of doing jobs that would develop the big muscles in shoulders and thighs.[23]

The legacy of literary naturalism is clear, yet there is something else here, an ecological orientation that is new. "Nature" is here, from the opening paragraphs, in the December wind: "It did everything it could to discourage the people walking along the street. It found all the dirt and grime on the sidewalk and lifted it up so the dirt got into their noses, making it difficult to breathe; the dust got into their eyes and blinded them; and the grit stung their skins."[24] Such passages carry metaphorical freight, but they also bring attention to the relationship between the "natural" and built environment in a treeless, grassless block of Harlem. Like Gwendolyn Brooks's "street in Bronzeville," Petry's Harlem street, "grayed in and gray," has been formed by an "involuntary plan."[25] Environmental injustice shapes the local ecosystem. Lutie Johnson knows that "Streets like the ones she lived on were no accident. They were . . . the method the big cities used to keep Negroes in their place. . . . From the time she was born, she had been hemmed into an ever-narrowing space, until now she was very nearly walled in and the wall had been built up brick by brick by eager white hands."[26]

After flourishing in Chicago in the 1920s and 1930s, the story goes, "urban ecology" languished until the aftermath of World War II, when it resprouted in studies of plant ecology in the urban rubble of England and Europe, concerned primarily with nonhuman nature in urban environments. Contrary to this story, from the mid-1930s through the 1940s, urban ecology was getting a thorough rearticulation and transformation not only in African American fiction like that of Wright and Petry but in the cultural criticism of Lewis Mumford. Mumford had started out as a cultural critic in the 1920s, one of the "Young Americans" associated with *The Dial* magazine and the likes of Van Wyck Brooks and Randolph Bourne. He had written one of the first books to bring attention to Melville and *Moby-Dick*, as well as *The Golden Day*, a major study of what came to be called the American Renaissance. But he also wrote pioneering architectural criticism and finally major books in the interconnected fields of urban studies, environmentalism, and regional planning. His four-volume Renewal of Life series (1934–1951) argued for reasserting the priority of human values over technology as an ecological necessity. His trajectory culminated in an argument for the transformation of human "personality" toward a dynamic balance in which "no one part of life should be segregated from another part, incapable of influencing it or being influenced by it"—away from its organization by profit and material accumulation toward what he called, idealistically, to be sure, "wholeness."[27] By this he meant wholeness of the individual, in which a balance of economic, emotional, aesthetic, and familial capacities could be nourished. But this wholeness could be achieved only in a society in which it was available to all, nourished as an ideal to all. Mumford believed that an epochal transformation in human culture was required, and possible.

An ecological orientation provided an anticapitalist alternative to Marxist discourse in Mumford's thinking; as American intellectuals grew wary of Marxism throughout the 1940s, this was not an unusual development.[28] In fact, Mumford's position can be usefully considered in relationship to Wright's. Mumford believed that Marx was a great critic and social historian, but his confusion about material relations as not only a basis but the singular cause of all relations led him astray. There was another, more valuable, side to Marx: his "sense of the whole man, as being the necessary goal of a fully humane system of production. . . . But . . . the concept of the whole man must rest upon a theory of production which itself takes into consideration the underlying needs of the human personality."[29] Here Mumford's thinking converges with that of Richard Wright at the time.

And it merges with his ecological perspective. What do workers need? Fellowship, work interest, esthetic stimulus, "not merely . . . a just share of the rewards after the work is done, but . . . an equal share of reward in the work itself."[30] How is this "ecological"? It places emphasis on process rather than end, and it has implications for the type of historicism that was pervasive in Marx's time. He had envisioned a "happy ending," an end of history in the ultimate withering away of the state after the proletariat triumphed. He did not recognize what his contemporary Whitman knew, that

"it is provided in the essence of things that from any fruition of success, no matter what, shall come forth something to make a greater struggle necessary." At the very moment that mankind as a whole is clothed, fed, sheltered adequately, relieved from want and anxiety, there will arise new conditions, calling equally for struggle, internal if not external conditions, derived precisely from the goods that have been achieved.[31]

By the mid-1940s, it was clear that well before humanity as a whole had been clothed, fed, and sheltered adequately, the technological means of producing such a result could lead to human extinction.

Mumford was not against technology and cities. Considering the city as an "earth form," Mumford interpreted urban and regional organization ecologically. His hero was the little-known Scottish botanist/ sociologist Patrick Geddes, but he also cited the work of the Chicago sociologists. Mumford's arguments in *The Culture of Cities* (1938) unsurprisingly comport with Richard Wright's and Ann Petry's treatment of urban ecology:

The autonomy of the organism, so characteristic of its growth, renewal, and repair, does not lead to isolation in either time or space. On the contrary, every living creature is part of the general web of life: only as life exists in all its processes and realities, from the action of the bacteria upward, can any particular unit of it continue to exist. As our knowledge of the organism has grown, the importance of the environment as a co-operative factor in its development has become clearer; and its bearing upon the development of human societies has become plainer, too. If there are favorable habitats and favorable forms of association for animals and plants, as ecology demonstrates, why not for men? If each particular natural environment has its own balance, is there not perhaps an equivalent of this in culture? Organisms, their functions, their environments: people, their occupations, their workplaces and living-places, form inter-related and definable wholes.[32]

Against the capitalist trajectory of continuous expansion, mechanical multiplication, imperialism, and power, Mumford stressed the need for balance, maintenance of diversity (both biological and cultural), a reorientation "not only from mechanism to organism, but from despotism to symbiotic association, from capitalism and fascism to co-operation and basic communism." The goal would not be to make humans more powerful but "to make them . . . more capable of carrying on the specifically human attributes of culture."[33] To achieve this required thinking beyond the boundaries separating not just nations and provinces or states but those separating "inner" from "outer" environments, or "nature" from "culture," regarding culture as an inherent function of human organisms (and thus a function of "nature" itself) that needs to develop in balanced relationship with the physical environment. From this mode of thinking Mumford came to focus on the region, anticipating more recent ecological emphases on bioregionalism.

Rob Nixon has recently mounted a powerful critique of American "ethics-of-place" environmentalism for nationalist myopia, hostility toward displaced persons, a tendency to transcendentalism rather than transnationalism, and spiritual amnesia toward the history of white

American complicity in the havoc wreaked outside the bioregion of the nation. In short, Nixon calls for a rapprochement between environmentalism and postcolonialism.[34] Mumford's bioregionalism was explicitly anti-imperialist and essentially postcolonial in outlook. He attacked the "Malthus-Darwin myth" of the nineteenth and early twentieth centuries for sanctioning imperialism: "the Americans robbing the Indians, the Belgians in the Congo, the Germans in Southwest Africa, the Boers and British in Transvaal, the united Western power in Peking. . . . To exterminate their rivals was to improve themselves—or so the gunmen thought."[35] The answer to the myth, Mumford argued, could be found in the "advance of ecological studies" and an end to expansionism. Notably, Ramachandra Guha—best known for his attack on American environmentalism's wilderness emphasis and blindness to Third World concerns—was the first scholar to bring attention to Lewis Mumford as "The Forgotten American Environmentalist," worth the attention of postcolonial scholars.[36]

In the wake of World War II, Mumford argued that the overwhelming challenge to human life—and to life on earth—was to develop universal values against the modern epoch's domination by the "mechanism, militarism, and mammonism" of Western civilization.[37] He was driven to sweeping statements about how Western man's pursuit of power through technology and technologically enabled conquest had led to a cul-de-sac made manifest by the horrors of World War II. This view matched, intriguingly enough, a main thesis of Max Horkheimer and Theodor Adorno's *Dialectic of Enlightenment*, which critiqued "the inescapable compulsion toward the social control of nature" and linked that compulsion to the "enforced self-alienation of individuals, who must mold themselves to the technical apparatus, body and soul."[38] Mumford and Aldo Leopold had nearly identical positions on this issue. "The pursuit of power," Mumford argued, "ceased to be a means of adding to the security and variety of human life: it became an end in itself, attached to a disengaged fragment of the human personality." By means of this worship of power, and the power that technology gave Western nations over the natural world, superficially the world was unified. "But this unity was not a genuinely inclusive one. Culturally, it was based on the dominance of Western man and Western modes of thought," which worked hand-in-glove with ruthless exploitation and inequality. "The gross inequalities between continents, between peoples, between social classes, upon which our entire economic scheme was based, cannot now be maintained except by terrorism and brute force."[39] Equilibrium, both cultural and economic, would be essential to human survival. Western imperialism and racist exploitation were inextricable from the advent of a growing ecological crisis that was finally brought to a point by the invention and use of the atomic bomb.

What Mumford termed the goal of "expansion" must be replaced by that of "equilibrium," "conquest" with "co-operation."[40] He defined the goals of what we call today "sustainability," and necessary to that sustainability was "social security and well-being" for all humans: "We must prepare for the time when both population and industry will be mainly on a replacement basis: when the principle of continuous yield, as applied in agriculture and forestry, will supplant the reckless mining economy of the period of expansion."[41] Again, Mumford could not separate "ecology" in the scientific sense from "cultural ecology" and planetary humanism, what he termed *organic humanism*:

> The guiding themes for the coming era cannot be derived from the needs and hopes of the era of expansion: we have to frame a whole new set of objectives in terms of balance, equilibrium, co-ordination, and cultivation, a many-sided organic development: above all, in terms of human balance, human co-ordination, human development.[42]

Ecology in the 1940s, then, was not about "nature" abstracted from culture or cities. Conversely, as geographers and ecologists from the sciences were pointing out, physiographic areas themselves were dynamic and contoured, whether directly or indirectly, by human processes as surely as those processes were contoured by nonhuman ones: "wherever man found even the primeval wilderness, up to the days of the airplane, his own footprints accompanied him, and participated in the definition."[43]

I would add that the inextricability of ecology as a scientific pursuit from "culture" inheres in the fact that social metaphors are ubiquitous in the biological sciences—indeed, biological sciences practically depend on social tropes to communicate—and scientific study is itself a social activity.

Different tendencies in culture will have different consequences for species survival—including human survival. In *Values for Survival*, Mumford argues that

> If we are to create balanced human beings, capable of entering into world-wide co-operation with all other men of good will—and that is the supreme task of our generation, and the foundation of all its other potential achievements—we must give as much weight to the arousal of the emotions and to the expression of moral and esthetic values as we now give to science, to invention, to practical organization. One without the other is impotent. And values do not come ready-made: they are achieved by a resolute attempt to square the facts of one's own experience with the historic patterns formed in the past by those who devoted their whole lives to achieving and expressing values. . . . Virtue is not a chemical product, as Taine once described it: it is a historic product, like language and literature; and this means that if we cease to care about it, cease to cultivate it, cease to transmit its funded values, a large part of it will become meaningless, like a dead language to which we have lost the key. That, I submit, is what has happened in our own lifetime.[44]

Culture is essential to ecological survival.

By 1940, Aldo Leopold, who specialized in game management and is considered the inspiration of much postwar "nature writing"—had come to think of land as a community of which humans are members.[45] Earlier, conservationists including Leopold had focused on eliminating "problematic" species and increasing those thought "useful." Beginning with the essay "A Biotic View of Land" (1939), Leopold shifted course, realizing that such judgments about "useful" and "harmful" species are always valid only according to specific conditions, and thus one must conclude only "the biota as a whole is useful," including soils and waters as well as plants and animals.[46] The impending war, and the rising awareness of the immensity of modern technology that it brought, significantly affected Leopold's views; concern about human violence emerges in the essay. Leopold writes that "Man's invention of tools has enabled him to make changes of unprecedented violence, rapidity, and energy."[47] Thinking of "land" as a community or organism led Leopold to speak of "land health" or "sickness," and in the 1940s he wrote and spoke often of "land health," which has been identified as his "culminating concept."[48] No part of nature could be separated from any other part, including human beings: this interdependence and complexity Leopold considered "the outstanding discovery of the 20th century."[49]

Leopold became increasingly concerned about the relationship of human culture to the bios and the need for cultural change, above all a change in ethics. In the late 1930s and early 1940s, as he grew increasingly alarmed at events in Europe, he took interest in the work of Carl O. Sauer, the cultural geographer who drew on ecology alongside economics and anthropology to talk about how cultures alter their environments and are in turn affected by those alterations, and vice versa in a continual dialectic. (Sauer had rebelled against the earlier environmental determinism of cultural geographers.) Curt Meine has illuminated how, as the U.S. entry into the war grew inevitable, Leopold applied ecological insights to society. His opening lecture to his Wildlife Ecology 118 class in March 1941 began with a reflection on how war disrupts "the give and take equation" of every living thing in relation to its total environment. That the

> collective account between the Earth and its creatures ultimately balances is implicit in the fact that both continue to live. It does not follow, however, that each species continues to live. Paleontology is a book of obsequies for defunct species. Man, for reasons sufficient to himself, would rather see than be one of the defunct.[50]

What can ecology say about war as a disruption of the ecological equation? "Not much, except by analogy with animals. . . . I shall try to sketch the human enterprise, in its relation to war, as it now appears to me." He went on to argue that technology increased the land's "carrying capacity," allowing a greater human "take," but this could only go so far before the balance broke down and humanity had degraded the conditions of its own survival to a point of no return.[51] In short, if human culture, specifically human ethics, could not get ahead of science and technology to direct them more intelligently, the war was showing us where we would all end up, in desperate battles for shrinking resources.

A Sand County Almanac, and Sketches Here and There is often referred to as the bible of the postwar environmental movement. It is also a self-consciously literary experiment. The inextricability of human culture from nature is not only a major theme of the book; it inheres in the book's method of presentation, its aesthetic form. At its center, as in Mumford's work, is an argument about the connection between ideologies of conquest, capitalist notions of property in land, and ecological catastrophe. The key term Leopold mobilizes against the reigning ideologies is "community": "We abuse land," he writes in his foreword, "because we regard it as a commodity belonging to us. When we see land as a community to which we belong, we may begin to use it with love and respect."[52]

The war deepened Leopold's commitment to this premise. In his famous essay "The Land Ethic," which became the concluding segment of *A Sand County Almanac*, he explains that all ethics rest upon the premise "that an individual is a member of a community of interdependent parts." The land ethic enlarges the concept of community "to include soils, waters, plants, and animals, or collectively: the land."[53]

> In short, a land ethic changes the role of *Homo sapiens* from conqueror of the land-community to plain member and citizen of it. . . .
>
> In human history, we have learned (I hope) that the conqueror role is eventually self-defeating. Why? Because it is implicit in such a role that the conqueror knows *ex cathedra*, just what makes the community clock tick, and just what and who is valuable, and what and who is worthless, in community life. It always turns out that he knows neither, and this is why his conquests eventually defeat themselves.[54]

To Leopold, an ecological interpretation of history reveals that human beings are only members of a "biotic team."

His book attempts to weld together three essential concepts: the "basic concept of ecology," "that land is a community"; the ethical concept that "land is to be loved and respected"; and the esthetic concept "that land yields a cultural harvest." The logic of the book also works in the converse direction: through aesthetic appreciation we come to love and respect land, which can lead us to view and experience it as a community of which we are a part rather than as a resource that belongs to us to use however we like. In his most famous motto for developing a land ethic, Leopold suggests one "examine each question in terms of what is ethically and esthetically right, as well as what is economically expedient. A thing is right when it tends to preserve the integrity, stability, and beauty of the biotic community. It is wrong when it tends otherwise."[55] This notion of "beauty" inherently privileges human perceptions of beauty, balance, and proportion. Leopold is very aware that what we call environmentalism cannot escape anthropocentrism. We are not concerned about the death of the dinosaurs, nor about the new forms of life that might spring up in our absence. Our attachment to forms of "nature" that coexist with us, and upon which we depend, has an inherent esthetic component; to extend that attachment also requires esthetic creation.

Leopold strives for a "shift of values" through esthetic appeal. As John Dewey might say, aesthetics precedes ethics. When we feel the beauty in something and come to love it, we become ethically bound to it. The relationship between Leopold's text and its environment goes further than delivering this message, however. The book, as a literary experiment only completed—published at the hands of others—after his death, demonstrates what Leopold calls the "cultural harvest" that land yields through human perception.

This insight may have resulted from the process of composition itself. Lawrence Buell argues that "Leopold, like Faulkner, came to embrace the literary as a way of exploring a style of ethical apprehension of the claims of the nonhuman on the human that surpassed his prior understandings and that he himself may not have grasped with full self-awareness."[56] Making a cultural harvest of the land is therefore essential to saving it. The cultural harvest inheres in the total ecology of a place, taking into proper account human beings' relationship to it. Esthetic creation is a natural human function. Whitman once referred to the "belch'd words" of his voice. Poems are emanations of human being as necessary as burps.

If the almanac is in some sense the product of a particular place and community, it is also an engagement with the human experience of time, and from early in the almanac—specifically, the month of February—Leopold's concern with human history transects natural history, like a saw cutting through an oak. One effect of this transection is to notice the connection of environmental changes with "history"; another is to put seemingly catastrophic moments in human history into a longer, ecological, perspective. Recent history has given Leopold fresh metaphors for shaping his response to the natural world around him. But at the same time, the process of using them while meditating on things "wild, natural, and free" becomes a way of domesticating the incomprehensible—the world war, the extermination of peoples, the atomic bomb.

World War II has fundamentally affected the way Leopold thinks about ecology, in addition to providing his guiding metaphors and funding much of the rhetorical power of his argument. His literary imagination is saturated with tropes deriving from the war.

> The erasure of a human subspecies is largely painless—to us—if we know little enough about it. A dead Chinaman is of little import to us whose awareness of things Chinese is bounded by an occasional dish of chow mein. We grieve only for what we know. The erasure of Silphium from western Dane County is no cause for grief if one knows it only as a name in a botany book.

Or again, "It is an irony of history that the great powers should have discovered the unity of nations at Cairo in 1943. The geese of the world have had that notion for a longer time, and each March they stake their lives on its essential truth."[57]

The most extended use of martial tropes comes in the section of the almanac on bur oaks, describing a form of ecological succession leading to what was known as a "climax stage," or state of equilibrium between competing life forms:

> Bur oaks were the shock troops sent by the invading forest to storm the prairie; fire is what they had to fight. Each April, before the new grasses had covered the prairie with unburnable greenery, fires ran at will over the land, sparing only such old oaks as had grown bark too thick to scorch. Most of these groves of scattered veterans, known to pioneers as "oak openings," consisted of bur oaks.
>
> Engineers did not discover insulation; they copied it from these old soldiers of the prairie war. Botanists can read the story of that war for twenty thousand years. The record consists partly of pollen grains embedded in peats, partly of relic plants interned in the rear of the battle, and there forgotten. The record shows that the forest front at times retreated almost to Lake Superior; at times it advanced far to the south. At one period it advanced so far southward that spruce and other "rear guard" species grew to and beyond the southern border of Wisconsin; spruce pollen appears at a certain level in all peat bogs of the region. But the average battle line between prairie and forest was about where it is now, and the net outcome of the battle was a draw.
>
> One reason for this was that there were allies that threw their support first to one side, then to the other. Thus rabbits and mice mowed down the prairie herbs in summer, and in winter girdled any oak seedlings that survived the fires. Squirrels planted acorns in the fall, and ate them all the rest of the year. June beetles undermined the prairie sod in their grub stage, but defoliated the oaks in their adult stage. But for this geeing and hawing of allies, and hence of the victory, we should not have today the rich mosaic of prairie and forest soils which looks so decorative on a map.

In another passage, a half-uprooted maple shelters raccoons: "Without this 'bombproof' shelter, my seed stock of coons would be cleaned out by hunters each year."[58]

Putting human history in the context of natural history, or an ecological interpretation of history, makes for a longer view of the world wars than other modes of thinking, such as those focused on history being defined by exceptional events—for example the French Revolution, the revolutions of 1848, the American Civil War, or the use of the first atomic bombs. Reading the spaces between succeeding whorls of pine branches, which indicate how well the tree grew in a given year, Leopold finds that "the 1941 growth was long in all pines; perhaps they saw the shadow of things to come, and made a special effort to show the world that pines still know where they are going, even though men do not."[59]

Of course, what men do can affect how pines grow, or even if they will grow at all. Leopold does not minimize the effect of human choices on the community that is the land. We learn early on that Leopold does not keep his hands off of his land. He chops down a tree, bands birds to study them, plants trees, favors pines over birches. His very presence inevitably affects the community. He picks and chooses based on aesthetics and personal references, and an ecological perspective, in his telling, must take such choices into account because there is no choice *not* to be involved in the community. The animals and plants themselves battle it out for survival; species annihilate each other. In the essay "On a Monument to the Pigeons," Leopold does not simply lament the extermination of the passenger pigeon; he also observes that

> for one species to mourn the death of another is a new thing under the sun. The Cro-Magnon who slew the last mammoth thought only of steaks. . . . But we, who have lost our pigeons, mourn the loss. Had the funeral been ours, the pigeons would hardly have mourned us. In this fact, rather than in Mr. DuPont's nylons or Mr. Vannevar Bush's bombs, lies objective evidence of our superiority over beasts.[60]

As the reference to the bombs designed by Vannevar Bush (who was in fact the author's good friend) implies, Leopold believes science has for too long been the servant of conquest, the sharpener of swords instead of a "searchlight on the universe," just as land has been treated as slave and servant rather than as "collective organism." To develop an "ethical relation to land" requires an "internal change in our intellectual emphasis, loyalties, affections, and convictions."[61] He charges that the conservation movement hitherto has made no attempt to touch these foundations of behavior: hence the need for an environmental literature.

Leopold opposes his "land ethic" to a conservationism that stresses the economic value of natural resources. Yet he also resists a purely instrumental view of literature's relationship to environmental activism. Echoing Thoreau, he places emphasis on aesthetic "harvesting." Literary expression is not simply a means of conveying an environmentalist message. It belongs to the ecological cycle of the local bios. That Leopold conceived of his writing as a natural product of Adams County inheres in his choice to call the first half of the book an almanac, paced by the months of a year. It is as much a natural product as the dropping from a goose winging its way overhead. Through the "international commerce of geese," he writes,

> the waste corn of Illinois is carried through the clouds to the Arctic tundras, there to combine with the waste sunlight of a nightless June to grow goslings for all the lands between. And in this annual barter of food for light, and winter warmth for summer solitude, the whole continent receives as net profit a wild poem dropped from the murky skies upon the muds of March.[62]

But it is of course Leopold's leavings that alert us to this poetry and thus inspire us.

Because of the war, too, Leopold (like Mumford) encouraged an international perspective on ecological issues. Rob Nixon, in the course of critiquing American environmentalism since the 1960s for its myopia concerning transnational perspectives, has pointed out that the American Wilderness Society moved in 1946 to integrate American environmental priorities with an agenda of world peace and named Leopold to chair a Committee on Foreign Relations. This outlook, however, was derailed when Truman announced in 1949 that the USSR had produced an atomic bomb. American internationalism, as Nixon observes, "became starkly militarized," and "American environmentalism incrementally retreated from a vision of a global human ecology premised on the notion of a viable environment as a fundamental human right"—an ironic counterpoint to Leopold's argument in the *Almanac*, published in that very year.[63] Leopold, meanwhile, had died while fighting a brush fire in 1948.

Leopold's concept of his writing as a product of a place invites association with William Carlos Williams's long poem *Paterson* and Charles Olson's developing concept of projective verse. Williams's later poems have been recognized recently as modernist examples of ecopoetics and "bioregionalism."[64] *Paterson* constitutes, among other things, an environmental history of its eponymous city and particularly of the Passaic River as it runs through the area in which that city grew. In a 1948 lecture, "The Poem as a Field Action," Williams characterizes the "American language" as a language of immigrants in contact with a new geography and other ethnic groups, "yawping speakers of a new language" reaching toward a new poetic measure.[65] The first three books of *Paterson* (1946, 1948, 1949) exemplify a poetics of place that comports with the notion of land as community, in which human speech is a common and irrepressible product. "Thought clambers up" the wet rocks by Passaic Falls,

> hedged in by the pouring torrent—
> and has its birth and death there
> in that moist chamber, shut from
> the world—and unknown to the world,
> cloaks itself in mystery—
>
> . . . .
> And standing, shrouded there, in that din,
> Earth, the chatterer, father of all
> speech.[66]

The earth does not itself utter human speech, but human speech emanates like birdsong from the rocks. The man who lies in the valley under the Passaic Falls, with his "head near the thunder / of the waters filling his dreams"[67] is a man who is himself a city and at times an alter ego of Dr. Williams, a dream fulfillment. Poems traffic in dreams, naturally.

In his Sunday walk through the park of book 2, Paterson as person comes in and out of focus as the landscape takes over. What Olson would call the "ego-position" is displaced. What makes the poem fundamentally incomprehensible (like any natural being?) is how Paterson is both a feature of the landscape and a man, moving.

The human beings are noticed in the way of flora and fauna, the flora and fauna described with precision, and Paterson's own body described in the act of walking as precisely as that of an animal in a textbook: "The body is tilted slightly forward from the basic standing / position and the weight thrown on the ball of the foot, / while the other thigh is lifted and the leg and opposite arm are swung forward (fig. 6B). Various muscles, aided."[68] The mind meanders as the man walks, observing, daydreaming, thinking about poetry, about the need for a new, relative measure in verse, a new line adequate to its place in the world. Without the invention of a new line, "well-spaced,"

> the necessity
> will not matriculate: unless there is
> a new mind there cannot be a new
> line, the old will go on
> repeating itself with recurring
> deadliness: without invention
> nothing lies under the witch-hazel
> bush, the alder does not grow from among
> the hummocks margining the all
> but spent channel of the old swale,
> the small foot-prints
> of the mice under the overhanging
> tufts of the bunch-grass will not
> appear: without invention the line

will never again take on its ancient
divisions when the word, a supple word,
lived in it, crumbled now to chalk.[69]

Tellingly, in this second book of *Paterson* Williams begins pacing on
what he would later call the variable foot, his alternative to English literary measure.

The poetic line is here presented as a functioning part of a biotic community and a person's physiology—dependent, however, on human invention. But this invention depends, in turn, not on an observance of
Western poetic tradition, as in T. S. Eliot, but on attention to the place
itself, the land and its inhabitants, including their intertwined history
(which is extensively documented in the poem itself, with extracts from
old newspapers and the like) and the body's movements through the
landscape. Walking down a slope,

The descent beckons
    as the ascent beckoned
            Memory is a kind
of accomplishment
        a sort of renewal
                even
an initiation, since the spaces it opens are new
places
        inhabited by hordes
                heretofore unrealized[70]

The approach to this place is equally ecological. Williams reports on the
discovery of fine freshwater pearls made by the profusion of mussels in
the river, which led to overharvesting and the destruction of the mussel
population. This is only one example of how the poem documents the
past fecundity of the area, severely damaged by human greed. As he later
said, "This was my river and I was going to use it. I had grown up on its
banks, seen the filth that polluted it, even dead horses."[71]

Someone is walking this ground, pacing himself, rejoining a path and seeing "on a treeless / knoll—the red path choking it—/ a stone wall, a sort of circular / redoubt against the sky."[72] Why not mount it? This is not merely a metaphorical park; it is the very park that Williams knew of a Sunday afternoon. (As he told an interviewer later, "he visited as far as possible every place in Paterson mentioned in the poem.")[73] Yet the poem extends the park into imaginations far away, through its pacing.

"The Poem as a Field of Action," composed as Williams was writing *Paterson*, sheds light on what he was striving for in his struggle for a new measure. An improvisational process itself drew the poet on: "I had to think and write, I had to invent the means to get said, in the pattern of the terms I employed, what appeared as called for." (Charles Olson would later refer to "composition by field," insisting at the same time on particularity, not altering actual things for symbolic accretions but putting them in the poem exactly as they are in a particular place and time.) *Paterson*, like a natural process, has no real conclusion: "It wouldn't do to have a grand and soul satisfying conclusion because I didn't see any in my subject."[74] There are no grand conclusions in biotic communities, either, only transformations, conditions that make further struggle necessary. *Paterson* is environmental literature, but it is not "nature writing." It is an urban poem, one as open-ended as your life.

Akin to Williams's view of poetry and anticipating Charles Olson's "projective verse" was the position Muriel Rukeyser enunciated in *The Life of Poetry* (1949), in which poetry is defined as "a transfer of human energy." Poetry is the art that allows "people to feel the meeting of their consciousness and the world, to feel the full value of the meanings of emotions and ideas in their relations with each other, and to understand, in the glimpse of a moment, the freshness of things and their possibilities." The dynamics and "meanings" of a poem do not inhere in the words or images but emerge in the relations among its elements:

The science of ecology, is only one example of an elaboration of the idea, so that the life of land may be seen in terms of its tides of growth, the feeding of one group on another, the equilibrium reached, broken, and the drive toward another balance and renewal.

We think of the weather now as a dance of airs, predictable in relationship, with its parades of clouds, the appetites of pressure areas, and aftermath of foreseen storms.

But in areas dealing with emotion and belief, there is hesitation. Their terms have not been invented . . . a poem, a novel, or a play *act emotions out* in terms of words, they do not describe.[75]

Initiated at the meeting point of individual consciousness and the world, Rukeyser stresses, poems are about the "*in*vironment, where live the inner relationships."

Objections to the divorce between human and nonhuman nature inhered in the dialectic that the geographer Carl O. Sauer saw in landscape and the growing field of "cultural ecology" and in the thinking and poetic theorizing of Charles Olson. Olson, while rector at Black Mountain College in the early fifties, would fasten onto the connection of Sauer's theories to his own ideas for revolutionizing the arts. In the late 1940s, having abandoned a career in the federal government in part because of American imperialist trajectories, Olson was coming to see the human maker/poet as merely a "force within a field of force containing multiple other expressions," attempting to move beyond what he termed the "ego-position." Meetings with Ezra Pound in the late 1940s caused him to break from his example in disgust, although the model of Pound's "poem containing history" remained powerful. In "The Resistance," Olson identified the importance of the Holocaust for his turning:

When man is reduced to so much fat for soap, superphosphate for soil, fillings and shoes for sale, he has, to begin again, one answer, one point of resistance only to such fragmentation, one organized ground, a ground he comes to by a way the precise contrary of the cross, of spirit in the old sense, in old mouths. It is his own physiology he is forced to arrive at. And the way—the way of the beast, of man and the Beast.

It is his body that is his answer, his body intact and fought for, the absolute of his organism in its simplest terms, this structure evolved by nature, repeated in each act of birth, the animal man.[76]

Ultimately, Olson is more a descendant of Williams than of Pound—politically, poetically, and ecologically. As Sherman Paul put it almost forty years ago, "Olson's world-poem differs [from Pound's] because its object, in the face of world destruction, is ecological: to give us again 'an actual earth of value.'"[77]

Call Me Ishmael, Olson's tour de force about *Moby-Dick* and America, drew attention to the word "ECOLOGY" in discussing the environment supporting whales and saw in Ahab's quest and what Melville himself presented as the early global capitalist formation known as the whaling industry (which was driving the whales to near extinction) the apocalypse toward which the "ego-position" of Western humanism was leading humanity. To escape the spiral that nearly sucked Ishmael to his death required a new aim, one that Olson called "postmodern" and that demanded a swerve from those forms of Western thought in which humanity, and especially Western "Man," was the measure of all things. Western humanity in the wake of the war was in the position of human beings in the late Pleistocene period.

This correspondence with Pleistocene people's separation from a prior mode of existence, in Olson's reckoning, does not suggest a separation from "nature" but immersion in process. The imposition of the ego makes process secondary to purpose and is where Western art went wrong long, long ago. Olson's influential manifesto "Projective Verse" (first published by Leroi Jones in 1950) would emanate from this conviction. Only in process can the creator enlist the power both within and outside himself, "that with which we are most familiar." This would lead to a view of artistic creation as "the chance success of a play of creative accident,"[78] a concept echoing abstract expressionism as much as evolutionary theory. The poem is a communicative function of the will to cohere, energy making a place for itself. It is an integrating capability that exists only as a community of forces cohering at a certain place in a certain instant. The forces are historical, of the place and the economics and the habits of people—the overall conditions inherent and adherent to a place and a people's relation to it. If a person bears relation to his place and can communicate that connection, expression merely voices that place in the way a human animal projects a new object into and out from it. Olson termed his poetic approach "objectism."

From this trajectory emerged a major vector of postmodernism. His first use of the term came in a letter to Robert Creeley of 1951 and connected it not with extreme alienation or the triumph of simulacra but with an ecological view of human culture in relation to the bios: "any POST-MODERN is born with the ancient confidence that he *does* belong."[79] The base of Olson's "post-modern" push was an ecological approach to artistic creation. His project aimed to connect artistic expression once again with "that with which we are most familiar" but from which Western thought since Socrates ("humanism") had detached its human subjects.

Like Charles Olson, A. R. Ammons came to "disagree" with Western culture and, in his own words, "tried to get rid of the Western tradition as much as possible."[80] He felt more comfortable with the pre-Socratics. This involved thinking of poetry physiologically, as an activity making use of the whole body: "The pace at which a poet walks (and thinks), his natural breath-length, the line he pursues, whether forthright and straight or weaving and meditative, his whole 'air,' whether of aimlessness or purpose—all these things and many more figure into the 'physiology' of the poem he writes."[81] From multiple sources, the movement toward "open form" evinced a new conception of the relationship between literary expression and the environment, along with a decentering of Western culture inspired by the war.

There is a back story. A young sailor with no college or literary training, raised on a southern Appalachian farm in an isolated Pentecostal Baptist community, "Archie" Ammons served in the Pacific during the war. One day in 1944 his ship was resting near an island when a vision of the shoreline—the land/marine ecotone—inspired, according to his later recollection, an epiphany. As he imagined the lives and processes first above, then below, the water level, his beliefs were overturned. At roughly the same time, he came upon an anthology of poetry. Whether these events were causally connected is hard to know, but he came to believe that they determined his future life:

> One day, when I was nineteen, I was sitting on the bow of the ship anchored in a bay in the South Pacific. As I looked at the land, heard the roosters crowing, saw the thatched huts, etcetera, I thought down to the water level and then to the immediately changed and strange world below the waterline. But it was the line inscribed across the variable landmass, determining where people would or would not live, where palm trees would or could not grow, that hypnotized me. The whole world changed as a result of an interior illumination—the water level was not what it was because of a single command by a higher power but because of an average result of a host of actions—runoff, wind currents, melting glaciers. I began to apprehend things in the dynamics of themselves—motions and bodies—the full account of how we came to be a mystery with still plenty of room for religion, though, in my case, a religion of what we don't yet know rather than what we are certain of. I was de-nominated. . . . It was on board this ship that I found an anthology of poetry in paperback. And I began to imitate those poems then, and I wrote from then on.[82]

Epilogue

ONE WORLD

....

I n the mid-1940s, attacks on the international hegemony of the nation-state grew clamorous. It was a theme in the novels and poems
about the war, heightened by memories of the first "world war"—
as the Great War now came to be called—which many people alive could
still remember. Particularly after mid-1943, when Americans began to
feel confident that the Allies would win, people began thinking of how
to build a world without war, believing that another war would spell the
end of humanity. John Berryman's poem "The Dangerous Year," referring to 1939, exemplifies how World War II made the world one: "It's
time to see the frontiers as they are, / Fiction, but a fiction meaning
blood, / Meaning a one world and a violent car."[1] Created and maintained by power elites through use of arms, nation-states were dangerous
to the whole.

The war had made Americans conscious of parts of the world they had
rarely thought of before, places that now seemed part of their own world.
Radio brought foreign lands home in ways that Martha Gellhorn captured in her novel *Liana*:

Pierre turned the range-finding dial very slowly, and watched the thin
thread move across the ruler-like face of the machine, and marveled

again that one tiny line suddenly became San Francisco and one tiny line quite near it would be Constantinople. He took no pleasure in the loud closeness of the world, all the world babbling and playing music, announcing destruction in ponderous or homely or falsely theatrical tones, all the world so hideously alike, so vocal, so sad. He would have liked the world to be again wide and full of privacy and quiet lives.[2]

The radio not only carried the sounds of far-off lands; it created simultaneity across oceans and continents—a new kind of "imagined community," to borrow Benedict Anderson's phrase for the growth of nationalism in the eighteenth century, affected by then-new media such as newspapers.

Strains of "One World" thinking, not universally popular, permeated American culture in many registers. Wendell Willkie, the businessman and Republican presidential candidate, published the hugely popular book of that title in 1943, which sold in the millions and heralded a future of global interdependence.[3] In the aftermath of Hiroshima and Nagasaki, Eleanor Roosevelt wrote for her newspaper audience, "we came into a new world—a world in which we had to learn to live in friendship with our neighbors of every race and creed and color, or face the fact that we might be wiped off the face of the earth."[4]

A "Christmas 'Round the World" issue of *Superman* in February 1946 recounted the Man of Tomorrow's holiday travels of 1945, proving that "Just as the Eskimo's fur parka differs from the bright South American mantilla, so languages and customs differ from country to country—but people's hopes and fears and joys are everywhere the same!" By flying westward at a thousand miles per hour, pulling a string of transport gliders, Superman visits every corner of the earth (with a specially featured stop in Russia) in the same day, delivering gifts to bombed-out cities and reuniting refugees with their families. In each place, Superman's gifts suit the customs of the people, and he carries the message that "The day is near when all nations will be neighbors!"[5] Bill Finger, who wrote the story, may have been riffing on FDR's last public address (which he did not live to deliver): "We are faced with the pre-eminent fact that if civilization is to survive we must cultivate the science of human relationship—the ability of peoples of all kinds to live together and work together in the same world, at peace."[6]

The refugee anthropologist Claude Lévi-Strauss and the émigré linguist Roman Jakobson met in Manhattan, giving birth to structural anthropology, a theory that found universal structures behind the diversity of human cultures. Joseph Campbell published his first and most influential book, *The Hero with a Thousand Faces* (1949), popularizing comparative mythology while finding "universal" motifs of the hero's journey in central myths of peoples around the globe and throughout recorded history. While the myths always developed from the particular conditions of life of human collectives, their common patterns and motifs proved the spiritual unity of humankind.

There was also a pessimistic view of this human commonality: that people were made to combat and exterminate one another, to lay waste to the planet on which their lives depended. Had *Homo sapiens*—or at least its conquering tribes—evolved like certain forms of insects, that is, with an overinvestment in bureaucratic institutions and armor that allowed the strong to conquer the weak, only to discover that the armor they could no longer shed would bring their extinction? Campbell's close friends and mentors, Edward F. Ricketts and John Steinbeck, had expressed this hypothesis in *Sea of Cortez* at the beginning of the decade.[7]

The entomologist Caryl P. Haskins offered a more hopeful vision, but one he considered by no means certain. The defeat of totalitarianism had proven the superiority of loose associative relationships and none-too-strict hierarchies among human beings (as compared with ants). The attempt to bureaucratize and perfectly coordinate human beings had failed. The war had undoubtedly failed to solve the problems of totalitarian ideology permanently, Haskins concluded, but it had "laid the danger for a time." Now came a larger and more vital question to ask: "Is mankind cohesive? If so, can we evolve an entirely new level of human associative living—the world organization? This is truly the greatest evolutionary step which has faced mankind since the emergence of the modern nation."[8]

The United Nations was founded in the midst of such musings. Even while hopeful and at times utopian strains played out over the defeat of fascism, the pervasive dread remained, revivified at the end of the decade by world events. In the popular culture of the 1940s a constant fear of "the next world war," combined with ecological warnings, anticipated not just the end of history but the end of humanity.

E. B. White captured the tension in the conclusion of his postwar paean *Here Is New York* (1949):

> It used to be that the Statue of Liberty was the signpost that proclaimed New York and translated it for all the world. Today Liberty shares the role with Death. Along the East River, from the razed slaughterhouses of Turtle Bay, as though in a race with the spectral flight of planes, men are carving out the permanent headquarters of the United Nations—the greatest housing project of them all. . . . This race—this race between the destroying planes and the struggling Parliament of Man—it sticks in all our heads. The city at last perfectly illustrates both the universal dilemma and the general solution, this riddle in steel and stone is at once the perfect target and the perfect demonstration of nonviolence, of racial brotherhood, this lofty target scraping the skies and meeting the destroying planes halfway, home of all people and all nations, capital of everything, housing the deliberations by which the planes are to be stayed and their errand forestalled.[9]

Such hopefulness was hard to sustain in the decade to come. As school-children we learned to dive under our desks and file in prescribed order to bomb shelters filled with canned food. Some of us had seen the photos accompanying John Hersey's *Hiroshima* (1946) and couldn't see the point.

The Bomb. In contrast to the hopeful message of Superman for Christmas 1945, his late-breaking origin story came out in the July-August 1948 issue, revealing that shortly before Superman's birth, Krypton's greatest scientist had discovered that the core of their home planet was composed of "a substance called *uranium!* . . . which, for untold ages,

FIGURE E.1 Bradley Walker Tomlin, *Interplanetary Greeting*, 1946. Oil on canvas. 38" x 30". *Source*: Herbert F. Johnson Museum of Art, Cornell University. Acquired through the generosity of Alice F. and Robert M. Palmer, with additional support from the Museum Membership Fund. Photography courtesy of the Herbert F. Johnson Museum of Art Cornell University.

has been setting up a cycle of chain-impulses, building in power every moment! Soon . . . very soon . . . every atom of Krypton will explode in one, final terrible blast! Gentlemen, *Krypton is one gigantic atomic bomb!*"[10] Superman thus became the first interplanetary refugee. And he began voyaging to planets other than Earth at about the same time the abstract expressionist Bradley Walker Tomlin created the resonant painting *Interplanetary Greeting* (1947; fig. E.1).

The thought of "planets" communicating with one another implied the unity of planet Earth, a concept differently conceived in Max Ernst's 1942 *The Bewildered Planet* (mentioned in chapter 4), which may have influenced Tomlin as he moved from cubist still-lifes through experiments with surrealist automatism, cryptic writing, and esoteric symbolism to a more recognizably abstract expressionist style.[11]

In the literary field, seemingly no one was capable of addressing the advent of the atomic age. Gertrude Stein could not even find it interesting. In an infamous statement for *Yale Poetry Review* that is rarely quoted in its entirety, Stein protested:

> They asked me what I thought of the atomic bomb. I said I had not been able to take any interest in it.
>
> I like to read detective and mystery stories. I never get enough of them but whenever one of them is or was about death rays and atomic bombs I never could read them. What is the use, if they are really as destructive as all that there is nothing left and if there is nothing there nobody to be interested and nothing to be interested about. If they are not as destructive as all that then they are just a little more or less destructive than other things and that means that in spite of all destruction there are always lots left on this earth to be interested or to be willing and the thing that destroys is just one of the things that concerns the people inventing it or the people starting it off, but really nobody else can do anything about it so you have to just live along like always, so you see the atomic [bomb] is not at all interesting, not any more interesting than any other machine, and machines are only interesting in being invented or in what they do, so why be interested. I never could take any interest in the atomic bomb, I just couldn't any more than in everybody's secret weapon. That it has to be secret makes it dull and meaningless. Sure it will destroy a lot and kill a lot, but it's the living that are interesting not the way of killing them, because if there were not a lot left living how could there be any interest in destruction. Alright, that is the way I feel about it. They think they are interested about the atomic bomb but they really are not not any more than I am. Really

not. They may be a little scared, I am not so scared, there is so much to be scared of so what is the use of bothering to be scared, and if you are not scared the atomic bomb is not interesting.

Everybody gets so much information all day long that they lose their common sense. They listen so much that they forget to be natural. This is a nice story.[12]

In the long run, Stein's statement has proved prescient. There was plenty of fear all around, but from the standpoint of the American and European literary imaginations it was a dead subject. (In Japan, on the other hand, it gave rise to what is called "atomic-bomb literature," a category in itself.) As Paul S. Boyer has written, "while some writers like James Agee struggled unsuccessfully to deal with the bomb, others seemed almost deliberately to avoid it."[13] In one of the few allusions to the bomb in contemporary fiction, after hearing from Frankie about the power of the bomb, Berenice Sadie Brown in McCullers's play version of *The Member of the Wedding* commented, "Twenty thousand tons? And there ain't but two tons of coal in the coal house—all that coal. . . . The figures these days have got too high for me. Read in the paper about ten million peoples killed. I can't crowd that many peoples in my mind's eye."[14] The enormity of the war, the death camps, the disemboweled cities, surpassed reason's grasp.

Even today, one looks back on the literature of the world and finds little "about" the bomb. Outrage aplenty, fear for the advent of a nuclear war, but what could be said about it? The greatest impact for those not immediately victimized came in photographs of individual human beings accompanying John Hersey's flat prose, focusing on six individuals, in a special issue of the *New Yorker*. Lawrence Ferlinghetti was one of the first American servicemen to see the devastation soon after the event. It made him a lifelong pacifist, yet he never wrote about it. It reminds one of Theodor Adorno's statement that there could be no poetry after Auschwitz. These were the black holes around which everything swirled, as if concentrating in horror the uncountable, faceless individuals consumed through all the years of the war. And for the living life went on.

While Americans were glad they had developed the atom bomb before anyone else, there was considerable ambivalence about the responsibilities it carried and a knowledge that what happened to "them" could happen to "us."[15] Louis Simpson's "The Men with Flame-Throwers" concludes:

Since Nagasaki
Turned into showers
Those clipped commanders
Have not had a smoke.

What was it broke
At that flashing stroke
Of planes playing polo?
No city but ours.[16]

In a long, bombastic poem published as a book, *The Bomb That Fell on America*, Herman Hagedorn (a poet best known as a biographer of Theodore Roosevelt) grieved for the people of Hiroshima and for the United States, pondering whether the first test in the Nevada desert was equivalent to the day of Creation or the day of Doom. In any case, it had marked, he thought, a break in history comparable only to the birth of Jesus Christ.

We know that we have dropped other bombs that killed the innocent
    by thousands,
But in our hearts we know that this bomb was not like those.
With the others we merely demolished cities, as we slaughtered,
    overturned governments, ended the lives of nations.
With this bomb we ended an age, we divided the waters of the sea of
    time, we fulfilled the dreams of generations, the patient labor of
    pioneers, learned, selfless and bold.
In a breathless, daring thrust into the unknown, we captured for
    ourselves—we speak it not boastingly, Lord, but with humility that
    is half prayer—we captured the radiant power of the sun!

In a splendor beyond any that man has known, the new age we have
claimed came to birth.

The brightness of its dawning was the fierce shining of three suns
together at noonday, shedding, for golden seconds, such beauty over
the earth as poets, painters, philosophers and saints have imagined
and striven in vain to reveal to man in symbols and parables.

And we used it to destroy a hundred thousand men, women and
children!

God have mercy on our own children!

God have mercy on America![17]

The "conscience of America" shudders, for the "blinding light that lighted
Hiroshima / Lighted, too, the empty caverns of our souls." Now the
country must grow in soul-power, the only thing mightier than the
bomb, or bring about the end of humanity.

Essay after essay, pamphlet after pamphlet, book after book featured
the unleashing of atomic energy as an epochal divide in human history.
The world could never be the same. The atomic age required nothing
less than "a rebirth of civilization."[18] The editors of Pocket Books hurriedly
cobbled together a mass-market paperback and published it in August
1945, in the belief that the bombing of Hiroshima meant "the beginning
of a new age. For, with this newly-released force, man can destroy himself or create a world rich and prosperous beyond all previous dreams."[19]
In the future, power might be free, cars could run on water, the people of
the world be fed.

Prometheus or Faust? In countless documents immediately following
the war, the discovery of how to unleash atomic energy was described as
harnessing "the secret of the sun"—an ageless aspiration of humanity.[20]
On the other hand, Karl Shapiro, in "The Progress of Faust," worried
that the United States had made a bad bargain, acquiring a "secret formula" from German refugees:

Backwardly tolerant, Faustus was expelled
From the Third Reich in Nineteen Thirty-nine.
His exit caused the breaching of the Rhine,

Except for which the frontier might have held.
Five years unknown to enemy and friend
He hid, appearing on the sixth to pose
In an American desert at war's end
Where, at his back, a dome of atoms rose.[21]

To control this incomprehensible force might require more than one nation's self-discipline. The advent of the atomic era gave enormous impetus to the idea, through 1949, that national sovereignty along Western lines had been the scourge of the world since the Enlightenment and must be countered by a worldwide government or, at the very least, a federation. Balance-of-power politics was, from now on, a "fairy-tale."[22]

The modern Prometheus himself, also known as Albert Einstein, weighed in on the matter in no uncertain terms. It was he who had written FDR early in the war about the possibility of creating an atomic bomb. His passion now was to replace nation-states with world government. Interviewed at a cabin in the Adirondacks by a reporter for the *New York Times*, Einstein said, "In my opinion the only solution for civilization and the human race lies in the creation of a world government, with security of nations founded upon law. As long as sovereign states continue to have separate armaments and armaments secrets, new world wars will be inevitable."[23] Again and again Einstein spoke up in public on the issue and involved himself intensely in current affairs. Following the logic of Emery Reves's *The Anatomy of Peace* (1945), which he urged all Americans to read, Einstein came out consistently and repeatedly through the late 1940s for a world government and for abrogating the sovereignty of nation-states. The United States should keep the secrets of the bomb until such a government was established and the separate nations' military organizations dissolved so that the world government would supersede all: "The method is the same that today makes the states of New York and California (nonproducers of atomic bombs) safe from annihilation by the states of Tennessee and New Mexico (producers of atomic bombs)."[24] Einstein was just one of many. Reves's book was an enormous success. Even Harry Truman was heard to say in Kansas City, "It will be just as easy for nations to get along in a republic of the world as it is for you to get along in the republic of the United States."[25]

Reves's argument was often repeated that the UN charter, by maintaining the sovereignty of the rival nation-states, would fail as miserably as the Articles of Confederation that preceded the U.S. Constitution. Nothing less than a federal constitution of the world, covering all human beings equally, could prevent atomic war. Seeing no positive uses of atomic energy in the near future, Einstein could only hope that it would "intimidate the human race into bringing order to its international affairs, which, without the pressure of fear, undoubtedly would not happen."[26] When the *New York Times* excerpted his remarks from the original *Atlantic Monthly* article but left out his mention of Reves's book, he objected in a letter to the editor published October 27, 1945: "To draw the attention of the American people to this book was one of the main reasons I wrote that article."[27]

Reves's book, first published a few weeks before Hiroshima's incineration, argued for the necessity of a Copernican revolution in social thought to solve the problem of war. It was time to give up what Reves called "nation-centric" thinking. His argument followed the logic of Boasian anthropology, Deweyan pragmatism, and the developing science of ecology:

> We still believe, in each one of the seventy or eighty sovereign states, that our "nation" is the immovable center around which the whole world revolves. . . . In order to understand the highly integrated and industrialized world, we have to shift our standpoint and see all the nations and national matters in motion, in their interrelated functions, rotating according to the same laws without any fixed points created by our own imagination for our own convenience.[28]

He faulted what he termed the "fallacy of internationalism" for failing to attack the disease of national sovereignty and to dismantle "the nation-state structure" of world politics.[29]

Reves was not considered a wild-eyed crackpot, although his supporters, including Einstein, eventually found themselves under attack from conservative congressmen. World- government thinking was fairly widespread, as Paul S. Boyer has argued at length in *By the Bomb's Early Light*.[30] *One World or None*, a book cobbled together with the thoughts of America's most esteemed thinkers and scientists, sold over one hundred thousand copies, frequently urging the necessity for a new global political system. The Nobel laureate Arthur H. Compton wrote in the introduction, "We now have before us the clear choice between adjusting the pattern of our society on a world basis so that wars cannot come again, or of following the outworn tradition of national self defense, which if carried through to its logical conclusion must result in catastrophic conflict."[31] General H. H. Arnold—who was taught to fly by the Wright Brothers in 1911, headed the Army Air Forces in World War II, and capped his career as chief of the air staff for the U.S. Army from 1943 to 1946—also contributed: "the time is at hand for the peoples of the world to admit that their warring power is too great to be allowed to continue. Through international collaboration we must make an end to all war for good and all."[32] Walter Lippmann's essay for the book concluded that the United Nations should be the seed of a "world state." Under American leadership many nations would rally around the cause: "an ideal for all mankind, not the United States of America as a nation state, may dominate and conquer the world."[33] But by 1950, Lippmann fell back to "the familiar ground of defending the national interest as the only means of navigating a perpetually divided world."[34] What was thought to be a decisive break turned out to be only another sharp bend in the road.

Even those unwilling to go as far as dissolving national sovereignty were impressed in the wake of the war. In 1946 the U.S. delegate to the United Nations proposed the creation of an Atomic Development Authority to prevent any further development or use of nuclear arms, by controlling all atomic-energy production under the auspices of the United Nations. The result was ultimately the UN Atomic Energy Commission, a considerably scaled-down (and relatively toothless) version of the original proposal. By 1949, the effort of scientists to awaken

Americans to the need for a new world government had been totally eclipsed by fear of the Soviet Union—which, ironically, their own rhetoric in warning of the horror of a nuclear apocalypse had only helped stoke.[35] By then, the scientists themselves who had called for world government were being called up for questioning about their loyalty; McCarthyism succeeded in painting the world-government movement as a communist plot.

Also affecting the shift were the arguments of George F. Kennan for a U.S. policy of "containment" of the Soviet Union. Kennan concluded, against the current wisdom, that if the Western nations could contain the Soviet Union's expansion, eventually it would collapse, and history would continue as before: "In his mind, the perennial challenges far outweighed the novel circumstances of the mid-century international scene." By the end of 1950 the Korean War appeared to have halted communist expansion without a nuclear event. According to Fritz Bartel:

As the "cold" conditions of the Cold War became permanent fixtures of the domestic and international scene by the end of 1950, reevaluations of the international system's fundamentals receded from the prominent place they held among liberal internationalists during the years of grace from 1945 to 1950.[36]

A rather similar drama played out in the effort to draft a Universal Declaration of Human Rights (UDHR), an extraordinary ideal and the most comprehensive such effort in history. While the international War Crimes Tribunal—another "first" in world history—was being created, the atrocities of World War II, and above all the extermination of European Jewry, inspired the belief that a new leaf in history must be turned over. If the atomic bomb demanded a rebirth of civilization and a uniting of humankind under equal rights, surely the Holocaust did as well. Charles Olson viewed the end of the war as a "Preface" to a new age, writing in 1948, in one of his first "projectivist" poems, written to accompany drawings of Buchenwald by a friend who had been among the first Allied soldiers to encounter it: " 'My name is NO RACE' address / Buchenwald new Altamira cave / With a nail they drew the object of the hunt."[37] The efforts of the present toward a planetary consciousness with new modes of expression reenact the Pleistocene humans' effort to break out of a "zoological mode of existence." Humanity in the wake of the war was in the position of the first people. As Olson would later put it, from now on one must take the context of the entire species for the self. Yet in the years immediately after the war, American literature was notably silent on the subject of the Holocaust, as on the subject of the bomb. Intense intellectual effort was being expended instead on drafting some global rules. There should be a worldwide covenant protecting "human rights"— whatever those were.

Berenice Sadie Brown, during a "queer conversation" in *The Member of the Wedding*, expressed some ideas on the subject that may have been shared by many at the time:

> No war, said Berenice. No stiff corpses hanging from the Europe trees and no Jews murdered anywhere. No war, and the young boys leaving home in army suits, and no wild cruel Germans and Japanese. No war in the whole world, but peace in all countries everywhere. Also, no starving. To begin with, the real Lord God had made free air and free rain and free dirt for the benefit of all. There would be free food for every human mouth, free meals and two pounds of fatback a week, and after that each able-bodied person would work for whatever else he wished to eat or own. No killed Jews and no hurt colored people. No war and no hunger in the world.[38]

The germ of the Universal Declaration of Human Rights is expressed here, in tune with FDR's Four Freedoms of 1941, enunciated in his State of the Union speech, almost a year before Pearl Harbor:

> In the future days, which we seek to make secure, we look forward to a world founded upon four essential human freedoms.
>
> The first is freedom of speech and expression—everywhere in the world.

The second is freedom of every person to worship God in his own way—everywhere in the world.

The third is freedom from want—which, translated into world terms, means economic understandings which will secure to every nation a healthy peacetime life for its inhabitants—everywhere in the world.

The fourth is freedom from fear—which, translated into world terms, means a world-wide reduction of armaments to such a point and in such a thorough fashion that no nation will be in a position to commit an act of physical aggression against any neighbor—anywhere in the world.

That is no vision of a distant millennium. It is a definite basis for a kind of world attainable in our own time and generation. That kind of world is the very antithesis of the so-called new order of tyranny which the dictators seek to create with the crash of a bomb.[39]

Freedom of Speech, Freedom of Worship, Freedom from Want, Freedom from Fear—"everywhere in the world"—and this in a State of the Union speech to a joint session of Congress. Melvin B. Tolson, prophesying a coming "Global Man," hailed FDR's vision: "From the gates of Chungking to the Potomac quays, / From the zenith zone to the nadir zone of the poles, / On the five continents and the isles of seven seas, / The Four Freedoms symphonize a billion souls."[40] All four freedoms were incorporated into the UDHR.

Once again, the protection of national sovereignty, especially for the United States and the USSR, intervened, and the UDHR became a document with no legally binding force. The results have been a crux of debate in recent years over the failings of the UDHR and the impossibility of protecting the rights of all human beings, including those left stateless, under the current international system. Hannah Arendt saw the problem as early as 1943. In the essay "We Refugees," published in the *Menorah Journal*, she coined the phrase "the right to have rights," which, to be universally applicable, would require going beyond familiar political categories having to do with states and national citizenship.[41] This ultimately led to her break with Zionism over its aim to secure Jews' rights by virtue of their citizenship in a Jewish state.

In addition to the stumbling block of national sovereignty, the problem arose of whose ideas of "human rights," and whose ideas of the relationship between individual rights and "group" rights, should be the standard. Were Enlightenment concepts of the individual and of "rights" adequate, or would their imposition amount to a form of imperialism? This dilemma has yet to be resolved, and it was fully anticipated at the very time the UDHR was being conceived.

During the drafting of the document, conceived as a path to a legal covenant, a "philosophers' committee" of UNESCO polled a vast range of thinkers from around the world for conceptions of human rights in their various cultures—and discovered many points of convergence as well as basic agreement in practical terms, but not necessarily based on the same theories of the "human" or of "rights." When someone expressed surprise that the group writing the UDHR was able to come to agreement, according to a well-known story, he was told, "Yes, we agree about the rights but on condition no one asks us why." This story is often repeated as a joke, yet it has a significant lesson. Maritain and his colleagues did not regard this lack of consensus on foundations as fatal. The only feasible goal for the UN, he maintained, was to achieve agreement "not on the basis of common speculative ideas, but on common practical ideas, not on the affirmation of one and the same conceptions of the world, or man, and of knowledge, but upon the affirmation of a single body of beliefs for guidance in action." In other words, they settled on nonfoundationalist pragmatism, as if straight out of William James—or, for that matter, Richard Rorty. Mary Ann Glendon summarizes: "If there are some things so terrible in practice that virtually no one will publically approve them, and some things so good in practice that virtually no one will oppose them, a common project can move forward without agreement on the reasons for those positions."[42]

Sumner Twiss has similarly argued that the framers avoided

> building into the declaration metaphysical conceptions and epistemological appeals, beyond those that could be commonly agreed upon, that might inhibit its acceptability to the peoples of the world. Thus, no

theological foundations, no invocations of natural law or any other contestable moral theory, no theories about the origins of society, no commitment to a singularly appropriate political system (other than a vague notion of democracy), no specification of the precise mechanisms and policies for implementing human rights norms, and no prioritization of one class of human rights as regnant over the other were included. What the framers did agree upon was this: there are certain social and material conditions which are absolutely requisite for human existence and flourishing in the world. . . . The framers thought these ought to be socially guaranteed by otherwise diverse social and political systems.[43]

In fact, it is striking how much pragmatist pluralism permeated the debates of the drafting committee chaired by Eleanor Roosevelt, especially through the contributions of the Chinese representative and elected co-chair, P. C. Chang. Chang had earned a doctorate at Columbia University under the direction of John Dewey in 1924 and pursued a career as an educational reformer and diplomat in China under the Kuomintang. In 1930, he also directed a Chinese classical theater tour of the United States, and in 1931 taught philosophy and Chinese art at the University of Chicago.[44] I do not mean to suggest that the framers were pragmatists, only that what they ended up with and the process by which they ended up with it demonstrate pragmatist hypotheses. Dewey's philosophy appealed not only to Chang but to many Chinese intellectuals of his generation because of what they perceived as its similarities to aspects of Confucianism.[45] Chang's introduction of Confucian concepts into the ultimate draft of the UDHR has been explored recently in nearly exhaustive detail, and it is clear that on many counts these concepts were also compatible with pragmatism, especially on the relationship between the individual and community. Lydia H. Liu has recently shown how "He was one of those Chinese intellectuals who sought to *reinvent* Confucianism (and Buddhism) by refashioning universals in conversation with modern European, American, Indian, and other great philosophical traditions of the world."[46] A conversation was happening across continents about how to think in terms of "one world," and it was happening at the level of a serious experiment, involving great minds and more nations than ever before, to create a species-wide institution protecting persons in their communal and individual particularity.

Eleanor Roosevelt recalled the intense debates between Chang and the Lebanese delegate on the drafting committee, a Thomist (follower of Thomas Aquinas, newly important in Christian circles) who wanted some statement that human rights are "natural" rights, grounded in human nature as such:

> Dr. Chang was a pluralist and held forth in charming fashion on the proposition that there is more than one kind of ultimate reality. The Declaration, he said, should reflect more than simply Western ideas and Dr. Humphrey would have to be eclectic in his approach. His remark, though addressed to Dr. Humphrey, was really directed at Dr. Malik, from whom it drew a prompt retort as he expounded at some length the philosophy of Thomas Aquinas. Dr. Humphrey joined enthusiastically in the discussion, and I remember that at one point Dr. Chang suggested that the Secretariat might well spend a few months studying the fundamentals of Confucianism![47]

As Mary Ann Glendon has pointed out, in the most comprehensive study of the drafting of the UDHR, "Malik believed the Declaration should be anchored more explicitly in 'nature,' Chang thought it better to leave it up to each culture to supply its own account of the philosophical underpinnings of human rights."[48] Chang's views, while originating in Confucianism, are entirely in keeping with Dewey's arguments against grounding rights in nature, which he argued is always a cover for political interests. Contrary to Rousseau, human rights are not "natural."

In recent years the UDHR has been routinely critiqued as an instrument of Western imperialism, based on a concept of the autonomous individual of classical liberalism. To give just one recent example, published in *American Quarterly*, Rosa-Linda Fregoso demands a decolonial "pluriversal" notion of human rights (unknowingly echoing William James's "Pluralistic Universe"):

> thinking beyond the conventional definition of human rights, premised on a Western cosmology that foregrounds the human as an autonomous individual/agent unyoked by the surrounding world; it involves thinking beyond a circular conception of rights as the individual possession of the human inhering in his very being.[49]

The framers of the declaration were not so naïve, and in fact there was already a solid critique of the position set up as a straw man here. The discussions around the issue of human rights in the late 1940s were every bit as sophisticated and pluralistic as the debates today.

The final draft of the UDHR, thanks chiefly to P. D. Chang and Eleanor Roosevelt, in fact bore no mention of natural rights, did not assume the classical liberal subject in its definition of the human, and understood each individual as formed in relation to others and with responsibilities to their community—a key Confucian concept incorporated in article 29: "Everyone has duties to the community in which alone the free and full development of his personality is possible." This phrasing is unfamiliar to those who think of rights as belonging to autonomous individuals or who think of "rights" in purely individual terms. The implications of one's responsibilities to "the community in which alone the free and full development of his personality is possible" amounts to a positive defense of the rights of "communities" against the imposition of a notion of the abstract liberal subject of English and French philosophy. This point is also supported by article 15, which asserts: "(1) Everyone has the right to a nationality. (2) No one shall be arbitrarily deprived of his nationality nor denied the right to change his nationality."

Citing Chang's influence, Sumner Twiss has rightly defended the UDHR from charges that it cemented a Western conception of the autonomous individual at the center of human-rights discourse:

So far as I can ascertain, the philosophical framework of the UDHR is very spare, proffering a pragmatic recognition of basic behavioral norms and human needs that is intended to be compatible with diverse cultural, philosophical, and religious traditions. Although spare, the UDHR does appear to forward as a self-conscious action taken in concert a conceptualization of person within community wholly at odds with the radically autonomous and self-interested individual. . . . Accordingly, I propose reading the UDHR as an instrument that advances a relational conception of the person that the framers were able to pragmatically agree upon.[50]

Twiss attributes these aspects of the UDHR to Chang's interventions primarily but at the same time notes their broad acceptance by the others involved in the drafting and unanimous adoption of the declaration, premised on

an understanding of human beings as both relationally free and basically social, destined to live for one another if they are to be truly human, rather than being radically autonomous and acting exclusively out of self-interest. . . . This is not just Chang's own idiosyncratic view of the UDHR, for the historical records show clearly that the majority (if not all) of the framers shared Chang's interpretation of the UDHR's underpinnings with respect to person and community.[51]

Lydia H. Liu, while confirming this view and dismissing critiques of the declaration as a "western" creation, also emphasizes Chang's successful rebuff to "civilizationist" discourse in the early stages of drafting.

This brings to a head a curious paradox, however, because the UDHR, according to common wisdom, was criticized by American anthropologists on the very bases that have been asserted in much recent critique of the document: that its concept of the "individual" was Western and not universal and that there is no universal standard for judging cultures and their conceptions of rights. This critique came from the executive council of the American Anthropological Association, authored by Melville

Herskovits, who had come of age in the midst of the Harlem Renaissance, published an essay in the famous anthology *The New Negro*, and for whom Zora Neale Hurston had worked as an assistant. However, it came before the UDHR was drafted in its final form; in fact, it could not have been written to counter the UDHR itself, because Melville Herskovits mailed it to Eleanor Roosevelt in June 1947, before John Peters Humphrey wrote the final version of the UN document.

The issues surrounding the Universal Declaration of Human Rights have gathered around two terms: *universalism* and *cultural relativism*. The opposition holds no more water than that between *individual* and *community*. And it has been considered leaky ever since the initial debates about the UDHR. Yet most critics of the UDHR have ignored the relationship between pragmatist philosophy, Confucianism, and the American anthropologists' concerns. Sent to Eleanor Roosevelt in June 1947 and published in *American Anthropologist* in late 1947 as a statement by the executive board of the American Anthropological Association, this document began from the assertion that each human being is born and raised within a culture. While all human beings share basic needs, those needs are met by an enormously diverse set of culturally shaped practices, and there is no "outside" or objective position from which to judge those practices—thus the "relativism" of the anthropologists' argument.

However, far from dismissing the possibility of coming up with a basic framework of human rights, Herskovits asserted his support for such a project, only insisting that Western values of individualism as postulated in service to capitalism under the false aegis of "natural rights" could not be the sole standard. (In this he was following Dewey's arguments, most recently in *Freedom and Culture* [1939], that appeals in Western philosophy to human "nature" as a basis for individual rights were historically specific to the European Enlightenment and thus ideological.) Chang's and the anthropologists' views were not far apart.[52]

Herskovits's opening postulate could come directly from John Dewey's essay for *Commentary*, "The Crisis of Human History: The Danger of a Retreat to Individualism," which I have discussed with reference to the relationship between universality, cultural particularism, and

individualism in literature by Jewish Americans in the 1940s.[53] To recap
part of Dewey's argument, remember that he had argued that no human
being is an abstract individual, a fallacy initiated in Western philosophy
by dividing "essential" spirit from "inessential" matter, mind and body,
contemplative and practical thought, the "consummatory" and the "useful." We are all, as Dewey countered, what we are in relation to others
and as embodied beings. Much of Dewey's thinking, going back to his
early books on education, was concerned with critiquing the mind/body
split and that between individuality and community. Behind Dewey's
thinking is Walt Whitman's insistence, as the premise of a "democratic"
culture respecting all human beings, on overturning the Western tradition's subordination of body to soul. The material, the social, and the
individual cannot be segregated from one another when taking into account the whole human being. In tune with Dewey's thought as it appeared in *Commentary* in 1945, a work like Isaac Rosenfeld's *Passage from
Home* (1946) or Jo Sinclair's *Wasteland* anticipates the very dilemmas facing the framers of a "universal" declaration—how to respect cultural
particularity, individuality, and the desire for human "universality" simultaneously. (Incidentally, Herskovits was Saul Bellow's college mentor
at Northwestern University; he was working on his now-classic book, *The
Myth of a Negro Past* at that time.)[54] Respect for the individual personality
and his or her right to fullest development as a member of a society—the
chief concern of the Commission on Human Rights—must include "respect for cultures of differing human groups," according to the anthropologists.[55] Respect for cultures and respect for individuals, to Herskovits, were two sides of the same human-rights coin:

> It is a truism that groups are composed of individuals, and human be-
> ings do not function outside the societies of which they form a part. The
> problem is thus to formulate a statement of human rights that will do
> more than just phrase respect for the individual as an individual. It must
> also take into full account the individual as a member of the social
> group of which he is a part, whose sanctioned modes of life shape his
> behavior, and with whose fate his own is thus inextricably bound.[56]

Given the cultural diversity of the human world, how could a universal declaration cover all human beings and not be couched in terms of the values of particular societies, specifically the United States and its Western allies? To quote from the statement again, "If the essence of the Declaration is to be, as it must, a statement in which the right of the individual to develop his personality to the fullest is to be stressed, then this must be based on a recognition of the fact that the personality of the individual can develop only in terms of the culture of his society."[57] Since people brought up in a society are trained to believe their ways are the best for them, they will tend (even when they adopt new customs) to look askance on others but are mostly willing to live and let live as long as their subsistence is secure.

However, economic expansion and evangelical religious traditions of the West have led to imperialist domination supported by "philosophical systems that have stressed absolutes in the realm of values and ends. Definitions of freedom, concepts of the nature of human rights, and the like, have thus been narrowly drawn."[58] The anthropologists expressed a pragmatist line of thinking that swerved from metaphysics, monistic views of historical causation, and foundational "absolutes" typical of the main lines of European philosophy.

Then comes an oft-neglected turn in the argument. Herskovits notes that alternative definitions and philosophies of human rights have been condemned and suppressed by imperialists to such an extent that "The hard core of *similarities* between cultures has consistently been overlooked."[59] Here, he implied, is where an experimental approach to universalism might begin.

The anthropologists' position was not, as it has been perpetually characterized, "relativist." If no "objective" view existed to adjudicate between different cultures' values and conceptions of rights, it was also true that no outside judge could say that they were all morally equal. And cultures change. They were patterned, yes, but they were not fixed or organic wholes. Within cultures one finds much debate about moral norms, often affected by outside pressures and inspirations. Cultures are always in process, changing in relationship to each other and to the natural environment. One of the Boasians' original interests was cultural diffusion—how elements of one culture spread through others. Thus cultures developed in relationship to one another. While the American anthropologists resisted judging other cultures by the values of their own, they were, for example, anti-imperialist—clearly not a value-neutral position.

> Doctrines of the "white man's burden" have been employed to implement economic exploitation and to deny the right to control their own affairs to millions of peoples over the world, where the expansion of Europe and America has not meant the literal extermination of whole populations. Rationalized in terms of ascribing cultural inferiority to these peoples, or in conceptions of their backwardness in development of their "primitive mentality," that justified their being held in the tutelage of their superiors, the history of the expansion of the western world has been marked by demoralization of human personality and the disintegration of human rights among the peoples over whom hegemony has been established.[60]

This is not a "relativist" argument. It is instead a humanist argument of a pluralistic sort placing primary value on protecting against the "demoralization of human personality," whether by imperialist imposition from without or similar forms of domination within particular cultures or nations.

Ultimately, the statement cannot avoid the *theoretically* irresolvable dilemma of respecting cultures while establishing a universal declaration: If there is no ground on which to base a judgment of when human rights are being violated except the values of one's own culture, yet one must avoid imposing one's values on others, the project can only collapse— unless commonalities can be found as a starting point of discussion and begin a pragmatic process in which diverse peoples participate in essentially inventing human rights as they go along because they must learn to come to some agreements for mutual self-preservation. We can see how the horrors of World War II and fears of ecological catastrophe brought urgency to the problem. The anthropologists' statement ends up affirming the aspiration for a universal declaration, which is hardly a "relativist" position:

> World-wide standards of freedom and justice, based on the principle that man is free only when he lives as his society defines freedom, that his rights are those he recognizes as a member of his society, must be basic. Conversely, an effective world-order cannot be devised except insofar as it permits the free play of personality of the members of its constituent social units, and draws strength from the enrichment to be derived from the interplay of varying personalities.[61]

It is a vague and idealistic statement because no *theory* can bridge the horns of the fundamental dilemma. Rather, processes of intercultural and international communication and cooperation in order to avoid war and environmental devastation might gradually weave peoples together in new and more "free" ways that will in turn lead to the diffusion across cultures of newly shared values and practices, including the protection of "human rights."[62] This is very close to what the committee drafting the UDHR finally settled upon in the version officially adopted on December 10, 1948, almost a year after the anthropologists' "Statement on Human Rights" was published and a year and a half after it was signed and sent to Eleanor Roosevelt. Whether it had any impact on the UN committee is unclear; what is clear is that the "Statement" and the "Declaration" had more in common than is usually supposed.

American slavery, so fundamental to American *culture*, comes to seem even to most white Americans wrong; anti-Semitism likewise, and in time antiblack racism. Human sacrifice in religious worship goes by the boards around the world. Some cultures abandon polygamy. Infanticide is given up in cultures where it was practiced for untold generations, girls start being allowed to go to school, female genital mutilation comes under opprobrium in parts of the world where it had long been practiced, capital punishment comes under attack, and so on.

How might these newly shared values and practices of mutual recognition develop and spread? Surely military and economic force had, over the centuries, been a main spur to cultural assimilation. But they seemed to have reached a limit, driving human life, like the corporate-owned, harpoon-barbed, planet-circling *Pequod* of Melville's imagining, to irreversible destruction. The argument was that now those forces must be subordinated to culture and noncoercive expression as the main engines of planetary human cohesion. Here what Herskovits termed the "aesthetic drive" in human beings as social creatures would have its role. Imaginative literature and other forms of creative expression, conceived on increasingly egalitarian terms within and between groups, must have their day.

The debate over individuality and cultural identity in human-rights discourse, and the route between aesthetics and ethics, had a parallel in the fledgling field of ecology at the same time. Comparing the approaches of Aldo Leopold and Ed Ricketts, Michael J. Lannoo has written, "While most biologists, including Leopold, tended (and still tend) to view ecology as individuals having relationships, Ricketts viewed ecology as relationships having individuals. That is, for Ricketts, the relationships were often primary; who or what was having them was secondary."[63] Like individuals in "cultures," organisms developed within biotic communities—thus biotic communities "have" organisms, and vice versa. Whether one put organism or community first was a matter of emphasis, not an either/or decision. Moreover, both men came up against the limits of science. Ricketts verged into an interest in archetypes of the imagination deriving from basic drives of the human animal and artistic expression as biological, affecting "science" itself; Leopold into questions about what might help bring ecological stability, which led to an emphasis on aesthetics—reviving an aesthetic interest in land and in biological diversity and relationships. Aesthetics would provide the practical route to the shared "land ethic" he envisioned.

The insights of the ecologists and the framers of the UDHR were soon swept away by rising neoimperial competition and national identity politics. While the Cold War can be said to have begun in the waning months of World War II, in 1949 it became frigid. The USSR successfully tested an atom bomb in August of that year—ending any remaining hope that a world government might be created. The nation-state triumphed, and the world would go back to balance-of-power politics. Samuel Moyn has argued that "the 1940s were much closer to the telos of the era of globalized nationalism than to that of the era of international human rights. . . . What needs to be explained is not just the exciting contingency of the era but also how overdetermined it was that nationalist solidarity would soon succeed so comprehensively."[64] Winston Churchill gave his "Iron Curtain" speech; the Communist Party of China won the final stage of the Chinese Civil War and established the People's Republic on October 1. The Korean War began in June 1950 and, in Norman Mailer's words,

> set us off on another of our clammy national hysterias. Anybody who worked and wrote for newspapers, magazines, television, movies, and advertising was discovering (if he were still innocent) that the natural work of his pen was to hasten our return to chastity, regularity, pomposity and the worship of the lifeless, the senseless, and the safe.[65]

The world-government movement died in the late 1940s, and the Universal Declaration of Human Rights never developed into a covenant with legal force; stateless persons would be left without protection. Ecological thinking did not get far, either, in the atmosphere of the Cold War. Both Edward F. Ricketts and Aldo Leopold died within weeks of each other in 1948, and their work had little impact until they were "rediscovered" in the 1960s and 1970s, when the Cold War culture was being assailed on college campuses and on the streets of cities. Rachel Carson's *Silent Spring* sparked, at the same time, a surge of ecological activism that has not yet let up, and it no doubt gave impetus to an iconic publication, *The Whole Earth Catalogue* (1968), featuring on its cover the first photograph of the globe from outer space. A powerful diversification and resurgence of American literature came, as well. This was not a return of the culture of the 1940s—its identity politics, for one, was vastly different—but the reverberations of that worldwide turning point can be found all through it, and beyond.

NOTES

....

INTRODUCTION

1. Warren French, "General Introduction: Remembering the Forties," in *The Forties: Fiction, Poetry, Drama*, ed. Warren French (Deland, Fla.: Everett/Edwards, 1969), 1.
2. Some excellent studies include Mark Greif, *The Age of the Crisis of Man: Thought and Fiction in America, 1933–1973* (Princeton, N.J.: Princeton University Press, 2015), although that book deals with the intellectual history of the 1940s and only treats American fiction of the fifties and after; Gordon Hutner, *What America Read: Taste, Class, and the Novel, 1920–1960* (Chapel Hill: University of North Carolina Press, 2009); Werner Sollors, *Ethnic Modernism* (Cambridge, Mass.: Harvard University Press, 2002); Paula Rabinowitz, *American Pulp: How Paperbacks Brought Modernism to Main Street* (Princeton, N.J.: Princeton University Press, 2014); and Lawrence P. Jackson, *The Indignant Generation: A Narrative History of African American Writers and Critics, 1934–1960* (Princeton, N.J.: Princeton University Press, 2013).
3. Mark Goble, review of *The Age of the Crisis of Man: Thought and Fiction in America, 1933–1973*, by Mark Greif, *Los Angeles Review of Books*, September 4, 2015, https://lareviewofbooks.org/article/good-literary-criticism-on-the-crisis-of-man/.
4. Roland Greene, "Presidential Address 2016: Literature and Its Publics: Past, Present, and Future," *PMLA* 131, no. 3 (May 2016): 597.
5. Greene, "Presidential Address," 597.
6. Greene, "Presidential Address," 599.
7. Allan Nevins, "Between Wars," in *Literary History of the United States*, vol. 2, ed. Robert E. Spiller, Willard Thorp, Thomas H. Johnson, and Henry Seidel Canby (New York: Macmillan, 1948), 1261.
8. Nevins, "Between Wars," 1262.

1. WHEN LITERATURE MATTERED

1. Gore Vidal, *Palimpsest: A Memoir* (New York: Random House, 1995), 115, 133, 169.

2. See Gordon Hutner, *What America Read: Taste, Class, and the Novel* (Chapel Hill: University of North Carolina Press, 2011), 205.

3. Office of War Information poster, 1942, qtd. in Nikola Von Merveldt, "Books Cannot Be Killed by Fire: The German Freedom Library and the American Library of Nazi-Banned Books as Agents of Cultural Memory," *Library Trends* 55, no. 3 (Winter 2007): 523, 524.

4. Muriel Rukeyser, *The Life of Poetry* (New York: A. A. Wyn, 1949), 62.

5. Kathy Lee Peiss, "Cultural Policy in a Time of War: The American Response to Endangered Books in World War II," *Library Trends* 55, no. 3 (Winter 2007): 370.

6. Muriel Rukeyser, *Beast in View* (New York: Doubleday Doran, 1944), dust jacket.

7. Jo Sinclair, *The Seasons: Death and Transfiguration* (New York: Feminist Press, 1993), 139.

8. Alfred Kazin, *New York Jew* (1978; Syracuse, N.Y.: Syracuse University Press, 1996), 4–5.

9. Karl Shapiro, "Public Library," in *V-Letter and Other Poems* (New York: Reynal & Hitchcock, 1944), 26.

10. Claude Lévi-Strauss, "New York in 1941," in *A View from Afar* (New York: Basic Books, 1985), 266–267.

11. Quoted in James L. W. West III, "The Expansion of the National Book Trade System," in *A History of the Book in America*, vol. 4, *Print In Motion: The Expansion of Publishing and Reading in the United States, 1880–1940*, ed. Carl F. Kaestle and Janice A. Radway, (Chapel Hill: University of North Carolina Press, 2009), 81.

12. Gertrude Stein, *Wars I Have Seen* (New York: Random House, 1945), 257, 256.

13. John W. Tebbel, *A History of Book Publishing in the United States* (New York: R. R. Bowker, 1981), 4:43.

14. Jay Satterfield, *The World's Best Books: Taste, Culture, and the Modern Library* (Amherst: University of Massachusetts Press, 2002), 9.

15. Bennett Cerf to Donald Klopfer, February 23, 1945, in Bennett Cerf and Donald Klopfer, *Dear Donald, Dear Bennett: The Wartime Correspondence of Bennett Cerf and Donald Klopfer* (New York: Random House, 2002), 203.

16. Cerf to Klopfer, April 27, 1945, in Cerf and Klopfer, *Dear Donald, Dear Bennett*, 209.

17. Ellen Gruber Garvey, "Ambivalent Advertising: Books, Prestige, and the Circulation of Publicity," in *A History of the Book in America*, 4:181.

18. James T. Farrell, *The Fate of Writing in America* (New York: New Directions, 1946), n.p.

19. Farrell, *The Fate of Writing in America*, n.p.

20. John W. Tebbel, *Between Covers: The Rise and Transformation of American Book Publishing* (Oxford University Press, 1987), 348–349.

21. Tebbel, *A History of Book Publishing in the United States*, 4:24.

22. John Jamieson, *Books for the Army: The Army Library Service in the Second World War* (New York: Columbia University Press, 1950), 156.

23. Jamieson, *Books for the Army*, 154–155.

24. Tebbel, *A History of Book Publishing in the United States*, 4:32.

25. A. J. Liebling, "Cross-Channel Trip," in *Reporting World War II, Part Two: American Journalism, 1944–1946* (New York: Library of America, 1995), 111, 112; originally published in *The New Yorker*, July 1, July 8, and July 15, 1944.

26. Qtd. in Jamieson, *Books for the Army*, 159.

27. Qtd. in Jamieson, *Books for the Army*, 159. Most of my information on the Armed Services Editions comes from Jamieson's history (142–160) and from John Y. Cole, *Books in Action: The Armed Services Editions* (Washington, D.C.: Library of Congress, 1984). The latter includes a complete list of the books published. More recently, Molly Guptill Manning has published *When Books Went to War: The Stories That Helped Us Win World War II* (Boston: Houghton Mifflin, 2014), a lively successor to the earlier studies.

28. Qtd. in Jamieson, *Books for the Army*, 160.

29. Qtd. in Cole, preface to *Books in Action*, viii.

30. Cole, "Armed Services Editions: An Introduction," in *Books in Action*, 10.

31. Irving Howe, *A Margin of Hope: An Intellectual Autobiography* (New York: Harcourt Brace Jovanovich, 1982), 98, 95.

32. Cole, "Armed Services Editions: An Introduction," in *Books in Action*, 18–19.

33. Matthew J. Bruccoli, "Recollections of an ASE Collector," in Cole, *Books in Action*, 26.

34. Bruccoli, "Recollections of an ASE Collector," 26.

35. Cerf to Klopfer, March 21, 1944, in Cerf and Klopfer, *Dear Donald, Dear Bennett*, 145.

36. Cass Canfield, *Up and Down and Around: A Publisher Recollects the Time of His Life* (New York: Harper & Row, 1971), 141.

37. See West, "Expansion," 84–85; Tebbel, *A History of Book Publishing in the United States*, 4:353.

38. Paula Rabinowitz, *American Pulp: How Paperbacks Brought Modernism to Main Street* (Princeton, N.J.: Princeton University Press, 2014), 42.

39. Gordon Graham, "Kurt Enoch: Paperback Pioneer," in *Immigrant Publishers: The Impact of Expatriate Publishers in Britain and America in the Twentieth Century*, ed. Richard Abel and Gordon Graham (New Brunswick, N.J.: Transaction, 2009), 41–46.

40. Graham, "Kurt Enoch," 46–47.

41. Weybright, qtd. in Thomas L. Bonn, *Heavy Traffic and High Culture: New American Library as Literary Gatekeeper in the Paperback Revolution* (Carbondale: Southern Illinois University Press, 1989), 14.

42. "About This Book," in William Faulkner, *Sanctuary* (New York: New American Library, 1947), n.p.

43. "A Note on Signet Giants," in Richard Wright, *Native Son*, 1st printing (New York: New American Library, 1950), n.p. (third-from-last page of book).

44. Weybright to Samuel Rapport, February 9, 1950, quoted in Bonn, *Heavy Traffic and High Culture*, 17.

45. Bonn, *Heavy Traffic and High Culture*, 18.

46. Qtd. in Ben Stoltzfus, *Hemingway and French Writers* (Kent, Ohio: Kent State University Press, 2009), xx, from Jean Paul Sartre, "American Novelists in French Eyes," *Atlantic Monthly* 178 (1946): 117.

47. See Renate Peters, "From Illusion to Disillusion: Sartre's Views of America," *Canadian Review of American Studies* 21, no. 2 (1990): 173–182; Richard Lehan, *A Dangerous Crossing: French Literary Existentialism and the Modern American Novel* (Carbondale: Southern Illinois University Press, 1973); Jean Paul Sartre, *Situations I* (Paris: Gallimard, 1947), 99–121, 7–25, 70–81; Harry R. Garvin, "Camus and the American Novel," *Comparative Literature* 3, no. 3 (1956): 194–204; Owen J. Miller, "Camus et Hemingway," *La revue des lettres modernes* 3 (1971): 9–42; Philippe Codde, *The Jewish American Novel* (West Lafayette, Ind.: Purdue University Press, 2007), 76–79.

48. Yang Jincai, "The Critical Reception of Herman Melville in China," *Leviathan: A Journal of Melville Studies* 14, no. 2 (June 2012): 54–66.

49. Alfred Kazin, *Writing Was Everything* (Cambridge, Mass.: Harvard University Press), 83–84.

50. Tebbel, *A History of Book Publishing in the United States*, 4:43.

51. On Pantheon, I am indebted particularly to Dan Simon and Tom McCarthy, "Editorial Vision and the Role of the Independent Publisher," in *A History of the Book in America*, David D. Hall, gen. ed., vol. 5: *The Enduring Book: Print Culture in Postwar America*, ed. David Paul Nord, Joan Shelley Rubin, and Michael Schudson (Chapel Hill: University of North Carolina Press, 2009), 212–213; and Hendrik Edelman, "Kurt Wolff and Jacques Schiffrin: Two Publishing Giants Start Over in America," in Abel and Graham, eds., *Immigrant Publishers*, 185–192.

52. Hendrik Edelman, "Other Immigrant Publishers of Note in America," in Abel and Graham, eds., *Immigrant Publishers*, 201–203.

53. Qtd. in Catherine Turner, *Marketing Modernism Between the Two World Wars* (Amherst: University of Massachusetts Press, 2003), 81.

54. James Laughlin, "A Few Random Notes from the Editor," in *New Directions 10* (New York: New Directions, 1948), 17.

55. Farrell, *The Fate of Writing in America*, n.p.

56. Norman Foerster, "The Study of Letters," in Norman Foerster et al., *Literary Scholarship: Its Aims and Methods* (Chapel Hill: University of North Carolina Press, 1941), 20.

57. Foerster, "The Study of Letters," 20.

58. Foerster, "The Study of Letters," 31.

59. Foerster, "The Study of Letters," 31.

60. Foerster, "The Study of Letters," 32.

61. Arthur Mizener, "Scholars as Critics," *Kenyon Review* 2 (Fall 1940): 422.

62. John Crowe Ransom, "Mr. Tate and the Professors," *Kenyon Review* 2, no. 3 (Summer 1940): 348–350.

63. Lionel Trilling, "Literary and Aesthetic," in Alexander Reid Martin, Lionel Trilling, and Eliseo Vivas, "The Legacy of Sigmund Freud: An Appraisal: Therapeutic, Literary and Aesthetic, Philosophical," *Kenyon Review* 2, no. 2 (Spring 1940): 165–166.

64. Richard M. Cook, ed., *Alfred Kazin's Journals* (New Haven, Conn.: Yale University Press, 2011), 47.

65. Mark McGurl, *The Program Era: Postwar Fiction and the Rise of Creative Writing* (Cambridge, Mass.: Harvard University Press, 2009), ix.

66. John W. Aldridge, *After the Lost Generation: A Critical Study of the Writers of Two Wars* (New York: McGraw-Hill, 1951), 244–245.

67. Howe, *A Margin of Hope*, 170–171.

2. POPULAR CULTURE AND THE AVANT-GARDE

1. Le Corbusier, *When the Cathedrals Were White: A Journey to the Country of Timid People*, trans. Francis E. Hyslop Jr. (New York: Reynal and Hitchcock, 1947), 42, 43. The original French edition is dated 1937.

2. William E. Cain, "Literary Criticism," in *The Cambridge History of American Literature*, vol. 5: *Poetry and Criticism, 1900–1950*, ed. Sacvan Bercovitch (Cambridge: Cambridge University Press, 2003), 396.

3. Daniel Aaron, "Parrington Plus," *Kenyon Review* 4, no. 1 (Winter 1942): 104.

4. Aaron, "Parrington Plus," 105.

5. Gertrude Stein, *Wars I Have Seen* (New York: Random House, 1945), 258.

6. Max Horkheimer and Theodor W. Adorno, "The Culture Industry: Enlightenment as Mass Deception," in *Dialectic of Enlightenment: Philosophical Fragments*, ed. Gunzelin Schmid Noerr, trans. Edmund Jephcott (1947; Stanford, Calif.: Stanford University Press, 2002), 94–136.

7. Langston Hughes, "Bop," in *The Best of Simple* (1961; New York: Hill & Wang, 1998), 118.

8. Ilya Bolotowsky, "An Abstract Mural for the Chronic Disease Hospital, Welfare Island," artist's proposal, in "Revealed: WPA Murals from Roosevelt Island" exhibition, Herbert F. Johnson Museum of Art, Cornell University, Spring 2016.

9. Paula Rabinowitz, *American Pulp: How Paperbacks Brought Modernism to Main Street* (Princeton, N.J.: Princeton University Press, 2014). See also David M. Earle's treatment of "pulp modernism" going back to the 1920s, *Re-Covering Modernism: Pulps, Paperbacks, and the Prejudice of Form* (Surrey: Ashgate, 2009). Earle argues that although pulps and "modernism" were and are often defined in polar terms, a fertile exchange between the two began early in the twentieth century.

10. Frederic Jameson, *A Singular Modernity* (London: Verso, 2012), 161–210.

11. Jameson, *A Singular Modernity*, 208–209.

12. Jameson, *A Singular Modernity*, 209.

13. Jameson, *A Singular Modernity*, 210.

14. Kenneth Rexroth, introduction to *The New British Poets*, ed. Kenneth Rexroth (New York: New Directions, 1949), xii.

15. Marianne Moore, *The Complete Prose of Marianne Moore*, ed. Patricia C. Willis (New York: Viking, 1986), 588. "Prompted in large part by the rise of totalitarianism and anti-Semitism," Rachel Buxton points out, "she moved away from an experimental modernist poetry and began to publish collections that were both more accessible to the reader and explicitly ethical in their outlook." Rachel M. Buxton, "Marianne Moore and the Poetics of Pragmatism," *Review of English Studies* 58, no. 236 (September 2007): 549–550.

16. William H. Pritchard, *Randall Jarrell: A Literary Life* (New York: Farrar, Straus & Giroux, 1990), 94.

17. Qtd. in Pritchard, *Randall Jarrell*, 127.

18. Stevens, qtd. in Alan Filreis, "Stevens' Home Front," *Wallace Stevens Journal* 14, no. 2 (Fall 1990): 109. See also Jacqueline Vaught Brogan, "Stevens in History and Not in History: The Poet and the Second World War," *Wallace Stevens Journal* 13, no. 2 (Fall 1989): 168–190.

19. Wallace Stevens, "Of Modern Poetry," lines 7–11, in *The Collected Poems of Wallace Stevens* (New York: Vintage/Random House, 1990), 240.

20. Filreis, "Stevens' Home Front," 106.

21. Martha Gellhorn, *A Stricken Field* (1940; London: Penguin/Virago, 1986), 313.

22. Alfred Kazin, *Writing Was Everything* (Cambridge, Mass.: Harvard University Press, 1995), 81–82.

23. Claude Lévi-Strauss, "New York in 1941," in *The View from Afar* (New York: Basic Books, 1984), 266, 261.

24. Lévi-Strauss, "New York in 1941," 267.

25. For a lively history of the people who created the superhero comics, see especially Gerard Jones, *Men of Tomorrow: Geeks, Gangsters, and the Birth of the Comic Book* (New York: Basic Books, 2004).

26. Gerald Gross, *Publishers on Publishing* (New York: R. R. Bowker, 1961), 333–334. Carlos Baker, *Ernest Hemingway: A Life Story* (New York: Bantam, 1970), 449. Friede started out working for Knopf, then moved to Boni & Liveright in the mid-1920s; in the summer of 1925 Liveright (struggling to pay off debts) sold him a one-half interest in the company and named him vice president at the age of twenty-four. That firm foundered, however, and in 1929 he joined Pascal Covici to found Covici-Friede, which specialized in limited editions. By 1940, that firm had also folded, and Friede had switched careers.

27. An excellent book on advertising and modernist publishers of the 1920s and 1930s is Catherine Turner, *Marketing Modernism Between the Two World Wars* (Amherst: University of Massachusetts Press, 2003). Several other books in the past twenty years have treated the promotion and marketing of modernism, including Kevin J. H. Dettmar and Stephen Watt, eds., *Marketing Modernisms: Self-Promotion, Canonization, and Rereading* (Ann Arbor: University of Michigan Press, 1996); and Warren E. Chernaik, Warwick Gould, and Ian Willison, eds., *Modernist Writers and the Marketplace* (New York: Palgrave Macmillan, 1996).

28. See Turner, *Marketing Modernism Between the Two World Wars*, 173.

29. James T. Farrell, *The Fate of Writing in America* (New York: New Directions, 1946), n.p.

30. Bennett Cerf to Donald Klopfer, March 27, 1944, in Bennett Cerf and Donald Klopfer, *Dear Donald, Dear Bennett: The Wartime Correspondence of Bennett Cerf and Donald Klopfer* (New York: Random House, 2002), 205.

31. Richard Wright, "Gertrude Stein's Story Is Drenched in Hitler's Horrors," *PM*, March 11, 1945, 5; qtd. in Michel Fabre, *The Unfinished Quest of Richard Wright*, trans. Isabel Barzun, 2nd ed. (Urbana: University of Illinois Press, 1993), 285.

32. Gertrude Stein, *Wars I Have Seen*, 245.

33. Gertrude Stein, "Off We All Went to See Germany," *Life*, August 6, 1945.

34. Stein, *Wars I Have Seen*, 256–257.

35. Gertrude Stein, *Blood on the Dining Room Floor* (Pawlet, Vt.: Banyan, 1948).

36. Stein, *Wars I Have Seen*, 244.

37. Stein, *Wars I Have Seen*, 258, 259. Worth pointing out here is Stein's opinion in the 1930s that no such mastery of the American language had yet taken place; she could only see such a breakthrough coming: "the pressure being put upon the same words to make them move in an entirely different way is most exciting, it excites the words it excites those who use them." Gertrude Stein, "Lecture I," in *Narration* (1935; Chicago: University of Chicago Press, 2010), 7.

38. Stein, *Wars I Have Seen*, 247.

39. Lévi-Strauss, "New York in 1941," 267.

40. Marshall McLuhan, "American Advertising," in *Essential McLuhan*, ed. Eric McLuhan and Frank Zingrone (New York: Basic Books, 1995), 13–15, 20.

41. Farrell, *The Fate of Writing in America*, n.p.

42. That this was a coordinated effort is clear from the correspondence between Laughlin and Farrell in 1946, New Directions Publishing Corporation records, Ms Am 2077, item 552, Houghton Library, Harvard University.

43. James Laughlin, "A Few Random Notes from the Editor," *New Directions 10* (Norfolk, Conn.: New Directions, 1948), 20.

44. Laughlin, "A Few Random Notes," 17–18.

45. Printed invitation to participate in a contest to choose the name of a Series of Monthly Poetry Pamphlets, New Directions Publishing Corporation records, Catalogs, circulars, and printed ephemera, MS Am 2077.3, item 6, Houghton Library, Harvard University. The pamphlet series was to begin January 1, 1941. For related printed materials from the 1940s, see items 6–15.

46. Printed advertisement, in New Directions Publishing Corporation records, Catalogs, circulars, and printed ephemera, MS Am 2077.3, item 6, Houghton Library, Harvard University.

47. James Laughlin to Paul Bowles, July 28, 1949, New Directions Publishing Corporation records, MS Am 2077, item 230, Houghton Library, Harvard University.

48. Paul Bowles to James Laughlin, August 4, 1949, correspondence between Laughlin and Bowles in the New Directions Publishing Corporation records, MS Am 2077, item 230, Houghton Library, Harvard University.

49. Laughlin to Bowles, August 16, 1949. New Directions Publishing Corporation records, MS Am 2077, item 230, Houghton Library, Harvard University.

50. Evan Brier, although he may not have known of Laughlin's deliberately "corny" sales pitch, emphasizes how the success of *The Sheltering Sky* demonstrated the emerging potential of a niche market for "art novels" in the postwar period, a niche that Laughlin appealed to precisely by pretending to be unconcerned with sales and resolutely anticommercial. Brier cannily shows how emphasizing disinterest in sales was a marketing ploy in its own right, accruing symbolic capital that could then be converted into financial returns. The point is somewhat compromised by Laughlin's tactics as discussed in his correspondence with Bowles, in which he distinguishes between New Directions fans who will buy the novel anyway and less highbrow readers the press normally could not attract. Laughlin clearly thought he could titillate such readers and thus open a new market for his books. Evan Brier, "Constructing the Postwar Art Novel: Paul Bowles, James Laughlin, and the Making of *The Sheltering Sky*," *PMLA* 121, no. 1 (January 2006): 186–199. The article, in revised form, is now a chapter in his book *A Novel Marketplace: Mass Culture, the Book Trade, and Postwar American Fiction* (Philadelphia: University of Pennsylvania Press, 2010), 19–44.

51. Finding aid for Banyan Press archive, Getty Research Institute, Special Collections.

52. Anna Grimshaw and Keith Hart, "*American Civilization*: An Introduction," in C. L. R. James, *American Civilization*, ed. Anna Grimshaw and Keith Hart (Cambridge, Mass.: Blackwell, 1993), 14.

53. Grimshaw and Hart, "*American Civilization*: An Introduction," 14.
54. James, *American Civilization*, 76.
55. James, *American Civilization*, 87, 91.
56. James, *American Civilization*, 118, 119, 121.
57. James, *American Civilization*, 122.
58. James, *American Civilization*, 123.
59. John A. Kouwenhoven, *Made in America: The Arts in Modern Civilization* (Garden City, N.Y.: Doubleday, 1949), 15.
60. Kouwenhoven, *Made in America*, 118.
61. Le Corbusier, *When the Cathedrals Were White*, 145.
62. Kouwenhoven, *Made in America*, 257, 256, 264, 266.

3. LABOR, POLITICS, AND THE ARTS

1. Mary McCarthy, *Intellectual Memoirs: New York, 1936–1938* (New York: Harcourt, Brace, Jovanovich, 1992), 22. This situation infuses her arch novel of 1942, *The Company She Keeps*.
2. Robert Warshow, "The Legacy of the 30s" (1947), in *The Immediate Experience: Movies, Comics, Theatre, and Other Aspects of Popular Culture* (Cambridge, Mass.: Harvard University Press, 2001), 3.
3. A classic critique by a philosopher once deeply attracted to Marxism is Karl Popper's *The Poverty of Historicism* (1957), originally published in *Economica* 11, no. 42 (May 1944): 86–103; 11, no. 43 (August 1944): 119–137.
4. Daniel Aaron, *Writers on the Left: Episodes in American Literary Communism* (1961; New York: Avon, 1965), 325.
5. Warshow, "Legacy," 8.
6. Cf. James Smethurst, *The New Red Negro: The Literary Left and African American Poetry, 1930–1946* (New York: Oxford University Press, 1999), 45–46.
7. "Negro Author Criticizes Reds as Intolerant," *New York Herald Tribune*, July 28, 1944. Reprinted in *Conversations with Richard Wright*, ed. Keneth Kinnamon and Michel Fabre (Jackson: University Press of Mississippi, 1993), 51, 52.
8. Richard Wright, untitled essay, in *The God That Failed: A Confession*, ed. Richard H. Crossman (1949; New York: Columbia University Press, 2001), 137. This passage had been included in Wright's autobiography *American Hunger*, ready for publication in 1944 until the Book-of-the-Month Club offered to make it a main selection if he dropped the second part of the book.
9. Richard Wright, *Native Son*, restored text ed. (New York: Harper Perennial, 1998), 429.
10. Richard Wright, *Black Boy*, in *Later Works* (New York: Library of America, 1991), 324, 325.
11. Warshow, "Legacy," 17, 15.
12. Lionel Trilling, "Reality in America," in *The Liberal Imagination* (1950; New York: NYRB, 2008), 12. This lead essay of the book originally appeared in two parts in 1940 (*Partisan Review*) and 1946 (*The Nation*).

13. This would include some of those Michael Denning identifies with the Popular Front while defending them against charges of propagandistic and uncomplicated "social realism." Michael Denning, *The Cultural Front: The Laboring of American Culture in the Twentieth Century* (1997; London: Verso, 2010), 115–159.

14. Muriel Rukeyser, prefatory statement to *The Life of Poetry* (New York: A. A. Wyn, 1949), n.p. In "Projective Verse" (1950), Olson defined a poem as "energy transferred from where the poet got it (he will have some several causations), by way of the poem itself to, all the way over to, the reader."

15. Rukeyser, prefatory statement to *The Life of Poetry*, n.p.

16. Thomas M. Alexander, *John Dewey's Theory of Art, Experience, and Nature: The Horizons of Feeling* (Albany: SUNY Press, 1987), 186.

17. Carlos Bulosan, *America Is in the Heart: A Personal History* (1946; Seattle: University of Washington Press, 1973), 270.

18. Carlos Bulosan, "The Writer as Worker" (from a letter of January 17, 1955), in *On Becoming Filipino: Selected Writings of Carlos Bulosan*, ed. E. San Juan Jr. (Philadelphia: Temple University Press, 1995), 143–144.

19. Bulosan, *America Is in the Heart*, 57.

20. Wright, *Black Boy*, 316. This portion of *Black Boy*, which was not included in the first edition of *Black Boy* due to Book of the Month Club requirements, was first published in the essay "I Tried to Be a Communist," *Atlantic Monthly* 174, nos. 2–3 (August/September 1944). Wright believed that the Book of the Month Club's requirement to drop the second part of his autobiography derived from communists' objections, according to his journal. See Arnold Rampersad's "Note on the Texts," in *Black Boy*, 869.

21. No doubt Trotsky's tolerance for the independence of the artist had a strong bearing on the communist accusations against writers as "Trotskyists." Art, he believed, must "remain faithful to itself" to be an ally of revolution. Nonetheless, it was secondary and subordinate. Alexander Bloom, *Prodigal Sons: New York Intellectuals and Their World* (New York: Oxford University Press, 1986), 109–110.

22. Wright, *Black Boy*, 319.

23. Chester Himes, *Lonely Crusade* (1947; New York: Thunder's Mouth, 1986), 25.

24. Himes, *Lonely Crusade*, 254–255.

25. Himes, *Lonely Crusade*, 238.

26. Wright, *Black Boy*, 309, 312.

27. Robert Motherwell and Harold Rosenberg, "Editorial Preface," *possibilities* 1 (1947–1948): 1. Reprinted in *Reading Abstract Expressionism: Context and Critique*, ed. Ellen G. Landau (New Haven, Conn.: Yale University Press, 2005), 153–154.

28. Norman Lewis, "Thesis, 1946," in *Reading Abstract Expressionism*, 134.

29. Lewis, "Thesis, 1946," 134. Lewis's widow, Ouida Lewis, following a lecture I delivered for a retrospective of his work at the Hartford Atheneum in 1999, told me that he knew Barnes, having spent time at the Barnes Foundation at Barnes's invitation, and admired Barnes's theories and practical contributions to the arts.

30. See Ann Eden Gibson, "Black Is a Color: Norman Lewis and Modernism in New York," in *Norman Lewis: Black Paintings, 1946–1977* (New York: Studio Museum in Harlem, 1998), 15.

31. Norman Lewis, "Letter to James Yeargens" (c. 1947), in *Norman Lewis: From the Harlem Renaissance to Abstraction* (New York: Kenkeleba Gallery, 1989); qtd. in David Craven, "Norman Lewis as Political Activist and Post-Colonial Artist," in *Norman Lewis: Black Paintings*, 56.

32. Norman Lewis, recorded interview with Vivian Browne, Camille Billops, and James Hatch, August 23, 1973, Hatch-Billops Archive, New York; qtd. in Jorge Daniel Veneziano, "The Quality of Absence in the Black Paintings of Norman Lewis," in *Norman Lewis: Black Paintings*, 32.

33. Letter of Adolph Gottlieb and Mark Rothko, qtd. in Edward Alden Jewell, "The Realm of Art: A New Platform; 'Globalism' Pops Into View," *New York Times*, June 13, 1943; reprinted in *Reading Abstract Expressionism*, 149.

34. Rene Wellek, *A History of Modern Criticism, 1750–1950*, vol. 6: *American Criticism, 1900–1950* (New Haven, Conn.: Yale University Press, 1986), 156–157.

35. John Dewey, *Art as Experience* (1934), in *The Later Works: 1925–1953*, ed. Jo Ann Boydston (Carbondale: Southern Illinois University Press, 1981), 10:63.

36. Alan M. Wald, *The New York Intellectuals: The Rise and Decline of the Anti-Stalinist Left from the 1930s to the 1980s* (Chapel Hill: University of North Carolina Press, 1987), 228.

37. I discuss this in *The Harlem Renaissance in Black and White* (Cambridge, Mass.: Harvard University Press, 1996), 89.

38. Wald, *The New York Intellectuals*, 230.

39. Wald, *The New York Intellectuals*, 229.

40. Dewey, *Art as Experience*, 10:12, 12, 14–15, 63.

41. John Dewey, *Experience and Nature*, in *The Later Works*, 1:159.

42. Dewey, *Experience and Nature*, 1:290–291.

43. Mark Greif, *The Age of the Crisis of Man: Thought and Fiction in America, 1933–1973* (Princeton, N.J.: Princeton University Press, 2015), 44. See also Robert Westbrook, *John Dewey and American Democracy* (Ithaca, N.Y.: Cornell University Press, 1991), 537.

44. "Editorial Statement," *Partisan Review* 4, no. 1 (December 1937): 3.

45. "Editorial Notice," *The Masses* 4, no. 4 (January 1913): 2.

46. Paul Grimstad, *Experience and Experimental Writing: Literary Pragmatism from Emerson to the Jameses* (New York: Oxford University Press, 2015).

47. For a similar point and another assertion of Trilling's pragmatist orientation, see Daniel T. O'Hara, *Lionel Trilling: The Work of Liberation* (Madison: University of Wisconsin Press, 1988), 24. Cornel West similarly emphasizes Trilling's pragmatist orientation (alongside Sidney Hook's) in *The American Evasion of Philosophy: A Genealogy of Pragmatism* (Madison: University of Wisconsin Press, 1989), chap. 4. John Patrick Diggins discusses Trilling's relationship to Deweyan pragmatism in the closing pages of *The Promise of Pragmatism: Modernism and the Crisis of Knowledge and Authority* (Chicago: University of Chicago Press, 1994), 382–385.

48. Adam Kirsch, *Why Trilling Matters* (New Haven, Conn.: Yale University Press, 2011), 23–35.

49. Wellek, *A History of Modern Criticism*, 6:146.

50. See Robert H. Brinkmeyer, *The Fourth Ghost: White Southern Writers and European Fascism, 1930–1950* (Baton Rouge: Louisiana State University Press, 2009), 27–29. In the opening manifesto of *I'll Take My Stand*, John Crowe Ransom cried that "The

true Sovietists or Communists . . . are the Industrialists themselves. . . . We therefore look upon the Communist menace as a menace indeed, but not as a Red one, because it is simply according to the blind drift of our industrial development to expect in America at last much the same economic system as that imposed by violence upon Russia in 1917." Ransom, in Twelve Southerners, *I'll Take My Stand: The South and the Agrarian Tradition* (1930; Baton Rouge: Louisiana State University Press, 1977), ii–xlii.

51. Brinkmeyer, *The Fourth Ghost*, 28, 37, 40.

52. James Matthew Wilson, "The Fugitive and the Exile: Theodor W. Adorno, John Crowe Ransom, and the *Kenyon Review*," in *Rereading the New Criticism*, ed. Miranda B. Hickman and John D. McIntyre (Columbus: Ohio University Press, 2012), 83–101.

53. Brinkmeyer, *The Fourth Ghost*, 52.

54. "Robert Penn Warren, The Art of Fiction XVIII," interviewed by Eugene Walter and Ralph Ellison, *Paris Review* 4, no. 16 (Spring/Summer 1957): 131–132.

55. John Crowe Ransom, "Criticism as Pure Speculation," in *The Intent of the Critic*, ed. Donald Stauffer (Princeton, N.J.: Princeton University Press, 1941), 108.

56. John Crowe Ransom, "We Resume" (editorial), *Kenyon Review* 4 (Autumn 1942): 405.

57. Allen Tate, "The Present Function of Criticism," *Southern Review* 6 (Autumn 1940): 238; qtd. in Brinkmeyer, *The Fourth Ghost*, 56.

58. See comments of Tate and John Crowe Ransom in the symposium "On the Brooks-MacLeish Thesis," *Partisan Review* 9 (January/February 1942): 38–47.

59. Brinkmeyer, *The Fourth Ghost*, 256.

60. Robert Penn Warren, "Pure and Impure Poetry," *Kenyon Review* 5 (Spring 1943): 254; qtd. in Brinkmeyer, *The Fourth Ghost*, 257.

61. Robert Penn Warren, "Paul Rosenfeld: Prompter of Fiction," *Commonweal*, August 15, 1947.

62. James H. Justus, *The Achievement of Robert Penn Warren* (Baton Rouge: Louisiana University Press, 1981), 194.

63. Robert Penn Warren, "All the King's Men" (introduction to Italian translation of the play); reprinted in *Robert Penn Warren's "All the King's Men": Three Stage Versions*, ed. James A. Grimshaw Jr. and James A. Perkins (Athens: University of Georgia Press, 2000), 9.

64. Warren, "All the King's Men," 9.

65. In a letter of November 1941, following the play, Warren wrote a friend that he was working on a novel partly based on "the Huey Long situation, but not an exposé—on the theme of power versus values, means versus ends." Robert Penn Warren to David M. Clay, November 8, 1941, in *Selected Letters of Robert Penn Warren*, Vol. 2: *The "Southern Review" Years*, ed. William Bedford Clark (Baton Rouge: Louisiana University Press, 2001), 341.

66. Robert Penn Warren, *All the King's Men* (New York: Harcourt, Brace, and World, 1946), 464.

67. Warren, *All the King's Men*, 200.

68. Randall Jarrell, "The Emancipators," in *Little Friend, Little Friend* (New York: Dial, 1945), 14.

69. John Berryman, "Thanksgiving, Detroit," in *Poems* (Norfolk, Conn.: New Directions, 1942), 16.

70. John Berryman, "Communist," in *Poems*, 15.

71. John Berryman, "Rock-Study with Wanderer," in *The Dispossessed* (New York: William Sloane Associates, 1948), 87–88.

72. Arthur Miller, "Regarding *Streetcar*," intro. to Tennessee Williams, *A Streetcar Named Desire* (New York: New Directions, 2004), xiii.

73. Karen Leick, "Ezra Pound v. *Saturday Review of Literature*," *Journal of Modern Literature* 25, no. 2 (Winter 2001/2002): 22, 37n7. An important earlier article on the controversy is Robert A. Corrigan, "Ezra Pound and the Bollingen Prize Controversy," in *The Forties: Fiction, Poetry, Drama*, ed. Warren A. French (Deland, Fla.: Everett/Edwards, 1969), 287–295.

74. Leick, "Ezra Pound v. *Saturday Review of Literature*," 23.

75. Robert Hillyer, "Treason's Strange Fruit: The Case of Ezra Pound and the Bollingen Award," *Saturday Review of Literature*, June 11, 1949.

76. Robert Hillyer, "Poetry's New Priesthood," *Saturday Review of Literature*, June 18, 1949.

77. Wai Chee Dimock, "Aesthetics at the Limits of the Nation: Kant, Pound, and the *Saturday Review*," *American Literature* 76, no. 3 (September 2004): 536.

78. Harrison Smith, editorial, *Saturday Review of Literature*, July 2, 1949; qtd. in Corrigan, "Ezra Pound and the Bollingen Prize Controversy," 289.

79. Allen Tate to Luther Evans, January 31, 1949; Allen Tate to Leonie Adams, January 31, 1949; qtd. in Leick, "Ezra Pound v. *Saturday Review of Literature*," 24.

80. Arthur Schlesinger Jr., *The Vital Center: The Politics of Freedom* (1949; New York: Da Capo, 1988), 79.

81. Malcolm Cowley, *New Republic* 71 (October 3, 1949): 17–20.

82. Karl Shapiro, "Trial of a Poet," in *Trial of a Poet and Other Poems* (New York: Reynal & Hitchcock, 1947), 55–58. The epigraph is from lines 237–240 of Milton's "Samson Agonistes."

83. Shapiro, "Trial of a Poet," 81.

84. Shapiro, "Trial of a Poet," 76–78.

85. Shapiro, "Trial of a Poet," 77.

4. THE WAR

1. Yvor Winters, "Before Disaster: Winter 1932–33," in *The Giant Weapon* (New York: New Directions, 1943), n.p.

2. W. H. Auden, "September 1, 1939," in *The English Auden: Poems, Essays, and Dramatic Writings: 1927–1939*, ed. Edward Mendelson (London: Faber and Faber, 1986), 245.

3. John Berryman, "The Dangerous Year," *Poems* (Norfolk, Conn.: New Directions, 1942), 2–3.

4. Dawn Powell, *A Time to Be Born* (1942; rpt. Hanover, N.H.: Steerforth, 1996), 1–3.

5. Charles Jackson, *The Fall of Valor* (New York: Rinehart, 1946), 12.

6. Edna St. Vincent Millay, *The Murder of Lidice* (New York: Harper & Bros., 1942), 30, 32. See also the shorter version in *Life*, October 19, 1942.

7. Thomas Howell, "The Writers' War Board: U.S. Domestic Propaganda During World War II," *Historian* 59, no. 4 (Summer 1997): 795–813; Howell quotes from the *Christian Science Monitor* and *Theater Arts* on 805. Information on the Writers' War Board comes chiefly from Howell.

8. Millay, *The Murder of Lidice*, 1.

9. Harry Brown, *A Walk in the Sun* (New York: Knopf, 1944), 33.

10. Carson McCullers, *The Member of the Wedding*, in *Complete Novels* (New York: Library of America, 2001), 479–480.

11. Martha Gellhorn, *Liana* (New York: Scribner, 1944), 176.

12. Eleanor Roosevelt, column of June 7, 1944, in *My Day: The Best of Eleanor Roosevelt's Acclaimed Newspaper Columns, 1936–1962* (New York: Da Capo, 2001), 342.

13. Anatole Broyard, *Kafka Was the Rage: A Greenwich Village Memoir* (1993; New York: Vintage, 1997), 80.

14. Karl Shapiro, "Recapitulations," in *The Trial of the Poet and Other Poems* (New York: Reynal & Hitchcock, 1947), 9.

15. Jackson, *The Fall of Valor*, 20.

16. Shapiro, poem XV of "Recapitulations," 20.

17. Randall Jarrell, "Mail Call," in *Little Friend, Little Friend* (New York: Dial, 1945), 35.

18. Harry Brown, *A Walk in the Sun* (New York: Knopf, 1944), 148.

19. Paul Ricoeur, *Time and Narrative*, vol. 1, trans. Kathleen McLaughlin and David Pellauer (Chicago: University of Chicago Press, 1990).

20. Brown, *A Walk in the Sun*, 185.

21. Brown, *A Walk in the Sun*, 187.

22. Brown, *A Walk in the Sun*, 184.

23. Richard Eberhart, "The Fury of Aerial Bombardment," in *Poems New and Selected* (Norfolk, Conn.: New Directions, 1945), 8.

24. Louis Simpson, "Carentan O Carentan," in *The Arrivistes: Poems 1940–1949* (New York: Fine Editions Press, 1949), 58–59.

25. Louis Simpson, "Arm in Arm," in *Arrivistes*, 20.

26. Martha Gellhorn, *A Stricken Field* (New York: Penguin/Virago, 1986), 301.

27. Irwin Shaw, *The Young Lions* (1948; Chicago: University of Chicago Press, 2000), 590.

28. Jarrell, "The Lines," in *Losses* (New York: Harcourt Brace, 1948), 21.

29. Randall Jarrell, "The Wide Prospect," in *Little Friend, Little Friend*, 57.

30. Randall Jarrell, "The Sick Nought," in *Little Friend*, 51.

31. Jarrell, "The Sick Nought," 51.

32. Randall Jarrell, qtd. in Stephen Burt, *Randall Jarrell and His Age* (New York: Columbia University Press, 2002), 55.

33. Randall Jarrell, "The Death of the Ball Turret Gunner," in *Little Friend*, 58.

34. Gwendolyn Brooks, "still do I keep my look, my identity . . ." in *A Street in Bronzeville* (New York: Harper & Brothers, 1945), 47.

35. Karl Shapiro, "Elegy for a Dead Soldier," in *V-Letter and Other Poems* (New York: Reynal & Hitchcock, 1944), 43.

36. Brown, *A Walk in the Sun*, 52.

37. Richard Eberhart, "Dam Neck, Virginia," in *Poems New and Selected*, 7.

38. Vincent Sheean, *This House Against This House* (New York: Random House, 1945), 123.

39. John Ciardi, "Take-Off Over Kansas," in *Other Skies* (Boston: Little, Brown, 1947), 21.

40. Dan Jaffe, "Poets in the Inferno: Civilians, C.O.'s, and Combatants," in *The Forties: Fiction, Poetry, Drama*, ed. Warren French (Deland, Fla.: Everett/Edwards, 1969), 57.

41. Yvor Winters, "By the Road to the Air-base," in *The Giant Weapon* (New York: New Directions, 1943), n.p.

42. Winters, "Summer Noon: 1941," in *The Giant Weapon*, n.p.

43. Eberhart, "Dam Neck, Virginia," 7.

44. Randall Jarrell, "The Emancipators," in *Little Friend, Little Friend*, 14.

45. Eberhart, "The Fury of Aerial Bombardment," 8.

46. Marianne Moore, "Keeping Their World Large," in *Collected Poems* (New York: Macmillan/Penguin, 1994), 145.

47. Randall Jarrell, *Kipling, Auden & Co.: Essays and Reviews, 1935–1964* (New York: Farrar, Straus & Giroux, 1980), 129.

48. Harry Brown, *A Sound of Hunting* (New York: Knopf, 1945), 121, 68, 124.

49. Louis Simpson, "Roll," in *The Arrivistes*, 19.

50. James Dawes, *The Language of War: Literature and Culture in the U.S. from the Civil War Through World War II* (Cambridge, Mass.: Harvard University Press, 2002), 2.

51. Mark Harris, *Five Came Back: A Story of Hollywood and the Second World War* (New York: Penguin, 2014), 226.

52. Harris, *Five Came Back*, 411.

53. Huston, qtd. in Harris, *Five Came Back*, 411.

54. Most recently, in Mark Harris's *Five Came Back*. See also, especially, Gregory D. Black, *Hollywood Goes to War: How Politics, Profits, and Propaganda Shaped World War II Movies* (New York: Free Press, 1987). Thomas Doherty defends the industry against charges of cynicism and profiteering, arguing for the artistic and political value of some World War II cinema, in *Projections of War: Hollywood, American Culture, and World War II* (New York: Columbia University Press, 1993). Charges of the ultimate "dishonesty" of the films, regardless of intention, remain convincing, however.

55. James T. Farrell, *The Fate of Writing in America* (New York: New Directions, 1946), n.p.

56. John Steinbeck, "Introduction," in *Once There Was a War* (New York: Penguin, 1958), xii–xiii. The book reprints Steinbeck's World War II journalism for the New York *Herald Tribune* of 1943.

57. Norman Mailer, "Preface," in *Some Honorable Men: Political Conventions, 1960–1972* (Boston: Little, Brown, 1976), ix.

58. See Martha Gellhorn, "Afterword," in *A Stricken Field*.

59. James Anderson Winn, *The Poetry of War* (Cambridge: Cambridge University Press, 2008), 212.

60. A fine recent exception is Diederik Oostdijk, *Among the Nightmare Fighters: American Poets of World War II* (Columbia: University of South Carolina Press, 2011), 4. Oostdijk takes a generational approach, discussing poems of the 1940s along with much later ones, finding four common themes of the white male "academic poets" of the war generation: "tradition, identity, masculinity, and afterlife." Another good book is Susan Schweik's *A Gulf So Deeply Cut: American Women Poets and the Second World*

War (Madison: University of Wisconsin Press, 1991), which discusses poetry by Marianne Moore, Edna St. Vincent Millay, Gwendolyn Brooks, Muriel Rukeyser, Elizabeth Bishop, and H.D. Sandra M. Gilbert and Susan Gubar devote a substantial chapter to women's poetry and fiction from the period in *No Man's Land: The Place of the Woman Writer in the Twentieth Century*, vol. 3: *Letters from the Front* (New Haven, Conn.: Yale University Press, 1994), 211–265.

61. James Dawes, "The American War Novel," in *The Cambridge Companion to the Literature of World War II*, ed. Marina MacKay (Cambridge: Cambridge University Press, 2009), 56.

62. This issue has recently been raised from a different vantage point in Vaughn Rasberry, *Race and the Totalitarian Century: Geopolitics in the Black Literary Imagination* (Cambridge, Mass.: Harvard University Press, 2016), which shows how African American authors used the battle against totalitarianism to push for decolonization, questioning the stark divide being drawn between existing democracies, Nazism, and Stalinism.

63. Marianne Moore, "In Distrust of Merits," in *Collected Poems*, 138. Originally published in Moore's *Nevertheless* (1944).

64. Moore, "In Distrust of Merits," 137.

65. Burt, *Randall Jarrell*, 56 (quoting the historian Ellen Herman).

66. Shaw, *Young Lions*, 294–295.

67. Harvey Shapiro, "Introduction," *Poets of World War II* (New York: Library of America, 2003), xxi.

68. Shaw, *Young Lions*, 137.

69. Howard Nemerov, "IFF," in *War Stories* (Chicago: University of Chicago Press, 1987), 29.

70. Howard Nemerov, "IFF," 29.

71. Randall Jarrell, note to "O My Name It Is Sam Hall," in *Losses*, 66.

72. Witter Bynner, "Defeat," in *Selected Poems*, ed. Richard Wilbur (New York: Farrar, Straus & Giroux, 1978), 185; published earlier in Bynner's war-focused book of poems, *Take Away the Darkness* (New York: Knopf, 1947).

73. John Frederick Nims, "Race Riot," in *The Iron Pastoral* (New York: William Sloane Associates, 1947), 51. First published in *Accent* 5, no. 3 (Spring 1945): 155.

74. Gwendolyn Brooks, "the white troops had their orders but the Negroes looked like men," in "Gay Chaps at the Bar," in *A Street in Bronzeville*, 52.

75. Gwendolyn Brooks, "the white troops," 52.

76. Gwendolyn Brooks, "Negro Hero," in *A Street in Bronzeville*, 32.

77. Gwendolyn Brooks, "the progress," final poem of "Gay Chaps at the Bar," 57.

78. Press release, "Paintings by Leading Negro Artist Shown at Museum of Modern Art," MoMA archives, http://www.moma.org/momaorg/shared/pdfs/docs/press _archives/955/releases/MOMA_1944_0041_1944–10–10_441010–34.pdf. Note these are not the same as his slightly later *War Series* (1946–1947), and most of these paintings have been lost since the end of the war.

79. Norman Mailer, *The Naked and the Dead* (New York: Henry Holt/Picador, 1998), 321–322.

80. Gore Vidal, "Speaking of Books: John Horne Burns," *New York Times*, May 30, 1965.

81. John Horne Burns, *The Gallery* (1947; New York: NYRB, 2004), 76.

82. Burns, *The Gallery*, 259.
83. Burns, *The Gallery*, 1.
84. Burns, *The Gallery*, 205.
85. Burns, *The Gallery*, 339. Ellipses in original.
86. Burns, *The Gallery*, 338–339. Ellipses in original.
87. Burns, *The Gallery*, 307.
88. Burns, *The Gallery*, 306.
89. Vidal, "Speaking of Books," 22.

5. AMERICA! AMERICA! A JEWISH RENAISSANCE?

1. Cecil Roth, "Jewish Culture: Renaissance or Ice Age?" *Commentary* 4 (1947): 329.
2. Roth, "Jewish Culture," 333.
3. Qtd. in Jonathan D. Sarna, "Two Ambitious Goals: American Jewish Publishing in the United States," in *A History of the Book in America*, vol. 4: *Print in Motion: The Expansion of Publishing and Reading in the United States, 1880–1940*, ed. Carl F. Kaestle and Janice A. Radway (Chapel Hill: University of North Carolina Press, 2014), 391.
4. Roth, "Jewish Culture," 333.
5. Leonard Dinnerstein, *Anti-Semitism in America* (New York: Oxford University Press, 1994), 151.
6. Irwin Shaw, *The Young Lions* (1948; Chicago: University of Chicago Press, 2000), 293.
7. Sarna, "Two Ambitious Goals," 390, 391.
8. Richard Abel and William Gordon Graham, *Immigrant Publishers: The Impact of Refugee Publishers in Britain and America in the Twentieth Century* (New York: Transaction, 2009), 191–192.
9. Charles A. Madison, *Jewish Publishing in America: The Impact of Jewish Writing on American Culture* (New York: Sanhedrin, 1976), 93. Madison discusses Schocken more generally on 91–94.
10. Isaac Rosenfeld, "Approaches to Kafka," *New Leader*, April 12, 1947; reprinted in Rosenfeld, *An Age of Enormity: Life and Writing in the Forties and Fifties* (New York: World, 1962), 174.
11. John A. Weigel, "Sinclair, Jo," in *Contemporary Novelists*, ed. James Vinson, 2nd ed. (New York: St. Martin's Press, 1976), 1248.
12. Werner Sollors, *Ethnic Modernism* (Cambridge, Mass.: Harvard University Press, 2008), 224.
13. Elliot E. Cohen, "Announcement," *Contemporary Jewish Record* 8, no. 3 (June 1945).
14. Irving Howe, *A Margin of Hope: An Intellectual Autobiography* (New York: Harcourt Brace Jovanovich, 1982), 122.
15. See George Hutchinson, *The Harlem Renaissance in Black and White* (Cambridge, Mass.: Harvard University Press, 1995), part 1, "The Transformation of Institutions."
16. Sarna, "Two Ambitious Goals," 390.
17. Madison, *Jewish Publishing in America*, 206.
18. See Madison's chapters "The Efflorescence of Yiddish Literature," and "Some Major Yiddish Writers," in *Jewish Publishing in America*, 156–205.

19. Stephen Katz, *Red, Black, and Jew: New Frontiers in Hebrew Literature* (Austin: University of Texas Press, 2009), 5.

20. Katz, *Red, Black, and Jew*, 226. See also Alan Mintz, "Hebrew Literature in America," in *The Cambridge Companion to Jewish American Literature*, ed. Hana Wirth-Nesher and Michael P. Kramer (Cambridge: Cambridge University Press, 2003), 92.

21. Alfred Kazin, preface to *On Native Grounds* (1942; New York: Harcourt Brace Jovanovich, 1970), ix.

22. Alfred Kazin, *A Walker in the City* (1951; New York: Harcourt/Harvest, 1979), 172.

23. Kazin, *A Walker in the City*, 176.

24. Kazin, *On Native Grounds*, x.

25. Theodore Solotaroff, "Introduction," in Rosenfeld, *An Age of Enormity*, 25.

26. Howe, *A Margin of Hope*, 160.

27. Kazin, *On Native Grounds*, 31.

28. "The Art of Poetry XXXVI: Karl Shapiro Interviewed by Robert Phillips, December 1984," http://www.departments.bucknell.edu/stadler_center/shapiro/interview.pdf.

29. Lewis Fried, "American Jewish Fiction, 1930–1945," in *Handbook of American-Jewish Literature*, ed. Lewis Fried (Westport, Conn.: Greenwood, 1988), 52.

30. Karl Shapiro, "Christmas Eve, Australia," in *V-Letter and Other Poems* (New York: Reynal & Hitchcock, 1944), 9.

31. Karl Shapiro, "New Guinea," in *V-Letter*, 10.

32. Shapiro, "New Guinea," 11.

33. Karl Shapiro, "Sunday, New Guinea," in *V-Letter*, 13.

34. Shapiro, "Jew," in *V-Letter*, 27.

35. Waldo Frank, "The Jew in Our Day: Preface to a Program," *Contemporary Jewish Record* 7, no. 1 (February 1944): 43.

36. "The Art of Poetry XXXVI."

37. Kazin, *A Walker in the City*, 162.

38. Kazin, *A Walker in the City*, 171.

39. Madison, *Jewish Publishing in America*, 180–186.

40. Muriel Rukeyser, "Holy Family," in *Beast in View* (Garden City, N.J.: Doubleday, Doran, 1944), 36.

41. Rukeyser, "Ninth Elegy: The Antagonists," in *Beast in View*, 95.

42. Rukeyser, "Note," in *Beast in View*, 98.

43. Rukeyser, "A Translation," in *Beast in View*, 39.

44. Rukeyser, "Letter to the Front," in *Beast in View*, 62.

45. Leslie A. Fiedler, "What Can We Do About Fagan? The Jew-Villain in Western Tradition," *Commentary* 8 (1949): 418. In contrast, in 1963, Fiedler charged that "Jewish writers have discovered their Jewishness to be eminently a marketable commodity, their much vaunted alienation to be their passport into the heart of Gentile American culture." Qtd. in Madison, *Jewish Publishing in America*, 272.

46. Leslie A. Fiedler, "What Can We Do About Fagan?" 418.

47. Philip Rahv, foreword to *A Malamud Reader* (New York: Farrar, Straus & Giroux, 1967); qtd. in Bonnie K. Lyons, "American-Jewish Fiction Since 1945," in *Handbook of American-Jewish Literature*, 61.

48. Frederick R. Karl, qtd. in Lyons, "American-Jewish Fiction since 1945," in *Handbook of American-Jewish Literature*, 61.

49. Allan Bloom, *Prodigal Sons: The New York Intellectuals and Their World* (New York: Oxford University Press, 1987), 151.

50. Alfred Kazin, August 14, 1948, in *Alfred Kazin's Journals*, ed. Richard M. Cook (New Haven, Conn.: Yale University Press, 2011), 119.

51. Alfred Kazin, September 27, 1948, in *Alfred Kazin's Journals*, 120–121.

52. Kazin, September 27, 1948, in *Alfred Kazin's Journals*, 121.

53. Saul Bellow, *The Victim* (1948), in *Bellow: Novels 1944–1953* (New York: Library of America, 2003), 158.

54. Martin Greenberg, "Modern Man as Jew," *Commentary* 5, no. 1 (January 1948): 87.

55. Bellow, *The Victim*, 379.

56. Greenberg, "Modern Man as Jew," 86.

57. Greenberg, "Modern Man as Jew," 86.

58. See Ben Siegel, "Bellow as Jew and Jewish Writer," in *A Political Companion to Saul Bellow*, ed. Gloria L. Cronin and Lee Trepanier (Lexington: University of Kentucky Press, 2013), 29–56.

59. Bellow, qtd. in Siegel, "Bellow as Jew and Jewish Writer," 47.

60. Christopher Bigsby, *Arthur Miller: 1915–1962* (Cambridge, Mass.: Harvard University Press, 2009), 311.

61. Miller, qtd. in Bigsby, *Arthur Miller*, 311; from Arthur Miller, "Concerning Jews Who Write," *Jewish Life* 2, no. 5 (March 1948): 7–10.

62. Muriel Rukeyser, in "Under Forty: A Symposium on American Literature and the Younger Generation of American Jews," *Contemporary Jewish Record* 7, no. 1 (February 1, 1944): 8.

63. Rukeyser, in "Under Forty," 9.

64. Alfred Kazin, in "Under Forty," 11.

65. Thorstein Veblen, "The Intellectual Pre-eminence of Jews in Modern Europe" (1919), reprinted in *Contemporary Jewish Record* 7, no. 5 (October 1944): 564–565; qtd. in Kazin, *A Walker in the City*, 131–132. Veblen's essay was originally published in *Political Science Quarterly* (March 1919).

66. Daniel Aaron, *The Americanist* (Ann Arbor: University of Michigan Press, 2007), 4.

67. Lionel Trilling, in "Under Forty," 15.

68. Trilling, in "Under Forty," 17.

69. Louis Kronenberger, in "Under Forty," 20, 23.

70. Howard Fast, in "Under Forty," 26.

71. Richard Wright to Jo Sinclair, qtd. in Jo Sinclair, *The Seasons: Death and Transfiguration* (New York: The Feminist Press, 1993), 140.

72. Jo Sinclair, *Wasteland* (New York: Harper & Bros., 1946), 307, 315.

73. Sinclair, *Wasteland*, 102, 110.

74. Sinclair, *Wasteland*, 194–195.

75. Sinclair, *Wasteland*, 219–220.

76. Sinclair, *Wasteland*, 282.

77. Sinclair, *Wasteland*, 289.

78. Sinclair, *Wasteland*, 290.

79. Isaac Rosenfeld, *Passage from Home* (New York: Dial, 1946), 115–116.

80. Rosenfeld, *Passage from Home*, 116.

81. Rosenfeld, *Passage from Home*, 116.

82. I owe a debt here to the final chapter of Paul Grimstad, *Experience and Experimental Writing: Literary Pragmatism from Emerson to the Jameses* (New York: Oxford University Press, 2015).

83. Steven J. Zipperstein, *Rosenfeld's Lives: Fame, Oblivion, and the Fury of Writing* (New Haven, Conn.: Yale University Press, 2009), 2.

84. Solotaroff, "Introduction," 17–18.

85. Zipperstein, *Rosenfeld's Lives*, 85.

86. Howe, *A Margin of Hope*, 112–113.

87. Diana Trilling, review of Isaac Rosenfeld's *Passage from Home*, in *The Nation*, May 18, 1946; reprinted in Diana Trilling, *Reviewing the Forties* (New York: Harcourt Brace Jovanovich, 1978), 167–168, my emphasis.

88. Leslie Fiedler, *Waiting for the End* (Dell, 1975); qtd. in Lyons, "American-Jewish Fiction Since 1945," 64. For an essay on shifts in the attention of Jewish critics toward Jewish identity and the Holocaust, particularly in Ivy League English departments, see Daniel R. Schwarz, "Eating Kosher Ivy: Jews as Literary Intellectuals," in *In Defense of Reading: Teaching Literature in the Twenty-First Century* (Chichester: Wiley-Blackwell, 2008), 94–111.

89. See George Ross, "'Death of a Salesman' in the Original: The Yiddish Version Reveals the Real Willy Loman," *Commentary* 11 (February 1951): 184–186.

90. Frantz Fanon, *Black Skin, White Masks*, trans. Charles Mam Markmann (New York: Grove, 1967), 110. Originally published in 1952 as *Peau noir, masques blancs*.

91. Fanon, *Black Skin, White Masks*, 109.

92. Fanon, *Black Skin, White Masks*, 122.

93. Gordon Lloyd Harper, "The Art of Fiction: Saul Bellow" (1966), in *Conversations with Saul Bellow*, ed. Gloria L. Cronin and Ben Siegel (Jackson: University Press of Mississippi, 1994), 74. Philippe Codde, in *The Jewish American Novel* (West Lafayette, Ind.: Purdue University Press, 2007), 146, asserts that Bellow misreads (perhaps willfully) Sartre's *Anti-Semite and Jew* here, but Bellow may instead be recalling the interchange in *Commentary*.

94. John Dewey, "The Crisis in Human History: The Danger of the Retreat to Individualism," *Commentary* 1 (December 1945): 1–9. The editors of *Commentary* published this as the fourth in a series of essays on "The Crisis in Human History" by contemporary thinkers including Dewey, Martin Buber, Andre Gide, Pearl S. Buck, Waldo Frank, Sidney Hook, and others. It was the lead article in the first issue of *Commentary* succeeding *Contemporary Jewish Record*.

6. A RISING WIND: "LITERATURE OF THE NEGRO" AND CIVIL RIGHTS

1. John W. Aldridge, *After the Lost Generation: A Critical Study of the Writers of Two Wars* (New York: McGraw Hill, 1951), 100.

2. Farah Jasmine Griffin makes this point in *Harlem Nocturne: Women Artists and Progressive Politics During World War II* (New York: Columbia University Press, 2013), 4. Martha Biondi has shown that "World War II was a watershed for the northern

civil rights movement": Martha Biondi, *To Stand and Fight: The Struggle for Civil Rights in Postwar New York City* (Cambridge, Mass.: Harvard University Press, 2003), 3.

3. J. Saunders Redding, *No Day of Triumph* (New York: Harper & Bros., 1942), 327, 43.

4. Redding, *No Day of Triumph*, 339.

5. Redding, *No Day of Triumph*, 340.

6. Lawrence P. Jackson, *The Indignant Generation: A Narrative History of African American Writers and Critics, 1934–1960* (Princeton, N.J.: Princeton University Press, 2011), 5.

7. Concerning Lawrence and his art education, see Patricia Hills, *Painting Harlem Modern: The Art of Jacob Lawrence* (Berkeley: University of California Press, 2009), 13–17. Leah Dickerman also traces Lawrence's artistic development in relationship to legacies of the Harlem Renaissance in "Fighting Blues," in *Jacob Lawrence: The Migration Series*, ed. Leah Dickerman and Elsa Smithgall (New York/Washington, D.C.: Museum of Modern Art/Phillips Collection, 2015), 10–31. Elsa Smithgall focuses on Lawrence's artistic development and the acquisition of his work by the MoMA and the Phillips Collection in "One Series, Two Places: Jacob Lawrence's Migration Series at the Museum of Modern Art and the Phillips Collection," in the same catalogue, 32–45.

8. Erik S. Gellman, "Chicago's Native Son: Charles White and the Laboring of the Black Renaissance," in *The Black Chicago Renaissance*, ed. Darlene Clark Hine and John McCluskey Jr. (Urbana: University of Illinois Press, 2012), 155–157.

9. Paul Nadler, "American Theater and the Civil Rights Movement, 1945–1965," Ph.D. diss., CUNY, 1996.

10. Headnote to Eleanor Roosevelt, "My Day," November 6, 1943, in Eleanor Roosevelt, *My Day: The Best of Eleanor Roosevelt's Acclaimed Newspaper Columns, 1936–1962* (New York: MJF, 2001), 315.

11. Errol G. Hill and James V. Hatch, *A History of African American Theater* (Cambridge: Cambridge University Press, 2003), 345. Information on black theater in the 1940s comes primarily from the chapter "Creeping Toward Integration," 335–374.

12. Hill and Hatch, *A History of African American Theater*, 350.

13. Langston Hughes, "Some Practical Observations: A Colloquy," *Phylon* 11, no. 4 (1950): 309.

14. Hughes, "Some Practical Observations," 308.

15. See, for example, Alain Locke, "Wisdom *de Profundis*: The Literature of the Negro, 1949," *Phylon* 11, no. 1 (1950): 5–14.

16. Thomas D. Jarrett, "Toward Unfettered Creativity: A Note on the Negro Novelist's Coming of Age," *Phylon* 11, no. 4 (1950): 313.

17. Arna Bontemps and Langston Hughes, eds., *The Poetry of the Negro, 1746–1949* (Garden City, N.Y.: Doubleday, 1949), vii.

18. See Ifeoma Kiddoe Nwankwo, "More Than McKay and Guillen: The Caribbean in Hughes and Bontemps's *The Poetry of the Negro* (1949)," in *Publishing Blackness: Textual Constructions of Race Since 1850*, ed. George Hutchinson and John K. Young (Ann Arbor: University of Michigan Press, 2013), 108–135.

19. "The Negro: 'New' or Newer,—A Retrospective Review of the Literature of the Negro for 1938," *Opportunity* 17 (January–February 1939); reprinted in Jeffrey Stewart, *The Critical Temper of Alain Locke* (New York: Garland, 1983), 273.

20. Ernie Julius Mitchell II, "Black Renaissance: A Brief History of the Concept," *Amerikastudien* 55, no. 4 (2010): 641–665.

21. Hughes, "Some Practical Observations," 307, 308.

22. Blyden Jackson, "Silver Foxes," *Journal of Negro Education* 15, no. 4 (Autumn 1946): 649–650.

23. Senator Theodore Bilbo, June 27, 1945, 79th Congress, 1st sess., *Congressional Record*, 91:6808.

24. Bucklin Moon, "Preface," in *Primer for White Folks* (Garden City, N.Y.: Doubleday, Doran & Co., 1945), xii.

25. Lillian Smith, "Addressed to White Liberals," in *Primer for White Folks*, 484. Originally published in the *New Republic*.

26. Cash wrote that the systematic social control of thought and behavior in the contemporary American South had taken such a form as "had not been established in any Western people since the decay of medieval feudalism, and almost as truly as it is established today in Fascist Italy, in Nazi Germany, in Soviet Russia—and so paralyzed Southern culture at the root." W. J. Cash, *The Mind of the South* (1941; New York: Vintage, 1991), 134. For a full and fascinating discussion of the response of Southern white writers to European fascism, see Robert H. Brinkmeyer, *The Fourth Ghost: White Southern Writers and European Fascism, 1930–1950* (Baton Rouge: Louisiana State University Press, 2009).

27. Irving Howe, "Black Boys and Native Sons," *Dissent* (Autumn 1963): 354.

28. Hugh Gloster, "Race and the Negro Writer," *Phylon* 11, no. 4 (1950): 370.

29. Richard Wright, *Native Son* (New York: Harper Perennial Classics, 1998), 288.

30. Wright, *Native Son*, 289.

31. Wright, *Native Son*, 290.

32. Wright, *Native Son*, 429.

33. Wright, *Native Son*, 429, 430. Ellipses in the original.

34. Richard Wright, *Twelve Million Black Voices* (1941; Boston: Thunder's Mouth, 1988), 146.

35. James Baldwin, "Everybody's Protest Novel," *Partisan Review*, June 16, 1949; reprinted in James Baldwin, *Collected Essays* (New York: Library of America, 1998), 18.

36. James Baldwin, "The Image of the Negro," *Commentary*, April 1948; reprinted in Baldwin, *Collected Essays*, 582.

37. James Baldwin, "History as Nightmare," *New Leader*, October 25, 1947; reprinted in Baldwin, *Collected Essays*, 580.

38. James Baldwin, "The Image of the Negro," 582.

39. James Baldwin, "History as Nightmare," 581.

40. James Baldwin, "The Discovery of What It Means to Be an American," in Baldwin, *Collected Essays*, 137.

41. Faulkner to Richard Wright, probably September 11, 1945, in Joseph Blotner, ed., *Selected Letters of William Faulkner* (New York: Random House, 1977), 201.

42. Cecile Gerletz, "S. Brown Considers Faulkner's Negroes," *Vassar Miscellany News* 41, no. 19 (March 13, 1957): 2. Lee Jenkins also emphasizes a major shift in Faulkner's depiction of black characters beginning with *Go Down, Moses* and further advanced in *Intruder in the Dust*. Lee Jenkins, *Faulkner and Black-White Relations: A Psychoanalytic Approach* (New York: Columbia University Press, 1981), 226–237, 261.

43. William Faulkner, *Go Down, Moses* (New York: Vintage, 1970), 346.

44. Faulkner, *Go Down, Moses*, 345.

45. William Faulkner to Malcolm A. Franklin, 4 July 1943, in Joseph Blotner, ed., *Selected Letters of William Faulkner* (New York: Random House, 1978), 175–76.

46. Blotner, ed., *Selected Letters of William Faulkner*, 415.

47. William Faulkner to Eudora Welty, April 27, 1943; qtd. in Suzanne Marrs, *Eudora Welty: A Biography* (New York: Harcourt, 2005), 98.

48. Concerning Mollie Beauchamp's relationship to Roth Edmonds, Faulkner (*Go Down, Moses*, 113–114) writes that she "had surrounded him always with care for his physical body and for his spirit too, teaching him his manners, behavior—to be gentle with his inferiors, honorable with his equals, generous to the weak and considerate of the aged, courteous, truthful and brave to all—who had given him, the motherless, without stint or expectation of reward that constant and abiding devotion and love which existed nowhere else in this world for him." Of Caroline Barr, Faulkner wrote, "She reared all of us from childhood. She stood not only as a fount of authority and information, but of affection, respect, and security." William Faulkner, "Funeral Sermon for Mammy Caroline Barr," in *Essays, Speeches, and Public Letters*, ed. James B. Meriwether (New York: Modern Library, 2004), 275. Blotner (*Selected Letters*, 414) writes that Mollie Beauchamp's portrayal in "The Fire and the Hearth" "was drawn directly from Mammy Callie, and her closeness to Edmonds was not unlike that of Mammy Callie to William Faulkner."

49. Blotner, ed., *Selected Letters of William Faulkner*, 413.

50. Blotner, ed., *Selected Letters of William Faulkner*, 414–415.

51. Ralph Ellison, "The Shadow and the Act," in *Shadow and Act*, 271. Originally published in *The Reporter*, December 6, 1949.

52. See R. Baxter Miller, ed., *Black American Literature and Humanism* (Lexington: University Press of Kentucky, 1981), for essays on a number of black authors, mostly of the midcentury, who embraced humanism and contested Eurocentric humanism in the Enlightenment tradition.

53. Richard Wright, review of *The Heart Is a Lonely Hunter*, in the *New Republic*, August 5, 1940.

54. Gertrude Stein to Richard Wright, April 22, 1945; qtd. in Hazel Rowley, *Richard Wright: The Life and Times* (New York: Henry Holt, 2001), 323.

55. *Chicago Defender*, October 27, 1945; qtd. in Rowley, *Richard Wright*, 324.

56. Qtd. in Rowley, *Richard Wright*, 239.

57. Baldwin, "The Image of the Negro," 578.

58. Only one critic has drawn attention to the first published version of "Middle Passage," and that quite recently: Carl Plasa, "Doing the Slave Trade in Different Voices: Poetics and Politics in Robert Hayden's First 'Middle Passage,'" *African American Review* 45, no. 4 (Winter 2012): 557–573. Plasa focuses on the relationship of the poem to Eliot's formal experiments and to earlier accounts of the *Amistad* mutiny and court case.

59. Robert Hayden, "Middle Passage," *Phylon* 6, no. 3 (3rd qtr., 1945): 250.

60. Hayden, "Middle Passage," *Phylon*, 251.

61. Robert Hayden, "Middle Passage," in *Collected Poems*, ed. Frederick Glaysher (New York: Liveright, 1985), 53–54.

62. Hayden, "Middle Passage," *Phylon*, 253.

63. Werner Sollors observes that despite their differences, "Both Wright and Hurston were part of the greater emphasis placed on universalism in the 1940s and 1950s and of which novels that crossed lines of expected racial representation were representative." Werner Sollors, *Ethnic Modernism* (Cambridge, Mass.: Harvard University Press, 2002), 166. Recent scholarship has begun drawing attention to "white life" novels by black authors. See especially Gene Andrew Jarrett, *Deans and Truants: Race and Realism in African American Literature* (Philadelphia: University of Pennsylvania Press, 2007); John C. Charles, "Talk About the South: Unspeakable Things Unspoken in Zora Neale Hurston's *Seraph on the Suwanee*," *Mississippi Quarterly* 62 (2009): 19–52; and Stephanie Li, *Playing in the White: Black Writers, White Subjects* (New York: Oxford University Press, 2015).

64. Robert Bone, *The Negro Novel in America* (New Haven, Conn.: Yale University Press, 1958), 169.

65. Hughes, "Some Practical Observations," 311.

66. Hugh M. Gloster, "Race and the Negro Writer," *Phylon* 11, no. 4 (1950): 371.

67. Stephani Li (*Playing in the White*, 22), discussing several midcentury "white life" novels by black authors, has recently critiqued critics of the 1940s such as Gloster for assuming "universality" is white and whiteness is nonracial. "Racial" (black) experience is therefore, for these critics, too particular to be "universal." While this was certainly true for some critics and readers, it was not for many of them. Writers and critics of the time were far more sophisticated than recent scholars have assumed.

68. Ann Petry to Kenneth Reeves, March 8, 1969; qtd. in Alex Lubin, "Introduction," in *Revising the Blueprint: Ann Petry and the Literary Left*, ed. Alex Lubin (Jackson: University Press of Mississippi, 2007), 9.

69. Nick Aaron Ford, "A Blueprint for Negro Authors," *Phylon* 11, no. 4 (1950): 376–377.

70. Elizabeth Boutelle, *Collier's*, April 3, 1944; in Dorothy West Papers, Schlesinger Library, Harvard University.

71. George T. Bye to Dorothy West, Dorothy West Papers, August 9, 1945. West failed to finish the novel in time, apparently, and ended up selling the completed novel to Houghton Mifflin in September 1946, according to later correspondence with Bye. Harper & Brothers also expressed strong interest in the novel but bowed out when Houghton Mifflin accepted it.

72. Blyden Jackson, "An Essay in Criticism," *Phylon* 11, no. 4 (1950): 341.

73. Ann Petry, *Country Place* (Boston: Houghton Mifflin, 1947), 231.

74. Petry, *Country Place*, 1.

75. Petry, *Country Place*, 1.

76. Petry, *Country Place*, 59.

77. Petry, *Country Place*, 132.

78. Petry, *Country Place*, 11.

79. Petry, *Country Place*, 10, 11, 20.

80. Petry, *Country Place*, 262.

81. Christopher Rieger, "The Working-Class Pastoral of Zora Neale Hurston's *Seraph on the Suwanee*," *Mississippi Quarterly* 56, no. 1 (Winter 2002–2003): 105–124.

82. Robert E. Hemenway, *Zora Neale Hurston: A Literary Biography* (1977; Urbana: University of Illinois Press, 1980), 314.

83. John C. Charles, "Talk About the South: 'Unspeakable Things Unspoken' in Zora Neale Hurston's *Seraph on the Suwanee*," *Mississippi Quarterly* 62 (2009): 30n15.

84. Zora Neale Hurston, *Folklore, Memoirs, and Other Writings* (New York: Library of America, 1995), 587–588.

85. Zora Neale Hurston, *Seraph on the Suwanee* (New York: Griot Editions, 1997), 27.

86. Zora Neale Hurston to Marjorie Kinnan Rawlings and Norton Baskin, postmarked December 22, 1948, in *Zora Neale Hurston: A Life in Letters*, ed. Carla Kaplan (New York: Doubleday, 2002), 577–578.

87. Zora Neale Hurston to Burroughs Mitchell, October 2, 1947, in *A Life in Letters*, 559.

88. Hurston to Mitchell, October 2, 1947, in *A Life in Letters*, 558.

89. Zora Neale Hurston, "What White Publishers Won't Print," *Negro Digest* 8 (April 1950): 85–89.

90. Representative of the criticism is Robert Hemenway's: "If the [black] novelist consciously seeks to portray whites in order to validate his talent, to prove to the world there are no limits to his genius, the very assumptions of the decision become self-defeating. . . . In writing *Seraph on the Suwanee* Zora Neale Hurston largely turned her back on the source of her creativity. She escaped the stereotype of the 'picturesque' black by giving up the celebration of black folklife, replacing the storytellers on Joe Clarke's porch with a family of upwardly mobile Florida crackers." Hemenway, *Zora Neale Hurston*, 307. Among other observations one might make of this stereotypical dismissal, one might point out that Hurston distinguishes Jim Meserve from the "crackers"; the psychological drama depends rather on his wife's difficulty in overcoming the sense of inferiority connected with her "cracker" origins and developing the self-confidence to love.

91. Hurston to Mitchell, "October Something Late 1947," in *A Life in Letters*, 563.

92. Hurston, "What White Publishers Won't Print," 85–89.

93. Baldwin, "Everybody's Protest Novel," 19, 16.

94. Smith, "Addressed to White Liberals," 485.

95. Richard Wright, qtd. in Charles J. Rolo, "This, Too, Is America," *Tomorrow* 4 (May 1945): 63; reprinted in *Conversations with Richard Wright*, ed. Keneth Kinnamon and Michel Fabre (Oxford: University Press of Mississippi, 1993), 70.

96. Jo Sinclair, *The Seasons: Death and Transfiguration* (New York: Feminist Press, 1993), 139.

97. Qtd. in Sinclair, *The Seasons*, 140–141.

98. Sinclair, *The Seasons*, 141.

99. Lillian Smith, *Strange Fruit* (1944; New York: Harcourt, 1992), 49.

100. Smith, *Strange Fruit*, 50.

101. Smith, *Strange Fruit*, 58, 60.

102. Johnson, "Introduction," xiii.

103. Zora Neale Hurston to Edwin Osgood Grover, November 7, 1943, in *A Life in Letters*, 496.

104. Bucklin Moon, *Without Magnolias* (Garden City, N.J.: Doubleday & Co., 1949), 68.

105. Moon, *Without Magnolias*, 69, 70, 68.

106. Moon, *Without Magnolias*, n.p.

107. Moon, *Without Magnolias*, 50.

108. Moon, *Without Magnolias*, 54, 56.

109. Moon, *Without Magnolias*, 192–193.

110. Moon, *Without Magnolias*, 254.

111. Moon, *Without Magnolias*, 250.

112. Moon, *Without Magnolias*, 272.

113. Ralph Ellison, "That Same Pain, That Same Pleasure," in *Shadow and Act* (1964; New York: New American Library, 1966), 39.

114. Ralph Ellison, "Richard Wright's Blues," in *Shadow and Act*, 104. Originally published in *Antioch Review* (Summer 1945).

115. Ralph Ellison, "Beating that Boy," in *Shadow and Act*, 106.

116. Ellison, "Beating that Boy," 110.

117. Michael Kreyling, *Inventing Southern Literature* (Jackson: University Press of Mississippi, 1998), 81, 82.

118. George Mayberry, "Underground Notes," *New Republic* 126, no. 16 (April 21, 1952): 19.

119. Kreyling, *Inventing Southern Literature*, 84.

120. Lawrence P. Jackson, "Bucklin Moon and Thomas Sancton in the 1940s: Crusaders for the Racial Left," *Southern Literary Journal* 40, no. 1 (Fall 2007): 94. I should add that this critique is left out of Jackson's full and nuanced discussion of Moon and Sancton in *The Indignant Generation*.

121. T. D. J., "Negroes, but Not Men," *Phylon* 10, no. 3 (1949): 275–276.

122. Marion T. Wright, "People Are That Way," *Journal of Negro Education* 18, no. 4 (1949): 500.

123. James Sallis, *Chester Himes: A Life* (New York: Walker, 2000), 91.

124. Anonymous, "To Take the Pressure Off," *Time* 61, no. 17 (April 27, 1953): 52.

125. "The Bucklin Moon Manuscript Collection," Winter Park History and Archives Collection, Winter Park Public Library, http://www.wppl.org/wphistory/Bucklin Moon/.

126. W. E. B. Du Bois, "Foreword," in Howard Fast, *Freedom Road* (1944; New York: Routledge, 2015), xviii. Originally published in an edition by Howard Fast's own Blue Heron Press in 1952.

127. Howard Fast, *Freedom Road* (New York: Duell, Sloan, & Pearce, 1944), 41.

128. Fast, *Freedom Road*, 199.

129. Fast, *Freedom Road*, 262–263.

130. See "About the Author," in Howard Fast, *Intellectuals in the Fight for Peace* (New York: Masses & Mainstream, 1949), 2.

131. William Attaway, *Blood on the Forge* (1941; New York: NYRB, 2005), 22.

132. Attaway, *Blood on the Forge*, 180.

133. Attaway, *Blood on the Forge*, 232–233.

134. Chester Himes, *If He Hollers Let Him Go* (1945; New York: Da Capo, 2002), 89.

135. Himes, *If He Hollers Let Him Go*, 151.

136. Himes, *If He Hollers Let Him Go*, 153.

137. Carl Van Vechten to John A. Williams, November 6, 1962; qtd. in Marc Gerald and Samuel Blumenfeld, "Editors' Notes," in Chester Himes, *Yesterday Will Make You Cry* (New York: Norton, 1998), 7.

138. Edward Margolies and Michel Fabre, *The Several Lives of Chester Himes* (Jackson: University Press of Mississippi, 1997), 33–34; Sallis, *Chester Himes*, 57.

7. QUEER HORIZONS

1. John W. Aldridge, *After the Lost Generation: A Critical Study of the Writers of Two Wars* (New York: McGraw Hill, 1951), 100.

2. Leslie A. Fiedler, "Come Back to the Raft Ag'n, Huck Honey," *Partisan Review* 15 (1948): 664.

3. John Costello, *Virtue Under Fire: How World War II Changed Our Sexual Attitudes* (Boston: Little, Brown, 1985), 1, 2.

4. Gore Vidal, *The City and the Pillar* (New York: Random House, 1995), 159.

5. Costello, *Virtue Under Fire*, 5.

6. John D'Emilio and Estelle B. Freedman, "Foreword," in Allan Berube, *Coming Out Under Fire: The History of Gay Men and Women in World War II* (1990; Chapel Hill: University of North Carolina Press, 2010), x. See also Berube's "Preface" to the same book, xiv.

7. Alfred Kazin, entry for December 29, 1941, in *Alfred Kazin's Journals*, ed. Richard M. Cook (New Haven, Conn.: Yale University Press, 2011), 28.

8. Robert Duncan, "The Homosexual in Society," *Politics* (August 1944): 209–211.

9. Duncan, "The Homosexual in Society," 210.

10. Duncan, "The Homosexual in Society," 210.

11. Duncan, "The Homosexual in Society," 210.

12. Duncan, "The Homosexual in Society," 210.

13. Duncan, "The Homosexual in Society," 211.

14. Duncan, "The Homosexual in Society," 211.

15. Jo Sinclair, *Wasteland* (New York: Harper Brothers, 1946), 307.

16. Jonathan Katz, *Gay/Lesbian Almanac: A New Documentary* (New York: Harper & Row, 1983), 161.

17. Willard Motley, *Knock on Any Door* (New York: D. Appleton-Century, 1947), 185.

18. Motley, *Knock on Any Door*, 297.

19. Lillian Smith, *Strange Fruit* (1944; New York: Harcourt, 1992), 243.

20. Smith, *Strange Fruit*, 244.

21. Smith, *Strange Fruit*, 245.

22. Smith, *Strange Fruit*, 245.

23. Smith, *Strange Fruit*, 246.

24. Smith, *Strange Fruit*, 247.

25. Charles Jackson, *The Fall of Valor* (New York: Rinehart, 1946), 254.

26. Jackson, *The Fall of Valor*, 308.

27. Jackson, *The Fall of Valor*, 310.

28. Qtd. in Anthony Slide, "Lost Gay Novels: Charles Jackson's *The Fall of Valor* (Rinehart, 1946)," *Harrington Gay Men's Quarterly* 6, no. 1 (January 2004): 105–110; from Diana Trilling, review of *The Fall of Valor*, in *The Nation*, October 19, 1946.

29. Edmund Wilson, "Another Hard Case by Charles Jackson," *New Yorker*, October 5, 1946.

30. Slide, "Lost Gay Novels," 108.

31. Gore Vidal, preface to *The City and the Pillar; and Seven Early Stories* (New York: Random House, 1995), xiii.

32. Vidal, *The City and the Pillar*, 3, 4.

33. Vidal, *The City and the Pillar*, 164.

34. Vidal, *The City and the Pillar*, 189.

35. Vidal, *The City and the Pillar*, 192.

36. James Baldwin, "Preservation of Innocence" (1949), in James Baldwin, *Collected Essays*, ed. Toni Morrison (New York: Library of America, 1998), 596. Originally published as "Preservation of Innocence: Studies for a New Morality," *Zero* 1, no. 2 (Tangier, Morocco, 1949): 14–22.

37. Baldwin, "Preservation of Innocence," 599.

38. Baldwin, "Preservation of Innocence," 600.

39. Truman Capote, *Other Voices, Other Rooms* (New York: Random House, 1948), dustjacket.

40. Joseph Valente, "Other Possibilities, Other Drives: Queer, Counterfactual 'Life' in Truman Capote's *Other Voices, Other Rooms*," *MFS/Modern Fiction Studies* 59, no. 3 (Fall 2013): 529. Other articles pointing out the significance of the novel for queer literary studies include Brian Mitchell-Peters, "Camping the Gothic: Que(e)ring Sexuality in Truman Capote's *Other Voices, Other Rooms*," *Journal of Homosexuality* 39, no. 1 (2000): 107–138; and William White Tison Pugh, "Boundless in a Nightmare World: Queer Sentimentalism and Southern Gothicism in Truman Capote's *Other Voices, Other Rooms*," *Mississippi Quarterly* 51, no. 4 (1998): 663–682. Studies that critique the novel's "failure" as unequivocally gay affirmative include Peter G. Christensen's "Capote as Gay American Author," in *The Critical Response to Truman Capote*, ed. Joseph J. Waldmeir and John C. Waldmeir (Westport, Conn.: Greenwood, 1999), 61–67; and Gary Richards, *Lovers and Beloveds: Sexual Otherness in Southern Fiction, 1936–1961* (Baton Rouge: Louisiana State University Press, 2005).

41. Only one article has so far focused on issues of race in the novel: Thomas Fahy's "Violating the Black Body: Sexual Violence in Truman Capote's *Other Voices, Other Rooms*," *Journal of the Midwest Modern Language Association* 46, no. 1 (Spring 2013): 27–42. Fahy focuses on the treatment of Zoo and the sexual violence she suffers, relating it to an actual rape that Capote would have known about. He also points out how whites refused to combat or even acknowledge Zoo's rape. Racial oppression, Fahy argues, is more egregious than the oppression of homosexuals in the novel.

42. Capote, *Other Voices*, 130.

43. Capote, *Other Voices*, 129, 48.

44. Capote, *Other Voices*, 45–46.

45. Capote, *Other Voices*, 9–10.

46. Capote, *Other Voices*, 173.

47. Capote, *Other Voices*, 56, 57, 177.

48. Capote, *Other Voices*, 113.

49. Capote, *Other Voices*, 57.

50. Capote, *Other Voices*, 57.

51. Capote, *Other Voices*, 58–59.

52. Capote, *Other Voices*, 63–64.

53. Capote, *Other Voices*, 64.

54. William W. Patton, "John Brown's Body" (1861).

55. Capote, *Other Voices*, 175.
56. Capote, *Other Voices*, 181.
57. Capote, *Other Voices*, 182.
58. Capote, *Other Voices*, 183.
59. Capote, *Other Voices*, 184, 185.
60. Capote, *Other Voices*, 52–53.
61. Capote, *Other Voices*, 186–187.
62. "Exotic Birds of a Feather: Carson McCullers and Tennessee Williams," *Tennessee Williams Annual Review*, 2000, http://www.tennesseewilliamsstudies.org/journal/work.php?ID=31.
63. Rachel Adams, "'A Mixture of Delicious and Freak': The Queer Fiction of Carson McCullers," *American Literature* 71, no. 3 (September 1999): 552.
64. Carson McCullers, *The Member of the Wedding*, in *Carson McCullers: Complete Novels* (New York: Library of America, 2001), 547, 546.
65. McCullers, *The Member of the Wedding*, 570.
66. José Esteban Muñoz, *Cruising Utopia: The Then and There of Queer Futurity* (New York: New York University Press, 2009), 32.
67. Hazel Rowley, *Richard Wright: The Life and Times* (New York: Henry Holt, 2001), 270, 282.
68. Carson McCullers, *Reflections in a Golden Eye*, in *Carson McCullers: Complete Novels* (New York: Library of America, 2001), 318, 314.
69. McCullers, *Reflections in a Golden Eye*, 344.
70. McCullers, *Reflections in a Golden Eye*, 366.
71. Melissa Free, "Relegation and Rebellion: The Queer, the Grotesque, and the Silent in the Fiction of Carson McCullers," *Studies in the Novel* 40, no. 4 (Winter 2008): 432.
72. Virginia Spencer Carr, *Understanding Carson McCullers* (Columbia: University of South Carolina Press, 1990), 90.
73. See Williams–Laughlin Correspondence, James Laughlin Papers, Houghton Library, Harvard University.
74. Qtd. in Joyce Durham, "Portrait of a Friendship: Selected Correspondence Between Carson McCullers and Tennessee Williams," *Mississippi Quarterly* (December 2005): 8.
75. Durham, "Portrait of a Friendship," 9.
76. Durham, "Portrait of a Friendship," 10.
77. Durham, "Portrait of a Friendship," 10; Joyce Savigneau, *Carson McCullers: A Life*, trans. Joan E. Howard (Boston: Houghton Mifflin, 2001), 246.
78. Williams to McCullers; qtd. in Durham, "Portrait of a Friendship," 10.
79. Savigneau, 91; qtd. in Durham, "Portrait of a Friendship," 10.
80. Durham, "Portrait of a Friendship," 9.
81. Gore Vidal, introduction to Tennessee Williams, *Collected Stories* (New York: New Directions, 1994), xxii.
82. Carlos Dews, in "Exotic Birds of a Feather."
83. An important exception is Francisco Costa, "'There was something different about the boy': Queer Subversion in Tennessee Williams's *A Streetcar Named Desire*," *Interactions: Ege Journal of British and American Studies/Ege İngiliz ve Amerikan İncelemeleri*

Dergisi 23, no. 1–2 (Spring/Fall 2014): 77–85. Costa helpfully interprets the play for its confrontation with heteronormativity, as I do here, although his reading differs in details and in its interpretation of the tragic qualities in Blanche, Mitch, and Stella. John M. Clum interprets the play as a "closet drama," in which Williams disguises the gay male character as a campy heterosexual woman, Blanche DuBois. This reading supports Clum's larger argument about the trajectory of male homosexuality in drama as a movement "from the unspoken to the spoken, from the unseen to the seen." John M. Clum, *Still Acting Gay: Male Homosexuality in Modern Drama* (1992; New York: St. Martin's Griffin, 2000), 122–126, 1.

84. John M. Clum, *Acting Gay*, 2nd ed. (New York: Columbia University Press, 1994), 150. See also the discussion of such interpretations in Alan Sinfield, *Out on Stage: Lesbian and Gay Theatre in the Twentieth Century* (New Haven, Conn.: Yale University Press, 1999), 186–187.

85. Tennessee Williams, *A Streetcar Named Desire* (New York: New Directions, 2004), 114–166. Ellipses in original.

86. Williams, *A Streetcar Named Desire*, 145.

87. Williams, *A Streetcar Named Desire*, 146–147.

88. Williams, *A Streetcar Named Desire*, 150.

89. Williams, *A Streetcar Named Desire*, 177.

90. Williams, *A Streetcar Named Desire*, 179.

91. John Lahr, *Tennessee Williams: Mad Pilgrimage of the Flesh* (New York: Norton, 2014), 180.

92. Lahr, *Tennessee Williams*, 135, 136.

93. Qtd. in Lahr, *Tennessee Williams*, 136, 137, from a personal interview.

94. Lahr, *Tennessee Williams*, 94–95.

95. Elia Kazan, *Elia Kazan: A Life* (New York: Knopf, 1988), 350.

96. George Jean Nathan, qtd. in Lahr, *Tennessee Williams*, 146.

97. Michael Paller, *Gentleman Callers: Tennessee Williams, Homosexuality, and Mid-Twentieth-Century Drama* (New York: Palgrave Macmillan, 2005), 50.

98. Alfred Kinsey et al., *Sexual Behavior in the Human Male* (1948; New York: Ishi Press International, 2010), 2:678, 659.

99. John D'Emilio, *Sexual Politics, Sexual Communities: The Making of a Homosexual Minority in the United States, 1940–1970*, 2nd ed. (Chicago: University of Chicago Press, 1983), 37.

8. WOMEN AND POWER

1. Pearl S. Buck, *On Men and Women* (New York: John Day, 1941), 155.

2. Elizabeth Bishop, "Roosters," in *North and South* (Boston: Houghton Mifflin, 1946), 36–37. Bishop dates the poem in 1941 in the text, to indicate to readers that it was written before Pearl Harbor.

3. George Starbuck, "'The Work': A Conversation with Elizabeth Bishop," in *Elizabeth Bishop and Her Art*, ed. Lloyd Schwartz and Sybil P. Estess (Ann Arbor: University of Michigan Press, 1983), 320–324.

4. Farah Jasmine Griffin, *Harlem Nocturne: Women Artists and Progressive Politics During World War II* (New York: Basic Books, 2013), 189.

5. Gordon Hutner, *What America Read: Taste, Class, and the Novel* (Chapel Hill: University of North Carolina Press, 2006), 219.

6. Gore Vidal, *Williwaw* (New York: E. P. Dutton, 1946), 130.

7. Griffin, *Harlem Nocturne*, 4.

8. Anatole Broyard, *Kafka Was the Rage: A Greenwich Village Memoir* (1993; New York: Vintage, 1997), 140.

9. Sandra M. Gilbert and Susan Gubar, *No Man's Land: The Place of the Woman Writer in the Twentieth Century*, vol. 3: *Letters from the Front* (New Haven, Conn.: Yale University Press, 1997), 211–265, details far more comprehensively than I can here what they call the "Blitz on Women" during World War II and the response of women writers to it. Also particularly notable is Susan Schweik, *A Gulf So Deeply Cut: American Women Poets and the Second World War* (Madison: University of Wisconsin Press, 1991).

10. Steven Dillon, *Wolf-Women and Phantom Ladies: Female Desire in 1940s U.S. Culture* (Albany: SUNY Press, 2015).

11. I was introduced to this photograph by Sarah Birmingham's fine Cornell honors thesis, "Framing and Posing in Eudora Welty's Fiction and Photography," which connects the "framing" of Welty's photographs with her use of corresponding techniques in fiction. She also draws attention to how the boys are being "hypnotized" in the photograph and to the erotic and exotic background posters.

12. Mark K. Wilson and Ann Petry, "A *MELUS* Interview: Ann Petry—the New England Connection," *MELUS* 15, no. 2 (Summer 1988): 75.

13. Gilbert and Gubar, *No Man's Land*, 265.

14. Ernest Hemingway, *For Whom the Bell Tolls* (1940; New York: Scribner, 2003), 26.

15. Hemingway, *For Whom the Bell Tolls*, 189, 190.

16. Hemingway, *For Whom the Bell Tolls*, 215.

17. Chester Himes, *If He Hollers Let Him Go* (1945; New York: Da Capo, 2002), 18.

18. Himes, *If He Hollers Let Him Go*, 19.

19. Himes, *If He Hollers Let Him Go*, 19.

20. Himes, *If He Hollers Let Him Go*, 123. First ellipses in the original.

21. Himes, *If He Hollers Let Him Go*, 124, 126.

22. Dawn Powell, *A Time to Be Born* (1942; Hanover, N.H.: Steerforth, 1999), 59.

23. Powell, *A Time to Be Born*, 36.

24. Powell, *A Time to Be Born*, 73.

25. Powell, *A Time to Be Born*, 24.

26. Powell, *A Time to Be Born*, 100.

27. Powell, *A Time to Be Born*, 127.

28. For an extended discussion of Powell's New York novels in relation to Menippean satire and Bakhtin's theory of carnival, see Marcelle Smith Rice, *Dawn Powell* (New York: Twayne, 2000), 63–108.

29. Dawn Powell, entry of March 23, 1943, in *The Diaries of Dawn Powell, 1931–1965*, ed. Tim Page (South Royalton, Vt.: Steerforth, 1995), 215.

30. Powell, *A Time to Be Born*, 145–146.

31. Catherine Keyser, *Playing Smart: New York Women Writers and Modern Magazine Culture* (New Brunswick, N.J.: Rutgers University Press, 2010), 113.

32. Powell, *A Time to Be Born*, 291.

33. Powell, *A Time to Be Born*, 312.

34. Dawn Powell, *The Locusts Have No King* (1948; Hanover, N.H.: Steerforth, 1995), 31.

35. Mary McCarthy, *The Company She Keeps* (1942; New York: Harcourt, 1970), 4, 6.

36. McCarthy, *The Company She Keeps*, 12.

37. McCarthy, *The Company She Keeps*, 18–19.

38. McCarthy, *The Company She Keeps*, 20.

39. Judith Brown, *Glamour in Six Dimensions: Modernism and the Radiance of Form* (Ithaca, N.Y.: Cornell University Press, 2009), 73, 87.

40. McCarthy, *The Company She Keeps*, 21.

41. Powell, *A Time to Be Born*, 280.

42. Evie Shockley, "Buried Alive: Gothic Homelessness, Black Women's Sexuality, and (Living) Death in Ann Petry's *The Street*," *African American Review* 40, no. 3 (Fall 2006): 439–460. Shockley focuses on the gothic qualities of the novel and Lutie Johnson as doppelganger for Petry herself.

43. Ann Petry, *The Street* (1946; Boston: Houghton Mifflin, 1974), 2.

44. Petry, *The Street*, 6, 10, 13.

45. Petry, *The Street*, 45, 15, 84, 133.

46. Petry, *The Street*, 150.

47. Petry, *The Street*, 270.

48. Petry, *The Street*, 283.

49. Black feminist readings of *The Street* going back to the 1980s include Thelma J. Shinn, "Women in the Novels of Ann Petry," *Critique: Studies in Modern Fiction* 16, no. 1 (1974): 110–120; Nellie Y. McKay, "Ann Petry's *The Street* and *The Narrows*: A Study of the Influence of Class, Race, and Gender on Afro-American Women's Lives," in *Women and War: The Changing Status of American Women from the 1930s to the 1950s*, ed. Maria Diedrich and Dorothea Fischer-Hornung (New York: Berg; 1990), 127–140; Lucy Robin, "Fables of the Reconstruction: Black Women on the Domestic Front in Ann Petry's World War II Fiction," *CLA Journal* 49, no. 1 (2005): 1–27; Farah Jasmine Griffin, *Who Set You Flowin': The African American Migration Narrative* (New York: Oxford University Press, 1996), 114–119.

50. Petry, *The Street*, 418.

51. Petry, *The Street*, 430.

52. Petry, *The Street*, 263.

53. Petry, *The Street*, 251.

54. Petry, *The Street*, 236–237.

55. Petry, *The Street*, 275–276.

56. Petry, *The Street*, 245–246.

57. Petry, *The Street*, 275–276.

58. Petry, *The Street*, 241.

59. Petry, *The Street*, 256.

60. Others have written about the relationship between Welty's photography and her fiction. See especially Louise Westling, "The Loving Observer of *One Time, One Place*," *Mississippi Quarterly* 39, no. 4 (Fall 1986): 587–604; and Matthew R. Martin, "Vision and Revelation in Eudora Welty's Fiction and Photography," *Southern Quarterly* 38, no. 4 (June 2000): 17–26. Martin discusses *Hypnotized, State Fair* and "Powerhouse" separately and interprets both very differently from me.

61. Eudora Welty, "Powerhouse," in *Eudora Welty: Stories, Essays, & Memoir* (New York: Library of America, 1998), 158.

62. Welty, "Powerhouse," 159.

63. Kenneth Bearden, "Monkeying Around: Welty's 'Powerhouse,' Blues-Jazz, and the Signifying Connection," *Southern Literary Journal* 31, no. 2 (Spring 1999): 65–79.

64. Welty, "Powerhouse," 160.

65. "Pagan Love Song," http://lyricsplayground.com/alpha/songs/p/paganlovesong .shtml.

66. Welty, "Powerhouse," 164.

67. Welty, "Powerhouse," 166.

68. Welty, "Powerhouse," 166–167.

69. Welty, "Powerhouse," 169.

9. ECOLOGY AND CULTURE

1. Arthur Schlesinger Jr., *The Vital Center: The Politics of Freedom* (1949; New York: Da Capo, 1988), 241–242.

2. Rachel Carson, *Under the Sea-Wind: A Naturalist's Picture of Ocean Life* (New York: Simon & Schuster, 1941). Other books in the trilogy were *The Sea Around Us* (New York: Oxford University Press, 1951) and *The Edge of the Sea* (Boston: Houghton Mifflin, 1954).

3. Susan Power Bratton, "Thinking Like a Mackerel: Rachel Carson's *Under the Sea-Wind* as a Source for a Transecotonal Sea Ethic," *Ethics and the Environment* 9, no. 1 (Spring 2004): 17, 1–22. See also Michael A. Bryson, *Visions of the Land: Science, Literature, and the American Environment from the Era of Exploration to the Age of Ecology* (Charlottesville: University of Virginia Press, 2002), 134–173.

4. John Steinbeck and Edward F. Ricketts, *Sea of Cortez: A Leisurely Journal of Travel and Research* (1941; New York: Penguin, 2009), 3.

5. Steinbeck and Ricketts, *Sea of Cortez*, 17, 16, 34.

6. Curt Meine, *Aldo Leopold: His Life and Work* (Madison: University of Wisconsin Press, 1988), 477.

7. Ivor Winters, "An Elegy," in *The Giant Weapon* (New York: New Directions, 1943), n.p.

8. Lawrence Buell offers a compelling reading of *Go Down, Moses* as a work of the "environmental unconscious," in connection with Aldo Leopold's work, in *Writing for an Endangered World: Literature, Culture, and Environment in the U.S. and the World* (Cambridge, Mass.: Belknap, 2001), 177–195. I want to stress that the environmental unconscious surfaces specifically in this work of the 1940s, not before, as does Leopold's emphasis on the aesthetics and ethics of environmentalism.

9. Robert Lowell, "Concord," in *Lord Weary's Castle* (New York: Harcourt Brace, 1946), 33.

10. Meine, *Aldo Leopold*, 393.

11. Quoted in Thomas Robertson, *The Malthusian Moment: Global Population Growth and the Birth of American Environmentalism* (New Brunswick, N.J.: Rutgers University Press, 2012), 37.

12. Richard Astro, *John Steinbeck and Edward F. Ricketts: The Shaping of a Novelist* (Minneapolis: University of Minnesota Press, 1973), 5.

13. See particularly Emanuel Graziano, "Ecological Metaphors as Scientific Boundary Work: Innovation and Authority in Interwar Sociology and Biology," *American Journal of Sociology* 101 (1996): 874–907; and Gregg Mitman, *The State of Nature: Ecology, Community, and American Social Thought, 1900–1950* (Chicago: University of Chicago Press, 1992).

14. Ernest W. Burgess, "The Growth of the City: An Introduction to a Research Project," in *Urban Ecology: An International Perspective on the Interaction Between Humans and Nature*, ed. J. M. Marzluff et al. (Springer, 2008), 73. Originally published in "The Trend of Population," *Publications of the American Sociological Society* 18 (1925): 85–97.

15. Buell, *Writing for an Endangered World*, 131–142.

16. Richard Wright, *Native Son* (New York: Harper Perennial Classics, 1998), 383. This is the "restored text" following the proofs preceding changes made for the Book-of-the-Month Club.

17. Wright, *Native Son*, 388.

18. Wright, *Native Son*, 391, 394.

19. Wright, *Native Son*, 382.

20. Wright, *Native Son*, 429.

21. Thomas Alexander, *The Human Eros: Eco-ontology and the Aesthetics of Existence* (New York: Fordham University Press, 2013), 6.

22. Richard Wright, "How Bigger Was Born," in *Native Son*, 442.

23. Ann Petry, *The Street* (1946; Boston: Houghton Mifflin, 1974), 248–249.

24. Petry, *The Street*, 2.

25. Gwendolyn Brooks, "kitchenette building," in *A Street in Bronzeville* (New York: Harper & Bros., 1945), 2. Buell also discusses *The Street* and *A Street in Bronzeville* in relation to *Native Son* and urban fiction of an environmental determinist bent.

26. Petry, *The Street*, 323–324.

27. Lewis Mumford, *The Condition of Man* (New York: Harcourt, Brace, 1944), 419.

28. See especially Philip Andrew Klobucar, "After Modernism: Charles Olson, Ecological Thought, and a Postwar Avant-Garde," PhD diss., University of British Columbia, 1999.

29. Lewis Mumford, *The Condition of Man* (New York: Harcourt Brace, 1944), 336.

30. Mumford, *The Condition of Man*, 336.

31. Mumford, *The Condition of Man*, 337–338.

32. Lewis Mumford, *The Culture of Cities* (New York: Harcourt, Brace, 1938), 302.

33. Mumford, *The Culture of Cities*, 303.

34. Rob Nixon, *Slow Violence and the Environmentalism of the Poor* (Cambridge, Mass.: Harvard University Press, 2011), 238–241.

35. Mumford, *The Condition of Man*, 350.

36. Ramachandra Guha, "Lewis Mumford, the Forgotten American Environmentalist: An Essay in Rehabilitation," in *Minding Nature: The Philosophers of Ecology*, ed. David Macauley (New York: Guilford, 1996), 209–228. Guha made a groundbreaking critique of the wilderness-oriented American environmental movement of the 1960s in "Radical Environmentalism and Wilderness Preservation: A Third World Critique"

(1989), reprinted in *The Great New Wilderness Debate*, ed. J. Baird Callicott and Michael P. Nelson (Athens: University of Georgia Press, 1998), 231–245. Ben A. Minteer has also brought new attention to Mumford as a "third-way" environmentalist (between anthropocentric "conservationism" and ecocentric "environmentalism") in a chapter of *The Landscape of Reform: Civic Pragmatism and Environmental Thought in America* (Cambridge, Mass.: MIT Press, 2006), 51–80. His focus on Mumford's work of the interwar period (1923–1933) makes for different emphases than mine, although I agree with his argument concerning the relationship of his thought to philosophical pragmatism. In the forties Mumford situated his thought much more comprehensively, and presciently, vis-à-vis ecology as such, Marxism, fascism, transnationalism, and anticolonialism.

37. Lewis Mumford, "The Unified Approach to Knowledge and Life," in *Values for Survival: Essays, Addresses, and Letters on Politics and Education* (New York: Harcourt Brace, 1946), 189.

38. Max Horkheimer and Theodor W. Adorno, *Dialectic of Enlightenment: Philosophical Fragments*, ed. Gunzelin Schmid Noerr, trans. Edmund Jephcott (Stanford, Calif.: Stanford University Press, 2002), 27, 23. The book was originally published in Amsterdam in 1947; it seems unlikely that Mumford knew of it.

39. Mumford, "The Unified Approach to Knowledge and Life," 190, 192, 193.

40. Mumford, *The Condition of Man*, 423.

41. Mumford, "Knowledge and Life," 194.

42. Mumford, "Knowledge and Life," 195.

43. Mumford, *The Culture of Cities*, 315.

44. Lewis Mumford, "Education for War and Peace," in *Values for Survival*, 183–184.

45. Julianne Lutz Newton, *Aldo Leopold's Odyssey* (Washington, D.C.: Shearwater Books/Island Press, 2006), 319.

46. Meine, *Aldo Leopold*, 393; Newton, *Aldo Leopold's Odyssey*, 316–322; Robertson, *The Malthusian Moment*, 26.

47. Qtd. in Robertson, *The Malthusian Moment*, 27.

48. Newton, *Aldo Leopold's Odyssey*, 319–320.

49. Aldo Leopold, "A Survey of Conservation," in *Round River: From the Journals of Aldo Leopold, Author of* A Sand County Almanac, ed. L. Leopold (New York: Oxford University Press, 1987), 146. Qtd. in Newton, *Aldo Leopold's Odyssey*, 318.

50. Qtd. in Meine, *Aldo Leopold*, 415.

51. Quotations from Meine, *Aldo Leopold*, 415.

52. Aldo Leopold, *A Sand County Almanac, and Sketches Here and There* (1949; New York: Oxford University Press, 1989), viii.

53. Leopold, *A Sand County Almanac*, 204.

54. Leopold, *A Sand County Almanac*, 204.

55. Leopold, *A Sand County Almanac*, viii–ix, 224–225.

56. Buell, *Writing for an Endangered World*, 186.

57. Leopold, *A Sand County Almanac*, 48, 22–23.

58. Leopold, *A Sand County Almanac*, 27, 73.

59. Leopold, *A Sand County Almanac*, 83.

60. Leopold, *A Sand County Almanac*, 110.

61. Leopold, *A Sand County Almanac*, 209–210.

62. Leopold, *A Sand County Almanac*, 23.

63. Nixon, *Slow Violence and the Environmentalism of the Poor*, 269–270.

64. See especially Buell, *Writing for an Endangered World*, 109–120. An extended study of William Carlos Williams as an ecopoet is Daniel E. Burke's dissertation, "From Pastorals to Paterson: Ecology in the Poetry and Poetics of William Carlos Williams," Marquette University, 2014.

65. William Carlos Williams, "The Poem as a Field of Action" (talk given at the University of Washington, 1948), in *Selected Essays of William Carlos Williams* (New York: New Directions, 1954).

66. William Carlos Williams, *Paterson*, book 1 (1946), rev. ed. by Christopher Mac-Gowan (New York: New Directions, 1995), 38–39.

67. Williams, *Paterson*, 6.

68. Williams, *Paterson*, 45.

69. Williams, *Paterson*, 50.

70. Williams, *Paterson*, 78.

71. William Carlos Williams, *I Wanted to Write a Poem: The Autobiography of the Works of a Poet*, ed. Edith Heal (Boston: Beacon, 1958), 73.

72. Williams, *Paterson*, 52.

73. Williams, *I Wanted to Write a Poem*, 83.

74. William Carlos Williams, "A Statement by William Carlos Williams about the Poem *Paterson*" (1951), in *Paterson*, xiv.

75. Muriel Rukeyser, prefatory statement in *The Life of Poetry* (New York: A. A. Wyn, 1949), n.p., 9–10.

76. Charles Olson, "The Resistance," in *Selected Writings*, ed. Robert Creeley (New York: New Directions, 1966), 13.

77. Sherman Paul, *Olson's Push: Origin, Black Mountain, and Recent American Poetry* (Baton Rouge: Louisiana State University Press, 1978), xvii.

78. Charles Olson, *The Special View of History* (1956 lecture), ed. Ann Charters (Berkeley: Oyez, 1970), 42.

79. Charles Olson to Robert Creeley, August 20, 1951, in *Charles Olson and Robert Creeley: The Complete Correspondence*, ed. George F. Butterick (New York: David R. Godine, 1987), 7:115. For a discussion of Olson's "archaic" postmodernism, see also Ralph Maud, "Charles Olson's Archaic Postmodern," *Minutes of the Charles Olson Society* 42 (September 2001); reprinted in "Looking for Oneself: Contributions to the Study of Charles Olson," http://charlesolson.org/Files/archaic1.htm.

80. David Lehman, "A. R. Ammons: The Art of Poetry LXXIII," *Paris Review* 38, no. 139 (Summer 1996): 62–91.

81. A. R. Ammons, "A Poem Is a Walk" (1967), in *Set in Motion: Essays, Interviews, and Dialogues*, ed. Zofia Burr (Ann Arbor: University of Michigan Press, 1996), 16.

82. Lehman, "A. R. Ammons," 62–91.

EPILOGUE: ONE WORLD

1. John Berryman, "The Dangerous Year," in *Poems* (Norfolk, Conn.: New Directions, 1942), 2.

2. Martha Gellhorn, *Liana* (New York: Scribner, 1944), 203.

3. John W. Tebbel, *Between Covers: The Rise and Transformation of American Book Publishing* (Oxford: Oxford University Press, 1987), 346.

4. Eleanor Roosevelt, qtd. in Blanche Wiesen Cook, *Eleanor Roosevelt*, vol. 2: *1933–38* (New York: Viking, 1999), 114–115.

5. Don Cameron, "Christmas 'Round the World," *Action Comics* 93 (February 1946); reprinted in *Superman in the Forties* (New York: DC Comics, 2005), 174, 181.

6. Franklin Delano Roosevelt, qtd. in *Einstein on Peace*, ed. Otto Nathan and Heinz Norden (New York: Schocken, 1968), 341.

7. John Steinbeck and Edward F. Ricketts, *Sea of Cortez: A Leisurely Journal of Travel and Research* (1941; New York: Penguin, 2009), 88.

8. Caryl P. Haskins, "Is Mankind Cohesive?" *Atlantic Monthly* 177, no. 3 (March 1946): 120.

9. E. B. White, *Here Is New York* (1949; New York: The Little Bookroom, 1999), 54–56.

10. Bill Finger, "The Origin of Superman," *Superman* 53 (July–August 1948); reprinted in *Superman in the Forties*, 49.

11. See especially Jeanne Chenault, "Bradley Walker Tomlin," in *Bradley Walker Tomlin: A Retrospective View* (Buffalo, N.Y.: Buffalo Fine Arts Academy, 1975), 20.

12. Gertrude Stein, "Reflection on the Atomic Bomb," in *Gertrude Stein: Writing, 1932–1946*, ed. Catharine R. Stimpson and Harriet Chessman (New York: Library of America, 1998), 823; originally published in *Yale Poetry Review*, December 1947.

13. Paul S. Boyer, *By the Bomb's Early Light: American Thought and Culture at the Dawn of the Atomic Age* (1985; Chapel Hill: University of North Carolina Press, 1994), 246.

14. Carson McCullers, *The Member of the Wedding: A Play* (1949; New York: New Directions, 2006), 90.

15. For a more extended discussion of ambivalence about the bomb as scientific achievement, see Boyer, *By the Bomb's Early Light*, esp. chap. 22, "Second Thoughts About Prometheus: The Atomic Bomb and Attitudes Toward Science," 266–274.

16. Louis Simpson, "The Men with Flame-Throwers," in *The Arrivistes: Poems, 1946–1949* (New York: Fine Editions Press, n.d.), 56–57; Simpson dates the poem March 1949.

17. Herman Hagedorn, *The Bomb That Fell on America* (Santa Barbara, Calif.: Pacific Coast Publishing Co., 1946), 8–9.

18. Editors of Pocket Books, *The Atomic Age Opens* (New York: Pocket Books, 1945), 174.

19. *The Atomic Age Opens*, back-cover marketing description.

20. Instances of this equivalence are many, but see, for example, the mass-paperback compendium of information about atomic energy and the bomb *The Atomic Age Opens*, 7–8. The book was published in August 1945.

21. Karl Shapiro, "The Progress of Faust," in *Trial of a Poet and Other Poems* (New York: Reynal & Hitchcock, 1947), 52.

22. Dorothy Thompson's syndicated column "On the Record," qtd. in *The Atomic Age Opens*, 248.

23. Qtd. in *Albert Einstein on Peace*, ed. Otto Nathan and Heinz Norden (New York: Schocken, 1968), 336, from an article in the *New York Times*, September 15, 1945.

24. Albert Einstein, letter of October 21, 1945, qtd. in *Albert Einstein on Peace*, 338.

25. Truman quoted in a letter to the *New York Times* signed by Thomas Mann, Supreme Court Justice Owen J. Roberts, and others, October 10, 1945; reprinted in *Einstein on Peace*, 341.

26. Albert Einstein as told to Raymond Swing, "Atomic War or Peace," *Atlantic Monthly*, November 1947; qtd. in *Einstein on Peace*, 351.

27. Qtd. in *Albert Einstein on Peace*, 352.

28. Emery Reves, *The Anatomy of Peace* (1945; New York: Harper & Bros., 1946), 29.

29. Reves, *The Anatomy of Peace*, 176.

30. Boyer, *By the Bomb's Early Light*, 27–46.

31. Arthur H. Compton, introduction to *One World or None*, ed. Dexter Masters and Katharine Way (New York: McGraw-Hill, 1946), v.

32. H. H. Arnold, "Air Force in the Atomic Age," in *One World or None*, 32.

33. Walter Lippman, "International Control of Atomic Energy," in *One World or None*, 75.

34. Fritz Bartel, "Surviving the Years of Grace: The Atomic Bomb and the Specter of World Government, 1945–1950," *Diplomatic History* 39, no. 2 (2015): 294.

35. Boyer, *By the Bomb's Early Light*, 93–106.

36. Bartel, "Surviving the Years of Grace," 299–300, 277.

37. Charles Olson, "La Preface," in *Selected Writings* (New York: New Directions, 1966), 160.

38. Carson McCullers, *The Member of the Wedding*, in *Complete Novels* (New York: Library of America, 2001), 546.

39. Franklin Delano Roosevelt, State of the Union Speech to the Congress of the United States, January 6, 1941.

40. Melvin B. Tolson, "Tapestries of Time," in *Rendezvous with America* (New York: Dodd, Mead, 1944), 121.

41. Hannah Arendt, "We Refugees," *Menorah Journal* 31, no. 1 (1943): 69–77.

42. Mary Ann Glendon, *A World Made New: Eleanor Roosevelt and the Universal Declaration of Human Rights* (New York: Random House, 2001), 77–78.

43. Sumner B. Twiss, "Confucian Ethics, Concept-Clusters, and Human Rights," in *Polishing the Chinese Mirror: Essays in Honor of Henry Rosemont Jr.*, ed. Marthe Chandler and Ronnie Littlejohn, ACPA Series of Chinese and Comparative Philosophy (New York: Global Scholarly Publications, 2008), 54.

44. Obituary for Peng Chun Chang, *New York Times*, July 21, 1957.

45. James Zhi Yang and William C. Frick, "When Confucius Encounters John Dewey: A Brief Historical and Philosophical Analysis of Dewey's Visit to China," *International Education* 44, no. 2 (Spring 2015): 7–22, 109–110.

46. Lydia H. Liu, "Shadows of Universalism: The Untold Story of Human Rights Around 1948," *Critical Inquiry* 40, no. 4 (Summer 2014): 415.

47. Eleanor Roosevelt, *On My Own* (New York: Harper, 1958), 77.

48. Glendon, *A World Made New*, 134.

49. Rosa-Linda Fregoso, "For a Pluriversal Declaration of Human Rights," *American Quarterly* 66, no. 3 (September 2014): 587–588.

50. Twiss, "Confucian Ethics," 54–55.

51. Twiss, "Confucian Ethics," 63. Chang's importance to the document has also been asserted recently by Liu, who emphasizes that Chang also fought "civilizationist" discourse in the drafting process and that the common view of the UDHR as a "western"-authored, Eurocentric document is incorrect.

52. Dewey and Franz Boas, who mentored Ruth Benedict, Melville Herskovits, Margaret Mead, Edward Sapir, and Zora Neale Hurston, among others, taught a seminar together in 1914–1915, and the views of Boas's students were deeply affected by

Dewey's work. Herskovits had also studied under Alexander Goldenweiser at the New School, another follower of Dewey whose anthropological approach was thoroughly pragmatist. I discuss this in *The Harlem Renaissance in Black and White* (Cambridge, Mass.: Harvard University Press, 1995), 88–89. See also Margaret M. Caffrey, *Ruth Benedict: Stranger in This Land* (Austin: University of Texas Press, 1989), 152–158; and Regna Darnell, *Edward Sapir: Linguist, Anthropologist, Humanist* (Berkeley: University of California Press, 1990), 172.

53. John Dewey, "The Crisis in Human History: The Danger of the Retreat to Individualism," *Commentary* 1 (December 1945): 1–9. Dewey had advanced the basic concepts behind the essay in earlier work, including *Freedom and Culture* (1939; Amherst, Mass.: Prometheus, 1989).

54. Zachary Leader, *The Life of Saul Bellow: To Fame and Fortune, 1915–1964* (New York: Knopf, 2015), 195.

55. Executive Board, American Anthropological Association, "Statement on Human Rights," *American Anthropologist* 49, no. 4 (October–December 1947): 539.

56. Executive Board, "Statement on Human Rights," 539.

57. Executive Board, "Statement on Human Rights," 540.

58. Executive Board, "Statement on Human Rights," 540.

59. Executive Board, "Statement on Human Rights," 540.

60. Executive Board, "Statement on Human Rights," 540–541.

61. Executive Board, "Statement on Human Rights," 543.

62. This line of thinking was powerfully enunciated decades later in the work of the neopragmatist Richard Rorty, particularly in *Contingency, Irony, and Solidarity* (Cambridge: Cambridge University Press, 1989), where he privileges the role of literature (especially novels) and the arts in creating solidarity across cultures.

63. Michael J. Lannoo, *Leopold's Shack and Ricketts's Lab: The Emergence of Environmentalism* (Berkeley: University of California Press, 2010), 125.

64. Samuel Moyn, "The Universal Declaration of Human Rights of 1948 and the History of Cosmopolitanism," *Critical Inquiry* 40, no. 4 (Summer 2015): 378.

65. Norman Mailer, *Advertisements for Myself* (New York: G. P. Putnam's Sons, 1959).

INDEX

....

CPSIA information can be obtained
at www.ICGtesting.com
Printed in the USA
LVHW032324100419
613744LV00002B/3